Acceptance and Commitment Therapy

Contemporary Theory Research and Practice

Edited by
J.T. Blackledge, Joseph Ciarrochi and Frank P. Deane

www.
AUSTRALIANACADEMICPRESS
.com.au

First published in 2009 from a completed manuscript presented to
Australian Academic Press
32 Jeays Street
Bowen Hills Qld 4006
Australia
www.australianacademicpress.com.au

National Library of Australia cataloguing-in-publication entry:

Title:	Acceptance and commitment therapy : contemporary theory research and practice / editors John T. Blackledge; Frank Deane; Joseph Ciarrochi.
Edition:	1st ed.
ISBN:	9781921513145 (pbk.)
Subjects:	Acceptance and commitment therapy.
Other Authors/ Contributors:	Blackledge, John T. Deane, Frank. Ciarrochi, Joseph.
Dewey Number:	616.89142

contents

acknowledgements

To my wife Cyndy and daughter Ava,
who matter most to me — JTB

To my family, Ann, Grace, and the baby on the way — JC

To Liz, James, Jake and Georgia.
An acknowledgement does not make up for all those times I have not
been entirely present, but I thought you would enjoy seeing your names
in a book and also enjoy my use of double negatives — FD

preface

In August of 2006, delegates from Oceania, Asia, Europe, and North America assembled at the University of Wollongong, Australia, for the first southern hemisphere conference on Acceptance and Commitment Therapy and Relational Frame Theory. ACT has rapidly grown in popularity in Australia and New Zealand over the past several years, with major ACT figures like Steve Hayes, Kelly Wilson, Robyn Walser, John Forsyth, and Georg Eifert making repeated trips here to provide 1- and 2-day workshops. While these expert forums were welcome, they were also necessarily few and far between. Most ACT experts live in the northern hemisphere, and this 'tyranny of distance' had historically conspired to prevent concentrated and extended doses of ACT and RFT training. This is one reason why we, as the conference organizers, were very pleased by the willingness of ACT experts from the United States, Sweden, Wales, and Australia to make this historic conference possible by asking for only bare minimum compensation — all in the interest of providing quality training to an extended community of therapists who clearly desired more. We would therefore like to publicly thank Ann Bailey, Sonja Batten, Joanne Dahl, Simon Dymond, Russ Harris, Tobias Lundgren, Patti Robinson, Kirk Strosahl, Robyn Walser, Kelly Wilson, Rob Zettle, and all the other co-presenters who made this fantastic event possible. So successful was the conference that there are firm plans to hold additional Oceanic ACT/ RFT conferences annually, with the second being held in Christchurch, New Zealand in August 2008.

If you were unfortunate enough to have missed this conference, you will be happy to know that the vast majority of chapters included in this book are written by ACT experts who participated in it, with several of the chapters directly mirroring presentations these authors made there. If you did attend the conference and have already fully absorbed what was said and done there, you will be pleased to know that most of the chapters contain entirely new content, ranging from detailed treatments of the scientific and theoretical aspects of the ACT model and research program, to several fully applied and wonderfully detailed discussions of how to apply ACT to a variety of human problems. As such, the book is divided into two parts, with the first section containing more theoretical treatments of ACT, and the second (and larger) section presenting extended descriptions of how to apply ACT in different contexts.

Michael Levin and Steven Hayes outline the broader research program that underlies ACT and Relational Frame Theory (RFT). Specifically, they describe the philosophical underpinnings and comprehensive approach to investigating the principles, processes, and outcomes embodied by ACT's contextual behavioral approach to science. The chapter will provide a full appreciation of the contextual behavioral science (CBS) research program and presents a challenge to the conventional, mainstream empirical approach to creating and evaluating psychotherapies.

Following on the heels of Levin and Hayes' insistence that middle level therapeutic constructs like 'acceptance' and 'defusion' be specified and researched in terms of basic behavioral processes and principles, JT Blackledge and Dermot Barnes-Holmes discuss the specific processes that may underlie each of ACT's six core, middle level processes. If you have ever wondered exactly how increased acceptance, increased contact with the present, an enhanced sense of self-as-context, cognitive defusion, and increased commitment to living a values-driven life might result in an increasingly effective and psychologically healthy life, tentative but behaviorally specific answers are suggested here.

Kirk Strosahl and Patti Robinson describe in detail how to 'take ACT to the streets', essentially providing a primer on making ACT so readily accessible that simplified forms of it might be effectively taught to and delivered by nonmental health professionals to exponentially higher numbers of nonclinical recipients. Drs Strosahl and Robinson have extensive experience in delivering brief forms of ACT in primary care settings, where therapist–client contact typically involves as little as one and no more than three sessions. Their expertise in distilling the essence of ACT into concentrated and readily ingested doses is clearly evident in this guide for disseminating ACT-consistent messages to the community and to the wider culture.

As the book segues from more theoretical treatments of ACT toward more applied discussions, Rhonda Merwin and Kelly Wilson provide a highly accessible primer on applying ACT to eating disordered clients, in addition to providing an extended modern behavioral conceptualization of eating disorders. The chapter serves as an excellent example of one of ACT's greatest strengths: the paramount importance of clear, theoretically guided conceptualization grounded in basic behavioral principles, and the direct impact this conceptualization has on treatment.

Joanne Dahl introduces us to the conflicting conceptualizations of epilepsy provided by the medical and behavioral therapy models of that disorder, noting the radically different treatment options flowing from these different views. Dr Dahl then both illustrates how behavior therapy for epilepsy proceeds, and how precisely ACT (as a modern form of behavior therapy) can be used to enhance the effect of traditional behavior therapy. Within the context of clinical depression, Rob Zettle, Stacey Barner and Suzanne Gird introduce forgiveness from an ACT perspective and also contextualise and contrast forgiveness from the view of several major world religions and from the standpoint of different therapeutic models (e.g., CBT, psychodynamic). Finally, the chapter describes how ACT interventions address forgiveness or can be adapted to help individuals 'enact forgiveness'. Although the chapter focuses on forgiveness in the context of clinical depression, it will provide readers with a rich insight into forgiveness interventions and the importance of forgiving as a therapeutic process.

Natalie Glaser, JT Blackledge, Louise Shepherd, and Frank Deane describe the preliminary results of a randomized controlled trial comparing group ACT and group CBT for anxiety disorders writ large. Adapted from an individual treatment protocol created by Georg Eifert and John Forsyth, the trial reported here suggests promising results for the ACT condition. Glaser and her co-authors go on to describe a number of issues to watch for while conducting ACT in a group format, with clients exhibiting a wide variety of anxiety symptoms, as well as specifically describing some of the exercises conducted.

Tobias Lundgren introduces an ACT approach in the treatment of self-destructive behavior using a detailed case example of an adolescent girl. The chapter starts with an outline of a functional behavioral account of self-destructive behavior and in particular the role of experiential avoidance. Understanding the functions of self-destructive behaviors is essential to the treatment approach forwarded in the chapter. There is a fascinating micro-analysis of transcripts from therapy sessions with 'Linda' that are linked with the original functional analysis provided for the case. The explicit application of learning principles 'in-session' are a timely reminder of the reinforcing power of the therapist 'in the present moment'. The chapter finishes by providing examples of ACT resources that can be used to facilitate processes such as values clarification and pursuit.

Scott Bethay, Kelly Wilson and Katherine Moyer walk through the nuts and bolts of applying ACT to the reduction of staff burnout, providing several wonderfully detailed examples of specific ACT techniques that will give the reader a clear idea of how to apply ACT. While the examples provided are directed specifically at staff working with the developmentally disabled, the suggestions and strategies discussed in the chapter should apply equally well to virtually any setting where mental health or behavioral support workers strive to help challenging clients in a demanding work environment.

Joseph Ciarrochi and Linda Billich provide an ACT-based theory of why people struggle so much to get along, even in the absence of observable deprivation and threat. They link this theory to an experiential-based approach to social skills training. This approach seeks to us all the ACT-related processes (e.g., acceptance, defusion) to help people achieve their social goals. Ciarrochi and Billich provide concrete examples and worksheets to help others apply experiential skills training to their clients.

Given ACT's increasing potential as a viable treatment for psychosis, Hamish McLeod (an expert on CBT for psychosis) compares and contrasts ACT and CBT in the treatment of this problem, and reviews existing data in support of both therapies. Unbeknownst to many, CBT for psychosis looks substantially different than the forms of CBT conducted for more mainstream psychological problems. It has been argued elsewhere that CBT and ACT exist on a continuum, with some similarities and some differences. Dr McLeod summarizes a number of these similarities and differences within the context of psychosis treatment and provides an overview of the current state of their evidence. He raises several interesting issues for future research, including the possibility that psychotic patients may show excessive sensitivity to contingencies and may not benefit from ACT interventions that seek to increase such sensitivity.

Ann Bailey, Diane Mooney-Reh, Lisa Parker and Sonja Temelkovski have attempted to respond to the clinical challenges of working with people diagnosed with Borderline Personality Disorder (BPD). They start by reviewing the treatment approaches of Dialectical Behaviour Therapy, Mentalization-Based Treatment and Transference-focused psychotherapy and compare the major components with ACT principles. In doing so, they provide a rationale and clearly outline the major treatment components that they draw from each approach in their own clinical work with BPD. A detailed ACT conceptualization of BPD is provided which highlights the importance of experiential avoidance, self-as-concept', 'self-as-process', and 'self-as-context'. A description of their graded exposure model (GEM-ACT) treatment for BPD is provided along with examples of various 'graded' ACT interventions that are used in their approach.

Sonja Batten, Jason DeViva, Andrew Santanello, Lorie Morris, Paul Benson, and Mark Mann have provided an ACT approach to dealing with the common comorbid problems of PTSD and Substance Use Disorders. They start by reviewing the literature that links the disorders and then suggest that it may be often difficult to treat these disorders in isolation. They outline an ACT theory of how both disorders may often have the same underlying cause, i.e., experiential avoidance. Finally, they provide the details of an ACT intervention for PTSD and substance abuse.

In sum, the mix of chapters speaks to the strengths of the contextual behavioral science (CBS) research program discussed by Levin and Hayes.

In the end, ACT is an applied treatment model, and as such, it lives and dies by its ability to effectively benefit a wide variety of clients. But from a CBS approach, it is not sufficient to have a treatment modality that has simply been assessed to be effective. In order to make the treatment increasingly effective and to maximize understanding about precisely how the treatment works, its tenets must be theoretically coherent, firmly based on empirically tried and true principles, and must have its active psychological processes clearly identified and sufficiently assessed. The chapters in this volume demonstrate a mix of full application, an appreciation of basic-applied research linkage, clear and behaviorally-consistent conceptualization of specific problem areas, and coherent explication of the ACT model. In other words, the pages that follow will not only tell you what to do with clients struggling with various problems, they will also tell you a fair bit about how those things work.

JT Blackledge
Mount Sterling, Kentucky

Joseph Ciarrochi & Frank Deane
Wollongong, Australia

chapter one

ACT, RFT, and Contextual Behavioral Science

Michael Levin and Steven C. Hayes

Acceptance and Commitment Therapy (ACT; Hayes, Strosahl, & Wilson, 1999) is part of a larger approach to psychology and related fields, which we have termed contextual behavioral science (CBS). In this chapter we want to describe the CBS approach and explain how it relates to the theory, philosophy and research strategy underlying ACT and Relational Frame Theory (RFT; Hayes, Barnes-Holmes, & Roche, 2001).

Even a cursory look at shortcomings in the dominant research paradigm in applied psychology suggests the need for this discussion. These shortcomings include the lack of integration between basic and applied psychology (Hayes, 1998a); the slow rate of improvement in the effect sizes of applied interventions, failures in component analyses of some of our most successful technologies (Dimidjian et al., 2006; Jacobson et al., 1996); the failure of syndromal diagnosis to lead to specific etiologies (Kupfer, First, & Regier, 2002); and the low rate of adoption of empirically supported treatments (ESTs) by practicing clinicians (Sanderson, 2002). A new approach to applied psychological research is needed.

Contextual Behavioral Science

Contextual behavioral science represents an evolutionary expansion of traditional behavior analysis into complex human behavior, based in part on advances in behavioral theories of language and cognition and the development of clinical behavior analysis. There are several key features of the CBS approach (Hayes, in press):

- explicating philosophical assumptions about science, units of analysis, the purpose of analysis and truth criteria
- creating a basic account with refined principles informing treatment and vice versa
- developing a model or theory of pathology, intervention and health tied to basic principles
- measuring of processes of change
- building and testing techniques and components linked to these processes and principles
- an emphasis on mediation and moderation in the analysis of applied impact
- early testing of effectiveness, dissemination and training strategies and developing linkage between these and the overall mode
- testing the research program across a broad range of areas and levels of analysis in search of limiting conditions and the need for further model development.

All of these characteristics are emphasized early and throughout the CBS research program, with each part building upon the others.

In what follows we will walk through each of these eight areas. Because the ACT/RFT research program has been consciously linked to a CBS approach, we will focus on this research program in describing it; but we believe that CBS is considerably broader and also encompasses the vast majority of traditional behavior analysis. Clarifying how ACT and RFT research fits within a CBS model may help to provide a framework in which to view past research and future directions, as well as to provide an example of the utility and progressivity of this inductive, functional approach.

There is another value to this exercise. There have been criticisms of ACT, but often these criticisms have attempted to evaluate the model separate from its scientific program and goals. For example, a recent review by Öst (2008) evaluated the efficacy of ACT interventions solely upon the methodological rigor of randomized controlled trials, without considering the larger research program. Such reviews miss important areas within the research program that lend support to it, such as analogue/component studies and mediational analyses. Other reviews have taken aspects of ACT theory and technologies out of the context of the larger, principle-focused model in an attempt to show it is the same as other CBT treatments (Arche & Craske, in press; Hofmann & Asmundson, 2008). Reviewing ACT within its own model of science can assist in placing these criticisms in the context of the larger research program.

1. Explicate Philosophical Assumptions

The purpose of science can be described as 'the construction of increasingly organized systems of verbal rules that allow analytic goals to be accomplished with precision, scope and depth, and [be] based on verifiable experience' (Hayes, 2004, p. 36). In science, verbal constructs are developed based upon systematic observations within a scientific domain that apply to a range of events (scope), cohere across analytical levels and domains (depth), and provide a limited subset that can be applied to the analysis of a given event (precision; Biglan & Hayes, 1996). Progressivity in science is marked by increases in the organization of these verbal concepts; by increases in their precision, scope and depth; and by increases in the degree to which analytic goals can be achieved.

Philosophical assumptions are critical to science because they specify the domain, units of analysis and analytic purpose that are necessary for this approach to knowledge to function. These, in turn, specify the truth criterion within an approach.

Assumptions about topics such as the purpose of science and the nature of truth provide the framework for theories, methodologies and techniques. That is the case whether or not a scientist identifies these assumptions. Philosophy of science is merely the process of owning or explicitly clarifying one's assumptions within a scientific approach. Owning assumptions helps the scientists weed out unintended inconsistencies, and vitalizes theoretical concepts and methodologies by enhancing their link with basic assumptions. It is important to note that this level of scientific program development occurs outside of the empirical realm. Core assumptions cannot be evaluated empirically because they are needed to engage in empirical analysis. Assumptions are chosen and explicated, not evaluated (Hayes, Hayes, & Reese, 1988).

Functional contextualism (Biglan & Hayes, 1996; Hayes, 1993; Hayes et al., 1988) represents the foundation of contextual behavioral science. Contextualism is based upon the root metaphor of the ongoing act in context (Pepper, 1942). From this perspective, psychological events are understood holistically as the 'whole organism interacting in and with a historical and situational context' (Hayes, 1993, p. 24). Contextualism differs from many other philosophical approaches used in science in that it avoids entirely ontological claims regarding the nature of reality, relying instead on the epistemological basis of knowledge claims. Like all forms of contextualism, functional contextualism assumes that 'truth' is a way of speaking about successful working toward one's scientific goals (Hayes et al., 1988). Thus, analytic goals are foundational in all forms of contextualism because they provide the concrete metric against which to apply a pragmatic truth criterion (Hayes, 1993). What is distinctive about functional contextualism is that its goal is the prediction and influence of events with precision, scope and depth (Hayes, 1993).

Contextual behavioral science is based on functional contextualism, as applied to the domain of behavioral science: the study of whole organisms acting in and with a context defined historically and situationally. Thus, the 'truth' of any concept, model, or technique in a CBS approach is ultimately demonstrated by its ability to effectively and efficiently lead to the prediction and influence of behavior — the actions between organisms and historical and situational contexts — and to do so with precision, scope and depth.

Functional contextualism provides the foundation for all observations, principles, theories and methodologies used within contextual behavioral science. Theories do not represent ontological truths, but are ways of speaking about how to predict and influence behavior in a particular way (Biglan & Hayes, 1996).

Viewing psychological events holistically within a historical and situational context leads to a functional conception of causality in terms of the determinants and consequences of a given behavior. This means that within a CBS approach an analysis is not complete until it has identified broadly useful manipulable variables that control behavior (Hayes, 1993).

Models that specify thought–action, emotion–action, or behavior–behavior relationships, although they can be quite useful in predicting behavior, are considered to be fundamentally incomplete until they identify controlling variables outside the psychological event that can be manipulated (Biglan & Hayes, 1996; Hayes & Brownstein, 1986). Any method can be useful provided it fits with the goals of CBS. For example, correlational research examining behavior–environment relations may assist more in identifying manipulable contextual factors. But the truth criterion of CBS means that experimental methods in which one tests functional environment–behavior relations by manipulating context and observing the effect on behavior are ultimately preferred (Biglan & Hayes, 1996).

The implications of functional contextualism for theory, methodology and applied technologies can be seen throughout the ACT/RFT research program and will be covered throughout this chapter, but a few notable areas are worth mentioning at this point. The ACT emphasis on client values makes sense because it allows a pragmatic truth criterion to be applied. The model does not take a stance that any behavior is a priori harmful because these behaviors may only be evaluated with regards to what is important and workable with the specific client. Within treatment, clinicians focus upon altering the contexts that regulate the causal relationship between thoughts, feelings and behaviors, rather than attempting to directly change private events as might seem to be necessary within a more ontological approach.

2. Develop a Basic Account With Refined Principles That Continuously Informs Treatment and Vice Versa

A primary problem of the dominant research paradigm in applied and clinical psychology is that it emphasizes precision, but not scope. Scope is particularly important as it relates to questions of concern to practitioners, because applying knowledge is inherently a matter of not just internal validity, but also external validity. Scope is achieved in a CBS approach through explicating theory that is tied to refined principles, which orient clinicians to functional, manipulable processes underlying the often complex set of problems seen in everyday clinical work.

Behavioral principles are high precision, high scope abstractions of functional environment–behavior relations. In a CBS approach, these principles are developed inductively in basic research in which simple, specific behavior–environment relations can be observed and manipulated. Systematic observations of these relations are organized into principles that specify functional relationships between behavior and contextual factors, which are subsequently refined to maximize their precision, scope and depth (Hayes, 2004; Waltz & Hayes, in press). Behavioral principles subsequently inform functional analyses of complex behavior, serving as the building blocks for analytic–abstractive theoretical models of human behavior and interventions (Hayes et al., 2007). Thus, behavioral principles are not ends in themselves, as their utility is demonstrated through their ability to account for complex behavior (Hayes & Berens, 2004; Skinner, 1938). The emphasis on scope and precision allows principles to apply across a broad array of topographically distinct behaviors of varying complexity, while maintaining coherence and parsimony within a theory. These refined principles are essential to establishing theoretical models with sufficient scope to adequately address the needs of clinicians.

This approach necessitates the integration of basic research developing refined principles with applied research in their effective application. Yet there have been few successful attempts at integrating these areas, due in part to difficulties with models commonly used for this work. For example, if clinical researchers need to apply basic knowledge across the board, an incredibly large breadth of knowledge needs to be assimilated by those outside the area that developed that knowledge (Hayes, 1998a). Contextual behavioral science avoids these problems by adopting a mutual interest model in which applied and basic research programs find a common ground within a shared theoretical interest area. The work of both basic researchers and applied scientists inform each other and yet researchers in one field are not in the position of depending upon the other field to answer their questions.

In the history of the development of CBS, the biggest stumbling block has been the development of an adequate account of language and cognition. This was also true in clinical behavior analysis. ACT is a behavioral approach and thus its principles are based in part on traditional behavior analytic direct contingency principles (e.g., reinforcement). Respondent and operant conditioning are applied to produce first order change in overt behaviors and emotion (Hayes et al., 2007). Behavioral technologies such as shaping and contingency management, which are based on traditional behavioral principles, may be applied when a clinician has some degree of control over the client's environment (Hayes et al., 2007). However, since therapists rarely have access to a client's environment outside of the clinic, therapeutic work consists mostly of verbally based interventions intended to produce clinical gains. Yet previous theoretical accounts of language and cognition were inadequate in regards to the analytic goals of prediction and influence (see Hayes et al., 2001, for a review of the criticism of Skinner's account of language).

Thus, in accord with the need in CBS to develop a basic account with refined principles that continuously informs treatment and vice versa, ACT researchers have, from the beginning, attempted to create a more adequate theory of language and cognition for applied work. This work fits within a mutual interest model in which much of the early research on rule-governed behavior (Hayes, 1989), derived stimulus relations (Hayes & Brownstein, 1985) and Relational Frame Theory (RFT; Hayes et al., 2001) was conducted by applied researchers. This research program was subsequently adopted by an experimental psychologist, Dermot Barnes-Holmes, and later by other basic researchers who have continued to publish a substantial amount of research on RFT. RFT proposes that relational responding is a functional operant that serves as the core of human language and cognition. From this approach, language and cognition are based on the learned and contextually controlled ability to arbitrarily relate events mutually and in combination, and to transform the functions of related events as a result. Relational operants — such as comparative, temporal and hierarchal frames — are generalized operants, meaning they have been abstracted over multiple exemplars and both the type of relating and the functions relevant to transformation are brought under contextual control such that they can be arbitrarily applied based upon one's verbal community and history.

A series of studies have been found to support the existence of relational operants. Studies have shown that derived relational responding develops over time (Lipkens, Hayes, & Hayes, 1991) and can come under both antecedent and consequential control (Healy, Barnes-Holmes, & Smeets, 2000; Roche, Barnes-Holmes, Smeets, Barnes-Holmes, & McGeady, 2000), each of which is a feature of operant behavior (Hayes et al., 2001).

Furthermore, recent studies have demonstrated that arbitrarily applicable derived relational responding can be trained through multiple exemplars (e.g., Barnes-Holmes, Y., Barnes-Holmes, D., Smeets, Strand, & Friman, 2004; Berens & Hayes, 2007),

The contextually-controlled transformation of functions produced through relational networks is a key feature of relational operants in accounting for verbal behavior. Studies have supported the existence of such a process in various types of relational frames by demonstrating derived transformation of functions including avoidance (Dymond, Roche, Forsyth, Whelan, & Rhoden, 2007), sexual arousal (Roche et al., 2000) and self-discrimination (Dymond & Barnes, 1995).

The findings from RFT studies have significant implications for both basic and applied behavioral research. A new behavioral principle is not necessary to account for the existence of relational operants. However, the implications of this operant, specifically derived transformation of stimulus functions, does appear to require a new principle (Berens & Hayes, 2007). There are currently no existing principles to account for how behavioral processes such as direct contingency principles can be altered through the derived transformation of functions that occurs in language-able humans (e.g., Dougher, Hamilton, Fink, & Harrington, 2007).

In addition to its implications for basic research, RFT has several implications for applied clinical work. First, the verbal processes that appear to be involved in psychological problems are also essential to critical activities such as problem-solving, suggesting that there is no healthy way to eliminate these processes. Rather, the task is to bring them under better contextual control. An operant account of verbal behavior also leads to the conclusion that one cannot actually eliminate cognitions. This is a simple extension of the additive nature of learning, in which aspects of an individual's relational history cannot simply be subtracted. Furthermore, direct attempts to alter thoughts can also elaborate a relational network and increase its importance rather than reduce its impact, because the relational cues designed to change the structure of a relational network may also serve as functional cues for the centrality of targeted events. Finally, because the transformation of functions produced through relational networks is under contextual control, one may be able to reduce the impact of harmful functions without reducing the content or frequency of relation (e.g., the form of thoughts) by manipulating the relevant context. Each of these implications has had a significant impact on the development of ACT (Hayes, Luoma, Bond, Masuda, & Lillis, 2006).

The RFT analysis of language and cognition co-evolved with ACT, forming the foundation of the theory of psychopathology and providing a naturalistic means to manipulating the impact of private events on overt behavior by altering the context of how one relates to thoughts and emotions (Hayes et al., 2007). New findings within RFT continue to inform current treatment models, as well as suggesting entirely new treatments and processes (e.g., Rehfeldt, Dillen, Ziomek, & Kowalchuk, 2007). The added complexity of studying verbal behavior in RFT suggests that applied researchers may be able to provide useful contributions to the basic research program, beyond what has occurred in the past with traditional behavior analysis. Traditionally, research has steered away from studying environment–behavior relations in applied settings due to the increased complexity and inclusion of confounding variables, instead developing principles largely through work with animals. Yet, many features of language can only be studied with complex human behaviors, and there are few adequate preparations currently available to do such work. RFT thus changes some of the more traditional relationships between basic and applied research, as the results from applied extensions of the basic analysis to complex behavior can have more of a direct impact on the basic research program (Hayes & Berens, 2004).

The ACT/RFT research program instantiates a successful 'mutual interest' model of how applied psychology can best progress, in which the applied domain is linked to progress in the basic domain and vice versa. Both applied and basic psychologists need a functional account of language and cognition and the shared goal of prediction and influence allows basic and applied contextual behavioral scientists to communicate and use their findings. Many of the findings in RFT have emerged from clinical laboratories (e.g., Berens & Hayes, 2007; Dougher et al., 2007; Steele & Hayes, 1991). Due to the shared theoretical area of research, the mutual interest model allows progress in basic research to further inform applied interventions and research in applied work to inform basic research. Further development and refinement of basic principles can be built into new models of treatment and intervention, as well as specific technologies. Alternatively, the successful application of refined principles in interventions provides an inductive test of the generality of principles and theory at higher levels of abstraction and complexity. The effects of specific intervention technologies or the application of treatment to new problems may also create additional questions regarding analytical concepts that are important to basic researchers.

3. Create a Model or Theory of Pathology, Intervention and Health Tied to Basic Principles

In the mainstream approach to applied psychology, assessment and intervention are largely atheoretical. This is typically enabled by mechanistic assumptions in which the goal of analysis is to model the underlying structure of an ontological reality. 'Theory' is not at issue: the need is to discover how a preorganized world is arranged. A classic example is the syndromal classification of psychological disorders, which represents an attempt to create precise ways of speaking regarding psychological problems, but without an emphasis on functional dimensions, principles and theories that would provide adequate scope for either a coherent theory or for use with applied workers (Hayes, 1997). The result is an increasingly expansive list of diagnostic labels based on subtler topographical distinctions and with little link back to any distinct etiological pathways.

Within current approaches to treatment development, technology is generally emphasized over theory. This lack of theoretical orientation leaves the research program without an efficient way to develop new techniques, treat new problems, or train the treatment in a coherent way. Instead, treatment developers rely on technologies that have been successful in treating other problems with little theoretical explanation for its new application and the mechanisms of change to be emphasized. Heterogeneous treatment packages are developed with, at times, minimal theory explaining how the components relate. The technique focus of these packages leads to the creation of highly specified manuals that do not provide the flexibility for applied workers to adapt them to the various multiproblem clients seen in everyday practice.

The combination of precise syndromes and treatment packages without theory and scope leads to a long list of large, unwieldy treatment packages for each disorder based upon topographical distinctions. This creates significant problems within treatment delivery as health care delivery systems and clinicians cannot possibly be trained and use the distinct treatment packages required for each problem. In addition, it creates a scientific problem for applied researchers who are left with no way to simplify their analytic task.

These problems are reflected in the ongoing debate regarding how best to classify a treatment as an EST, in which there is an increasing emphasis being placed on theory testing and examining the process of change in therapy (Castonguay & Beutler, 2006; Kazdin, 2001; Rosen & Davison, 2003). Funding sources such as the National Institute of Mental Health (NIMH) have also increased their focus on basic processes related to psychopathology and translational research that integrates this basic work with applied research (National Advisory Mental Health Council, 2000; Tashiro & Mortensen, 2006).

Contextual behavioral science is a theory-driven approach, and thus holds the creation of a theoretical model of pathology, health and intervention as essential. In a traditional behavior analytic approach, specific problems for specific people are analyzed in terms of behavioral principles — a process known as functional analysis. The problem with functional analysis is scope: a functional analysis needs to be conducted one person at a time. In a CBS approach theories are 'analytic abstractive' — which means that they are sets of functional analyses within a behavioral domain.

Theories of this kind organize the contextual factors related to the development and maintenance of psychological problems (of health) and the processes through which intervention produces its effects. The connection to refined principles allows such theories to produce analyses that are high scope, parsimonious and coherent. This is as distinct from entity postulating, hypothetico-deductive models in which theory is minimally linked to manipulable or even observable variables (Hayes, 2004).

Middle-level, gerundive concepts are often needed to provide a link between basic principles and theories of pathology, health and intervention. Core processes to target in interventions are specified with middle-level concepts that organize and describe the relationship between principles, contextual factors and behaviors.

Theories provide a framework detailing how psychological health/ distress is defined, how it is measured/assessed and how techniques should be applied to clinical problems (Waltz & Hayes, in press). Functional core processes and mechanisms of change are clearly identified within the theoretical model, which can inform the creation of new technologies or the application of an existing treatment to new problems (Hayes, 1998b). Middle-level concepts may function as flexible rules for assessment and intervention, increasing the ability for clinicians to adapt treatment to current setting and client characteristics (Waltz & Hayes, in press). An organized body of knowledge can be established based on these core principles and processes, reducing the dependence on highly technical language and increasing the ease of training and dissemination of treatments (Hayes, 1991; Rosen & Davison, 2003).

ACT bases its theory of psychopathology and treatment upon principles derived from both traditional behavior analysis and RFT (see Hayes et al., 2006 or Hayes et al., 2007 for a review). Within ACT, the hexaflex (see Figure 1.1) represents a system of middle-level gerundive concepts that serves both as a model of psychopathology and treatment (Hayes et al., 2006; Hayes et al., 2007). Several reviews have been conducted describing the mid-level concepts within the hexaflex at various levels including its link to basic RFT principles (Hayes et al., 2007), case conceptualization (Bach & Moran, 2008; Wilson, 2007) and treatment technologies (Luoma, Hayes, & Walser, 2007).

ACT is an approach to psychological intervention defined in terms of certain theoretical processes, not a technology per se. The seven core ACT processes together provide a model of pathology, health and intervention. These concepts will be reviewed extensively in other chapters and thus we will review them only briefly here. Our primary interest is in showing how ACT and RFT instantiate a CBS approach.

Commitment and Behavior
Change Processes

Contact with the
Present Moment

Acceptance

Values

Psychological
Flexibility

Defusion

Committed
Action

Self as
Context

Mindfulness and
Acceptance
Processes

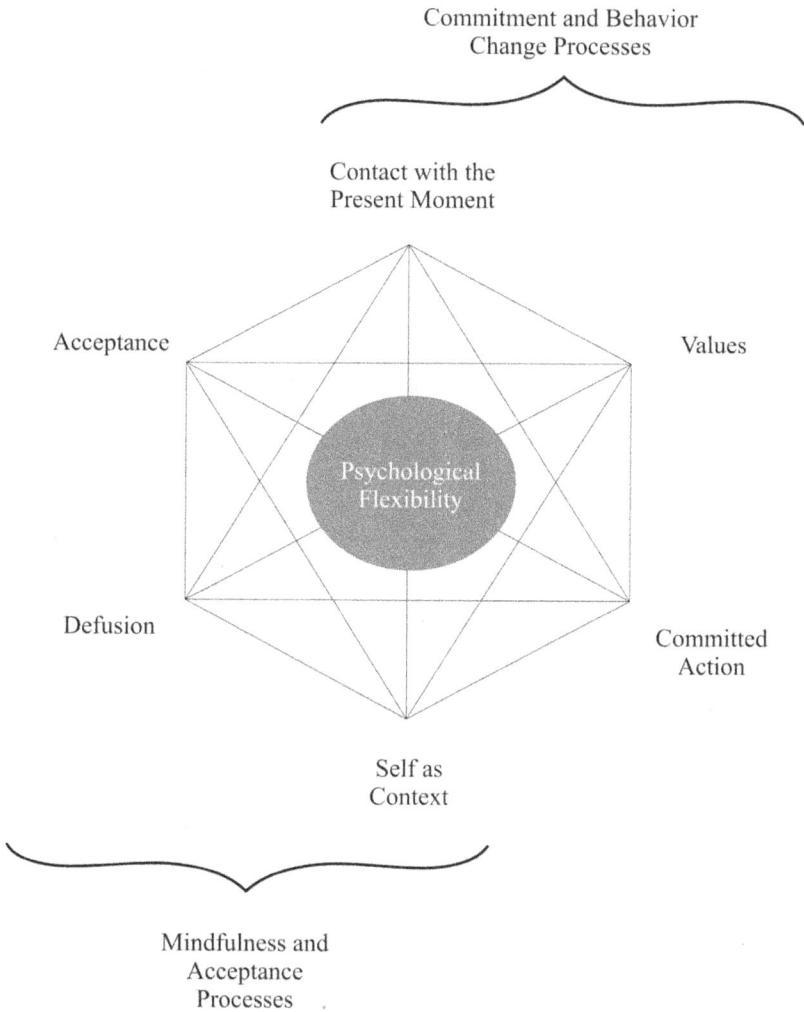

FIGURE 1.1
The hexaflex.

Cognitive defusion. There is a tendency for verbal events to be treated literally, and in that context they often considerably alter the functions of other events. In an ACT model this is termed 'cognitive fusion'. Often that process is clinically unhelpful. In ACT, cognitive defusion and mindfulness techniques attempt to alter the undesirable functions of thoughts and other private events, rather than trying to alter their form, frequency or situational sensitivity. In technical RFT terms, ACT uses functional more so than relational contexts to alter the impact of unhelpful verbal events. Said another way, ACT attempts to change the way one *interacts with* or *relates to* thoughts by creating contexts in which their unhelpful functions are diminished. There are scores of such techniques that have been developed for a wide variety of clinical presentations (Hayes & Strosahl, 2005). For example, a negative thought could be watched dispassionately, repeated out loud until only its sound remains, or treated as an externally observed event by giving it a shape, size, color, speed, or form. The result of defusion is usually a decrease in believability of, or attachment to, private events, rather than an immediate change in their frequency.

Acceptance. Experiential avoidance refers to the unwillingness to experience 'negative' emotions, thoughts, memories, or physical sensations as they are, even though avoiding these experiences creates behavioral harm (Hayes, Wilson, Gifford, Follette, & Strosahl, 1996). This is argued in ACT/RFT to emerge from the overdominance of comparative frames as applied to private events, and the resulting problem-solving steps focused on changing these events. From a RFT perspective, attempts to reduce the occurrence of relational framing serve to paradoxically increase the strength of the contexts that occasion their impact. Acceptance is taught as an alternative to experiential avoidance. Acceptance involves the active and aware embrace of those private events occasioned by one's history without unnecessary attempts to change their frequency or form, especially when doing so would cause psychological harm. For example, anxiety patients are taught to feel anxiety, as a feeling, fully and without defense; pain patients are given methods that encourage them to let go of a struggle with pain, and so on. Acceptance in ACT is not an end in itself. Rather, acceptance is fostered as a method of increasing values-based action.

Being present. Because of the domination of temporal and causal frames, in part due to the usefulness of relational framing for problem solving, language and cognition often lead to the loss of contact with the present moment, and increased contact with the conceptualized past and future. ACT promotes ongoing nonjudgmental contact with psychological and environmental events as they occur. The goal is to have clients experience the world more directly so that their behavior is more flexible, and thus their actions more consistent with the values that they hold. This is accomplished by allowing workability to exert more control over behavior; and by using language more as a tool to note and describe events, not simply to predict and judge them. A sense of self, called 'self-as-process', is actively encouraged: the defused, nonjudgmental ongoing description of thoughts, feelings and other private events.

Self-as-context. When literal language is applied to the 'self,' a conceptualized self emerges that is then defended. This considerably enhances psychological rigidity, since the reinforcers for this sense of self (e.g., being right) are often orthogonal to natural and chosen reinforcers. The solution is to undermine attachment to a conceptualized self and enhance contact with a sense of perspective taking — or 'self as context'. Because of relational frames such as *I* vs. *You, Now* vs. *Then,* and *Here* vs. *There,* human language leads to a sense of self as a locus or perspective, and provides a transcendent, spiritual side to normal verbal humans. This idea was one of the seeds from which both ACT and RFT grew (Hayes, 1984), and there is now growing evidence of its importance to language functions such as empathy, theory of mind, sense of self, and the like (e.g., McHugh, Barnes-Holmes, & Barnes-Holmes, 2004). In brief, the idea is that 'I' emerges over large sets of exemplars of perspective-taking relations (termed in RFT 'deictic relations'), but since this sense of self is a context for verbal knowing, not the content of that knowing, its limits cannot be consciously known. Self-as-context is important, in part because from this standpoint, one can be aware of one's own flow of experiences without attachment to them or an investment in which particular experiences occur: thus defusion and acceptance is fostered. Self-as-context is fostered in ACT by mindfulness exercises, metaphors, and experiential processes.

Values. Values are chosen qualities of purposive action that can never be obtained as an object but can be instantiated moment by moment. In RFT terms, values are formative and motivative augmentals that alter and enhance the consequential properties of streams of behavioral events. ACT uses a variety of exercises to help a client choose life directions in various domains (e.g., family, career, spirituality) while undermining verbal processes that might lead to choices based on avoidance, social compliance, or fusion (e.g., 'I should value X' or 'A good person would value Y' or 'My mother wants me to value Z'). In ACT, acceptance, defusion, being present, and so on are not ends in themselves; rather they clear the path for a more vital, values-consistent life.

Committed action. Finally, ACT encourages the development of larger and larger patterns of effective action linked to chosen values. In this re-gard, ACT looks very much like traditional behavior therapy, and almost any behaviorally coherent behavior change method can be fitted into an ACT protocol, including exposure, skills acquisition, shaping methods, goal setting, and the like. Unlike values, which are constantly instantiated but never achieved as an object, concrete goals that are values-consistent can be achieved, and ACT protocols almost always involve therapy work and homework linked to short-, medium-, and long-term behavior change goals. Behavior change efforts, in turn, lead to contact with psychological barriers that are addressed through other ACT processes (acceptance, defusion, and so on).

Psychological flexibility. Psychological inflexibility occurs as a result of the dominance of certain kinds of rule-governed behavior leading to avoidance, fusion, loss of the present, attachment to a conceptualized self, lack of values clarity, and lack of committed action. This is the ACT model of pathology. The model of health and intervention is the exact opposite — in which psychological flexibility is the core result of acceptance, defusion, contact with the present moment, self-as-context, values, and committed action. Psychological flexibility can be defined as contacting the present moment fully and without defense, and persisting or changing in behavior in the service of chosen values.

These concepts orient practitioners to particularly relevant clinical behaviors and contextual factors. The use of these concepts helps deal with the considerable complexity of RFT and of the inclusion of language and cognition into an analysis of human behavior and intervention. Metaphorically, middle-level concepts can be seen as a kind of computer interface or operating system that does not require users to fully understand the refined principles that are more like the lines of code that programmed the operating system (Muto, 2008b; Waltz & Hayes, in press). The interface is built from the source code, but one may use the system in an efficient, effective way without necessarily needing to understand all of the code.

Despite the utility of middle-level concepts in organizing theories of psychopathology and treatment, it is important to not let them become hypothetical constructs that *replace* the basic principles they represent. Continued work needs to be conducted on linking these middle-level concepts to basic behavioral principles and concepts, both theoretically and experimentally. The chapter by Blackledge and Barnes-Holmes in this volume speculates as to what many of these basic behavioral principles may be.

Experimental psychopathology research has served to test the theoretical model of psychopathology based on these mid-level concepts, as well as their connection to basic principles. The breadth of problems found to relate to ACT processes is consistent with the theoretical model in which problematic features of language (e.g., overextensions of evaluative framing and problem-solving) can lead to a number of functionally equivalent, but topographically distinct problems.

One area of research supporting the ACT model has been within the thought suppression literature. Thought suppression can be viewed as a result of both fusion and experiential avoidance, or the dominance of literal, evaluative functions and subsequent attempts to avoid this relational repertoire. A meta-analysis of 28 studies found that although thought suppression may initially reduce the frequency of thoughts, attempts over time result in an increase in their occurrence (i.e., rebound effect; Abramowitz, Tolin & Street, 2001). These findings help to support the ACT model of psychopathology and treatment in which ineffective control strategies may paradoxically increase the occurrence of the event being avoided. Other studies have also demonstrated the impact of cognitive fusion on distress. For example, a study by Gaudiano and Herbert (2006b) found that the relationship between frequency of hallucinations and distress is mediated by believability in hallucinations.

Findings within the distress tolerance and task persistence literature have also supported the ACT model. Studies have examined people's ability to persist in difficult tasks including aversive visual images (e.g., Cochrane, Barnes-Holmes, Barnes-Holmes, Stewart, & Luciano, 2007), cold pressors (e.g., Feldner et al., 2006), breath-holding (Brown, Lejuez, Kahler, & Strong, 2002) and math tasks (e.g., Gratz, Rosenthal, Tull, Lejuez, & Gunderson, 2006). Task persistence has been found to relate to a number of problems including substance use (Brandon et al., 2003; Brown et al., 2002; Daughters, Lejuez, Kahler, Strong, & Brown, 2005), gambling (Daughters, Lejuez, Strong, et al., 2005), a history of childhood abuse (Gratz, Bornovalova, & Delany-Brumsey, 2007), and borderline personality disorder (Gratz et al., 2006). This behavioral measure fits coherently into the ACT process of experiential avoidance. In support of this assertion, several studies have found the Acceptance and Action Questionnaire (AAQ; Hayes, Strosahl et al., 2004), a self-report measure of ACT processes, including experiential avoidance, moderated participants' ability to persist in distressing tasks (Cochrane et al., 2007; Feldner et al., 2006; Zettle et al., 2005; Zettle, Petersen, Hocker, & Provines, 2007). In addition, studies have found the AAQ to moderate subjective distress and emotional reactivity in distressing tasks (Cochrane et al., 2007; Karekala, Forsyth, & Kelly, 2004; Sloan, 2004; Spira, Zvolensky, Eifert, & Feldner, 2004; Zettle et al., 2007). These studies suggest the role of ACT processes in determining both people's ability to persist in a difficult task and their reactivity to distressing stimuli.

In the service of further developing the theory of psychopathology, additional experimental research is needed to specify the relationship of other processes, such as values and self, as content to psychological problems. Other features of behavior may also be examined, including delayed discounting (Waltz, Follette, & Drossel, 2007) and behavioral variability (Muto, 2008a). Behavioral measures may be especially promising as they avoid problems related to self-report and provide more direct observation of the behaviors of interest.

4. Measure Processes of Change
Within contextual behavioral science, the assessment of processes of change is emphasized. Processes of change represent the actual targets of treatment

that are hypothesized to produce clinical gains (Follette, 1995). Measures of processes of change can be used to test the theoretical model of psychopathology and intervention. One can examine whether theoretically important processes account for observed treatment effects through meditational analysis. Treatment packages or specific components may also be tested to see if they successfully impact the processes they are designed to. This aspect of contextual behavioral science is vital as it provides a link between the basic research on refined principles, analytic abstractive theories, and subsequent applied research with treatment technologies and packages. Recent criticisms of ACT have often focused on the claim that it is not different to the existing CBT treatment packages (Arch & Craske, in press; Hofmann & Asmundson, 2008). Examining the mechanisms of change within treatment packages provides one useful avenue to distinguish between therapies (O'Donohue & Yeater, 2003) and is thus important in the establishment of ACT as a unique therapy.

The development of ACT-specific process measures such as the AAQ (Hayes, Strosahl et al., 2004) have been used to examine the relationship between ACT processes and psychological/behavioral problems. The AAQ has been shown to relate to areas of psychopathology including a variety of anxiety disorders (e.g., Begotka, Woods, & Wetterneck, 2004; Flessner & Woods, 2006; Roemer, Salters, Raffa, & Orsillo, 2005; Tull, Gratz, Salters, & Roemer, 2004), depression (Hayes et al., 2006; Spira, Beaudreau, & Jimenez, 2007), chronic pain (e.g., McCracken, Vowles, & Eccleston, 2004), problem drinking (Stewart, Zvolensky, & Eifert, 2002), and self-harm (Chapman, Specht, & Cellucci, 2005). A recent meta-analysis (Hayes et al., 2006) showed that AAQ scores could account for 16 to 25% of the variance in behavioral health problems generally.

A variety of other process measures have been created within the ACT literature. Population-specific measures of the AAQ have been designed that are more sensitive to specific behaviors and contexts including body image (BI-AAQ; Sandoz & Wilson, 2006), diabetes management (AADQ; Gregg, Callaghan, Hayes, & Glenn-Lawson, 2007), weight (Lillis, Hayes, Bunting, & Masuda, under review), chronic pain (CPAQ; McCracken, Vowles, & Eccleston, 2004), auditory hallucinations (VAAS; Shawyer et al., 2007) and epilepsy (AAEpQ; Lundgren, Dahl, & Hayes, in press). The use of these disorder-specific measures is supported by their success over the general AAQ in accounting for treatment effects within clinical trials (e.g., Gifford et al., 2004; Gregg et al., 2007; Lillis et al., under review; Lundgren et al., in press). Measures of cognitive fusion have focused on the believability of thoughts related to depression (ATQ-B; Zettle & Hayes, 1986), substance abusing clients (SAB; Hayes, Bissett, et al., 2004), psychotic symptoms (Bach & Hayes, 2002; Gaudiano & Herbert, 2006a), and barriers to using empirically supported treatments (STA-B; Varra, Hayes, Roget, & Fisher, in press) and the belief that symptoms are caused by work (Dahl, Wilson, & Nilsson, 2004). A number of values measures have recently been developed, including the Personal Values Questionnaire (Blackledge, Ciarrochi, Bilich, & Heaven, 2007), Valued Living Questionnaire (Wilson, Sandoz, Kitchens, & Roberts, under review), and the Bulls-Eye instrument about valued life (Lundgren, 2006), which measure various features of values including valued domains of living, pliance, success in achieving values and persistence towards values despite barriers. Mindfulness measures such as the Five Facet Mindfulness Questionnaire (Baer, Smith, Hopkins, Krietemeyer, & Toney, 2006) and Mindfulness Attention Awareness Scale (Brown & Ryan, 2003) assess a combination of several ACT processes including present moment contact, fusion, experiential avoidance, and sense of self. Finally, there are several established measures from other research areas that fit well within ACT theory, including certain subfactors of the COPE (Carver, Scheier, & Weintraub, 1989) that assess experiential avoidance and measures of thought suppression (e.g., White Bear Suppression Inventory; Wegner & Zanakos, 1994).

The broad range of ACT-relevant process measures demonstrates the continuous work within ACT on identifying valid and reliable measures of processes of change. Yet, further development is needed in many of these areas. Fusion measures focusing on believability may miss several essential facets of this process including the tendency for literal, evaluative language to influence subsequent behavior. Values measures are still relatively new and have not received adequate empirical support regarding reliability and validity. Clear measures of processes such as self as context and present moment awareness have yet to be created. These limitations may be due, in part, to an emphasis on developing process measures related to mid-level concepts. Processes such as fusion and contact with the present moment overlap considerably, making the development of precise and mutually exclusive measures extremely difficult. Furthermore, all of the above process measures use self-report, which include additional auxiliaries and conditions that make it difficult to assess whether findings are due to the theory being tested or other features of assessment.

Behavioral measures may assist with some of these limitations. Preparations have been created to assess a number of processes, including distress tolerance (e.g., Lejuez, Kahler, & Brown, 2003), experiential avoidance (e.g., Herzberg, Forsyth, Dispenza, & Acheson, 2007), and behavioral variability (Muto, 2008a). These behavioral measures provide a tighter link between the theory and auxiliaries and have begun to be used as process measures in clinical trials (Lillis et al., under review). Yet, a great deal of research is still required in identifying the processes and principles being observed with these measures. If behavioral tasks are used as process measures, then additional research is needed to examine their properties (including reliability and training effects) as assessment tools.

5. Testing Techniques and Components Linked to Processes

Within an inductive approach, refined principles and processes specified in the theoretical model are built into intervention technologies, leading to a strong knowledge of the treatment elements within a package. Interventions are specifically designed to target theoretical processes of change related to problem behaviors. Existing treatment technologies originating from other sources that are tightly linked to relevant processes of change may also be included, as exemplified by the use of mindfulness exercises from Buddhist traditions in ACT. Building techniques tightly connected to these basic elements helps to avoid creating large, heterogeneous packages in which technologies are included with little link to theory and thus minimal understanding of each component's effect on mechanisms of change or outcome. This method also provides practicing clinicians with the flexibility of adapting existing technologies to more adequately fit specific client or setting characteristics, while keeping the emphasis on the relevant process of change being targeted.

Components and specific technologies can subsequently be tested in smaller analogue and experimental formats to explore the effects of treatment technologies on outcome variables and theoretical processes of change. These studies help to refine treatment packages by identifying inactive components, or components that do not have a specified process through which they produce treatment effects (Borkovec & Castonguay, 1998). Results can further test and inform the theoretical model as to the relevant processes of change and how they are best manipulated. Conducting these small, experimental studies provides an advantage over other approaches that typically emphasize expensive dismantling studies (e.g., Jacobson et al., 1996; Dimidjian et al., 2006), which often occur late in treatment development after the therapy has been well established and developers are more resistant to making modifications (Hayes et al., 2006).

Over the past 10 years, a number of experimental studies have been conducted using a variety of ACT treatment components. Some of these used clinical populations and clinically relevant tasks (e.g., Levitt, Brown, Orsillo, & Barlow, 2004). Some were component treatment studies (e.g., Williams, 2007). Others used experimental tasks such as task persistence in the presence of pain.

Performance in these tasks provides a means to test the influence of ACT components on mid-level processes that are tightly linked to specific behavior. In a recent meta-analysis of 16 studies testing ACT components on task persistence (Levin, Yadavaia, Hildebrandt, & Hayes, 2007), the acceptance component of ACT alone or in combination with other components (e.g., values, defusion) demonstrated a large effect size overall on increasing both task persistence and willingness to engage in the task again, as well as a small to medium effect size on subjective distress. These effects were demonstrated both in comparison to attention controls as well as suppression/distraction conditions, which sometimes used techniques taken directly from standard CBT protocols (e.g., Gutiérrez, Luciano, Rodríguez, & Fink, 2004). These interventions did not reduce physiological reactivity during the tasks despite the effects on other behaviors, which supports the hypothesis that these treatment components may work in part by creating desynchrony between behavior and other private events such as distressing physical sensations. Studies found minimal effects on task persistence when participants were only given a rationale for acceptance (e.g., McMullen et al., 2008), lending support for the emphasis in ACT on metaphors and experiential exercises (Levin et al., 2007). These studies also support the use of other ACT components such as values (Páez-Blarrina et al., 2008) and defusion (Gutiérrez et al., 2004), alone and in combination with acceptance components. The use of multiple treatment components in many of these studies is due, in part, to the inclusion of multiple processes in many treatment technologies (i.e., the chessboard metaphor) and the large degree of overlap between mid-level concepts.

Research has also been conducted on the effects of defusion on difficult thoughts. A study by Masuda and colleagues (2004) found that the use of the milk, milk, milk exercise — a standard defusion technique — reduced the impact of negative, self-relevant thoughts in college students. Marcks and Woods (2005) found another defusion exercise, soldiers on parade, to reduce distress related to personally relevant intrusive thoughts compared to a suppression condition. A subsequent study found the same exercise did not reduce anxiety related to intrusive thoughts, but did increase the willingness to re-experience the intrusive thought provoking task (Marcks & Woods, 2007).

Findings from other research areas may be used to support the efficacy of particular ACT components. For example, a series of studies have been conducted within the self-affirmation literature that provides some support for the broad impact of values-based interventions. Studies have found that a brief writing exercise in which participants write about important, personally-relevant values can produce a variety of effects — including reduced stress while engaging in a distressing task (Creswell et al., 2005), improved grades for stigmatized minority students (Cohen, Garcia, Apfel, & Master, 2006), and increased responsiveness to health messages (Harris & Napper, 2005). Within the pain coping literature, a series of studies have found that sensate focus interventions, in which participants are instructed to attend to the sensations of a pain task, reduce the level of pain experienced (e.g., Cioffi & Holloway, 1993; Logan, Baron, & Kohout, 1995), lending support for the potential impact of the present moment component of ACT (at least in response to physical pain). Finally, there are numerous studies demonstrating the positive impact of mindfulness-based interventions for a variety of problems (Baer, 2003; Toneatto & Nguyen, 2007), which support the combined use of self-as-context, present moment, defusion, and acceptance components.

Overall, these published studies lend support for the impact of ACT components on processes of change and clinically relevant behaviors. Due to the link between ACT components and RFT, these results also support RFT by demonstrating the impact of processes related to relational operants on behavior at higher abstractive levels. Future research may continue to test ACT components in various combinations and sequences to further test the ACT model, specific technologies, and their link with processes of change. With some exceptions, component research so far has emphasized a limited number of behaviors and processes including task persistence, emotional reactivity, and reductions in thought-related distress. Further work could examine additional relevant outcomes and processes through behavioral tasks such as delayed discounting (Waltz et al., 2007) or sensitivity to changing contingencies with a behavioral variability preparation (Muto, 2008). The difficulty of trying to parse out the middle-level concepts in the hexaflex can be problematic when attempting to precisely test specific components of ACT such as acceptance and present moment contact. Yet, this is not necessarily problematic in a functional contextual approach as these middle-level concepts do not represent 'true', independent processes. Rather middle-level concepts such as acceptance and values are ways of speaking that orient therapists to relevant features of behavior and context. Thus, one does not necessarily have to 'prove' the utility of each component in complete isolation as no claim is made regarding these as mutually distinct entities.

6. Strong Emphasis on Mediation/Moderation in Testing Treatment Impact

Group designs such as randomized clinical trials (RCTs) provide a test of the generalization of context–behavior relationships across a number of individuals (Biglan & Hayes, 1996). This approach allows one to answer important questions regarding the source of treatment effects, as well as to compare processes and outcomes to other active treatments. In addition, group designs represent the standard for demonstrating the effectiveness of a treatment within the larger domain of clinical psychology. Given the pragmatic truth criterion, it is thus extremely important to contribute to this area of research in order to impact other research programs, receive funding, and to increase dissemination.

Unfortunately, the emphasis within group design methodology is often narrowly focused on controlling for internal validity (Borkovec & Castonguay, 1998; Follette & Beitz, 2003) and does not comport well with the analytic goals of contextual behavioral science. This is demonstrated with a recent criticism of ACT that focused on its lack of tightly controlled RCTs (Öst, 2008), missing the larger strategy within the contextual behavioral approach in which both the treatment model and technologies are tested at multiple levels of abstraction using a variety of methodologies. EST standards specifically focus on what treatment is effective for a specific problem (Chambless & Ollendick, 2001; Follette & Beitz, 2003). Although this methodology removes many confounding variables, such as placebo and maturation effects, it often only tests whether some unspecified components of a treatment package produced effects through an unknown process in a very specific setting (Borkovec & Castonguay, 1998). This leaves several of the most critical questions for both clinicians and researchers unanswered, including identifying who will respond to treatment and how treatment effects are produced. Critiques of current EST standards have often emphasized this lack of attention to processes of change (Rosen & Davison, 2003). Solely testing treatment packages without examining theoretical models and processes of change represents a more brute force empirical approach that is unlikely to be progressive due to reasons described throughout this chapter.

Including mediational analyses within outcome studies allows for a more complex analysis of treatment effects by examining the relation between processes of change and treatment outcomes. Mediator variables represent the processes through which an intervention produces an effect on outcome variables (MacKinnon, Fairchild, & Fritz, 2007). These analyses allow researchers to test both the efficacy of the treatment package in targeting processes of change and the strength of the theoretical model in accounting for observed outcomes. Mediational analysis involves testing the degree of variance in treatment effects accounted for by changes in the mediators when controlling for treatment (MacKinnon et al., 2007). If a treatment package fails to alter the mediator or produce clinical outcomes, one may change the method of intervention as it is ineffective at influencing what it is designed to (Follette, 1995; MacKinnon et al., 2007). However, if the mediator repeatedly fails to account for the treatment effects it suggests a problem with the overall model in accounting for clinical improvements (Follette, 1995). Furthermore, if a treatment successfully alters the mediator, but does not produce improvements in outcome, one may infer that the model is incorrect as changes in the mediator did not produce changes in outcome (Follette, 1995). Prior to making these assumptions, however, it is important to consider whether treatment effects were assessed for a sufficient time span, as there may be a delay between changes in mediators and observed changes in outcome (MacKinnon et al., 2007). This also necessitates reliable and valid process measures as one would not want to mistakenly attribute problems with measurement auxiliaries and conditions to problems with the theory. As ACT can be conceptualized more as a model of treatment than a specific set of techniques, the success of mediation as a test of the model is essential. Even if ACT technologies are able to produce clinical outcomes, it is very important to identify the mediators through which these techniques produce their effects in order to develop and refine the theoretical model upon which this approach is based. Almost every ACT RCT has explored processes of change or mediation, although with varying degrees of methodological rigor. These studies have fairly consistently shown a differential impact of ACT interventions on the ACT theoretical processes of change and for these processes of change to relate to or account for treatment outcomes (see Hayes et al., 2006 for a review of specific studies). A recent meta-analysis of 12 studies calculated an effect size of the proportion mediated through ACT processes using the cross-product of the coefficients (MacKinnon et al., 2007) in order to provide a more quantitative summary of these studies. The meta-analysis found ACT processes accounted for approximately 50% of the variance of changes in primary outcome measures (Hayes, Levin, Yadavaia, & Vilardaga, 2007). These findings provide strong support for the ACT theoretical model as well as the technologies designed to produce clinical gains.

Direct comparisons of ACT to other active treatments, such as CBT, provide useful information regarding the relative efficacy of treatments as well as distinguishing treatments on the basis of the mechanisms of change. When comparing ACT to CBT/CT, studies have found ACT treatment effects to be mediated/correlated with changes in the AAQ (Forman, Herbert, Moitra, Yeomans, & Geller, 2007; Lappalainen et al., 2007), the acceptance and acting with awareness subscales of the Kentucky Inventory of Mindfulness Skills (KIMS; Forman et al., 2007), believability of depressive thoughts and reason giving (Zettle & Hayes, 1986; Hayes et al., 2006), and the mental disengagement subscale of the COPE (Branstetter et al., 2004; Hayes et al., 2006). In contrast, CBT/CT effects were mediated/correlated with self-confidence (Lappalainen et al., 2007), the observing and describing subscales of the KIMS (Forman et al., 2007), and reductions in dysfunctional attitudes (Zettle & Rains, 1989). None of the processes that mediated or correlated with ACT did so for CBT and the same was true with the CBT processes for ACT. These studies have also provided information regarding the relative efficacy of ACT compared to CBT and CT. Overall, ACT outcomes have been found to be comparable to CBT

(Forman et al., 2007; Zettle & Rains, 1989) or better (Block & Wulfert, 2000; Branstetter et al., 2004; Hayes et al., 2006; Lappalainen et al., 2007; Zettle & Hayes, 1986), although various methodological features of the studies may limit what can be concluded from these findings (Forman et al., 2007). ACT has also been found to demonstrate effects through different processes of change when compared to multicultural education (Hayes et al., 2004) and workplace innovation (Bond & Bunce, 2000).

Mediation has failed to fully support the model in a few ACT outcome studies. For example, Blackledge and Hayes (2006) did not find a significant change on the AAQ after an ACT workshop for parents of autistic children, although the believability scale of the Automatic Thoughts Questionnaire (ATQ-B; Zettle & Hayes, 1986) did function as a mediator. Another study comparing ACT and systematic desensitization found improvements on the AAQ with both interventions (Zettle, 2003). Yet overall, findings suggest that ACT technologies are more effective at moving the ACT-relevant processes than some other active treatments and that these processes account for the observed outcomes with treatment. Furthermore, ACT appears to produce its effects through different pathways than other active treatments such as CBT.

The positive findings regarding mediation are somewhat attenuated due to an inability to conduct a full meditational analysis in some studies because of methodological limitations. The methodological rigor of the ACT RCT studies fluctuates greatly, perhaps in part due to differences in stages of treatment development and testing. Some studies have only demonstrated the effect of ACT on processes of change (Bach & Hayes, 2002; Gratz & Gunderson, 2006), with others also demonstrating an association of these changes with clinical outcomes (Dalrymple & Herbert, 2007; Forman et al., 2007; Gaudiano & Herbert, 2006a; Lappalainen et al., 2007; McCracken, Vowles, & Eccleston, 2005; Woods, Wetterneck ,& Flessner, 2006), but not controlling for treatment, which is essential for full meditational analysis. This was often due to the use of pilot data that did not include a control condition (e.g., Dalrymple & Herbert, 2007) or did not have a sufficient number of participants (e.g., Woods et al., 2006). In addition, many studies did not measure changes in process measures prior to changes in outcome (e.g., Blackledge & Hayes, 2006). Other studies have used Baron and Kenny's (1986) causal steps method for demonstrating mediation (Gifford et al., 2004) or a modified version by MacKinnon (2003; Hayes et al., 2004; Hayes et al., 2006). However, causal steps methods are difficult to use with multiple mediators, do not account for suppressor variables, have low power with small samples, and create difficulties in estimating the size of the indirect effect (MacKinnon, Lockwood, Hoffman, West, & Sheets, 2002). Using the cross-product of the coefficients for the a and b paths (indirect effect) to test mediation (MacKinnon et al., 2007; Preacher & Hayes, 2006) helps to correct for these problems and a series of recent ACT outcome studies have successfully shown mediation through ACT processes using this approach (Gifford et al., 2002; Gregg et al., 2007; Lillis et al., under review; Lundgren, Dahl & Hayes, in press; Varra et al., in press).

Future research on mediation may continue to use the cross-product approach (Preacher & Hayes, 2006) as it appears to account for many of the limitations in the more commonly used causal steps method (Baron & Kenny, 1986). Further work on testing the model is somewhat dependent on the development of adequate process measures. As previously mentioned, almost all of the available process measures are based on self-report and are generally highly face valid. Reliable and valid measures of many ACT processes have not yet been developed, but this will be important as it will allow researchers to more fully test the ability of the model to account for treatment effects.

Moderation is another important characteristic to examine with group designs as it identifies differences in response to treatment due to relevant variables such as client characteristics. Moderation provides the opportunity to explore treatment responders and nonresponders, which has implications for the theory of psychopathology as well as for increasing effectiveness through treatment matching. Tests of moderation are much less frequent within ACT RCTs. To date there have been only a few published studies examining moderation with ACT (Masuda et al., 2007; Zettle, 2003). The study by Masuda and colleagues (2007) found the AAQ moderated treatment effects, such that the education condition was only effective in reducing mental health stigma with individuals who were more psychologically flexible. The lack of treatment effects on psychologically inflexible participants was not observed in ACT, suggesting this treatment is more effective at reducing stigma with individuals who are highly inflexible. Another study by Zettle (2003) found that 'participants who had higher levels of experiential avoidance ... benefitted the most from ACT' while this was not true of desensitization (p. 211).

The use of the AAQ as a moderator raises empirical questions regarding whether this is a behavioral predisposition or trait versus a process through which therapeutic change is made. In the study by Zettle (2003) the AAQ did not function as a mediator that distinguished it from systematic desensitization, although it appeared to moderate treatment effects in ACT.

7. Test Effectiveness, Dissemination and Training and Link These to the Model

Within the dominant, stage-based approach, dissemination and effectiveness research often occurs late in treatment development after multiple

RCTs have been conducted. This leads to critical features of application not being tested until very late in treatment development (Hayes, 2002). Researchers often consider these larger scale studies as extensions of efficacy research that further test the generality of a treatment package in more heterogeneous populations and less controlled settings. This stands in contrast to what is needed by applied workers and health care delivery systems that require information regarding characteristics such as the cost of training, the best method to train effective therapists, and the acceptability of the treatment to both clinicians and patients (Hayes, 1998b). Restraints such as training costs may require changes in the treatment package in order to to allow for effective dissemination of an intervention. Thus, it would benefit researchers to identify these characteristics early in treatment development before a package has been finalized and tested in multiple RCTs (Hayes, 1998b).

Effectiveness studies are conducted early on in treatment development within the contextual behavioral approach. From a functional contextual perspective, the success of a research program can be evaluated ultimately by its ability to effectively predict and influence behavior in the context of how it is actually applied. Thus, a practical application model (Hayes, 2002) is taken in which researchers focus on the characteristics of applied work that relate to how a treatment can be effectively applied and produce optimal clinical gains. From this pragmatic perspective, the effectiveness of the treatment may also be assessed by criteria that include ability to disseminate, ease of training, cost effectiveness, and acceptability of the treatment.

The first treatment study conducted after the long hiatus from the Zettle and Rains outcome study in 1989 was a training effectiveness study. Strosahl, Hayes, Bergan and Romano (1998) conducted a manipulated training method (Hayes, 2002) study that involved extensive training in ACT for self-selected participants. The study found that participants who chose to engage in the training produced better outcomes than non-trained therapists as related to higher therapists' rating of patients' ability to cope, fewer medication referrals, and higher probability of having completed treatment. Recently, two new effectiveness studies have been conducted, which directly compare ACT to CBT/CT. A study by Lappalainen and colleagues (2007) found that student therapists receiving training in both CBT and ACT demonstrated better clinical effects with ACT in a heterogeneous sample of clients seeking treatment. The study found equivalently high ratings in client satisfaction and therapist satisfaction with treatment at post assessment, suggesting ACT is a fairly acceptable treatment. However, the data also suggests ACT may be less acceptable to clinicians at first compared to CBT, judging by the lower initial rating of knowledge regarding ACT, lower self-confidence in using the methods, and higher fear ratings when using these methods. Another effectiveness study conducted by Forman and colleagues (2007) trained doctoral student therapists in ACT and CT. The study demonstrated equivalent effects of ACT and CT in treating a heterogeneous population of anxious and depressed individuals.

Although these three studies provide initial information regarding the application of ACT in 'real world' settings, further research is needed to test a number of features related to effectiveness and dissemination. There is a general lack of information regarding how to effectively train clinicians in ACT or psychotherapy in general. Studies can examine the utility of books, workshops, consultation, and other methods — in combination or alone — for training effective clinicians. The claim that mid-level concepts assist in efficiently training effective clinicians can be tested to determine whether therapists who are not trained in basic behavioral principles and RFT can effectively conduct ACT. These studies may test characteristics that relate to successful dissemination and adoption, including knowledge and competency with ACT, cost effectiveness of training, ease of training, acceptability/satisfaction of ACT with clinicians and clients, and the subsequent adoption of ACT by clinicians (Hayes, 1998b). The use of case conceptualization is another important area to consider in the application of ACT. Various models of case conceptualization have been proposed (Bach & Moran, 2008; Wilson, 2007) and future studies may examine the treatment utility of these conceptualization and assessment methods.

Effectiveness studies may also continue to examine important questions related to implementing treatment in everyday practice settings. Studies examining the ability of ACT to produce improvements in outcome across a broad range of problems including treatment-resistant and/or multi-problem clients will be important in testing whether the treatment comports well to the needs of everyday, practicing clinicians in outpatient settings. Evaluating the impact of ACT technologies when combined with other treatment components (e.g., cognitive disputation, emotion regulation strategies) may be important as well since it is inevitable in applied settings and may create adverse effects for clients (Hayes, 1998b). With this level of treatment testing it is important to consider the primary questions clinicians need answered, best put by Gordon Paul's question 'What treatment, by whom, is most effective for this individual with that specific problem under which set of circumstances, and how does this come about?' (Paul, 1969, p. 44). Research needs to identify the various client, therapist, and setting characteristics that relate to which treatment package or methods would be most effective for treating a specific problem. Although many aspects of contextual behavioral science assist in answering these questions, at this level of treatment testing it becomes apparent that there is a substantial amount of research that needs to be conducted, and that group-based designs are unlikely to adequately meet these needs. Many of these questions may be best answered by practicing clinicians who are likely to encounter the various multi-problem and treatment resistant clients, clients requiring particularly effective treatments.

Thus, the contextual behavioral science approach requires a mutual interest model of sorts between researchers and clinicians. The specific questions regarding clients that are seen by clinicians may be best tested within these settings by the clinicians themselves. Time series designs provide a potential method for clinicians to conduct such work. Time series studies provide the advantage of investigating treatment effects while avoiding group designs that create significant barriers including their size and time requirements, costs, recruitment problems, and ethical concerns regarding non-treatment controls. These designs fit well with good clinical practices, such as monitoring treatment effects, and can be implemented with little additional work. These methods are also more sensitive to individual client differences in response to treatment and allow for the idiographic analysis of treatment impact with multi-problem clients. Furthermore, clinicians conducting single subject research are not as bound to strict, manualized treatment protocols and can be more responsive to the client's progress or lack of progress. In addition, clinicians are able to more systematically monitor the impact of certain therapeutic methods and techniques on clients, which can assist in developing innovative methods for helping difficult to treat populations (Hayes & Blackledge, 1998). A number of time series studies have recently been conducted with ACT (e.g., Twohig, Hayes, & Masuda, 2006a, 2006b; Twohig, Shoenberger, & Hayes, 2007; Twohig & Woods, 2004), but in order to adequately answer the questions relevant to clinicians this method needs to be adopted by applied workers outside of the university setting.

8. Test the Analysis Across a Broad Range of Applicable Areas and Levels of Analysis

In an inductive approach, the model of psychopathology and treatment is tested through predictive verification in increasingly complex situations and across abstractive levels. In essence, this is a search for limiting conditions and the need for further model development. As treatment is successfully applied to a broader range of areas, the model is supported more and more through a series of unlikely coincidences. Thus, the application of a treatment model to a broad range of areas is essential within a contextual behavioral approach. Refined principles are tested for both their precision and scope across a range of problems, and the overall utility and progressivity of the theoretical model in predicting and influencing behavior is examined. The success of a treatment across a broad range of outcomes matches the needs of health care delivery systems and applied workers who cannot afford to be trained in specific treatment packages for each syndrome (Hayes, 1998b). This contextual behavioral approach goes beyond the common EST emphasis on DSM diagnoses that has been criticized by some researchers (Herbert, 2003) with the inclusion of samples that do not clearly fit into a specific diagnosis and non-clinical problems. Treatment effects are also assessed in terms of psychological health, which goes beyond a syndromal understanding of psychological health defined as the absence of symptoms. This allows researchers to more comprehensively assess treatment effects, avoiding ceiling effects that occur when only assessing symptom reduction.

A review of the outcome literature shows that the ACT model has been progressively applied to new problems and populations with each of these applications, serving to further test the theory of psychopathology and treatment. ACT outcome research originally focused on the areas of depression (Zettle & Hayes, 1986; Zettle & Rains, 1989), and pain (Hayes et al., 1999). Since the recurrence of ACT outcome studies in 1998, ACT has been successfully applied to a number of psychological disorders including psychosis (Bach & Hayes, 2002), social anxiety disorder (Block & Wulfert, 2000; Dalrymple & Herbert, 2007), math anxiety (Zettle, 2003), obsessive compulsive disorder (Twohig et al., 2006b), trichotillomania (Twohig & Woods, 2004; Woods et al., 2006), skin picking (Twohig et al., 2006a), borderline personality disorder (Gratz & Gunderson, 2006), polysubstance abuse (Hayes, Wilson, et al., 2004), marijuana use (Twohig et al., 2007), anxiety and general mood disorders (Forman et al., 2007), and related areas such as worksite stress (Bond & Bunce, 2000; Hayes, Bissett, et al., 2004; Lazzarone et al., 2007) and distress in parents of children diagnosed with autism (Blackledge & Hayes, 2006). ACT has also demonstrated efficacy in treating a number of problems within behavioral medicine including weight maintenance (Lillis et al., under review), smoking (Gifford et al., 2002; Gifford et al., 2004), diabetes self-management (Gregg et al., 2007), chronic pain (Dahl et al., 2004; McCracken et al., 2005; Wicksell, Melin, & Olsson, 2007), cancer (Branstetter et al., 2004), and epilepsy (Lundgren, Dahl, Melin, & Kies, 2006; Lundgren et al., under review).

A further test of the ACT model has been to apply treatment to new, nonclinical areas such as stigma, prejudice, and barriers to learning. If the ACT theory of psychopathology and the RFT account of language are 'correct' then ACT technologies should be applicable to other areas where verbal behavior can become problematic. In support of this notion, studies have shown ACT to influence the impact of stigma and prejudice towards ethnic minorities (Lillis & Hayes, 2007), stigma towards substance abusers in drug counselors (Hayes, Bissett et al., 2004), stigma towards mental health problems (Masuda et al., 2007), and self-related stigma regarding weight (Lillis et al., under review). In addition, recent studies have suggested that front-end ACT workshops and continuing ACT-based consultation groups targeting barriers to adoption of treatment technologies subsequently increase the use of empirically supported therapies by clinicians (Luoma et al., 2007; Varra et al., in press). Examining the impact of the treatment model across various modes of delivery also serves to test the overall theory and the limiting conditions of the treatment. This is accomplished by examining whether the treatment can still produce effects using theoretically important principles and processes without specific setting features such as individual therapist contact. In support of this, ACT has been conducted with a variety of modes of delivery, demonstrating positive effects in group formats (e.g., Bond & Bunce, 2000), workshop interventions as short as 2½ hours (Masuda et al., 2007), varying lengths of individual therapy (e.g., Gaudiano & Herbert, 2006a), and with bibliotherapy either alone (Lazzarone et al., 2007) or in conjunction with other ACT components (Lillis et al., under review).

The success of ACT across this broad range of problems and modes of delivery lends strong empirical support for the model. The ability of ACT to produce positive effects outside of individual therapy and even without any therapist contact suggests that effects are not dependent on therapeutic alliance or other 'nonspecific' factors. The success of ACT across a variety of topographically distinct problems supports the theoretical functional processes believed to be underlying these problems (e.g., experiential avoidance, fusion) and the application of principles and mechanisms of change believed to produce clinical gains (e.g., acceptance, defusion). This has been further supported by the results in mediation analysis showing that effects are often produced by these commonly targeted processes (Hayes, et al., 2007). From this perspective, ACT has really been replicated over 25 times, with the targets differing topographically, but not functionally. The ability for ACT to be successfully applied to such a wide range of problems involving language and cognition provides a strong test of the scope of the RFT analysis of language and cognition and a useful demonstration of RFT principles at a high level of abstraction.

Future studies may continue to expand the application in areas beyond the normal realm of clinical psychology including worksite functioning, prejudice, and stigma. In addition, a useful test of the model would be to determine whether the ACT processes may also serve to prevent the development of psychological problems through prevention studies. Continuing the broad application of ACT across various methods and modes of delivery will also serve to strengthen the model. For example, future studies may test the number of recently developed self-help books alone or in conjunction with therapy, as well as the effectiveness of ACT through internet treatments. These future studies can continue to rely on the methods of contextual behavioral science by examining the processes of change to see if the model works in treating new problems and using new modes of delivery. If treatment is not successful in these areas then the flexible nature of the model will allow the creation of new methods or the adoption of methods invented elsewhere.

Conclusion

A systematic review of how the ACT/RFT research program fits within contextual behavioral science helps to demonstrate the utility of this approach for both researchers and clinicians. The contextual behavioral approach provides somewhat new models of conducting basic research, treatment development, and treatment testing that are more likely to meet the needs of both basic and applied areas. Beginning at philosophy of science, this approach integrates multiple levels of research in order to adequately achieve the goals of prediction and influence of behavior with precision, scope, and depth. ACT and RFT research has addressed each of these levels in such a way that researchers are able to continue to progressively build upon the model simultaneously at multiple levels of research, while maintaining an emphasis on the overall analytical goals. This emphasis on a pragmatic truth criterion has led to a focus on the concerns of applied clinical workers, addressing many of the limitations in the current model of clinical psychology research. However, further work is needed within both ACT and RFT in order to continue towards these goals. This review suggests certain areas that might particularly benefit from increased attention. For example, the continued development of the link between middle-level concepts and behavioral principles will be important in developing basic RFT research, theory, interventions, and process measures. Increasing the emphasis on conducting full meditational analyses in group designs is also essential as it provides a test of the model, which arguably may be almost as important as the actual treatment outcomes. Continuing to conduct large scale effectiveness, training, and dissemination studies as well as time series designs will help to address many concerns regarding the training, adoption, and application of ACT in clinical settings.

Finally, this review helps to address recent criticisms of ACT (Arche & Craske, in press; Hofmann & Asmundson, 2008; Öst, 2008) by placing these comments within the larger context of the research program. For example, Öst (2008) focused specifically upon the methodological rigor of ACT RCTs in evaluating ACT as an EST, while missing many other relevant research areas supporting the efficacy of ACT that have been reviewed in this chapter. The statement that ACT is the same as other existing CBT treatment packages (Arch & Craske, in press; Hofmann & Asmundson, 2008) can be addressed by pointing to the fundamental differences between these approaches at multiple levels including philosophy, theory, methodology, and treatment technologies (Hayes, in press; Waltz & Hayes, in press) as well as through the meditational analyses showing how ACT works through different processes. These criticisms may be viewed, in part, more as a clash between the dominant approaches to science within clinical psychology and contextual behavioral science. Overall, these types of discussions may be more progressive if they are placed at the broader level of the larger research program where the success of the research is evaluated based on its own goals and assumptions, rather than evaluating one approach based on the assumptions and goals of the other.

References

Abramowitz, J. S., Tolin, D. F., & Street, G. P. (2001). Paradoxical effects of thought suppression: A meta-analysis of controlled studies. *Clinical Psychology Review, 21*(5), 683–703.

Arch, J. J., & Craske, M. G. (in press). ACT and CBT for anxiety disorders. *Clinical Psychology: Science and Practice.*

Bach, P., & Hayes, S. C. (2002). The use of Acceptance and Commitment Therapy to prevent the rehospitalization of psychotic patients: A randomized controlled trial. *Journal of Consulting and Clinical Psychology, 70*(5), 1129–1139.

Bach, P., & Moran, D. (2008). *ACT in Practice: Case conceptualization in Acceptance and Commitment Therapy.* Oakland, CA: New Harbinger.

Baer, R. A. (2003). Mindfulness training as a clinical intervention: A conceptual and empirical review. *Clinical Psychology: Science and Practice, 10*(2), 125–143.

Baer, R. A., Smith, G. T., Hopkins, J., Krietemeyer, J., & Toney, L. (2006). Using self-report assessment methods to explore facets of mindfulness. *Assessment, 13,* 27–45.

Barnes-Holmes, Y., Barnes-Holmes, D., Smeets, P. M., Strand, P., & Friman, P. (2004). Establishing relational responding in accordance with more-than and less-than as generalized operant behavior in young children. *International Journal of Psychology and Psychological Therapy, 4,* 531–558.

Baron, R. M., & Kenny, D. A. (1986). The moderator-mediator variable distinction in social psychological research: Conceptual, strategic, and statistical considerations. *Journal of Personality and Social Psychology, 51,* 1173–1182.

Begotka, A. M., Woods, D. W., & Wetterneck, C. T. (2004). The relationship between experiential avoidance and the severity of trichotillomania in a nonreferred sample. *Journal of Behavior Therapy and Experimental Psychiatry, 35,* 17–24.

Berens, N. M., & Hayes, S. C. (2007). Arbitrarily applicable comparative relations: Experimental evidence for a relational operant. *Journal of Applied Behavior Analysis, 40*(1), 45–71.

Biglan, A., & Hayes, S. C. (1996). Should the behavioral sciences become more pragmatic? The case for functional contextualism in research on human behavior. *Applied and Preventive Psychology: Current Scientific Perspectives, 5,* 47–57.

Blackledge, J. T., & Hayes, S. C. (2006). Using Acceptance and Commitment Training in the support of parents of children diagnosed with autism. *Child & Family Behavior Therapy, 28,* 1–18.

Blackledge, J. T., Ciarrochi, J., Bilich, L., & Heaven, P. (2007, May). *Continuing validation of the social values survey.* Paper presented at the Association for Behavior Analysis Conference, San Diego, CA.

Block, J. A., & Wulfert, E. (2000). Acceptance or change: Treating socially anxious college students with ACT or CBGT. *The Behavior Analyst Today, 1*(2), 3–10.

Bond, F. W., & Bunce, D. (2000). Mediators of change in emotion-focused and problem-focused worksite stress management interventions. *Journal of Occupational Health Psychology, 5,* 156–163.

Borkovec, T. D., & Castonguay, L. G. (1998). What is the scientific meaning of empirically supported therapy? *Journal of Consulting and Clinical Psychology, 66*(1), 136–142.

Brandon, T. H., Herzog, T. A., Juliano, L. M., Irvin, J. E., Lazev, A. B., & Nath, V. (2003). Pretreatment task-persistence predicts smoking cessation outcome. *Journal of Abnormal Psychology, 112*(3), 448–456.

Branstetter, A. D., Wilson, K. G., Hildebrandt, M., & Mutch, D. (2004). *Improving psychological adjustment among cancer patients: ACT and CBT.* Paper presented at the Association for Advancement of Behavior Therapy, New Orleans.

Brown, R. A., Lejuez, C. W., Kahler, C. W., & Strong, D. (2002). Distress tolerance and duration of past smoking cessation attempts. *Journal of Abnormal Psychology, 111*(1), 180–185.

Brown, K. W., & Ryan, R. M. (2003). The benefits of being present: Mindfulness and its role in psychological well-being. *Journal of Personality and Social Psychology, 84*(4), 822–848.

Carver, C. S., Scheier, M. F., & Weintraub, J. K. (1989). Assessing coping strategies: A theoretically based approach. *Journal of Personality and Social Psychology, 56*(2), 267–283.

Castonguay, L. G., & Beutler, L. E. (2006). Principles of therapeutic change: A task force on participants, relationships, and technique factors. *Journal of Clinical Psychology, 62*(6), 631–638.

Chambless, D. L., & Ollendick, T. H. (2001). Empirically supported psychological interventions: Controversies and evidence. *Annual Review of Psychology, 52,* 685–716.

Chapman, A. L., Specht, M. W., & Cellucci, T. (2005). Borderline personality disorder and self-harm: Does experiential avoidance play a role? *Suicide and Life Threatening Behavior, 35,* 388–399.

Cioffi, D., & Holloway, J. (1993). Delayed costs of suppressed pain. *Journal of Personality and Social Psychology, 64,* 274–282.

Cochrane, A., Barnes-Holmes, D., Barnes-Holmes, Y., Stewart, I., & Luciano, C. (2007). Experiential avoidance and aversive visual images: Response delays and event related potentials on a simple matching task. *Behaviour Research and Therapy 45,* 1379–1388.

Cohen, G. L., Garcia, J., Apfel, N., & Master, A. (2006). Reducing the racial achievement gap: A social-psychological intervention. *Science, 313,* 1307–1310.

Creswell, J. D., Welch, W. T., Taylor, S. E., Sherman, D. K., Gruenewald, T. L., & Mann, T. (2005). Affirmation of personal values buffers neuroendocrine and psychological stress responses. *Psychological Science, 16*(11), 846–851.

Dahl, J., Wilson, K. G., & Nilsson, A. (2004). Acceptance and Commitment Therapy and the treatment of persons at risk for long-term disability resulting from stress and pain symptoms: A preliminary randomized trial. *Behavior Therapy, 35,* 785–802.

Dalrymple, K. L., & Herbert, J. D. (2007). Acceptance and Commitment Therapy for Generalized Social Anxiety Disorder: A pilot study. *Behavior Modification, 31,* 543–568.

Dimidjian, S., Hollon, S. D., Dobson, K. S., Schmaling, K. B., Kohlenberg, R. J., Addis, M. E. et al. (2006). Treatment of depression and anxiety — randomized trial of behavioral activation, cognitive therapy, and antidepressant medication in the acute treatment of adults with major depression. *Journal of Consulting and Clinical Psychology, 74,* 658–670.

Daughters, S. B., Lejuez, C. W., Kahler, C., Strong, D., & Brown, R. (2005). Psychological distress tolerance and duration of most recent abstinence attempt among residential treatment seeking substance abusers. *Psychology of Addictive Behaviors, 19*(2), 208–211.

Daughters, S. B., Lejuez, C. W., Strong, D. R., Brown, R. A., Breen, R. B., & Lesieur, H. R. (2005). The relationship among negative affect, distress tolerance, and length of gambling abstinence attempt. *Journal of Gambling Studies, 21*(4), 363–378.

Dougher, M. J., Hamilton, D., Fink, B., & Harrington, J. (2007). Transformation of the discriminative and eliciting functions of generalized relational stimuli. *Journal of the Experimental Analysis of Behavior, 88*(2), 179–197.

Dymond, S., & Barnes, D. (1995). A transformation of self-discrimination response functions in accordance with the arbitrarily applicable relations of sameness, more than, and less than. *Journal of the Experimental Analysis of Behavior, 64,* 163–184.

Dymond, S., Roche, B., Forsyth, J. P., Whelan, R., & Rhoden, J. (2007). Transformation of avoidance response functions in accordance with same and opposite relational frames. *Journal of the Experimental Analysis of Behavior, 88,* 249–262.

Feldner, M. T., Hekmat, H., Zvolensky, M. J., Vowles, K. E., Secrist, Z., & Leen-Feldner, E. W. (2006). The role of experiential avoidance in acute pain tolerance: A laboratory test. desensitization in treatment of mathematics anxiety. *The Psychological Record, 53,* 197–215.

Flessner, D. A., & Woods, D. W. (2006). Phenomenological characteristics, social problems, and the economic impact associated with chronic skin picking. *Behavior Modification, 30,* 1–20.

Follette, W. C. (1995). Correcting methodological weaknesses in the knowledge base used to derive practice standards. In Hayes, S. C., Follette, V. M., Dawes, R. M., & Grady, K. E. (Eds.), *Scientific Standards of Psychological Practice: Issues and Recommendations* (pp. 229–247). Reno, NV: Context Press.

Follette, W. C., & Beitz, K. (2003). Adding a more rigorous scientific agenda to the empirically supported treatment movement. *Behavior Modification, 27*(3), 369–386.

Forman, E. M., Herbert, J. D., Moitra, E., Yeomans, P. D., & Geller, P. A. (2007). A randomized controlled effectiveness trial of Acceptance and Commitment

Therapy and Cognitive Therapy for anxiety and depression. *Behavior Modification, 31*(6), 1–28.

Gaudiano, B.A., & Herbert, J.D. (2006a). Acute treatment of inpatients with psychotic symptoms using Acceptance and Commitment Therapy. *Behaviour Research and Therapy, 44*, 415–437.

Gaudiano, B., & Herbert, J. D. (2006b). Believability of hallucinations as a potential mediator of their frequency and associated distress in psychotic inpatients. *Behavioural and Cognitive Psychotherapy, 34*, 497–502.

Gifford, E. V., Kohlenberg, B. S., Hayes, S. C., Antonuccio, D. O., Piasecki, M. M., Rasmussen-Hall, M. L. et al. (2004). Acceptance theory-based treatment for smoking cessation: An initial trial of Acceptance and Commitment Therapy. *Behavior Therapy, 35*, 689–705.

Gifford, E. V., Kohlenberg, B. S., Piasecki, M. P., Palm, K. M., Antonuccio, D. O., & Hayes, S. C. (November, 2002). *Bupropion SR in combination with acceptance-based behavioral therapy for smoking cessation: Results from a randomized controlled trial.* Paper presented at the meeting of the Association for Advancement of Behavior Therapy, Reno.

Gratz, K. L., Bornovalova, M. A., & Delany-Brumsey, A. (2007). A laboratory-based study of the relationship between childhood abuse and experiential avoidance among inner-city substance users: The role of emotional nonacceptance. *Behavior Therapy, 38*(3), 256–268.

Gratz, K. L., Rosenthal, M. Z., Tull, M. T., Lejuez, C. W., & Gunderson, J. G. (2006). An experimental investigation of emotion dysregulation in borderline personality disorder. *Journal of Abnormal Psychology, 115*(4), 850–855.

Gratz, K. L., & Gunderson, J. G. (2006). Preliminary data on an acceptance-based emotion regulation group intervention for deliberate self-harm among women with borderline personality disorder. *Behavior Therapy, 37*, 25–35.

Gregg, J. A., Callaghan, G. M., Hayes, S. C., & Glenn-Lawson, J. L. (2007). Improving diabetes self-management through acceptance, mindfulness, and values: A randomized controlled trial. *Journal of Consulting and Clinical Psychology, 75*(2), 336–343.

Gutiérrez, O., Luciano, C., Rodríguez, M., & Fink, B. C. (2004). Comparison between an acceptance-based and a cognitive-control-based protocol for coping with pain. *Behavior Therapy, 35*, 767–784.

Hayes, S. C. (1984). Making sense of spirituality. *Behaviorism, 12*, 99–110.

Hayes, S. C. (Ed.). (1989). *Rule-governed behavior: Cognition, contingencies, and instructional control.* New York: Plenum.

Hayes, S. C. (1991). The limits of technological talk. *Journal of Applied Behavior Analysis, 24*, 417–420.

Hayes, S. C. (1993). Analytic goals and the varieties of scientific contextualism. In S. C. Hayes, L. J. Hayes, H. W. Reese, & T. R. Sarbin (Eds.), *Varieties of scientific contextualism* (pp. 11–27). Reno, NV: Context Press.

Hayes, S. C. (1997). Technology, theory, and the alleviation of human suffering: We still have such a long way to go. *Behavior Therapy, 28*, 517–525.

Hayes, S. C. (1998a). Building a useful relationship between 'applied' and 'basic' science in behavior therapy. *The Behavior Therapist, 21*, 109–112.

Hayes, S. C. (1998b). Market-driven treatment development. *The Behavior Therapist, 21*, 32–33.

Hayes, S. C. (2002). Getting to dissemination. *Clinical Psychology: Science and Practice, 9,* 424–429.

Hayes, S. C. (2004). Falsification and the protective belt surrounding entity postulating theories. *Journal of Applied and Preventive Psychology, 11,* 35–37.

Hayes, S. C. (in press). Climbing our hills: A beginning conversation on the comparison of ACT and traditional CBT. *Clinical Psychology: Science and Practice.*

Hayes, S. C., Barnes-Holmes, D., & Roche, B. (Eds.). (2001). *Relational frame theory: A post-Skinnerian account of human language and cognition.* New York: Plenum.

Hayes, S. C., & Berens, N. M. (2004). Why relational frame theory alters the relationship between basic and applied behavioral psychology. *International Journal of Psychology and Psychological Therapy, 4,* 341–353.

Hayes, S. C., & Blackledge, J. T. (1998). Single case experimental designs: Clinical research and practice. In A. Bellack & E. Hersen (Eds.), *Comprehensive clinical psychology.* New York: Elsevier Science.

Hayes, S. C., Bissett, R. T., Korn, Z., Zettle, R. D., Rosenfarb, I. S., Cooper, L. D., et al. (1999). The impact of acceptance versus control rationales on pain tolerance. *The Psychological Record, 49*(1), 33–47.

Hayes, S. C., Bissett, R., Roget, N., Padilla, M., Kohlenberg, B. S., Fisher, G., Masuda, A., Pistorello, J., Rye, A. K., Berry, K., & Niccolls, R. (2004). The impact of acceptance and commitment training and multicultural training on the stigmatizing attitudes and professional burnout of substance abuse counselors. *Behavior Therapy, 35,* 821–835.

Hayes, S. C., & Brownstein, A. J. (1985). *Verbal behavior, equivalence classes, and rules: New definitions, data, and directions.* Invited address presented at the meeting of the Association for Behavior Analysis, Columbus, OH.

Hayes, S. C., & Brownstein, A. J. (1986). Mentalism, private events, and scientific explanation: A defense of B. F. Skinner's view. In S. Modgil & C. Modgil (Eds.), *B. F. Skinner: Consensus and controversy* (pp. 207-218). Sussex, England: Falmer Press.

Hayes, S. C., Hayes, L. J., & Reese, H. W. (1988). Finding the philosophical core: A review of Stephen C. Pepper's *World Hypotheses. Journal of the Experimental Analysis of Behavior, 50,* 97–111.

Hayes, S. C., Levin, M., Yadavaia, J. E., & Vilardaga, R. V. (November, 2007). *ACT: Model and processes of change.* Paper presented at the Association for Behavioral and Cognitive Therapies, Philadelphia.

Hayes, S. C., Luoma, J., Bond, F., Masuda, A., & Lillis, J. (2006). Acceptance and Commitment Therapy: Model, processes, and outcomes. *Behaviour Research and Therapy, 44,* 1–25.

Hayes, S. C., Masuda, A., Shenk, C., Yadavaia, J. E., Boulanger, J., Vilardaga, R., et al. (2007). Applied extensions of behavior principles: Applied behavioral concepts and behavioral theories. In D. Woods & J. Kantor (Eds.), *Understanding behavior disorders* (pp. 47–80). Reno, NV: Context Press.

Hayes, S. C. & Strosahl, K. D. (2005) (Eds.), *A practical guide to Acceptance and Commitment Therapy.* New York: Springer-Verlag.

Hayes, S. C., Strosahl, K., & Wilson, K. G. (1999). *Acceptance and Commitment Therapy: An experiential approach to behavior change.* New York: Guilford Press.

Hayes, S. C., Strosahl, K. D., Wilson, K. G., Bissett, R. T., Pistorello, J., Toarmino, D., et al. (2004). Measuring experiential avoidance: A preliminary test of a working model. *The Psychological Record, 54*, 553–578.

Hayes, S. C., Wilson, K. G., Gifford, E. V., Follette, V. M., & Strosahl, K. (1996). Experiential avoidance and behavioral disorders: A functional dimensional approach to diagnosis and treatment. *Journal of Consulting and Clinical Psychology, 64*(6), 1152–1168.

Hayes, S. C., Wilson, K. G., Gifford, E. V., Bissett, R., Piasecki, M., Batten, S. V., Byrd, M., & Gregg, J. (2004). A randomized controlled trial of twelve-step facilitation and acceptance and commitment therapy with polysubstance abusing methadone maintained opiate addicts. *Behavior Therapy, 35*, 667–688.

Harris, P. R., & Napper, L. (2005). Self-affirmation and the biased processing of threatening health-risk information. *Personality and Social Psychology Bulletin, 31*, 1250–1263.

Healy, O., Barnes-Holmes, D., & Smeets, P. M. (2000). Derived relational responding as generalized operant behavior. *Journal of the Experimental Analysis of Behavior, 74*, 207–227.

Herbert, J. D. (2003). The science and practice of empirically supported treatments. *Behavior Modification, 27*, 412–430.

Herzberg, K. N., Forsyth, J. P., Dispenza, F., & Acheson, D. T. (2007, November). *Toward the development of a behavioral measure of experiential avoidance: The experiential avoidance task (EAT) and distress intolerance.* Paper presented at the Association for Behavioral and Cognitive Therapies, Philadelphia.

Hofmann, S. G., & Asmundson, G. J. G. (2008). Acceptance and mindfulness-based therapy: New wave or old hat? *Clinical Psychology Review, 28*, 1–16.

Jacobson, N. S., Dobson, K. S., Truax, P. A., Addis, M. E., Koerner, K., Gollan, J. K., et al. (1996). A component analysis of cognitive behavioral treatment for depression. *Journal of Consulting and Clinical Psychology, 64*, 295–304.

Karekla, M., Forsyth, J. P., & Kelly, M. M. (2004). Emotional avoidance and panicogenic responding to a biological challenge procedure. *Behavior Therapy, 35*(4), 725–746.

Kazdin, A. E. (2001). Progression of therapy research and clinical application of treatment require better understanding of the change process. *Clinical Psychology: Science and Practice, 8*, 143–151.

Kupfer, D. J., First, M. B., & Regier, D. A. (2002). *A research agenda for DSM V.* Washington, DC: American Psychiatric Association.

Lappalainen, R., Lehtonen, T., Skarp, E., Taubert, E., Ojanen, M., & Hayes, S. C. (2007). The impact of CBT and ACT models using psychology trainee therapists: A preliminary controlled effectiveness trial. *Behavior Modification, 31*(4), 488–511.

Lazzarone, T. R., Hayes, S. C., Louma, J., Kohlenberg, B., Pistorello, J., Lillis, J., et al. (2007). *The effectiveness of an Acceptance and Commitment Therapy self-help manual: Get out of your mind and into your life.* Paper presented at the meeting of the Association for Behavioral and Cognitive Therapies, Philadelphia, PA.

Levitt, J. T., Brown, T. A., Orsillo, S. M., & Barlow, D. H. (2004). The effects of acceptance versus suppression of emotion on subjective and psychophysiological response to carbon dioxide challenge in patients with panic disorder. *Behavior Therapy, 35*, 747–766.

Lejuez, C. W., Kahler, C. W., & Brown, R. A. (2003). A modified computer version of the Paced Auditory Serial Addition Task (PASAT) as a laboratory-based stressor. *Behavior Therapist, 26*, 290–293.

Levin, M., Yadavaia, J. E., Hildebrandt, M. J., & Hayes, S. C. (November 2007). *A meta-analysis of acceptance-based interventions for behavioral challenges requiring task persistence.* Paper presented at the Association for Behavioral and Cognitive Therapies, Philadelphia.

Lillis, J., & Hayes, S.C. (2007). Applying acceptance, mindfulness, and values to the reduction of prejudice: A pilot study. *Behavior Modification, 31*(4), 389–411.

Lillis, J., Hayes, S. C., Bunting, K., & Masuda, A. (under review). A randomized controlled trial of acceptance and commitment therapy for weight control: preliminary test of a theoretical model. *Annals of Behavioral Medicine.*

Lipkens, G., Hayes, S. C., & Hayes, L. J. (1991). Longitudinal study of derived stimulus relations in an infant. *Journal of Experimental Child Psychology, 56,* 201–239.

Logan, H. L., Baron, R. S., & Kohout, F. (1995). Sensory focus as therapeutic treatments for acute pain. *Psychosomatic Medicine, 57*, 475–484.

Lundgren, T. (2006, July). *Validation and reliability data of the Bull's-Eye.* Presentation at the second world conference on ACT/RFT, London.

Lundgren, A. T., Dahl, J., Melin, L., & Kies, B. (2006). Evaluation of Acceptance and Commitment Therapy for drug refractory epilepsy: A randomized controlled trial in South Africa. *Epilepsia, 47*, 2173–2179.

Lundgren, T., Dahl, J., & Hayes, S. C. (in press). Evaluation of mediators of change in the treatment of epilepsy with Acceptance and Commitment Therapy. *Journal of Behavioral Medicine.*

Luoma, J. B., Hayes, S. C., & Walser, R. D. (2007). *Learning ACT: An acceptance & commitment therapy skills-training manual for therapists.* Oakland, CA: New Harbinger.

Luoma, J. B., Hayes, S. C., Roget, N., Fisher, G., Padilla, M., Bissett, R., et al. (2007). Augmenting continuing education with psychologically-focused group consultation: Effects on adoption of Group Drug Counseling. *Psychotherapy Theory, Research, Practice, Training, 44*(4), 463–469.

MacKinnon, D. P. (2003, November). *Mediator and moderator methods.* Paper presented at the meeting of the Association for Advancement of Behavior Therapy, Boston, MA.

MacKinnon, D. P., Lockwood, C. M., Hoffman, J. M., West, S. G., & Sheets, V. (2002). A comparison of methods to test mediation and other intervening variable effects. *Psychological Methods, 7*, 83–104.

MacKinnon, D. P., Fairchild, A. J., & Fritz, M. S. (2007). Mediation analysis. *Annual Review of Psychology, 58*, 593–614.

Marcks, B. A., & Woods, D. W. (2005). A comparison of thought suppression to an acceptance-based technique in the management of personal intrusive thoughts: A controlled evaluation. *Behaviour Research and Therapy, 43*, 433–445.

Marcks, B. A., & Woods, D. W. (2007). Role of thought-related beliefs and coping strategies in the escalation of intrusive thoughts: An analog to obsessive-compulsive disorder. *Behaviour Research and Therapy, 45*, 2640–2651.

Masuda, A., Hayes, S. C., Fletcher, L. B., Seignourel, P. J., Bunting, K., Herbst, S. A., et al. (2007). The impact of Acceptance and Commitment Therapy versus education on stigma toward people with psychological disorders. *Behaviour Research and Therapy, 45*(11), 2764–2772.

Masuda, A., Hayes, S. C., Sackett, C. F., & Twohig, M. P. (2004). Cognitive defusion and self-relevant negative thoughts: Examining the impact of a ninety-year-old technique. *Behaviour Research and Therapy, 42*, 477–485.

McCracken, L. M., Vowles, K. E., & Eccleston, C. (2004). Acceptance of chronic pain: Component analysis and a revised assessment method. *Pain, 107*, 159–166.

McCracken, L. M, Vowles, K. E., & Eccleston, C. (2005). Acceptance-based treatment for persons with complex, long-standing chronic pain: A preliminary analysis of treatment outcome in comparison to a waiting phase. *Behaviour Research and Therapy, 43*, 1335–1346.

McHugh, L., Barnes-Holmes, Y., & Barnes-Holmes, D. (2004). Perspective-taking as relational responding: A developmental profile. *The Psychological Record, 54*, 115–144.

McMullen, J., Barnes-Holmes, D., Barnes-Holmes, Y., Stewart, I., Luciano, C., & Cochrane, A. (2008). Acceptance versus distraction: Brief instructions, metaphors, and exercises in increasing tolerance for self-delivered electric shocks. *Behaviour Research and Therapy, 46*, 122–129.

Muto, T. (2008). The impact of 'operant variability' for applied behavior analysis: Some new implications of bridge studies. *Japanese Journal of Behavior Analysis, 22*(2), 154–163.

Muto, T. (May, 2008b). Switch your clinical-psychological OS!: From DSM to 'Turtle'". In *Beyond categorical thinking: Using the hexaflex for diagnosis, assessment, and intervention.* Workshop conducted at ACT Summer Institute 4th, Chicago.

National Advisory Mental Health Council. (2000). *Translating behavioral science into action: Report of the National Advisory Mental Health Council Behavioral Science Workgroup.* Bethesda, MD: National Institute of Mental Health.

O'Donohue, W., & Yeater, E. A. (2003). Individuating psychotherapies. *Behaviour Modification, 27*, 313–321.

Öst, L. (2008). Efficacy of the third wave of behavioral therapies: A systematic review and meta-analysis, *Behaviour Research and Therapy, 46*(3), 296–321.

Páez-Blarrina, M., Luciano, C., Gutierrez-Martinez, O., Valdivia, S., Ortega, J., & Valverde, M. (2008). The role of values with personal examples in altering the functions of pain: Comparison between acceptance-based and cognitive-control-based protocols. *Behaviour Research and Therapy, 46*, 84–97.

Paul, G. L. (1969). Behavior modification research: Design and tactics. In C. M. Franks (Ed.), *Behavior therapy: Appraisal and status* (pp. 29–62). New York: McGraw-Hill.

Pepper, S. C. (1942). *World hypotheses: A study in evidence.* Berkeley, CA: University of California Press.

Preacher, K. J., & Hayes, A. F. (2006). *Asymptotic and resampling strategies for assessing and comparing indirect effects in simple and multiple mediator models.* Manuscript submitted for publication.

Rehfeldt, R. A., Dillen, J. E., Ziomek, M. M., & Kowalchuk, R. K. (2007). Assessing relational learning deficits in perspective-taking in children with high-functioning autism spectrum disorder. *The Psychological Record, 57*, 23–47.

Roche, B., Barnes-Holmes, D., Smeets, P. M., Barnes-Holmes, Y., & McGeady, S. (2000). Contextual control over the derived transformation of discriminative and sexual arousal functions, *The Psychological Record, 50,* 267–291.

Roemer, L., Salters, K., Raffa, S. D., & Orsillo, S. M. (2005). Fear and avoidance of internal experiences in GAD: Preliminary tests of a conceptual model. *Cognitive Therapy and Research, 29,* 71–88.

Rosen, G. N., & Davison, G. C. (2003). Psychology should list empirically supported principles of change (ESPs) and not credential trademarked therapies or other treatment packages. *Behaviour Modification, 27,* 300–312.

Sanderson, W. C. (2002). Are evidenced-based psychological interventions practiced by clinicians in the field? *Medscape Mental Health, 7,* 1–3.

Sandoz, E. K., & Wilson, K. G. (2006). *Assessing body image acceptance.* Unpublished manuscript, University of Mississippi.

Shawyer, F., Ratcliff, K., Mackinnon, A., Farhall, J., Hayes, S. C., & Copolov, D. (2007). The voices acceptance and action scale (VAAS): Pilot data. *Journal of Clinical Psychology, 63*(6), 593–606.

Skinner, B. F. (1938). *Behavior of organisms.* New York: Appelton-Century-Crofts.

Sloan, D. M. (2004). Emotion regulation in action: Emotional reactivity in experiential avoidance. *Behaviour Research and Therapy, 42,* 1257–1270.

Spira, A. P., Beaudreau, S. A., & Jimenez, D. (2007). Experiential avoidance, acceptance, and depression in dementia family caregivers. *Clinical Gerontologist, 30*(4), 55–64.

Spira, A. P., Zvolensky, M. J., Eifert, G. H., & Feldner, M. T. (2004). Avoidance-oriented coping as a predictor of anxiety-based physical stress: A test using biological challenge. *Journal of Anxiety Disorders, 18,* 309–323.

Steele, D. L., & Hayes, S. C. (1991). Stimulus equivalence and arbitrarily applicable relational responding. *Journal of the Experimental Analysis of Behavior, 56,* 519–555.

Stewart, S. H., Zvolensky, M. J., & Eifert, G. H. (2002). The relations of anxiety sensitivity, experiential avoidance, and alexithymic coping to young adults' motivations for drinking. *Behavior Modification, 26,* 274–296.

Strosahl, K. D., Hayes, S. C., Bergan, J., & Romano, P. (1998). Assessing the field effectiveness of Acceptance and Commitment Therapy: An example of the manipulated training research method. *Behavior Therapy, 29,* 35–64.

Tashiro, T., & Mortensen, L. (2006). Translational research: How social psychology can improve psychotherapy. *American Psychologist, 61*(9), 959–966.

Toneatto, T., & Nguyen, L. (2007). Does mindfulness meditation improve anxiety and mood symptoms? A review of the controlled research. *The Canadian Journal of Psychiatry, 52*(4), 260–266.

Tull, M. T., Gratz, K. L., Salters, K., & Roemer, L. (2004). The role of experiential avoidance in posttraumatic stress symptoms and symptoms of depression, anxiety, and somatization. *Journal of Nervous & Mental Disease, 192*(11), 754–761.

Twohig, M. P., Hayes, S. C., & Masuda, A. (2006a). A preliminary investigation of Acceptance and Commitment Therapy as a treatment for chronic skin picking. *Behaviour Research and Therapy, 44,* 1513–1522.

Twohig, M. P., Hayes, S. C., & Masuda, A. (2006b). Increasing willingness to experience obsessions: Acceptance and Commitment Therapy as a treatment for obsessive compulsive disorder. *Behavior Therapy, 37,* 3–13.

Twohig, M. P., Shoenberger, D., & Hayes, S. C. (2007). A preliminary investigation of Acceptance and Commitment Therapy as a treatment for marijuana dependence in adults. *Journal of Applied Behavior Analysis, 40(4)*, 619–632.

Twohig, M. P., & Woods, D. W. (2004). A preliminary investigation of Acceptance and Commitment Therapy and habit reversal as a treatment for trichotillomania. *Behavior Therapy, 35(4)*, 803–820.

Varra, A. A., Hayes, S. C., Roget, N., & Fisher, G. (in press). A randomized control trial use evidence-based pharmacotherapy. *Journal of Consulting and Clinical Psychology*.

Waltz, T. J., Follette, B. F., & Drossel, C. (2007, May). *Understanding psychopathology and psychological health in terms of basic behavioral processes*. Paper presented at the meeting of the Association for Behavior Analysis, San Diego, CA.

Waltz, T. J., & Hayes, S. C. (In press). Acceptance and Commitment Therapy: A unique theoretical model within the CBT tradition. In N. Kazantis, M. A. Reinecke, & A.Freeman. (Eds.), *Cognitive behavior therapy: Using theory and philosophy to strengthen science and practice*. New York: Guilford Press.

Wegner, D. M., & Zanakos, S. (1994). Chronic thought suppression. *Journal of Personality, 62*, 615–640.

Wicksell, R. K., Melin, L. & Olsson, G. L. (2007). Exposure and acceptance in the rehabilitation of children and adolescents with chronic pain. *European Journal of Pain, 11*, 267–274.

Williams, L. (2007). Acceptance and Commitment Therapy: An example of third-wave therapy as a treatment for Australian Vietnam War veterans with post-traumatic stress disorder. *Salute, 19*, 13–15.

Wilson, K. G. (2007, July). *Using the hexaflex for diagnosis, assessment, and treatment*. Paper presented at the 3rd ACT Summer Institute, Houston, TX.

Wilson, K. G., Sandoz, E. K., Kitchens, J. & Roberts, M. E. (under review). The valued living questionnaire: Defining and measuring valued action within a behavioral framework. *The Psychological Record*.

Woods, D. W., Wetterneck, C. T., & Flessner, C. A. (2006) A controlled evaluation of Acceptance and Commitment Therapy plus habit reversal for trichotillomania. *Behaviour Research and Therapy, 44*, 639–656.

Zettle, R. D. (2003). Acceptance and commitment therapy (ACT) vs. systematic desensitization in the treatment of mathematics anxiety. *The Psychological Record, 53*, 197–215.

Zettle, R. D., & Hayes, S. C. (1986). Dysfunctional control by client verbal behavior: The context of reason giving. *The Analysis of Verbal Behavior, 4*, 30–38.

Zettle, R. D., Hocker, T. R., Mick, K. A., Scofield, B. E., Petersen, C. L., Hyunsung S., & Sudarijanto, R. P. (2005). Differential strategies in coping with pain as a function of level of experiential avoidance. *The Psychological Record, 55(4)*, 511–524.

Zettle, R. D., Petersen, C. L., Hocker, T. R. & Provines, J. L. (2007). Responding to a challenging perceptual-motor task as a function of level of experiential avoidance. *The Psychology Record, 57*, 49–62.

Zettle, R. D., & Raines, J. C. (1989). Group cognitive and contextual therapies in treatment of depression. *Journal of Clinical Psychology, 45*, 438–445.

chapter two

Core Processes in Acceptance and Commitment Therapy

John T. Blackledge and Dermot Barnes-Holmes

Acceptance and commitment therapy (ACT; Hayes, Strosahl, & Wilson, 1999) has received empirical support in well over 20 randomized controlled trials as a psychotherapeutic treatment for psychological problems as diverse as depression (Zettle & Hayes, 1986; Zettle & Raines, 1989), anxiety (Block, 2002), substance abuse (Hayes, Wilson, Gifford, Bissett, Piasecki, Batten, Byrd, & Gregg, 2004), psychosis (Bach & Hayes, 2002) and the treatment of chronic pain (Dahl, Wilson, & Nilsson, 2004; Robinson, Wicksell, & Olson, 2005). ACT is offered as a modern but thoroughly behavioral approach to the treatment of complex psychological problems — one that honors the strengths of more conventional behavioral treatment strategies, but incorporates a new behavioral conceptualization of language and cognition (Relational Frame Theory, or RFT; Hayes, Barnes-Holmes, & Roche, 2001).

Hayes, Strosahl, Bunting, Twohig and Wilson (2004) and Wilson and Murrell (2004) describe the primary goal of ACT as achieving increased psychological flexibility, defined as 'the ability to contact the present moment more fully as a conscious human being, and to either change or persist when doing so serves valued ends' (Hayes et al., 2004, p. 5). According to the authors, six core processes work to establish increased psychological flexibility: enhancing client *acceptance* of distressing experiential content; increasing the client's ability to maintain *contact with the present moment*; establishing a sense of *self-as-context* in the client; using *cognitive defusion* strategies to disrupt the effects of problematic cognitions; clarification of client *values* in multiple domains; and enhancement of the client's effective and *committed action* toward these valued ends. Breaking ACT down to these six core elements appears to do much in capturing the applied essence of the treatment, and in guiding a more detailed and precise exploration of the specific processes that underlay these elements. From the initial stages of ACT's development, a primary emphasis was put on conceptualizing ACT from an internally consistent, coherent theoretical perspective, and on amplifying the feedback loop between clinical applications of ACT and basic experimental findings that bear upon the treatment's strategies and processes. In this spirit, the current chapter offers a functional–contextual conceptualization of these six core ACT components. It is hoped that this effort will both provide a more technically precise picture of core ACT processes than has been previously advanced, and ultimately work to direct more focused research on these processes.

Values

Hayes et al. (1999) offered an initial definition of values as 'verbally construed global desired life consequences' (p. 206). In other words, values are verbal statements about what states of affairs an individual desires to experience throughout his life. This definition sets a valuable guideline for how to most usefully conceptualize values from an ACT perspective, though it somewhat de-emphasizes how values are operationalized within ACT therapy. For practical purposes, values are typically approached by an ACT therapist as process variables (ways of behaving) rather than outcome variables (desired life consequences). For example, if an ACT client stated she valued close, intimate relationships (an outcome), her ACT therapist would help her clarify qualities that are brought to bear within the context of a close relationship — qualities or ways of behaving that she can unilaterally bring to bear in her relationships that increase the likelihood of developing and maintaining close relationships. The reason for this is that (colloquially speaking), while the consequences for any given behavior is ultimately 'out of one's hands', one always has the ability to act unilaterally in a predetermined fashion. Thus, thinking of values as ways of behaving affords more utility to a behavior therapist attempting to shape the increased emission of specific responses in her client.

Valued Living: A Definition

Wilson and Murrell (2004) coined a progressive turn of phrase on *values* (a static noun that implies a focus on outcome) by emphasizing that the ultimate goal of ACT is increasing the frequency of *valued living* (which implies a focus on the process of behaving consistently with one's values). From our perspective, valued living (and, by implication, values) might be technically defined as ways of responding that give increased access to relatively stable, long-term sources of positive nonverbal and verbal reinforcement. An emphasis on *stable* and *long-term* sources of *positive* reinforcement as an adequate way of defining a value is highlighted for several reasons. First, it is obviously assumed that for any set of consequences (exemplified by personally held values) to maintain behavior instrumental in achieving them, these consequences are by definition reinforcers. However, competent ACT therapists go to great pains to make values-directed behavior come under appetitive rather than aversive control, due to a long experimental behavior-analytic tradition documenting the undesirable side effects of aversive control (see, e.g, Sidman, 2000). In other words, value-driven behavior is not about 'musts' and 'shoulds' and 'have-tos' (which imply escaping negative consequences), but about 'want-tos' (which imply approaching positive consequences). Thus, values reflect sources of positive reinforcement rather than reinforcement broadly defined.

Of course, it is also assumed that many positive reinforcers have a debilitating effect over time. Use of drugs or alcohol is, typically, immediately positively reinforcing, yet chronic consumption of such reinforcers typically deteriorates quality (and duration) of life over time, as well as decreasing one's ability to respond skillfully in a broad range of circumstances. Thus, given that the ACT concept of values appears to reflect a collective goal of shaping client behavior that is both sustainable and minimally under aversive control, values must refer to behaviors that yield access to *stable* and *long-term* sources of positive reinforcement. As what functions as a reinforcer differs according to individual and context, so values assessment in ACT comprises a sort of expanded 'stimulus preference assessment', where each client is free to choose her own reinforcers (values) from an unlimited array, and where prompts referring to more specific contexts (e.g., values domains like family relationships, spirituality and career) aid in the selection of reinforcers within a relatively broad variety of contexts.

Vital Living

Given only the definition of values and valued living proposed in the previous section, it would be appropriate to speculate that values refer to nothing more than the kinds of tangible reinforcers and attention that can be achieved through a basic token economy — that essentially, the ACT construct of values adds nothing to the basic behavior-analytic maxim of 'use positive reinforcement to manage the four basic behavioral functions of acquisition, attention, avoidance and self-stimulation'. However, ACT therapists conducting values clarification with clients seek to help the client identify ways of valued living that confer an increased sense of vitality, meaning and purpose in them. The subjective qualities referred to by these terms are difficult to pin down in precise terms, but greater precision seems essential for analytic purposes. So, the question arises: from a behavioral perspective, what is meant by terms like 'vitality', 'meaning' and 'purpose'?

Vitality has been defined as 'physical or intellectual vigor', with the term vigor referring to 'strong feeling; enthusiasm or intensity' (*The American Heritage Dictionary of the English Language*, 2000, p. 1919). Thus, it may be assumed that a sense of vitality refers to ways of living that tend to co-occur with or lead to strong, positively valenced emotions.

More to the point, vitality may result from engagement in behaviors most likely to yield positive reinforcement that is associated with feelings of enthusiasm and other strong and positively valenced emotions. Intensity and vigor also imply that such positive consequences are sufficient (and delivered often enough) to control relatively sustained and focused patterns of behavior instrumental in achieving them. It is likely that positive emotions would not be the only positive reinforcer in action. Such emotions might often be linked to reinforcers involving increased social support, greater harmony in relationships, and increased success at work, school and a variety of aspects of life. Verbal processes would undoubtedly be involved in transforming the functions of more mundane or taxing actions linked to vital outcomes. For example, a formative augmental like, 'I'm doing this for my daughter, whom I love dearly and love to see happy', might transform some of the verbal functions of a frustrating race home from work to drop her off at dance practice into an act where positive feelings of love are experienced. ACT is designed, in part, to help clients stop grasping directly at positive feelings and rather focus their attention on behaving in a way that increases vitality. Perhaps ironically, it would seem that letting go of feeling good allows one to act in ways that increases the frequency and intensity of good feelings over time. In other words, one of the goals of ACT is to transform the functions of perhaps mundane and even unpleasant activities into verbally reinforcing events, if such events are deemed to be in frames of coordination or causality with the client's verbally discriminated values.

Like a sense of vitality, a sense of *meaning* and *purpose* in life appears to be often linked to strong positive feelings and a relatively rich schedule of other types of positive reinforcement as well. But a sense of meaning and purpose may be of more exclusively verbal origin than raw vitality. The prefix of *purpose* derives from the Latin prefix *pro-*, which means 'acting in the place of; substituting for' (American Heritage Dictionary, 2000). According to the same source, to *pose,* means 'to put forward or present'. This brief etymological lesson is helpful in illustrating how *purpose* is viewed from a more existential perspective — as putting forward effort in the place of or on behalf of a greater good, or putting forward effort that leads to a collectively positive outcome. Once collective outcomes or abstract concepts like 'a greater good' are considered, the verbal nature of 'purpose' becomes more clearly apparent. Perhaps one of the reasons a sense of purpose becomes reinforcing is because one is typically socially reinforced for behaving in a constructive manner. A second reason a sense of purpose may be reinforcing is because such behavior is typically framed as 'important', 'worthwhile', 'good', 'necessary' and so forth. More direct reasons for the reinforcing nature of a sense of purpose may present themselves when one is able to link one's actions to the creation of conditions yielding other forms of reinforcement. For example, a sense of purpose may be found in a job because of the positive effects of the salary in contributing to a secure, safe and more harmonious family life. Or, a person's community conservation efforts might directly result in the preservation of a park where he or she engages in many reinforcing activities.

It is worth noting that *purpose* and *meaning* appear to be highly interrelated verbal constructs. An activity framed as *meaningful* may also be likely to be framed as 'important', 'significant', or in coordination with a 'greater plan', 'greater purpose' or 'larger pattern'. Thus, any action that is placed in a frame of coordination with such terms would likely serve to transform the verbal functions of that action in relatively positive ways. Furthermore, social reinforcement might also be expected to follow the emission of behavior framed as *meaningful* or rich with *purpose*. Finally, actions may be framed as meaningful, or serving a greater purpose, in part, simply because they are instrumental in receiving relatively rich and stable rates of positive reinforcement.

In summary, therefore, the concept of vitality in ACT appears to be focused on transforming the verbal functions of 'mundane', 'boring' or 'unpleasant' activities into reinforcing events in and of themselves. Although the transformation effects occur, in part, because such activities participate in relational frames with an individual's values, the term 'vital' only seems appropriate when many of the emotional or eliciting functions of valued activities transfer to the mundane action itself (e.g., when driving one's child to a dance lesson acquires some of the emotional functions of holding the child in a loving embrace).

In contrast, the concepts of purpose and meaning appear to be more focused on the extent to which specific actions lead to highly valued outcomes. In this case, the actions may continue to be discriminated verbally as generally negative, but are emitted simply because they are seen to participate in frames of causality with valued outcomes. Thus the action is not vital, in the sense of producing many of the emotional functions of a valued activity itself, but it does have purpose and meaning because the action facilitates access to highly valued states of affairs (e.g., doing overtime at work may be unpleasant, but has meaning and purpose because it may pay for an extended family holiday).

Values as Motivative and Formative Augmentals

Any discussion of values or valued living from an RFT perspective would be incomplete without considering the concept of augmentals. Hayes et al. (1999) stated that a verbally stated value may function as a motivative or formative augmental (p. 35). Motivative augmenting has been defined briefly as 'behavior due to relational networks that temporarily alter the degree to which previously established consequences function as reinforcers or punishers' (Barnes-Holmes, O'Hora, Roche, Hayes, Bissett, & Lyddy, 2001, p. 110). Consider, for example, the following rhetorical question, 'Even though it's frightening, doesn't a big part of you really want to open up to your partner and tell her exactly how you're feeling — to really connect with her, be close to her?' Such a question might serve to increase the likelihood that a client would behave accordingly, given that he has often found psychological intimacy reinforcing in the past. In effect, motivative augmentals are verbal stimuli that increase the likelihood of responses that are instrumental in receiving the reinforcer coordinated with the augmentative stimuli, because those stimuli possess some of the appetitive functions of the actual reinforcing events. In principle, motivative augmentals could also possess aversive stimulus functions, but in general these are avoided in ACT-based therapeutic interactions because such augmentative control tends to be rather coercive (e.g., 'If you don't open up to your wife she may well leave you').

By contrast, formative augmentals 'establish some new event as an important consequence' (Hayes et al., 1999, p. 31), or more technically, refer to 'behavior due to relational networks that establish given consequences as reinforcers or punishers' (Barnes-Holmes et al., 2001, p. 110). Whereas motivative augmentals work to verbally enhance the salience of events that are already reinforcing, formative augmentals seek to establish previously neutral (or even aversive) stimuli as reinforcing. For example, the formative augmental 'discussing unpleasant conflicts with your spouse in a careful and considerate manner will facilitate the closeness you desire' might verbally establish careful and considerate discussion of heated conflicts as reinforcing, even though it was previously aversive. Within the context of values, formative augmentals are verbal stimuli that serve to transform the consequential functions of specific events, such that those events now reinforce responses that are instrumental in working towards values. Without such augmental control, these responses would otherwise be too weak (or absent) to maintain values-consistent action.

Where Do Values Come From?

From an ACT perspective, most (if not all) clients are assumed to enter treatment having already experienced moments of meaning and vitality. As with any other behavior, valuing is assumed (from a behavioral perspective) to be determined by one's current and historical contexts. Multiple sources of control are assumed to exist over a given client's verbal articulation of values. When a client is asked what she values, one potential source of control over the response involves pliance, a form of 'rule-governed behavior under the control of a history of socially mediated reinforcement for coordination between behavior and antecedent verbal stimuli' (Barnes-Holmes, et al., 2001, p. 108). In other words, the client might state she values something simply because the statement of such values has been socially reinforced in the past. Or in other words, the client simply articulates a particular value because she expects the therapist will approve of what she says. Thus, a ply masquerading as a value would refer to behavior(s) that please others from time to time but do not provide increased access to stable long-term sources of positive reinforcement.

A second potential source of control over a client's verbal articulation of a value involves avoidant tracking. A track 'is rule-governed behavior under the control of a history of coordination between the rule and the way the environment is arranged independently of the delivery of the rule' (Barnes-Holmes et al., 2001, p. 109). Thus, avoidant tracking involves responses that function solely to avoid aversive consequences, regardless of how ineffective such responses might be in garnering short- or long-term positive consequences. For example, a client might state that he values professional achievement at work, in part, because it provides 'an excuse' for avoiding dealing with his wife's excessive drinking.

The competent ACT therapist works diligently to eliminate the influence of pliance and avoidant tracking over client valuing, because ACT assumes that simply pleasing others and avoiding discomfort are not the most effective ways of gaining long-term access to stable sources of positive reinforcement. In effect, we assume that clearly articulated values that are not plys or avoidant tracks (a) have been emitted by the client in the past and have been associated with a variety of highly salient reinforcing consequences, (b) have been modeled by others who were seen to receive highly desired forms of reinforcement as a result, (c) mirror forms of behavior emitted toward the client that the client found reinforcing and/or (d) are the result of verbal derivations regarding behavior(s) the client believes may be instrumental in living a life that is meaningful, vital, and/or purposeful.

Commitment

The notion of commitment in ACT appears to refer to multiple phenomena. At a basic level, commitment refers to a verbal statement that one will emit behavior consistent with one or more stated values. From a technical perspective, the act of verbally stating one's intent to move toward a given value may involve, in any given instance, the enactment of one or more behavioral processes. First, if made publicly, such a statement may increase the probability that one will act in accordance with that verbal statement, given a long history in which positive consequences ensued following concordance between words and action, and negative consequences ensued following discordance. To a lesser degree, even a private commitment might increase probability of concordant behavior due to the effects of the aforementioned history of differential reinforcement. Second, commitment to a specific values-consistent act (e.g., 'I'm committing to spending this Saturday afternoon playing with my children') may function as a track by specifying behavior within a specific context likely to receive reinforcement. Such verbal commitments may also function as tracks in other useful ways. Often, in ACT, commitments to pursue stated values also involve commitments to accept distressing thoughts and emotions as they arise, and to engage in ACT-specific processes (such as defusion and self-as-context strategies) to pass effectively through such verbal and emotional barriers. Consider the rather ubiquitous ACT question — 'Given the distinction between you and the stuff you struggle with, are you willing to have that stuff, as it is and not as what it says it is, and do what works in this situation?' (Hayes, 2005). This clearly exemplifies how a commitment of 'yes' to this statement might comprise a track (as well as increase the probability of such behavior).

The word 'commitment' may function as a track within ACT in another fashion. Many clients may view commitment as an all-or-nothing response that is violated and permanently preempted by a failure to honor it. To counter this view, an ACT therapist may engage in strategies intended to help the client view commitment as a moment-to-moment choice that, if not followed through in the last moment, may always be followed through in the next. For example, committed action toward a value may be metaphorically likened to learning how to ride a bicycle. In such a context, falling off the bike does not permanently end the process of riding it. Rather, after a fall, one always has the choice of getting back on the bicycle and riding again. Given the virtual impossibility of *always* acting consistently with a value in the real world, transforming the function of the word 'commitment' may allow an actual commitment to function as a track effective in guiding persistent behavior in the face of setbacks.

Additionally, a commitment made within an ACT context may function as a formative augmental. Given the discussion of formative augmentals in the Values section, above, this should come as no surprise. Since commitments often involve choosing to emit behavior that may not be intrinsically reinforcing but is instrumental in achieving valued aims, linking this behavior verbally to established reinforcers via formative augmenting may be an effective strategy.

At a more generic level, one might be said to have committed to the pursuit of a stated value if one is actually, in a given moment, acting consistently with that value. This perspective of 'commitment as action' seems very consistent with ACT's relentless focus on the emission of effective values-consistent behavior, regardless of how consistent or inconsistent such behavior is with whatever 'talk' is occurring in the moment. In effect, one is ultimately committed to moving toward a value when one is actually doing so.

Cognitive Defusion

A relatively complete functional contextual conceptualization of cognitive defusion is offered in Blackledge (2007); as such, the process will be described only briefly here. Within ACT therapy, defusion techniques involve a variety of actions designed to expose thoughts simply as thoughts, rather than binding realities. Paradox, mindfulness, cognitive distancing and a variety of other strategies are used to help clients experience problematic thoughts in a new context — one where the debilitating *functions* of such thoughts are disrupted even when the *form* (or content) of these thoughts remain the same. Within traditional behavioral psychology, stimuli take on functions through direct contingency processes such as operant and respondent conditioning, and stimulus generalization. A stimulus function essentially describes how the organism in question will respond when presented with the designated stimulus. From an RFT perspective, uniquely verbal operant processes (relational and derived relational responding; see, e.g., Hayes, Barnes-Holmes, & Roche, 2001; or Blackledge, 2003, for an introduction to RFT) can also lead to changes in stimulus functions. While procedures like exposure, extinction and response prevention have been devised to address problematic stimulus functions that arise through direct operant and respondent conditioning, cognitive defusion procedures are intended to alter problematic functions arising through verbal processes.

Thus, from a technical perspective, defusion can be conceptualized as a process in which well-established verbal stimulus transformations are disrupted via the displacement of contextual conditions that control relational responding in general. More research needs to be conducted on what these contextual conditions are, but several hypotheses have been advanced. It would seem these contextual conditions may include a focus on the content of speech or thinking (rather than the process of speaking or thinking), the use of relatively standardized grammar and speech parameters, and the provision of at least intermittent reinforcement for arbitrary verbal stimulus transformations (i.e., for nonformal stimulus transformations arising through relational/derived relational responding). At moments when conditions such as these are displaced, disruption of established verbal transformations of function via defusion is thought to occur. For example, meditation and mindfulness techniques used in ACT move the client's attention from a focus on the content of individual thoughts to a focus on the process of thinking. When thoughts are repeatedly identified as thinking and viewed from a greater psychological distance, the contextual control typically established over an individual's stream of private verbal behavior is altered and thus the established verbal transformations normally associated with these thoughts are temporarily disrupted. Similarly, when a thought is repeated over and over (as in ACT's 'Milk' exercise), or spoken very quickly or very slowly, contextual parameters regarding rate and frequency of speech may be sufficiently violated, with atypical verbal transformations of function ensuing. As a final example, a systematic and strategic failure on the therapist's part to reinforce a client's established arbitrary/abstract verbal stimulus transformations may effectively lower the rate of reinforcement for these transformations for the time these conditions are in place — such as when a client is repeatedly asked 'why' she cannot perform an action because of excessive anxiety, regardless of the content of each reason provided by the client.

Self-as-Context

The concept of self-as-context is an important one in ACT and RFT. The basic idea is that this type of verbal self emerges primarily through the establishment of three relational frames; I–You, Here–There, and Now–Then. Specifically, ongoing interactions with the verbal community serve to establish relational responding in the young child that allows him or her to verbally discriminate the location of self and others in space and time. Learning to respond to and ask the following types of questions are critical; 'Where are you now?' 'Where were you then?' 'Where was I when you were here?' 'Where were you when I was there?' Across many such questions, the relevant times and locations, and the other persons involved, may differ but the perspective from which the questions are asked and answered remains constant. In other words, each of us is *always* responding verbally from 'Here, and Now' (about events and others located There and Then). This verbal invariance thus establishes, across the first 3 to 5 years of normal development, a sense of perspective from which all of one's life will be viewed or experienced. This invariant relational, or verbal perspective, is referred to as self-as-context — the context from which an individual's earliest and very last verbal activities will be discriminated. Although many, many things will change during the course of a complete lifetime, in a very deep sense the 'I' that experiences a first day at school, is the same 'I' that says goodbye to the world while lying on a death-bed, aged 90 years.

Interestingly, the verbally ubiquitous nature of self-as-context can render it almost invisible, psychologically. Insofar as self-as-context (I–Here–Now) is always present in all verbal behavior, it fades appropriately into the background of our everyday verbal activities. Consequently, the verbal content of our lives (e.g., Am I a good or bad person? Am I happy or sad? Am I a failure or a success?) comes to dominate, and in a sense we lose touch with that deep, invariant and constant sense of verbal self that transcends the best and the worst of us. In other words, we fail to appreciate that no matter how wonderful or awful we discriminate our lives to be at any given point in time, all verbal discriminations occur within the wider arena of self-as-context. As such, self-as-context is neither good nor bad, neither hopeful nor despairing, neither loving nor hateful, and neither giving nor selfish. Self-as-context is the uncontaminated verbal 'I-ness' that transcends all the other verbal content in our lives. Put simply, self-as-context simply *is*. Critically, from an ACT/RFT perspective, targeting self-as-context in therapy can be very effective.

How might shaping a sense of self-as-context facilitate effective ACT? First, discriminating and framing one's 'self' as distinct from the content of aversive thoughts, feelings and other experiences would be expected to disable problematic transformations of function occurring when one's 'self' is framed in coordination with these same events. Someone with a clearly discriminated self-as-context who experienced guilt and thoughts of inadequacy would frame these stimuli as the product of one's mind and one's history, rather than as equivalent to one's inherent nature, effectively altering the stimulus transformations that would occur in the latter case. Second, framing one's 'self' as the context rather than the content of experiencing might result in the development of effective tracks that correspond to the way contingencies work when defusion is established. For example, a client who had experienced defusion and discriminated a sense of self-as-context several times might think something like 'I know these are just thoughts I'm having right now — I'll just notice them for what they are' when next faced with a series of negatively evaluative thoughts. A bout of thought observation might then ensue, serving to disrupt established verbal transformations of function associated with these thoughts. This points to a third set of helpful functions that discriminating a sense of self-as-context may serve — both serving as a cue for emitting defusive responses and verbally extending the 'lessons learned' from actual incidents of defusion.

As suggested by the previous paragraph, a sizeable overlap between *self-as-context* interventions and *defusion* interventions is evident. In fact, given how defusion has been conceptualized by Hayes et al. (1999) and Blackledge (2007), it would appear that therapeutic operations designed to help the client discriminate her 'self-as-context' or 'observing self' (Hayes et al., 1999) would also serve to instantiate defusion. In other words, when a person is viewing thoughts as thoughts from an observer perspective, this is tantamount to focusing attention on the process versus the content of thinking. Nevertheless, it seems important to distinguish the concept of defusion from self-as-context, because experiencing the former does not necessarily produce the latter.

Self-as-context, once established, is relatively constant in the behavioral stream, whereas cognitive defusion is relatively sporadic. Even when a client is fused with a particular thought, we would assume that this instance of fusion is being discriminated from self-as-context, although at that time the discrimination of self-as-context would be very weak (if self-as-context was completely absent, then the client would be unable to report that he or she was fused or had been fused with a particular thought). If a defusion exercise is then introduced, the client might well experience a transformation of functions for the specific thought, but self-as-context may still remain weak. For example, the client might report that the thought 'I am a bad person' seemed less aversive or threatening following a defusion exercise, but go on to argue 'Okay, I don't feel bad right now, but overall I am a bad person'. If, however, the therapist has worked on shaping up the discrimination of self-as-context, then even the functions of the 'overall bad person' thought may be transformed into 'OK, that's just another thought I can note and observe'.

In summary, therefore, it seems important to distinguish defusion from self-as-context because experiencing an example of the former does not automatically produce the latter. On balance, it is certainly the case that defusion exercises may well serve to help improve the discrimination of self-as-context and, moreover, discriminating self-as-context could certainly be seen as possessing some of the critical properties of any cognitive defusion exercise.

Contact with the Present Moment

An ACT therapist makes a sustained effort to put the client in contact with *current* experiences — sensations, thoughts, feelings, even sensory perceptions that are occurring *right now*. In fact, it is thought that the other five core ACT components are often best implemented when tied directly in to the client's *current* experience, rather than applied to reports of past behavior or verbal speculation about the future. When viewed from a basic behavioral perspective, one of the reasons such synchronicity between this and the other five ACT components should exist becomes readily apparent. Repeatedly modeling and shaping various ACT-consistent skills *in the moment* might be expected to enhance response generalization. In other words, skills associated with defusion, acceptance and values-consistent action must be applied *in the moment*, as cognitive and affective barriers arise and values-relevant opportunities present themselves. To the extent that these skills have been repeatedly practiced *in the moment* in therapy, the client would be expected to bring them to bear fluently.

Further, sustained attention to physical sensations and other experiences occurring in the present moment may facilitate defusion from problematic verbal stimulus transformations (Blackledge, 2007). Such attention involves an explicit focus on the formal properties of direct experience, rather than on often abstract 'languaging' about direct experience. This, in and of itself, may provide a very important contextual shift that helps to undermine the context of literality. There is a fundamentally different quality to direct experiencing than there is to describing direct experiencing. Feeling the air entering and exiting your body when you breathe, for example, is quite different from thinking about your breathing. Directly experiencing your breath involves the formal stimulus property of tactility. There is a perceptual solidity to the experience that cannot be achieved entirely by thought. In lay terms, the direct experience simply feels more 'real' and 'tangible' than the stimulus products of relational framing. Repeated experiential contact with the discrepancies between language and direct experience may thus help undermine the literal belief that language describes reality, that the transformed stimulus functions connected to words are tangible and immutable. Colloquially, one may then begin recognizing that words are words, and direct experience is something entirely different. This violates an implicit feature of the context of literality, which arguably establishes that, to some extent, words share the tangible and directly perceivable quality of direct experience.

Attending to the present moment may also involve the discrimination of the contingencies currently exerting control over behavior. Once various aspects of such contingencies are discriminated, several beneficial outcomes may unfold. First, such increased awareness of present experience could facilitate maximal consideration of values-consistent behavior that may be relevant to current circumstances. If one is intimately aware of what is happening right now, one's opportunity to select behaviors consistent with relevant values should increase. Second, when problematic verbal processes (e.g., those that block effective values-consistent behavior) are noticed, one can engage in various ACT-consistent responses to address them (such as defusion or acceptance). In other words, increased awareness of distressing thoughts and emotions in the present moment would facilitate emission of defusion and acceptance strategies designed to cut through those thoughts and emotions. Finally, discrimination of various aspects of the contingencies arising from increased contact with the present moment may facilitate action that is more effective in manipulating those contingencies to one's advantage. Metaphorically speaking, an increased awareness of how the road in front of you is laid out puts you in a better position to successfully navigate its cracks, curves and potholes. Such an increased awareness of the parameters of the present moment would be expected to facilitate the effective emission of 'nuts and bolts' skills involving communication, problem solving, empathy and so forth.

What Consequences Serve to Reinforce Contact With the Present Moment?

Effective movement toward values as a partial result of increased contact with the present moment would be expected to serve as positive reinforcement for this active awareness. Social reinforcement resulting, in part, from increased awareness (via increasingly effective social interaction) could also be a source of potential positive reinforcement. To the extent that increased contact with the present moment facilitates defusion from distressing verbalizations, negative reinforcement resulting from the attenuation or elimination of this aversive stimulation may also play a consequential role. Additionally, increased attention to the present moment might be expected to typically precede both positive and negative reinforcement — and perhaps make one more aware of contingencies preceding punishment so that such contextual antecedents could be more effectively avoided in the future. Through these channels, increased attending to the present moment could become established as a conditioned reinforcer. On a related note, it also seems plausible that punishment might more often result from a relative lack of contact with the present moment, thus working to establish lack of attending to the present as a conditioned punisher for those able to discriminate these contingencies.

Acceptance

From an ACT perspective, the construct of acceptance takes on a more conditional connotation than the word more commonly has. Within ACT, acceptance of psychological distress is only indicated when active avoidance of this distress is impeding more maximally effective movement toward personally held values. Acceptance of all psychological distress at all times is not suggested (unless, of course, a client's value indicates this, as some spiritually oriented values might). Thus, we conceive of acceptance as the act of approaching aversive stimuli, when that act is in an if–then frame with valued outcomes and/or a frame of coordination with valued actions. Conversely, acceptance can be said to involve a lack of verbally based avoidance occurring in the context of valued action.

Creative Hopelessness: The Functional Assessment of Control

A behavioral conceptualization of acceptance would be arguably incomplete without explicit discussion of the construct's antithesis. The opposite of acceptance, of course, involves active attempts to change, attenuate or eliminate aversive thoughts, feelings, physical sensations and other private experiences. The beginning stage of ACT typically involves attempts to draw out a sense of 'creative hopelessness' from the client, where the client's specific experiential avoidance strategies are articulated, and these strategies' short- and long-term effectiveness and effects on movement toward personal values are assessed. This stage in treatment is intended to comprehensively highlight the futility and counterproductivity of client avoidance attempts (taken individually and collectively), and to enhance client motivation to minimize engagement in such experientially avoidant behavior.

From a more precise behavioral perspective, what is the nature and purpose of a creative hopelessness intervention? Creative hopelessness (CH) enjoys a clear precedent in the classic applied behavior-analytic practice of *functional assessment*, although the CH process in ACT is conducted with some marked differences. In a standard functional assessment, the contingencies surrounding a problematic behavior are systematically assessed and manipulated, and the function(s) of the behavior is then determined. This typically sets the stage for the teaching of more appropriate replacement behaviors (i.e., more appropriate behaviors that serve the same function as the problematic behavior) and/or the rearrangement of behavioral antecedents and consequences to support the emission of less problematic behavior. For example, contextual conditions surrounding a child who aggresses in the classroom might be assessed to see what function this aggressive behavior serves (e.g., does it result in increased attention, or termination of aversive demands placed upon the child, or increased access to a tangible reinforcer?). Assuming this functional assessment indicates the child aggressed solely to avoid demands (such as the teacher asking the child to work on his math), this would set the stage for teaching the child more appropriate means of dampening the aversive aspects of the task (e.g., by asking for help) and for rearranging antecedents and/or consequences to support more appropriate behavior (e.g., by breaking the math work down to smaller component tasks, and/or by withholding reinforcement for aggressive behavior). Thus, traditional functional assessment uses direct observation, in the relevant environment(s), to (a) determine the function of a problematic behavior or behaviors, (b) produce data regarding the frequency with which such behavior receives reinforcement that serves this function and (c) sets the stage for the development of behavior(s) that will more appropriately serve the same function.

Creative hopelessness work is both similar and different to more conventional functional assessment. First, CH seeks only to assess the effects of behaviors that function as experiential avoidance strategies (e.g., the client is specifically asked what he does to 'get on top of' or 'deal with' his distressing thoughts and feelings). Second, initial CH work tends to rely solely on verbal reports of what the client does when distressed, rather than being the sole product of direct observation (though the therapist may observe and address specific instances of client experiential avoidance (EA) in vivo as he comes to know the client better). Third, the ACT therapist is not in a position to rearrange the client's environment outside of (and often inside) the therapy room so that EA behaviors are not reinforced. Rather, therapist and client are talking about the client's perceptions of whether or not the behavior works over the short and long term (i.e., whether each example of an experientially avoidant response receives negative reinforcement over the short term and long term). And fourth, ACT does not provide the client with more 'appropriate' or effective replacement behaviors that serve the same function of EA behaviors. On the contrary, one of the primary intentions of ACT is to minimize the client's emission of EA behaviors (at least those that interfere with effective values-consistent movement).

Thus, CH may be conceptualized as a verbal endeavor intended to accomplish several things. First, it may help the client view a variety of topographically different behaviors as a discrete functional class of behaviors. Once these behaviors have been explicitly tagged and grouped together, it might more effectively allow the client to notice in the moment when he is attempting to experientially avoid, so that he may instead engage in ACT-consistent behaviors involving acceptance, defusion and values-consistent movement. Second, CH may result in shaping the client's emission of increasingly accurate tracks regarding the short- and long-term effects of EA behaviors. In other words, undergoing a CH intervention may help the client more clearly articulate what are the actual short- and long-term effects of his EA behaviors. A verbal rule in the form of a track like the following might emerge: 'When I try to avoid my anxiety, it doesn't work and it actually makes the anxiety worse — I should lean into the anxiety and do what matters to me instead'. CH may additionally participate in the creation of increasingly accurate tracks regarding EA behaviors and movement toward/away from values (assuming the impact of EA behaviors on client movement toward values is assessed and discussed). Interestingly, however, since CH is a verbal endeavor (and thus does not involve systematic observation and manipulation of actual EA across contexts), CH may not result in tracks that are fully accurate. Finally, when CH is successful, it might result in the creation of motivative augmentals. That is, when a client is explicitly aware that EA is not working (e.g., thinks it is pointless to try and fight his anxiety) and is not moving him toward his values, he may be less motivated to try to avoid.

Summary/Conclusion

At the beginning of the current chapter we stated that our purpose here was to offer a functiona–contextual conceptualization of the six core ACT components. Our hope is that this work will add some technical precision to the ACT model, which will thus help to bridge the gap between basic and applied knowledge. We do not pretend that what we offer here is in any way definitive — we have simply provided some examples of how the six ACT components may be usefully, and admittedly sometimes loosely, interpreted from a more basic behavior-analytic perspective. We fully recognize, therefore, that far higher levels of precision will be needed to satisfy the 'hard-nosed' basic experimental researcher. Thus, the current work should be seen as an example of how we might begin to think about the six ACT processes in more basic behavioral terms, rather than as the final word on the issue.

References

*The American heritage dictionary of the English la*nguage (4th ed.). (2006). Boston: Houghton Mifflin.

Bach, P., & Hayes, S. C. (2002). The use of acceptance and commitment therapy to prevent the rehospitalization of psychotic patients: A randomised controlled trial. *Journal of Consulting and Clinical Psychology, 70*(5), 1129–1139.

Barnes-Holmes, D., O'Hora, D., Roche, B., Hayes, S., Bissett, R., & Lyddy, F. (2001). Understanding and verbal regulation. In S. Hayes, D. Barnes-Holmes, & B. Roche (Eds.), *Relational frame theory: A post-Skinnerian account of human language and cognition* (pp. 103–118). New York: Kluwer Academic/Plenum Publishers.

Blackledge, J. T. (2003). An introduction to relational frame theory: Basics and applications. *The Behavior Analyst Today, 3*(4), 421–433.

Blackledge, J. T. (2007). Disrupting verbal processes: Cognitive defusion in acceptance and commitment therapy and other mindfulness-based psychotherapies. *Psychological Record, 57,* 555–576.

Block, J. A. (2002). *Acceptance or change of private experiences: A comparative analysis in college students with public speaking anxiety.* Unpublished doctoral dissertation, State University of New York, Albany.

Dahl, J., Wilson, K. G., & Nilsson, A. (2004). Acceptance and commitment therapy and the treatment for persons at risk for long-term disability resulting from stress and pain symptoms: A preliminary randomized trial. *Behavior Therapy, 35*(4), 785–801.

Gifford, E. V., Kohlenberg, B. S., Hayes, S. C., Antonuccio, D. O., Piasecki, M. M., Rasmussen-Hall, M. L., & Palm, K. M. (2004). Acceptance-based treatment for smoking cessation. *Behavior Therapy, 35*(4), 689–705.

Hayes, S. C. (2005). *Choosing willingness: The willingness question.* Message posted to http://www.contextualpsychology.org/acceptance

Hayes, S. C., Barnes-Holmes, D., & Roche, B. (2001). *Relational frame theory: A post-Skinnerian account of human language and cognition*. New York: Kluwer Academic/Plenum Publishers.

Hayes, S. C., Strosahl, K. D., Bunting, K., Twohig, M., & Wilson, K. G. (2004). What is acceptance and commitment therapy? (pp. 1–30). In S. Hayes & K. Strosahl (Eds.), *A practical guide to acceptance and commitment therapy*. New York: Springer.

Hayes, S. C., Strosahl, K., & Wilson, K. G. (1999). *Acceptance and commitment therapy: An experiential approach to behavior change*. New York: Guilford.

Hayes, S. C., Wilson, K. G., Gifford, E. V., Bissett, R., Piasecki, M., Batten, S. V., Byrd, M., & Gregg, J. A. (2004) A preliminary trial of twelve-step facilitation and acceptance and commitment therapy with polysubstance-abusing methadone-maintained opiate addicts. *Behavior Therapy, 35*(4), 667–688.

Robinson, P., Wicksell, R. K., & Olson, G. L. (2005). ACT with chronic pain patients. In S. Hayes & K. Strosahl (Eds.), *A practical guide to acceptance and commitment therapy* (pp. 315–345). New York: Springer.

Sidman, M. (2000). *Coercion and its fallout*. Boston, MA: Authors Cooperative, Inc.

Wilson, K. G., & Murrell, A. R. (2004). Values work in acceptance and commitment therapy: Setting a course for behavioral treatment (pp. 120–151). In S. Hayes, V. Follette, and M. Linehan (Eds.), *Mindfulness and acceptance: Expanding the cognitive-behavioral tradition*. New York: Gilford.

Zettle, R. D., & Hayes, S. C. (1986). A component and process analysis of cognitive therapy. *Psychological Reports, 61*, 939–953.

Zettle, R. D., & Raines, J. C. (1989). Group cognitive and contextual therapies in treatment of depression. *Journal of Clinical Psychology, 45*, 438–445.

chapter three

Teaching ACT:
To Whom, Why and How

Kirk D. Strosahl and Patricia J. Robinson

Acceptance and commitment therapy (ACT; Hayes, Strosahl, & Wilson, 1999) is an empirically supported treatment that combines acceptance and mindfulness strategies with commitment and behavior change strategies to increase psychological flexibility. Unlike traditional cognitive behavioral therapy (CBT), ACT focuses on changing the function, rather than the form, of private experience. The goal is to change the functional properties of unwanted internal experience by developing a mindful and accepting posture toward thoughts, feelings, memories and sensations. Accepted for what they are (just thoughts, feelings, memories, etc.) rather than what they appear to be (dominating displays that require either obedience to a response rule, or conscious control or suppression), even unwanted private experiences can be effectively integrated into the fabric of daily human experience. In effect, they assume their appropriate role in the overall contextual array that is present as a basic function of self-awareness. To this end, ACT strategies promote development of present moment awareness and an encompassing transcendent self that can help the person separate the 'human from the mind'. Once this distinction is forged, ACT helps the patient get in touch with basic personal values and helps the patient develop committed actions based in those values.

From an ACT perspective, psychological suffering is often caused by experiential avoidance and an overidentification with the content of private experience, both of which act as barriers to acting in ways that promote vitality, purpose and meaning. The FEAR mnemonic summarizes the ACT formula for suffering.

- Fusion with rules about healthy living
- Evaluation of events/states of mind in good–bad terms
- Avoidance of unwanted private experience
- Reason giving to explain behavioral excesses or deficits

The name of the therapy itself suggests an algorithm for achieving psychological flexibility.

- Accept (what is present inside and outside the skin)
- Choose (a valued direction)
- Take action (consistent with those values)

ACT has been evaluated in over 30 randomized clinical trials. In comparison with other active treatments known to be helpful for various problems, the effect size for ACT is a Cohen's d of around 0.6 and this is considered to be a medium effect size. In a series of recent studies, ACT has been demonstrated as an effective treatment for depression, addictions, anxiety, smoking cessation, chronic pain, psychosis, diabetes management and job stress (Hayes, 2006). Mediational analyses have provided evidence for the possible causal role of core ACT processes (acceptance, defusion and values) in producing beneficial clinical outcomes. Deficient levels of these core processes have also been shown to correlate with psychopathology.

There are many features of ACT that make it somewhat unique among the growing list of 'third wave' cognitive behavioral treatments. First, ACT is based on relational frame theory (Hayes, Barnes-Holmes, & Roche, 2001), a post-Skinnerian contextual theory of language and cognition. Most ACT intervention principles were first identified in basic research studies examining the functional properties of language and thought. There is really no other cognitive behavioral treatment that can make the claim that is so tightly linked to basic research. Indeed, the disconnect between basic science and most traditional CBT treatments has been posited as one principle reason why we have seen a plateau in treatment effect sizes over the last 15 years. It is one thing to claim that a treatment works for some type of psychological problem; it is a completely different undertaking to explain why it works at a level of analysis that promotes continuous improvements in treatment effects. In this arena, ACT stands tall and is arguably setting a new standard for how basic research and clinical models can feed each other.

There are other unique features of ACT that make it an intriguing model for a wider audience of service settings. For one, ACT does not view human suffering as abnormal or out of the pale of daily experience, making it a far less stigmatizing approach. We maintain that there is something in the 'water supply' of social training that sets us up for suffering. One is the culturally transmitted belief that healthy living is freedom from any type of mental pain; consequently, the goal when faced with some type of personal adversity is to suppress, eliminate and/or avoid unwanted private experiences in the service of reaching 'good health'. From the ACT perspective, human suffering originates not from biomedical disease states or psychiatric syndromes, but rather from culturally supported attempts to escape from or avoid the experience of pain per se. It is the attempt to avoid, escape and control unwanted private experience that traps us in the cycle of suffering. Further, ACT proposes that the phenomenon of experiential and behavioral avoidance is a widespread cultural practice that essentially guarantees an unparalleled epidemic of human misery. In the United States alone, we are now witnessing annual rates of mental disorders and addictions nearing 30%, meaning almost one out of three Americans is developing a serious emotional health problem each year. This sobering finding brings us to question how we can best use what we have learned over the last 2 decades of developing ACT. You can treat the victims of this badly misguided philosophy of avoidance one at a time in therapy, or you can take ACT to the streets and use it as a type of social movement designed to restore the dignity of daily human experience. Or, you can do both. With the publication of such books as *Get Out of Your Mind and Into Your Life* (Hayes, 2007), *The Happiness Trap* (Harris, 2006) and *The Mindfulness and Acceptance Workbook for Depression* (Strosahl & Robinson, 2008), we seem poised to take on the culture of 'feel goodism'. To do this requires preparation of a new army of foot soldiers; people who do not think or act like therapists (and are probably glad they do not), but who play important roles in the community of service that surrounds us.

The single biggest challenge to promulgating ACT in the service community is that ACT was developed by therapist types for a therapist-type audience. One frequent complaint is that the treatment approach can come across as intellectually intimidating and even counterintuitive. Even experienced ACT providers can get lost in the nuances of core processes that require not just attention to the verbal behavior of the client, but also the culturally conditioned reactions of the therapist. ACT can easily turn into a 'hall of mirrors' in which everything is a reflection of everything else, and nothing ends up being real. This type of intellectual challenge may stimulate interesting discussions within the academic or therapy practitioner community, but it is a real turn-off when trying to disseminate core ACT concepts to the wider community. Here, we might be wise to remember the '80–20' rule of quality improvement, namely, the first 80% of 'results' is gained with the first 20% of effort. Another acronym that applies here is 'KISS', or Keep It Simple Stupid! If we can find simple, useful ways to condense core ACT concepts into simple, easy to digest 'soundbites', it is far more likely that health care practitioners, social services professionals, and even lay helpers will adopt the approach. There is much that ACT has to offer the service community, if only we can find a way to translate it into everyday concepts that anyone can grasp.

This chapter will focus on the issue of taking ACT 'to the streets'. We will describe various stakeholder groups that might benefit from training in ACT, both from the perspective of helping others and promoting personal growth. The old saying 'the devil is in the details' will bring us to the 'how-to' issues concerning widespread dissemination and training. To be accepted as useful to a larger community, a treatment model must exhibit certain qualities that give it 'sticking power'. We will examine these issues in some detail and propose a specific methodology for teaching untrained service professionals core ACT concepts and interventions. One major, unintended benefit of learning to translate ACT for the uninitiated is that it will help the translators understand their language in a totally different light. If we can reformulate ACT in simpler, easier to understand ways, we might discover that many of the complexities of the treatment are not really necessary to perform good deeds with people who need help.

To Whom

As we noted earlier, we are facing a virtual pandemic of mental disorders, addictions and problems in living. There is hardly anyone who is immune to one or more of these pitfalls of living, particularly in our socially disconnected world. This means that any real hope we have of reversing this destructive trend resides in our ability to propose an alternative that is not only easily to understand, but has a ring of common sense to it. So, who is the target audience? Potentially, all providers of services to humans — particularly humans who behave in challenging ways — stand to gain from learning ACT strategies. When we refer to humans who behave in challenging ways, we are alluding to the large and growing group of people who are suffering psychologically, attempting to avoid direct experience of their angst, entangled in cognitions about the unreasonableness of suffering and/or blaming others, driven to impulsive and unorganized behavior and unable to choose fresh, new patterns of behavior that could bring them closer to what they truly value in life. This group of challenged humans is a large one and they have contact with others in numerous contexts, starting early in life and continuing until life ends. Providers of various human services are usually drawn to their vocation because of an underlying compassion for humans who are suffering, but their vocational success is often limited by their preparation, particularly as it applies to the very most challenging people they come to serve.

One very natural idea is to promote ACT within the mental health and addiction treatment community. In this endeavor, the goals must be to stimulate interest in learning more about ACT, rather than turning people off. How do you turn people off? You can present ACT in impossibly complicated terms that simply overwhelm the senses, or you can provide ACT trainings in a way that offends young trainees by being overly intrusive, provocative or condescending. ACT can easily be presented in a way that borders on cultism, and although a certain percentage of people will develop into zealots, the more sobering question is, 'How many potential ACT practitioners dropped out of the process because they were either offended or simply felt the treatment was too complicated to master?' The question of how many people you lose to training is actually far more important than how many people you gain. Given that we develop training experiences that highlight many upsides of ACT, most psychologists, social workers, and counselors will pursue further training after receiving an introduction. Graduate schools are increasingly exposing young therapists in training to ACT and this provides a far better continuity training option, provided that faculty themselves understand core ACT principles. It is not clear at this point whether we have been successful on this front. Graduate schools have long been the bastion of warring schools of thought, where the goal is for one school to win out and put the other out to pasture. With the increasing emphasis on evidence-based care, perhaps this disappointing reality will give way to a new philosophy of equipping new mental health neophytes with all of the tools they will need to be effective in practice, not just effective in a specific professor's therapy approach.

Most mental health professionals mistakenly believe that the mental health of the population is in the hands of the mental health system, including mental health and addiction treatment settings. In reality, this system is microscopically small in comparison to the de facto treatment systems, the health care system and the public school system. Nearly 75% of all people with mental health or addiction issues circulate entirely within the health care system and are never seen by a mental health professional (Narrow, Reiger, Rae, Manderscheid, & Locke, 1993). Primary care providers, in particular, spend the majority of their practice time addressing these types of issues, often with disappointing results. Primary health care seems like an ideal place to deliver a new social message about the need to accept personal pain as part of living. Instead, primary care has become the flagship of the 'control and eliminate' philosophy. At least in the United States, people are trained at an early age to believe that if something is physically or emotionally painful, the doctor will surely have a pill that can eliminate the problem. Drug companies, through direct market-ing to consumers, have been very effective at creating the impression that better living through chemistry is the real solution.

Contemporary medical students graduate from schools where courses on biomedical diagnosis and treatment predominate and course work focused on psychological and social aspects of health is typically minimal. Residency programs often fail to integrate the psychosocial perspective into physician training, and it is only relatively late in residency training that physicians see patients and realize that little of what they learned in the biomedical world will work with the amazing varieties of psychological suffering that are seen during medical encounters. Training experiences for mid-level health care providers and nurses may be similar, although experience suggests that there is a little more credence given to the role of psychological and social factors in nursing and physician assistant training programs. It is no wonder that many health care providers focus primarily on medicating various symptoms of psychological suffering and feel frustrated when patients fail to comply with treatment and/or do not improve. The irony is that the acceptance message is highly applicable to a wide range of medical situations, such as living with chronic disease, managing preventable causes of health risk or dealing with the ultimate reality that we all are going to die. Both of us work as psychologists in primary care settings and have for many years. The reality is that most medical providers are intrigued with ACT and at the same time cannot deal with the highly complex aspects of it. They are looking for 2 to 5-minute 'soundbites' that can help a patient make a difficult situation more bearable. The message from primary care is a wake-up call for how to disseminate a philosophy like ACT. You have to get down to a limited set of core messages that can capture the imagination of both the provider and the patient. If the provider does not really understand (or believe in) ACT, the message to the patient will be garbled, the results will be equiv-ocal and the provider will conclude that this ACT stuff did not really work with his or her patients. We have spent much of the last 15 years focusing on ways to simplify ACT so that when primary care providers take a chance on learning to use ACT, they experience positive results. A sea-soned ACT therapist would be shocked by the seemingly primitive sim-plicity of how the primary care provider explains something like acceptance to a patient, and this highlights one of the real challenges in taking ACT to the streets. From setting to setting, the message will be spun differently; the helping interactions will vary dramatically in length and pace. Posi-tioned underneath these phenotypic differences will be a core message that does not stray too much from the point. This is the cardinal principle of the 80–20 rule.

Educators, day-care providers, and parents also stand to benefit from acceptance and commitment training. Teachers face larger classrooms and increasing pressure to prepare students to pass standardized academic tests. More and more students have behavioral problems, and special education resources are often reserved for select groups of students with educationally handicapping conditions. Day-care providers and early childhood education specialists report more children with conduct problems and feel frustrated in their efforts to involve parents in collaborative development of behavior change programs. Parents, most of whom work full time, often feel their relationships with their children are lacking. Tired and discouraged, they can easily slide into patterns of turning the television on and serving fast food — not at all what they had planned when they decided to have children. These large and diverse groups of people deserve the best tools available for their mission — creating the adults of tomorrow — and ACT strategies need to be in their bag of tricks.

Why

The reason to share ACT with as many providers of human services as possible is simple — to empower their efforts to deliver beneficial services. ACT strategies can foster greater awareness and intention in their work. While members of this group differ in significant ways, they share common values, and exposure to ACT principles can assist them with developing and maintaining the patience, acceptance, egalitarian stance and flexibility needed to explore, encourage, educate and promote healing. Service providers who use ACT are more likely to be effective, to experience satisfaction in their work and to be more resilient to the burnout that is all too common among providers of human services.

How

As we mentioned previously, the main thrust of this chapter is to develop guidelines for taking ACT to new helpers, with differing educational backgrounds and in differing service settings. Given our years of practice in primary care, we have learned that everything important has to be put forward in an algorithm, described by an acronym. Along with having illegible handwriting at this point, this is the badge of honor for someone working in primary care! But, we have also learned a lot of other important lessons about teaching ACT to non-mental health professionals and, particularly to people who do not immediately resonate to 'touchy, feely' principles. The algorithm we have developed is appropriately named TRANSLATE. In the sections that follow, we will describe the core features of this approach, with a focus on showing the immediate value of the principle to working with a challenging human.

Transparent

The first step in the *TRANSLATE* process is making ACT *transparent*. If ACT is to receive widespread acceptance in the helping community, we have to create an intervention philosophy that is far more transparent than is the case with the current model. This means we have to strip away needless complexities and focus on core messages that appeal to common sense. The difficulty of course is that 'common sense' could also be defined in terms of cultural norms (if you are unhappy with the way you are feeling, figure out what is causing you to feel this way and eliminate or change it) that are being targeted by ACT interventions. This caveat in place, it is possible to simplify ACT principles so that they are more readily understood by both the providers of human services, as well as the recipients of those services.

The Three-Legged Stool

Let us take the example of the six core processes thought to underpin ACT. These processes are represented in the 'hexaflex' figure shown in Figure 3.1. At the top, there are the processes of acceptance and defusion. In the middle are the processes of present moment awareness and contact with a bigger self that is transcendent. At the bottom are the twin processes of valuing and committed action. All six processes are interrelated and interact. This level of complexity is well beyond the tolerance limit of most primary care

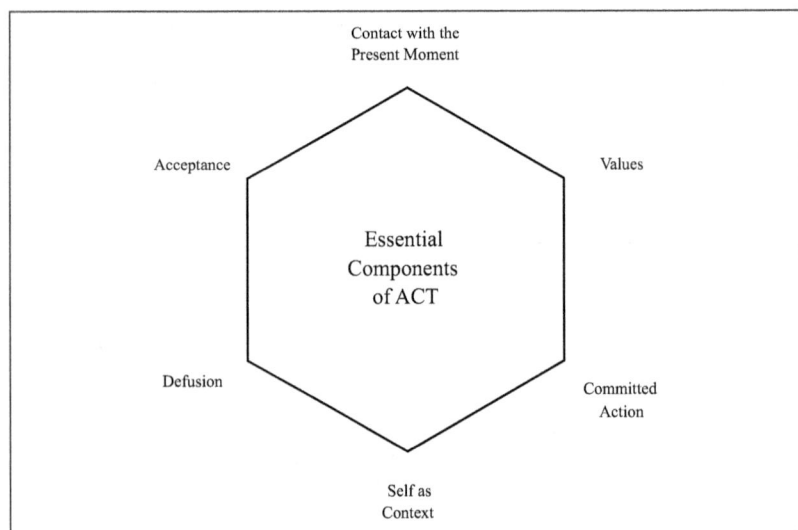

FIGURE 3.1
ACT hexaflex.

providers, who are likely to ask, 'So, what should I focus on and what should I say to my patient?'

The answer is to simplify the six core processes by consolidating them into three global 'response styles' that will be the focus of interventions. Response styles can best be thought of as tendencies (more technically speaking, these are behavioral predispositions) the person brings to the game of life. These tendencies are underpinned by the six core processes identified in the ACT model. It will be useful to briefly describe each response style, much as we would to one of our health care colleagues.

- *Accepting–Rejecting Stance* describes the extent to which the person is willing to experience personal pain with a welcoming, understanding posture, rather than being unwilling to feel pain, trying to run from it, or numb it out.

- *Purposeful–Autopilot Living Style* describes the extent to which the person is aware of daily lifestyle choices and makes purposeful choices, rather than simply following rules and living on autopilot. Purposeful living automatically includes contact with one's values as the key organizing principle.

- *Approach–Avoidance Oriented Problem Solving* describes the extent to which the person approaches difficult situations with the intention of fixing them in accordance with personal beliefs and values, rather than being passive, checking out of the situation altogether or engaging in actions that detract from personal confidence.

Each response style exists on a continuum and, collectively, they define a patient's psychological flexibility, a term that no-one outside the mental health community understands. Thus, we use the term 'resilience', a word that most lay people understand and see as a positive personal attribute. We urge physicians and other human service providers to think of resilience as a three-legged stool (see Figure 3.2). If all three legs are strong, then the stool will be perfectly stable and will not shift around when weight is applied. Appropriately designed, such a stool can handle an enormous amount of weight, far more than one would think by just looking at it. In contrast, if even one leg is shorter than the other two, the stool will be unstable and rock back and forth when even the lightest weight is applied. The goal when helping someone in distress is to measure each leg of their stool to see if they are in balance and to begin strengthening the leg(s) that seem weak and contribute to imbalance and a lack of resilience.

It does not take an advanced degree in education to see the differences between the hexaflex and the three-legged stool as teaching tools. Most lay people look at the hexaflex and mention that it looks interesting but they do not know what all those lines mean (even some mental health

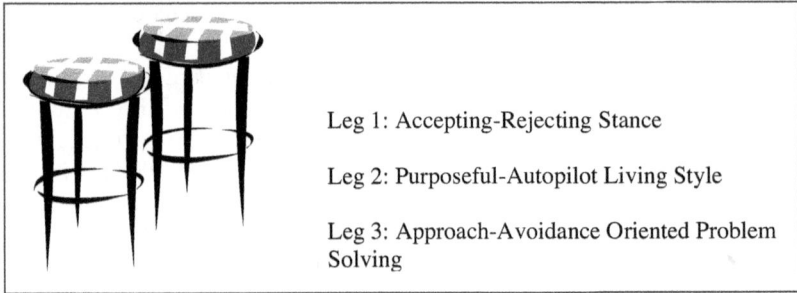

Leg 1: Accepting-Rejecting Stance

Leg 2: Purposeful-Autopilot Living Style

Leg 3: Approach-Avoidance Oriented Problem Solving

FIGURE 3.2
ACT three-legged stool.

professionals make this comment!). Those same people look at the three-legged stool and rather instantly understand the point we are trying to make. To make ACT transparent requires that we construct metaphors that may in fact hide many nuances that the ACTophile might find objectionable, but that deliver a simple, limited set of usable ideas to the non-mental health professional or lay helper.

Relevance

The second step in the TRANSLATE process is *relevance*. If people do not feel that ACT principles are relevant to the types of problems they are responsible for handling, they will not be motivated to continue learning them. The fact is that most professionals already have a 'bag of tricks' that they have assembled to address a variety of behavioral problems. The question is whether an ACT approach will be value added. For example, schoolteachers might already know the basics of behavior modification and so want to know how ACT is going to add potency to their results. A health care provider might already have some skill with motivational interviewing and will have questions about what ACT can do over and above the existing plan.

A simple metaphor like the three-legged stool does more than just assist a person with understanding what the three response styles are; it makes a more universal personal point. Specifically, response styles do not just describe the suffering of others; they describe a process by which others come to suffer. This makes suffering a lot less mysterious and intimidating, something that most people in helping professions struggle with. One virtue of ACT is that our perspective on human suffering is actually quite simple, when you boil it down to its essence. Most people will be attracted to simple messages that take what looks like a complicated problem and makes it quite simple to understand. We would argue that this is the hall-mark of a really good therapist as well!

To get an 'audience' with a professional who might potentially benefit from ACT principles, you need a hook. In our experience, ACT principles become intriguing in situations where the professional's interventions are not really working or there is a personality clash developing. In these cases, we gain an entrée by using the principle of workability, which is effectively the method used to discriminate between responses that have some potential longevity, and those that are destined to fail. If we could get every challenging human, and those who try to help them, to use the workability principle in daily living, there would be a lot less suffering in the world. This is because workability is not about what should work in one's life, it is about what is working. The worksheets below show how a simple re-sults analysis can be used with almost any professional in almost any set-ting to bring the relevance of ACT strategies to their work. Notice that we use the term 'results' rather than workability, because most non-mental health professionals and lay helpers understand the concept of results at a very basic level. It is easy to teach the distinction between immediate results and long-term results and this is what we call a second-level ACT principle. The first level is to begin looking at what is working and what is not in the first place. The second level is to realize many unworkable strate-gies persist because they seem to work in the short run, but fail in the long run. The ACT Short- and Long-Term Results Worksheet for Helping Professionals is a tool that various providers of human services can use to look closely at their efforts to address interactions with people they find challenging. Figure 3.3 presents this worksheet, and we encourage you to try it out. Figure 3.4 provides an example of a teacher's responses to this tool, and Figure 3.5 provides an example of a primary care provider's re-sponses. Looking over these examples may stimulate your thinking con-cerning your responses and the relevance of ACT to your work.

As these examples show, this tool demonstrates that it can be relatively easy to conduct a 'quick and dirty' workability analysis for a variety of interactions with challenging humans. From a motivation enhancement perspective, this type of assessment allows the provider to take several steps back and really think about what s/he is doing. Taking an honest look at how short-term strategies work in the long run often provides the hook necessary for a person new to ACT strategies to see their potential relevance to her or his work.

ACT Short- and Long-Term Results Worksheet for Helping Professionals

Column 1: Choose a challenging human to use as the focus of this exercise. Think of someone that you are trying to help, but haven't really been able to. Make a few notes to describe this person (age, gender) and several specific examples of behavior s/he demonstrates that you find challenging.

Column 2: How do you currently respond? What exactly do you do when the behavior occurs? Write your answers in column 2.

Column 3: What results are you getting? Write out both short-term and long-term results that you are seeing with your current responses.

1, Challenging human	2. Your current response	3. Results (short-term and long-term)	
Challenging behaviors		Short-term	Long-term

FIGURE 3.3
ACT Short- and Long-Term Results Worksheet for helping professionals.

**ACT Short- and Long-Term Results Worksheet for Helping Professionals:
A Schoolteacher's Responses**

(See Instructions in Figure 3.3)

1. Challenging human *10-year-old student*	2. Your current response	3. Results (short-term and long-term)	
Challenging behaviors		Short-term	Long-term
1. *Threatens or pushes other students when playing four square*	*I get really annoyed with this because I'm responsible if anyone gets hurt. I put him in time-out in the classroom, talk to him about rules for playing with others and try to get him to agree not to do this anymore.*	*He will stop for a while until I'm not looking and then will bully students again; he argues with me and tells me I'm being unfair; he will sometimes even curse at me, which scares me.*	*He is getting more aggressive with me in his words and is being more challenging. The bullying continues at about the same rate. I don't look forward to teaching class anymore because I know it is going to be a struggle.*
2. *Interrupts me in classroom either by blurting out answers or comments or not waiting his turn.*	*This really annoys me because he is challenging my control of the class. I silence him and put him in the back of the classroom; on some occasions I refer him to the principal.*	*I think he relishes getting my attention this way and I feel both sorry for him and angry because he really hasn't stopped.*	*Referrals to principal have made his parents have to leave work and now they are angry with me because they think I'm singling him out. I'm not but he is just such a problem that it seems that way to them.*

FIGURE 3.4
ACT Short- and Long-Term Results Worksheet for helping professionals:
A schoolteacher's responses.

ACT Short- and Long-Term Results Worksheet for Helping Professionals: A Physician's Responses

(See Instructions in Figure 3.3)

1. Challenging human	2. Your current response	3. Results (short-term and long-term)	
Patient with BPD and chronic pain		Short-term	Long-term
She comes in complaining of pain, wanting more narcotics and telling me that I'm not helping and her life is falling apart.	*I tell her she's drug seeking and that I'm not going to prescribe more narcotics. I tell her that she needs to take responsibility for her life and start exercising and get back to work.*	*She will quiet down for a while; she gives lots of excuses about why she can't go back to work; she insists her back pain gets worse when she stretches or exercises. She's less demanding, cries.*	*We are not getting anywhere. Her pain ratings are just as high as when we started, even though I've upped her narcotics; she looks more depressed and angry every time I see her.*
She tells me that she thinks about suicide a lot, particularly on days when her pain is bad and her depression worsens.	*I try to get her to give me reasons why she wouldn't kill herself. I try to get her to look at the good things going on in her life.*	*She will stop talking about suicide but I know she isn't convinced. She has trouble giving me sincere reasons for wanting to stay alive.*	*She continues to have crises and gets suicidal. She seems less willing to talk to me about this.*

FIGURE 3.5
ACT Short- and Long-Term Results Worksheet for helping professionals:
A physician's responses.

Analyze

The next TRANSLATE step is to encourage the use of simple *ACT*. Analytical tools that drive the professional back to the three-legged stool. Since many helping professionals simply do not have the time to engage in elaborate forms of behavior analysis, we need methods that are simple to complete and yet informative. While not yielding the precision of what is typically possible in a specialty behavioral health setting, adaptations of analytical tools can make them user-friendly to our colleagues in helping professions other than psychology. The three response style dimensions can again provide a starting and ending point for an analysis that can lead the helping professional to a new way of responding to challenging interactions. The ACT Patient Analysis Worksheet for Helping Professionals in Figure 3.6 provides a format for analyzing a challenging person's relative strengths on each of the three legs. We encourage you to use this tool with the patient you identified in the ACT Short-and Long-Term Results Worksheet.

The ACT Patient Analysis Worksheet for Helping Professionals

FIRST LEG: ACCEPTING POSTURE

Acceptance Behavior

What do I know about this person's ability to accept her sensations, thoughts, and feelings?

Strength of Acceptance Behavior: *Weak*   *Medium*   *Strong*

Rejecting Behavior

What do I know about this person's tendency to reject or shut-down in response to internal sensations, thoughts, and feelings?

Strength of Acceptance Behavior: *Weak*   *Medium*   *Strong*

SECOND LEG: PURPOSEFUL LIVING

Purpose-Driven Behavior

What behaviors or behavioral patterns demonstrate this person's commitment to live a purpose-driven life?

Strength of Purpose-Driven Behavior: *Weak*   *Medium*   *Strong*

Autopilot Behavior

What do I know about this person's tendency to behave on autopilot without thinking it through (e.g., desiring to just 'follow the rule' and hope for the best) or alternatively to act impulsively (e.g., to lash out when others interfere with her/his autopilot actions)?

Strength of Autopilot Behavior: *Weak*   *Medium*   *Strong*

THIRD LEG: APPROACH-ORIENTED PROBLEM SOLVING

Approach Behavior

What do I know about this person's ability to approach problems in a way that furthers resolution (e.g., taking the time to define the problem, looking at options, developing and evaluating action plans)?

Strength of Approach Behavior: *Weak*   *Medium*   *Strong*

Avoidance Behavior

What do I know about this person's tendency to avoid problems in general, including emotional and interpersonal problems (e.g., settling for the status quo, avoiding risks in an effort to control emotional discomfort or distress)?

Strength of Avoidance Behavior: *Weak*   *Medium*   *Strong*

FIGURE 3.6
The ACT Patient Analysis Worksheet for helping professionals.

The ACT Patient Analysis Worksheet for Helping Professionals:
A Physician's Analysis

FIRST LEG: ACCEPTING POSTURE

Acceptance Behavior

What do I know about this person's ability to accept her sensations, thoughts, and feelings?

She seems to understand that her pain is chronic and will be there forever. She seems to accept me as her provider.

Strength of Acceptance Behavior: *Medium*

Rejecting Behavior

What do I know about this person's tendency to reject or shut-down in response to internal sensations, thoughts, and feelings?

What do I know about this person's tendency to reject or shut-down in response to internal sensations, thoughts, and feelings? She is not willing to be in physical pain to exercise or work. She is very afraid of conflict and easily goes into crisis. She is unwilling to talk about her childhood and teen traumas; she just shuts down when I bring them up as something that might be making her depression worse.

Strength of Rejecting Behavior: *Strong to Very Strong*

SECOND LEG: PURPOSEFUL LIVING

Purpose-Driven Behavior

What behaviors or behavioral patterns demonstrate this person's commitment to live a purpose-driven life?

She has two dogs that she lavishes with attention.

Strength of Purpose-Driven Behavior: *Weak*

Autopilot Behavior

What do I know about this person's tendency to behave on autopilot without thinking it through (e.g., desiring to just 'follow the rule' and hope for the best) or alternatively to act impulsively (e.g., to lash out when others interfere with her/his autopilot actions)?

She frequently overdoes it on her household chores and ends up lying in bed for a day or two. She is convinced that the only way she can have a good life is to be free of pain. Nothing else I say matters if it contradicts this belief. She complains of being bored and lonely all the time and seems to have very few outside interests.

Strength of Autopilot Behavior: *Very Strong*

FIGURE 3.7
The ACT Patient Analysis Worksheet for helping professionals: A physician's analysis.

Figure 3.7 provides an example of a primary care physician's use of this tool to analyze the behavior of a chronically depressed, primary care patient with chronic pain.

What is apparent in this example is that all three legs of this stool are out of balance, but in particular the approach–avoidance problem-solving leg. The provider was unable to think of a single approach-oriented, value-based problem-solving behavior this patient was using.

**The ACT Patient Analysis Worksheet for Helping Professionals:
A Physician's Analysis** (continued)

THIRD LEG: APPROACH-ORIENTED PROBLEM SOLVING

Approach Behavior

What do I know about this person's ability to approach problems in a way that furthers resolution (e.g., taking the time to define the problem, looking at options, developing and evaluating action plans)?

Strength of Approach Behavior: *Weak*

Avoidance Behavior

What do I know about this person's tendency to avoid problems in general, including emotional and interpersonal problems (e.g., settling for the status quo, avoiding risks in an effort to control emotional discomfort or distress)?

She thinks about suicide a lot. She refuses to leave her dysfunctional family situation. She pressures me to give her more narcotics and refuses to really try physical therapy.

Strength of Avoidance Behavior: *Strong*

FIGURE 3.7 (continued)
The ACT Patient Analysis Worksheet for helping professionals: A physician's analysis.

Needs-Based

The fourth step in the TRANSLATE process concerns prioritizing the *needs* of the patient concerning deployment of ACT strategies. In the time-pressured world of social service work, it is imperative that the provider has a method for figuring out exactly what a challenging human needs to generate some positive momentum. This is because there are so many challenging humans to help that overtreating one person means someone else will get nothing. This is particularly true in primary care, where a typical practice day might consist of seeing 25 to 30 patients, at least half of whom will have psychological issues. Taking the three-legged stool model a step further, the results of a simple response style analysis should also point to a needs-based intervention that is likely to have a positive impact. As mentioned previously, these interventions are likely to be delivered in very brief interactions between the helper and the challenging human. Figure 3.8 offers an example of the ACT Needs-Based Change Plan and its use to benefit the work between the physician and his challenging patient. Repeated use of this tool can prepare helpers to make quick decisions about ways to target one or more legs and support the person's development of resilience over time. It can also assist the provider or helper in efforts to change her own behaviors that have not yielded good long-term results with the patient, as well as clarify behavior change targets for the patient. In this example, the primary care physician and patient agreed to target the least strong leg, acceptance, and to work to further develop skills in this response area over time.

This simple planning tool helped clear the emotional clutter of the physician's interaction with this patient and provided a visit-to-visit focus based on the previous analysis. Prior to each visit, the physician reviewed the intervention targets and picked one area to focus on, while always assessing the three targets. She noticed that this had a calming influence on the patient's emotional volatility during medical visits. She noticed that the more she focused the discussion on these specific goals, the more the patient was trying to engage in meaningful activities between visits.

The ACT Needs-Based Change Plan: A Physician's Example

Response style (leg) target	Goal	Exercises	Evaluation	
			Now	Later
Accepting posture	*Acceptance of the fact that she will likely have pain the rest of her life and that at times she will think she cannot have a good life because of her pain. Accepting that I cannot stop her pain.*	*Read the serenity prayer and think about how it might apply to our work together and her pain experiences. Talk about acceptance at every visit.*	*Pain Acceptance Rating (baseline is 2 on 7-point scale)*	*Pain Acceptance Rating (most recent rating is 4 on 7-point scale)*
Approach driven problem-solving	*Use more non-narcotic strategies for dealing with pain and less reliance on drugs. Accept that she may be angry with me about this at times.*	*Present physical therapy for 10 weeks and at-home practice on a daily basis as an experiment; teach present moment strategies with exercises at our visits.*	*Goal of completing five home exercises per week (baseline is zero)*	*Adherence rating at each medical visit (most recent visit is 2 on 0–7)*
Purposeful living	*Encourage her to engage in life pursuits, even with pain, understanding she will have pain no matter what.*	*Identify one thing she will do at every visit that engages her interest in spite of her pain.*	*Life engagement rating (baseline is 1 on 7-point scale)*	*Life engagement rating (most recent visit is 3)*

FIGURE 3.8
The ACT Needs-Based Change Plan: A physician's example.

Self-Improvement

The fifth step in the ACT TRANSLATE process concerns *self-improvement*. ACT is unique in that it levels the playing field between the provider and the challenging human. The fact that 'we are in this stew together' means that the same ACT principles that influence the challenging human also impact the helper. Like those they seek to help, most helpers are likely to encounter substantial life stresses and disappointments. Very often, the burnout seen in social service providers is not the result of working with challenging humans; it results from the underuse of acceptance strategies, taking an autopilot approach to helping others and failing to recognize forms of avoidance that are being used to cope with the stress of caregiving. In our experience, most primary care providers are intrigued about the potential utility of acceptance, purposeful living and approach-driven problem solving. This is because these messages speak to us all; almost anyone would benefit from a consistent application of these strategies for healthy living. Because of this, we encourage providers to conduct an inventory of acceptance, purpose and approach orientation in their own lives, and the ACT Personal Inventory for Helping Professionals provides such a supportive structure (see Figure 3.9). Reviewing the responses of the physician from our previous example to this inventory may help clarify questions you may have about how to use this tool (see Figure 3.10).

Based upon this self-inventory, the physician was able to identify a few 'red flags' that she could focus on. In particular, she realized that her not wanting to be a disappointment and avoidance of conflict and expression of feelings might be 'birds of a feather'. You can use the results of your work to make a change plan by using the ACT Self-Improvement Plan in Figure 3.11. The physician's responses to this tool are presented in Table Figure 3.12 and may stimulate your thinking about your own change plan.

The physician really struggled with making some of these changes, particularly opening up to her husband. She mentioned that her struggles with this seemingly simple goal gave her a much greater appreciation of how difficult it is to change. She noted that this experience had dramatically changed her approach to change-oriented discussions with her patients. She was much more open to allowing her patients to 'set the level' of their behavioral commitments, rather to impose her own solutions.

Learning Curve

The sixth step in the ACT TRANSLATE process is to anticipate that there will be a *learning curve* that is unique to each individual helping professional. Put another way, we do not expect providers to immediately understand all ACT principles and, in fact, they may put their own 'spin' on some of these ideas. However, their learning curve must be such that the

ACT Personal Inventory for Helping Professionals

FIRST LEG: ACCEPTING POSTURE

Acceptance Behavior

What behaviors or behavioral patterns in your life provide examples of an accepting response style?

Strength of Acceptance Behavior:

Rejecting Behavior

What behaviors or behavioral patterns in your life provide examples of a response style characterized by rejection of your thoughts, feelings, sensations, and memories?

Strength of Rejecting Behavior:

SECOND LEG: PURPOSEFUL LIVING

Purpose-Driven Behavior

What behaviors or behavioral patterns demonstrate your commitment to live a purpose-driven life?

Strength of Purpose-Driven Behavior:

Autopilot Behavior

What behaviors or behavioral patterns in your life provide examples of a response style characterized by going through life on autopilot (i.e., without questioning what you do, making intentional choices and/or reflecting on the results of your choices)?

Strength of Autopilot Behavior:

THIRD LEG: APPROACH-ORIENTED PROBLEM SOLVING

Approach Behavior

What in your life demonstrates your ability to take an approach orientation to solving life problems (e.g., taking the time to define the problem, looking at options, developing and evaluating action plans)?

Strength of Approach Behavior:

Avoidance Behavior

What behaviors or behavioral patterns in your life provide examples of an avoidance approach to problems in living (e.g., settling for the status quo, avoiding risks in an effort to control emotional discomfort or distress)?

Strength of Avoidance Behavior:

FIGURE 3.9
ACT Personal Inventory for Helping Professionals.

ACT Personal Inventory for Helping Professionals: A Physician's Responses

FIRST LEG: ACCEPTING POSTURE

Acceptance Behavior

What behaviors or behavioral patterns in your life provide examples of an accepting response style?

I accept that I am often 'guessing' when I treat a patient and that guessing is what I'm paid to do. I accept that, as a mother, I'm not going to be there as much for my children because of my career.

Strength of Acceptance Behavior: Strong

This is something I remind myself of every day before work. I definitely go back and forth as to whether I made the right decision when I picked medicine. It's not easy to do both jobs and still I choose it.

Rejecting Behavior

What behaviors or behavioral patterns in your life provide examples of a response style characterized by rejection of your thoughts, feelings, sensations, and memories?

I feel badly about disappointing patients and sometimes cave in to unreasonable requests. When my children get mad at me or express disappointment about my not being able to spend time with them, I feel awful and just want to scream or walk out of the house. I can feel my blood pressure increase, and I want to say, 'Enough, stop it!'

Strength of Rejecting Behavior: Medium

There is probably one visit every day where I do something like this and it makes me feel like a bad doctor. When this happens in the morning, I'm more likely to eat lunch at my desk and not work out. This sort of thing happens at least weekly, and I think it leads me to back down on limits I've set because I feel guilty about not being there for them.

SECOND LEG: PURPOSEFUL LIVING

Purpose-Driven Behavior

What behaviors or behavioral patterns demonstrate your commitment to live a purpose-driven life?

My religious faith is a very important part of my life. I really believe in my role as a mother even though I have a very tight schedule.

Strength of Purpose-Driven Behavior: Strong

I participate in my church in as many ways as I can, given my schedule. I'm pretty good at spending quality time with each of my kids when I'm home.

Autopilot Behavior

What behaviors or behavioral patterns in your life provide examples of a response style characterized by going through life on autopilot (i.e., without questioning what you do, making intentional choices and/or reflecting on the results of your choices)?

I daydream a lot when I have free time that I could be spending a lot more productively. I don't let myself think about my career choices. I just pedal as fast as I can to keep up with the demands.

Strength of Autopilot Behavior: Medium

I have always been a daydreamer and probably always will be; it works for me — I think. This is something my husband has commented on when I'm really stressed out. I know this treadmill approach leads me to be tense and have problems with sleeping well; maybe also makes me irritable.

FIGURE 3.10
ACT Personal Inventory for Helping Professionals: A physician's responses.

ACT Personal Inventory for Helping Professionals: A Physician's Responses (cont)

THIRD LEG: APPROACH-ORIENTED PROBLEM SOLVING

Approach Behavior

What in your life demonstrates your ability to take an approach orientation to solving life problems (e.g., taking the time to define the problem, looking at options, developing and evaluating action plans)?

I do try to arrange my schedule so that I can be with my kids as much as possible. I'm very good at getting myself educated about the latest medical knowledge.

Strength of Approach Behavior: Strong

I feel I'm very good at this, even though there still isn't as much time as I would like. Every night when I pray, I express gratitude for each of my children and reflect on time I spent with each, what they might need. I've always been very motivated to improve my medical knowledge and skills. I am proactive in planning professional reading time.

Avoidance Behavior

What behaviors or behavioral patterns in your life provide examples of an avoidance approach to problems in living (e.g., settling for the status quo, avoiding risks in an effort to control emotional discomfort or distress)?

I won't deal with conflicts with my nurses or other physicians. I find it really hard to express my feelings to my husband, particularly my frustrations.

Strength of Avoidance Behavior: Medium to Strong

My tendency is to just let these things slide and hope they get better. Retreating to my office and rolling my eyes is quite automatic for me. I also complain a lot about office problems to my husband. This has been a sticking point in our relationship since the beginning. I wish I could do better, but I feel so uncomfortable with it that I settle for the status quo. When we disagree, I go silent and then busy myself with some task — reading, cleaning, etc.

FIGURE 3.10 (continued)
ACT Personal Inventory for Helping Professionals: A physician's responses.

ratio between the effort required to learn and the perceived benefits of learning creates a motivation to continue exposure to ACT principles. Our philosophy has been to plant whatever seed the provider is interested in and let it grow. Each provider's journey with ACT is a different one and we do not try to apply a formulaic way of moving providers through ACT. If one provider is enthusiastic about acceptance strategies and the next one is keen about approach-oriented problem-solving, that is fine. Insisting that ACT principles must be learned in a specific, preordained way is a formula for failure in the real world. While a polished ACT therapist might wince at hearing this, there are going to be providers who really do not care as much about values as they do about acceptance and vice versa. The 'spin' they put on this during their helping discussions might not even seem recognizable to a therapist who specializes in ACT. This is the reality of following the 80–20 rule.

ACT Self-Improvement Plan for Helping Professionals

Response style	Goal	Exercises	What will be different?	
			Pre	Post
Accepting posture				
Purposeful living				
Approach-oriented problem-solving				

FIGURE 3.11
ACT Self-Improvement Plan for Helping Professionals.

An example of the 80–20 rule is the ACT Behavioral Prescription Pad developed for use by primary care medical providers and nurses (Robinson & Reiter, 2007). Figure 3.13 presents this simple, yet potentially more complex teaching and intervention tool. Providers and nurses can learn a few or many of the nuances of using this pad at any given brief encounter with a primary care psychologist or other ACT-trained behavioral health provider. Briefing a medical provider on all of the following teaching points can easily be done in less than 20 minutes. If less time is available, three or four teaching points can be covered in 8 to 10 minutes.

ACT Behavioral Prescription Teaching Points

- The bull's-eye represents a person's value; you can have a patient select one area for each visit. Relationships, Health, and Work/Play/Spirituality cover a lot of what is important to most people.
- A value is different from a goal. Values are global and abstract statements; goals are specific, measurable and attainable. An example of a

ACT Self-Improvement Plan for Helping Professionals: A Physician's Responses

Response Style	Goal	Exercises	What Will Be Different?	
			Pre	Post
Accepting Posture	*Accepting my children's disappointment or anger and my own guilt feelings*	*Just allow myself to feel guilty and keep setting limits*	*Caving in because of guilt*	*Having guilt feelings but enforcing limits*
Purposeful Living	*Make better use of my free time*	*Practice interrupting my daydreaming and chose to do something more productive at that exact moment*	*Loss of free time to daydreaming*	*Daydreaming will not prevent me from productive use of free time*
Approach-Oriented Problem Solving	*Open up with my husband more often*	*Practice sharing at least one care and one concern with him at dinner or when we get together each day*	*Too closed off to sharing my cares and concerns with my husband*	*Able to regularly speak with him about my cares and concerns*

FIGURE 3.12
ACT Self-Improvement Plan for Helping Professionals: A physician's responses.

value statement is 'I care a great deal about the environment'. An example of a goal is 'I plan to exercise 30 minutes daily'.

- Values provide direction for goal-setting.
- Values support committed action and resilience in pursuing goals over long periods of time. For example, a person who avoids going out of their home because they feel anxious in public situations might pursue such in the service of a value about being a mother who wants the best for her children (and hence may set goals to go to specific community events with the children).
- Most of the time, our behavior is less than perfectly consistent with our values. In fact, we have to work very hard at times to keep up the effort to make our day-to-day behaviors reflect our values. We are not looking for perfection here; we are looking for direction and persistence.

- Many things get in the way of our plans, and it takes more than commitment to keep going at times. It often takes learning new skills.
- New skills that help us persist in pursuing valued directions include learning:
  - how to get unstuck from doing the same old thing (like learning how to just take a deep breath and accept the urge to shut down, give up, hide out or whatever)
  - be present in the moment (and notice our thoughts about the past and future)
  - be still with painful emotions, sensations, and memories.
- For today, what area of life do you want to address in our visit? What is your value statement? Let us form a goal. What can I teach you in the way of a new skill that might help you pursue this goal?

Accessibility

The seventh step in the ACT TRANSLATE process concerns *accessibility*. To successfully promulgate ACT principles requires that social service providers have easy access to these ideas and the teaching tools that promote them. We believe that this is one of the major challenges facing the

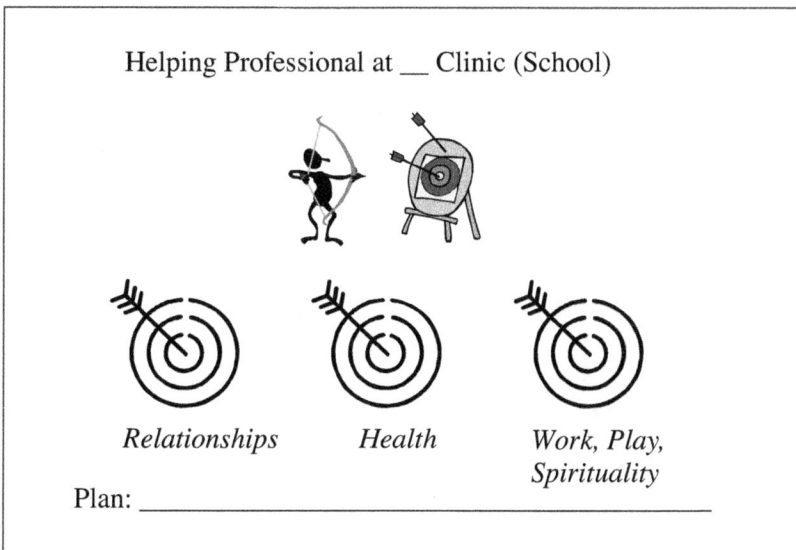

Helping Professional at __ Clinic (School)

Relationships   *Health*   *Work, Play, Spirituality*

Plan: _____

FIGURE 3.13
ACT Behavioral Prescription Pad.

ACT community at this point in time. If you cannot get the message in front of the people who provide the help to challenging humans, there is little chance that ACT principles will get into the equation. Publication of self-help books does not necessarily guarantee that the target audience will get the message. One question is whether these are the same people that buy self-help books. The answer is probably a mixed result. Some of these providers might get their first exposure to ACT through a self-help book, but probably a small minority. Another question is how the ACT model is presented in these books. Are the ACT principles simple and easy to digest? Will they intrigue the reader enough to expand the hunt for more information about ACT? Another strategy that has not really been used, to our knowledge, is to begin directing ACT readings toward audiences that we previously have not reached. This might involve directing monographs on ACT to physicians, medical schools, schools of education and so forth. These products would probably look a lot different than self-help books and would be much more focused on delivering the core ACT message and how it can be useful to that type of professional.

Trustworthy

The eighth step in the ACT TRANSLATE process concerns *trustworthiness*. One of the hallmarks of the ACT community has been the egalitarian stance taken toward training, certification and other issues related to dissemination. Rather than being a 'for profit' movement, ACT has been a 'not-for-profit' activity. Applied to dissemination efforts, this philosophy would mean we should try to 'give ACT away'. This would involve making ACT teaching tools available at little or no cost, providing support in low cost ways, and building a bond of trust between the ACT community and the service professionals we are trying to reach. Creating a version of the ACT website that contains free, downloadable teaching tools would be another positive achievement.

Evaluate

The ninth step in the ACT TRANSLATE process concerns *evaluation*. As exemplified in the clinical examples previously presented, a key aspect of dissemination is to help providers evaluate the results of their ACT interventions. These evaluation methods do not necessarily have to involve using empirically developed self-report inventories, but rather could be customized for each patient and based on the goal attainment scaling approach. Our experience is that focusing the provider on evaluation tends to also focus the intervention. When goals are unclear, asking the provider a question such as, 'If your intervention worked, how would the client behave differently, and in what situations', can help. As an empirically based treatment, ACT should ultimately be judged on the results it produces. If we model a willingness to look at what is working, then the target audiences we are trying to reach will recognize that we are just trying to help them be better at what they do. The key question is always whether the application of ACT principles adds value and insisting on evaluation of results is the only way that question can be answered.

Summary

In this chapter, we have examined many of the core issues involved in taking ACT to the streets. Thus far, we have penetrated only a small fraction of the helping community, particularly in general medicine, education and the long-term care community. ACT principles can be condensed and simplified so they can be applied in virtually any service setting. We described a specific methodology for building and disseminating simplified versions of ACT. If these steps are pursued rigorously, the chances that we can influence the helping community will be greatly improved.

References

Harris, R. (2006). *The happiness trap*. Wollombi, Australia: Exsile Publishing.

Hayes, S. (2007). *Get out of your mind, get into your life*. Oakland, CA: New Harbinger Publishing.

Hayes, S. (2006). *State of the ACT Evidence*. Retrieved April 17, 2008, from http://www.contextualpsychology.org/state_of_the_act_evidence

Hayes, S., Barnes-Holmes, D., & Roche, B. (2001), *Relational frame theory: A post Skinnerian account of human language and cognition*. New York: Plenum Kluwer.

Hayes, S., Strosahl, K., & Wilson, K. (1999). *Acceptance and commitment therapy: An experiential approach to behavior change*. New York: Guilford Press.

Narrow, W., Reiger, D., Rae, D., Manderscheid, R., & Locke, B. (1993). Use of services by persons with mental and addictive disorders: Findings from the National Institute of Mental Health Epidemiologic Catchment Area Program. *Archives of General Psychiatry, 50*, 95–107.

Robinson, P. J., & Reiter, J. T. (2007). *Behavioral consultation and primary care: A guide to integrating services*. New York: Springer.

Strosahl, K., & Robinson, P. (2008). *The mindfulness and acceptance workbook for depression: Using acceptance and commitment therapy to move through depression and reclaim your life*. Oakland, CA: New Harbinger Publishing.

chapter four

Understanding and Treating Eating Disorders: An ACT Perspective

Rhonda M. Merwin and Kelly G. Wilson

The Problem of Eating Disorders

Dissatisfaction with appearance is commonplace, so much so that it is increasingly being referred to 'normative discontent' (Mazzeo, 1999). Population-based studies indicate over half of women and girls hold negative global evaluations of their bodies (Shelly & Hyde, 2006). A great majority of these individuals are actively trying to change their body through diet and exercise. For some, however, this discontent is associated with *life-threatening* eating and exercise behavior and an *all-consuming* preoccupation with food, weight and one's body at the expense of other life values and goals. Effective interventions are unacceptably sparse, particularly for those with the most deadly variant of eating pathology, anorexia nervosa (AN; Agras et al., 2004). According to current estimates, up to 20% of these individuals will die as a result of self-starvation or suicide (Birmingham, Su, Hlynsky, Goldner, & Gao, 2005; Franko & Keel, 2006; Neumarker, 2000). Their risk of dying prematurely is significantly greater than that of the general population (Berkman, Lohr, & Bulik, 2007; Keel, Dorer, Eddy, Franko, Charatan, & Herzog, 2003), and for adolescents it is 57 times that of age-matched controls (Gillberg, Rastam, & Gillberg, 1994).

Unfortunately, the current diagnostic system is limited in its ability to make meaningful distinctions among variants and severity of eating pathology (Crow, Agras, Halmi, Mitchell, & Kraemer, 2002; Hebebrand, Casper, Treasure, & Schweiger, 2004; McIntosh, Jordan, Carter, McKenzie, Luty, Bulik et al., 2004). Although the *Diagnostic and Statistical Manual, Fourth Edition — Text Revision* (DSM-IV-TR) distinguishes two specific eating disorder presentations (anorexia and bulimia nervosa), diagnostic crossover is common (Fichter & Quadflieg, 2007) and the most prevalent eating disorder is Eating Disorder Not Otherwise Specified (ED NOS) (Machado, Machado, Gonclaves, & Hoek, 2007). An NOS diagnosis is most often due to a menstrual cycle, or bingeing–purging that occurs at a frequency less than twice a week. Despite an inability to make diagnostic threshold, lives are significantly narrowed by under- or over-control of eating (i.e., dietary restriction, bingeing), engagement in compensatory behaviors (i.e., excessive exercise, purging), and body preoccupation (i.e., checking, hiding).

Eating disorders (ED) are perplexing when considered from a biological or evolutionary perspective. Excessive dietary restriction when food is readily available, for example, defies natural physiological drives to ingest life-sustaining nutrients. When similar behavior is seen in nonhumans it often has a clear survival or evolutionary advantage (e.g., a mother that forgoes eating in order to nourish her young). Humans, however, starve themselves in the service of aesthetics, control, a sense of accomplishment and pride, and the like. They persist in this and other problematic eating and exercise behaviors in the face of the significant health consequences. These include, but are not limited to, chronic bradycardia, hypotension, hypothermia, loss of cardiac muscle, decreased bone density and frequent fractures, dehydration, reproductive problems and amenorrhea, hair loss, growth of laguno, and cortical atrophy associated with caloric restriction. Bingeing and purging confers additional risks, such as electrolyte imbalances that can produce potentially fatal cardiac arrhythmias, inflammation and possible rupture of the esophagus, tooth decay and profound gastrointestinal distress, to name a few of the most significant outcomes (Mitchell, Pomeroy, & Adson, 1997). How is it that humans can respond so ineffectively to sensations of hunger, satiety, and fatigue (in the case of excessive exercise)?

Conceptual Framework

Regulation of Eating

Initial Regulation of Eating

As an infant, eating is regulated primary by hunger and satiety and, everything being equal (i.e., no aberrant experiences or developmental issues), human infants will eat when they are hungry and stop when they are full. Of course, mealtime behavior is impacted by external as well as the internal environment, and a normally developing infant will be more likely to cry for food if an appropriate caregiver is present, and so forth. Over time, infants will learn that an array factors are reliably associated with food and eating, and these events will take on additional meaning, such as physical closeness to a caregiver, comfort or relief from distress. In some contexts, these directly learned associations will influence eating behavior. However, this perhaps pales in comparison to the range and reach of stimuli that will exert control over eating when a child becomes verbal.

The Emergence of Verbal Regulation of Eating

A child's use of language signals the ability to derive and combine relations among stimulus events of almost any form or modality (Carr, Wilkinson, Blackman, & McIlvane, 2000; DeGrandpre, Bickel, & Higgins, 1992; Lipkens, Hayes, & Hayes, 1993). This skill will exponentially increase the number of associations one has for food, eating, and the sensations of hunger and satiety; and, as a result, rapidly expand or alter the psychological functions of these events (Barnes & Keenan, 1993; Dougher, Augustson, Markham, Greenway, & Wulfert, 1994; Dymond & Barnes, 1994; Roche & Barnes, 1997). For example, one may derive a relation between sweet tastes and 'indulgence'. Indulgence, in turn, may have positive or negative psychological functions as a result of individual learning history. In the appropriate context, sweet tastes will take on the psychological functions of 'indulgence', leading to either increased or decreased consumption. Responding to sweets in this way is not the result of some direct training experience; rather it reflects relational conditioning processes or derived relational responding (Hayes, Wilson, & Barnes-Holmes, 2001 for a more extensive discussion of Relational Frame Theory; RFT).

During this same developmental period, children demonstrate an increased awareness of body (Brownell, Zerwas, & Ramani, 2007) and the body will, for the first time, enter into complex relations with other verbal and nonverbal events. Children will learn what it means to be of a particular size or shape, what is healthy and what is desirable (Kostanski & Gullone, 1999; Tiggemann & Wilson-Barrett, 1998). The psychological functions of the body will continue to expand and diversify across the lifespan as one interacts with parents (Annus, Smith, Fischer, Hendricks, & Williams, 2007; Haworth-Hoeppner, 2000), peers (Krones, Stice, Batres, & Orjada, 2005), and mass media (Kostanski, Fischer, & Gullone, 2004), and experiences body changes associated with puberty (McCabe, & Ricciardelli, 2004), and aging.

As progressively more sophisticated language abilities develop, eating and exercise behavior will become *increasingly regulated* by relational stimulus control. For example, one might choose to eat breakfast despite a lack of appetite because she/he has been told that *breakfast is the most important meal of the day*. Or, alternatively, one might limit particular food types and increase exercise in order to achieve a verbally ascribed weight goal that has been associated with fitness or a particular physique. This process is advantageous in many ways and has greatly improved the health and longevity of humans. Responding to rules regarding appropriate intake and exercise allows us to forgo a long process of trial and error. As long as individuals are able to respond directly to internal cues (e.g., hunger/satiety) and flexibly to rules, then there is a harmonious integration between these two types of stimulus control. For some, however, relational conditioning processes will be the source of significant psychological or behavioral inflexibility around food, eating, and one's body.

Disordered Regulation of Eating

Just as relational conditioning processes can result in food or eating functioning as a celebratory activity, a marker of social–cultural identity, or a medium for artistic expression, these processes can result in these same events psychologically representing the possibility of isolation, worthlessness, gluttony, failure, imperfection, unpredictability, loss of control or some other dreaded experience or feared outcome. In some contexts, the aversive properties of food/eating/body will become psychologically present and (as with all conditioned aversives) the effect will be decreased behavioral variability, with behaviors that function to eliminate or diminish contact with these difficult psychological events at extraordinarily high strength. Although the defining topography of experiential avoidance in this population is ruminative or obsessive focus on calories and food, repetitive body checking, excessive exercise, and ritualized or out-of-control eating, avoidance and control of difficult thoughts, feelings, and other private events may take many other forms (e.g., self-harm, social isolation, over-scheduling).

Verbal processes (i.e., relational conditioning) may also contribute to behavioral or psychological inflexibility around food, eating, or one's body by way of decreased sensitivity to environmentally available information. As verbal relations are elaborated, eating and exercise behavior may become increasingly regulated by *verbally* constructed rules and contingencies, rather than directly experienced events (cognitive fusion). This is problematic to the extent that verbal rules contradict experience, such as in the case of rigid adherence to dietary rules that do not correspond to hunger and satiety. Indeed, a lack of sensitivity to changing internal states and the inability to respond effectively to bodily cues or sensations is core to the eating disorder clinical presentation. Evidence from laboratory-based studies suggests that rule-based insensitivity may be potentiated in populations with high levels of rigidity and perfectionism (Wulfert, Greenway, Parkas, Hayes, & Dougher, 1994), such as the case of ED (Bardone-Cone, et al., 2007; Halmi, 2005).

This is not to say that over- or under-eating is solely maintained by the verbal properties of stimuli. One of the known effects of starvation is downregulation of autonomic arousal (Sodersten, Bergh, & Zandian, 2006), which some may directly experience as highly rewarding. In addition, consuming particular macro or micronutrients during a binge may have a physiologic analgesic effect (Steiger & Bruce, 2007; Walker, 2005) independent of other derived psychological functions. Thus, it is likely that under- or over-control of eating is maintained by a complex interplay between both nonverbal and verbal functions of stimulus events. ACT provides a way to target overregulation of behavior by verbal relations, in addition to more directly experienced maintaining factors.

Compensatory Behaviors

Thus far, the theoretical framework outlined above has focused primarily on over- or under-control of eating. However, it is easily applicable to mal-adaptive compensatory behaviors such as excessive exercise, purging or fasting in response to perceived overeating.

As a result of derived relational responding, exercising past exhaustion may come to represent self-discipline or moral aptitude (e.g., ability to override physical or worldly desires). Engaging in this behavior may thus produce increased feelings of self-worth, or be negatively reinforced as following rules of an exercise regimen allows one to avoid contact with thoughts of being a horrible, lazy person. Again, verbal stimuli likely work in conjunction with other directly experienced events, such as the decreased physiological reactivity to psychological stressors that has been reported to follow exercise (Alderman, Arent, Landers, & Rogers, 2007).

Purging may be maintained in much the same way. Self-induced vomiting following a binge may immediately reduce distress associated with (1) digressing from rules regarding appropriate intake (Urbszat, Herman, & Polivy, 2002), and (2) the verbally constructed implications of losing control over eating (or of one's behavior more generally). Such factors may operate along with directly experienced events that accompany self-induced vomiting, such as relief from the physical discomfort of overeating.

Body Image Concerns

Body image disturbance, first described by Hilde Bruch in 1962, is currently recognized as a central feature of eating disorders (Fairburn, Cooper, & Shafran, 2003; Garner & Garfinkel, 1997). Although the precise nature of the disturbance is unclear, body image remains a clinically meaningful construct that predicts outcome and risk of relapse. Historically, there has been considerable attention to the perceptual aspects of body image. Although data have been mixed, this work has been taken to indicate that individuals with ED perceive their bodies to be larger than objectively true (Smeets, 1997). Certainly this assertion made sense of the denial of the seriousness of low body weight and the all-consuming preoccupation with weight loss. More recently, a growing body of evidence has indicated that body image can be better understood as a state rather than a trait (Cash, Fleming, Alindogan, Steadman, & Whitehead, 2002) and body dissatisfaction (rather than distortion) is most consistently related to ED symptoms (Polivy & Herman, 2002).

From an ACT perspective, the primary issue of body image is not whether perception of body is objectively distorted, or even whether body-related thoughts and feelings are positive or negative. Rather, ACT is primarily concerned with the *contexts* in which body-related thoughts and feelings are accompanied by behavioral excesses (e.g., body checking, eating or exercise rituals) or behavioral deficits (e.g., avoidance of particular people, places, or activities because of one's body, concentration difficulties) that interfere with movement toward one's values. For example, in the context of emotional control, one might have difficulty engaging with friends at an outing because she/he is continuously checking the size of various parts of their body in order to temporarily reduce distress. The same context may generate behavioral rigidity that has a very different form but same function, and ultimately the same life-narrowing effects. For example, one might stay home, wear baggy clothes and avoid mirrors in order to decrease body shame, behaviors that only result in increased isolation.

Western culture is inundated with the message that the way to change your life is to change your body or appearance. There is little escape from this cognitive programming. For the ED client, the thought that changing one's body will lead to increased happiness and life satisfaction is taken literally and associated with extreme eating and exercise behaviors. When responding literally to this thought does not deliver the expected outcome, it is not uncommon for ED clients to attribute this to the idea that they have not worked hard enough, lost enough weight, or perfected their bodies. Thus, they employ a 'work harder' strategy, a strategy that has been effective in other areas of their life. However, as they work harder to change their body, they actually get *further away* from what they want their lives to be about, and a particular body size or shape becomes a prerequisite for living a full, meaningful life.

The underlying theoretical or conceptual work of ACT points to other sources of difficulty relevant to eating disorders. These processes are related to experiential avoidance and cognitive fusion, but unique and tied to other core components of the model.

Lack of Values Clarity

It may seem as if individuals with eating disorders value appearance above all else. In the early stages of therapy, they will often have difficulty articulating anything other than concerns about how they look, what others think of them and the discomfort of gaining weight. Or, by contrast, they may work hard to avoid conversations about anything other than eating or body, or appear to comply with the goals of therapy if they have a history of important people in their lives exerting control over them in the context of such conversations. Self-doubt and low self-directedness, common among ED clients (Cassin & von Ranson, 2005), may contribute to a lack of values clarity by making it more likely that they will adopt others' values (or the values exposed by mass media) without personal connection or awareness of why they deem these things important. Core values may be hidden in layers of language and If/Then relations (e.g., *If* I have a particular body size or shape, *then* I can pursue interpersonal relationships).

Values clarity may be particularly difficult to achieve in this highly risk-averse population (Fassino, Amianto, Gramaglia, Facchini, Daga, & Abbate, 2004). ED clients may fear caring about things that are less tangible than body shape and weight, or they may have difficulty articulating values because doing so may make expectations, the possibility of failure and other feared outcomes psychologically present.

From an ACT perspective, values, vulnerabilities and defensiveness are linked. If we know what someone cares about, we also know how they can be hurt. Thus, conversations about values, although nominally about positive things, carry with them the potential for loss and pain. Such conversations frequently raise the likelihood of both experiential avoidance and fusion with thoughts about potential negative outcomes. Building a therapeutic contract centered on client values requires the clinician to be sensitive to the emergence of both the desirable impact of psychological contact with valued patterns of activity and also the potential narrowing impact of closely related aversives.

TABLE 4.1
On the Nature of Eating Disorders from an ACT Perspective

Governed by Fat
Many women have thoughts about the size and shape of their bodies, and it is not uncommon for women to report feeling *fat*.
What is different for women with an eating disorder is that they *can't have fat* (as a thought, or a feeling, or anything else).
Fat means something. Something very important. Something life-dependent. It is associated with the most difficult aspects of psychological experience.
So they work to keep *fat* away. They work so hard that their lives begin to narrow. And life essentially becomes all about *fat*.

Extracted from conversation with Tyler Beach, licensed clinical social worker working in the area of eating disorder.

Weak Self-Knowledge
Conceptualized Self

Individuals with an ED often report an impoverished conceptualized self. They describe confusion regarding their likes, dislikes and interests, and report that the ED gives them an identity. Such a limited conceptualized self may be a function of a highly controlled and externally focused environment in which decisions were made by others and appearance was viewed as defining of individuals. The same pattern might also emerge in a highly chaotic environment, in which an individual is not asked about his/her experiences or preferences. Both types of home environments have been noted in ED populations (Steiner & Lock, 1998). Such environmental variables would be expected to not only contribute to a lack of expansion of the conceptualized self but also reinforce inflexible fusion with that narrow definition of self.

Knowing Self–Present Moment Processes

Individuals with ED may lack awareness of a full range of private experience, particularly early in treatment. This most typically manifests as access to only ED-specific content or awareness of only somatic correlates of emotion. For example, when anxious, an individual with AN may only be aware of sensations of stomach tightness or feelings of fatness, or the BN client may only be aware of intense urge to binge.

This narrowed attentional focus likely functions to diminish contact with other, more distressing content. This interpretation has been supported by studies that indicate bingeing allows escape from aversive self-awareness (Heatherton & Baumeister, 1991) and under- or over-eating may alleviate aversive affective experiences, such as feelings of boredom, dysphoria, or guilt (Davis & Jamieson, 2005; Macht, 2008). It is also supported by clinical observations. As therapy progresses ED clients begin to report thoughts about self-worth, feelings of loneliness and isolation, and other evocative content that reliably precedes problem behavior.

Limited awareness of experience observed in ED clients might represent a deficit in skills related to tuning into and decoding internal cues. Like an impoverished conceptualized self, limited awareness of ongoing thoughts and feelings might be shaped in an under- or over-controlled environment. In such contexts, individuals would be less likely to receive the training necessary to monitor and respond effectively to internal experiences. An inability to stay present and be fully aware of dynamic moment-to-moment fluctuations in hunger, fatigue, or affect would be expected to support maladaptive eating and exercise behavior in vulnerable individuals. The ED literature has captured deficits in awareness and clarity of internal experience with constructs such as alexythymia (Zonnevylle-Bender, van Goozen,

Cohen-Kettenis, van Elburg, & van Engeland, 2004) and poor interoceptive awareness (Fassino, Piero, Gramaglia, & Abbate-Daga, 2004).

Transcendent Self

Many individuals who struggle with an ED report oppressive self-awareness. They describe being hyperaware of their actions and bodies, and observing themselves from an external vantage point. This suggests difficulty with the transcendent self (i.e., the ability to look from one's own eyes and observe internal and external events from a stable perspective). This deficit has been observed in socially anxious clients who describe taking the perspective of an external viewer and judging how they are presenting to others (Spurr & Stopa, 2002). Individuals with ED also demonstrate difficulty experiencing a self independent of one's physical body. This lack of distinction between 'I' as a stable perspective and the physical body likely supports maladaptive eating and exercise behavior. If self is equivalent to body, then physical appearance is the only indicator of self-worth.

Functional Assessment

Functional assessment is core to an ACT intervention. The following are key considerations when completing a functional assessment with an ED population.

Parsing the Impact of Starvation on Behavior

The effects of starvation or malnourishment have to be parsed out as maintaining factors. Individuals with eating disorders are often malnourished to some degree. Some will clearly be in a starved state, others will be engaging in periods of fasting punctuated by episodes of consumption of large quantities of poor quality foods that may be subsequently purged, and still others will demonstrate some pattern in between these two extremes. Appreciation for the impact of aberrant eating behavior on cognitive, emotional and social functioning is credited to a study conducted by Ancel Keys during World War II. The aim of the study was to determine how best to go about refeeding soldiers and other starved populations. In the study, volunteers experienced a 50% reduction in food intake for 6 months, followed by 3 months of refeeding. Experimenters observed a dramatic increase in food preoccupations (conversations, reading, daydreams, collections), the emergence of odd eating behavior and food rituals (concoctions, cutting into small pieces), an increase in the importance of food/eating that came to elicit strong emotional reactions, and binge-eating followed by self-reproach. The experimenters also noted that the men became progressively more withdrawn and isolated. They demonstrated reluctance to plan activities, make decisions and participate. They experienced decreases in sexual desire, humor, camaraderie, and there was an emergence of feelings of inadequacy.

Other cognitive and emotional changes included a subjective sense of decreased concentration, alertness, comprehension and judgment; and increased irritability, anger, anxiety, apathy, psychosis and suicidal ideation.

Keys' seminal work suggests that some behaviors observed in the ED client may be maintained by malnourishment. Thus, it is essential that the effects of poor nutrition be continually assessed and incorporated into a functional assessment of target behaviors.

Changes in Maintaining Factors

Factors that maintain ED behaviors may change significantly over time. For some, ED onset may have followed an event such as weight loss due to a physical illness (Eisenbarth, Polonsky, & Buse, 2003; Mitchell & Crow, 2006) or dieting (Stice, 2001). In this case, the individual may receive initial reinforcement related to the change in their appearance and continue to work to lose weight. Over time, weight or weight loss acquires other psychological functions (Vitousek, Watson, & Wilson, 1998). For example, it becomes the source of an identity, or the one thing that provides relief from difficult thoughts or feelings.

Factors that maintain the ED may also change over time as a result of developmental stage or life transitions (Neumark-Sztainer, Wall, Eisenberg, Story, & Hannan, 2006). For example, early in adolescence, ED behaviors may function to help an individual cope with challenges associated with puberty and increased complexity of social relationships. In later adolescence or in young adulthood, the ED may help the individual cope with academic or occupational pressures. In middle to late adulthood, the ED may be maintained by factors associated with aging or divorce. The nonstatic nature of maintenance factors highlights the importance of dynamic assessment throughout treatment.

Positive and Negative Reinforcement of ED

The ACT model focuses primarily on the role of negative reinforcement in the maintenance of problem behaviors (i.e., experiential avoidance). Indeed, ED behaviors often function as avoidance or escape from chaos, uncertainty or aversive arousal states. However, it is essential that clinicians also identify positive reinforcement for ED behaviors, such as the sense of pride that is experienced when ED clients, who are often highly self-critical and feel generally ineffective (Frederick & Grow, 1996; Cervera et al., 2003), are able to overcome bodily urges and maintain low weight. Other positive reinforcers reported by ED clients include a sense of being superior or special, feelings of safety (ED is dependable, consistent, looks after them), simplification of life (ED provides structure, dictates behavior, provides certainty), and feelings of euphoria (Serpell, Treasure, Teasdale, & Sullivan, 1999).

Many clients will indicate reinforcers that are interpersonal in nature; stating that the ED provides them with a means of communication, dominance or care-taking (Serpell et al., 1999). Some of these positive reinforcers may play an important role in treatment, since they are suggestive of values in the domains of interpersonal and social relationships. Values work in ACT may provide the means to link social reinforcers to patterns of activity other than eating and body shape. In assessing these areas, it is important that the clinician gain not only information about these reinforcers, but also some in-the-present-moment, felt sense of appreciation for the meaning of the reinforcers.

Assessing the Limitations of Reinforcers

The ability of ED behaviors to positively shift internal experience may be extremely time-limited. This includes both positive reinforcers such 'feeling proud' and negative reinforcers, such as a momentary lessening of 'feeling fat.' The function of ED behaviors should be assessed in a way that captures moment-to-moment fluctuations in internal experience. The importance of such a time-sensitive assessment is highlighted by studies examining the function of binge-eating. These studies appear to call into question the emotion-regulatory function of bingeing because participants report feeling worse, rather than better, after they binge. However, closer examination suggests that bingeing does provide relief from dysphoria, but effects are temporary and individuals who binge often experience a rebound of negative affect (Wegner, Smyth, Crosby, Wittrock, Wonderlich & Mitchell, 2002). Assessment of the impact of ED behaviors, carried out by a slow, mindful, present-moment focused walk through an ED episode can provide both information and appreciation for the moment-by-moment effects of ED behaviors. This information and appreciation is an asset to both the therapist and the client.

Barriers to Accurate Reporting

There are barriers to self-disclosure and accurate records. Individuals with BN often react with shame and embarrassment regarding their lack of restraint and bingeing behavior. Individuals with AN may react to their life-threatening caloric restriction with denial of illness, or pride and a sense of accomplishment (Kaplan & Garfinkel, 1999). As a result, ED clients may avoid reporting particular behaviors when completing diaries and food logs. Such psychological barriers to self-disclosure and accurate recording will need to be addressed for successful intervention.

Variability in Topography of Avoidance

The topography of an avoidant repertoire may be quite variable. Obsessive thinking about calories, food and body, for example, may not look like avoidance in terms of topography. It may appear as if clients are contacting the psychological events that are most distressing. However, it is likely that ED-related thoughts or feelings are the *preferred* foci and that thinking about counting calories and obsessing about one's body shape likely takes attention away from other, more distressing, content (e.g., feelings of low self-worth).

It may also be that thinking about food, eating, or one's body is seen as a means to an end of emotional suffering (i.e., 'If I just figure our how to solve the problem of my appearance, then life will be good or easier, or I will feel better about myself'). In this case, the avoided event is emotional suffering and the avoidant repertoire is the ED-related thoughts and feelings. It should also be noted that ED behaviors that look very different from *one another* in terms of topography may be functionally equivalent. Bingeing and caloric restriction, for example, are both ways in which clients alter food intake in order to shift from a less preferred to a more preferred context.

Although clinicians conducting an ACT-based functional assessment may readily see ED-specific behaviors as avoidance strategies, they may miss other functionally equivalent behaviors. Table 4.2 provides an overview of ED-specific and non-ED-specific behaviors that may comprise a client's avoidant repertoire.

Unique Treatment Challenges with this Population

One of the most difficult, and most essential, aspects of the treatment of eating disorders is refeeding. By the time they present for treatment, some individuals with ED will be significantly malnourished. As described previously, it is important that this is addressed early in intervention. Some behavior problems will remit merely as a result of increasing intake and improving nutritional status, and minimally adequate nutrition is necessary for individuals to have the cognitive capacity to participate fully in therapy.

Challenges in the Refeeding Process

In addition to the significant psychological barriers to refeeding that are directly related to ED pathology, the Keys (1950) study points to physiological changes that occur during renourishment that intensify existing psychological barriers. During refeeding, participants in the Keys study ate more or less continuously, reported increases in hunger after even large meals, and gained up to 110% of their original body weight and 140% original body fat. They became concerned about sluggishness, general flabbiness and tendency for fat to accumulate in the abdomen and buttocks. Some participants continued to binge eat for months (Keys, Brozek, Henschel, Mickelsen, & Taylor, 1950).

TABLE 4.2
Behaviors Which May be Part of the Avoidant Repertoire of an ED Client

ED-specific behaviors	Non-ED-specific behaviors
Over/Under Control of Eating	*More commonly associated with AN*
Dietary restriction (calories or portion size)	Social isolation (particularly unstructured social activities)
Eating rituals	
Eliminating particular types of food	Overscheduling
Eating only at certain times of day or after exercise	Achievement striving (awards, leadership roles)
Following other idiosyncratic rules for intake	Excessive compliance
Bingeing (subjective or objective)	Rumination
Maladaptive Compensatory Strategies	Extremely measured decision-making
Purging	Perfectionistic persistence
Use of laxatives	Self-degradation or inflation
Use of diuretics	Working long hours
Self-induced vomiting	*More commonly associated with BN*
Excessive exercise	Alcohol and drug use
Fidgeting, frequent unnecessary movement	Self-harm (e.g., cutting or scratching skin)
Body Preoccupation	Sexual promiscuity
Body checking	Excessive social engagement
Mirror avoidance	Lack of sustained participation in academics, occupation, or other activities
Hiding or displaying body with clothing choice	Impulsive decision-making
Other	Sleeping more frequently or longer hours
Chewing and spitting food	Engagement in rote activities that allow one to 'zone out'
Hoarding or storing excess food or food items	
Excessive meal planning or calorie counting	
Avoidance of meal situations	

For patients who are already fearful of weight gain and loss of control over-eating, and have significant body concerns, this can make the process of refeeding even more intimidating and aversive. ACT clinicians can address some of the challenges associated with refeeding by quickly laying a foundation to develop a self independent of body, putting clients into experiential contact with the cost of continuing to restrict, and flexibly shifting between defusing difficult thoughts and feelings associated with refeeding and using values to increase willingness to have such events as an inevitable part of recovery. Such interventions can help bring eating into the realm of choice in the service of values, rather than it being driven by prevention of aversive thoughts and emotions or as the sole means of achieving a sense of worthiness.

Challenges in Motivation to Change Among ED Clients

Motivation to change ED behaviors is a significant challenge when work-ing with this population (Kaplan & Garfinkel, 1999; Treasure & Schmidt, 2001). Individuals with AN often do not come to treatment on their own accord. Rather they are typically brought into treatment by a loved one, at the insistence of an employer, following a medical destabilization and the like. This is, in part, due to the ego-syntonic nature of their symptoms (Vitousek, Watson, & Wilson, 1998). Individuals with AN typically see their exceedingly low weight as consistent with their preferred self and report little distress regarding eating and exercise rituals or significant weight loss, despite health consequences or impact on other domains of life. If they note areas of life that are less than ideal, they often have difficulty acknowledging that their eating or exercise behavior is partly responsible.

Individuals with BN may present for treatment on their own accord; however, they most often present in response to distress associated with bingeing or depressive symptoms. Rarely do individuals with BN come to treatment with concern regarding their strict dietary rules or the fact that they often fast between binges. Thus, BN clients may not be motivated to address these behaviors in treatment, even after being told that their strict dietary rules and fasting are likely contributing to bingeing (Treasure & Schmidt, 2001). They may be reluctant to let go of fasting and normalize eating because they fear they will continue to binge despite these changes and thus gain weight. Fear of potential weight gain often interferes with BN clients making necessary changes to disrupt the restrict–binge cycle.

A lack of desire to change particular ED behaviors presents significant challenges to the therapeutic alliance. This can be overcome by forming a therapeutic contract around what the patient wants most in their life and a frank exploration of how ED behaviors are interfering with the client's cho-sen values. This will be a hard discussion for most clients and it will likely necessitate repeated experiential contact with the costs of severe restriction, excessive exercise, bingeing-purging and the like. The therapeutic alliance can be strengthened by the therapist's explicit acknowledgment of the func-tion that ED has served and an honoring of the ways in which it has helped the client cope. Willingness or motivation to change ED behaviors will grow as the therapeutic work turns to exposure and defusion processes.

ACT Principles and the ED Clinician

The ED clinical presentation can be quite evocative. Emaciation captures attention. The lack of appreciation for the seriousness of weight loss and the excessive attachment to appearance that we observe in our ED clients can be disconcerting. It may be difficult to understand how an individual could eat so far past satiation, only to self-induce vomiting. Clients might appear physically and psychologically fragile. They may exhibit considerable pride in the behaviors we see killing them and make provocative statements about other people who do not demonstrate the same degree of control. They might demonstrate unnerving active passivity in which they request help but are not willing to actively make changes.

These presentations will likely precipitate psychological reactions from clinicians, and ACT emphasizes the fact that the same psychological processes that trap our clients trap us. In the context of emotional control, for example, our feelings of fear, disgust or bewilderment may narrow our behavior in the therapy room and render us clinically ineffective. We might doggedly go after a line of inquiry that is not bearing fruit. We may begin to work to *convince* our client about the lack of workability and acceptance. We might shy away from difficult content because we are afraid that this might 'cause' further restriction or elicit a binge–purge episode. The solution: seek supervision and consultation, regularly check in with oneself, be utterly aware of the fact that this is the human condition and we are not removed from it. Practice acceptance and defusion regarding difficult reactions to clients. Make time to revisit and appreciate your own values in the therapy room and recommit to them on an ongoing basis.

ED clients tend to be highly verbal and they will produce a lot of material in sessions. However, the range of topics is often impoverished and their descriptions tend to lack a richness of experience. Undirected, they may spend the session talking about what they ate, how much, or what their body feels like. Such disclosure often has a ruminative or circular quality to it, a strong past or future orientation, and is filled with reasons (i.e., why they could not eat or did not work to prevent a binge). As a therapist working with an ED client, it is easy to get pulled into this content and digress from the ACT model. The key is to remember that this narrow focus on food, eating and body is often *the avoidant repertoire* manifesting in the therapy room. Thus, the goal from an ACT perspective is to disrupt this pattern in such a way that novel behavior can emerge. Doing so will involve persistent flexible movement among domains, including both client difficulties and client values.

Working in an Interdisciplinary Team

The medical and nutritional complexity of ED pathology often necessitates an interdisciplinary treatment approach. However, there is limited information about how to most effectively use ACT in the context of an interdisciplinary team. The primary issue associated with a team approach is that other treatment providers may not be familiar with the model and may use strategies that, while consistent with mainstream CBT, may be contraindicated from an ACT perspective (e.g., teaching distraction as a way to manage eating-related distress). This can be addressed by frequent communication regarding treatment strategies and providing some degree of ACT training to familiarize key staff.

ACT in Action with ED

The early phase of ACT serves two interdependent functions: (1) drawing out the system and clearing the way for something new to emerge (sometimes referred to as creative hopelessness), and (2) conducting a functional assessment in which avoided events and avoidant repertoires are identified and examined. There is considerable variability among ED clients in both acknowledgment of the futility of their current avoidance and control strategies and the extent to which they have made experiential contact with the cost of avoidance and control. It is not uncommon for ED clients to have low motivation to change their eating or exercise behavior, even if they are aware of how the ED has narrowed their life. This is due, in part, to the significant benefits and relief they get from their ED.

ED clients also differ significantly in their awareness of the functions that their ED serves. Some clients present with an awareness of only the surface thoughts and feelings related to eating/food/body; others will be clear about what the ED allows them to escape or avoid (through distraction or some other mechanism) or what the ED promises to deliver if they work hard enough (in terms of benefits or rewards). The functions of the ED will be highly individualistic, and the more client-specific avoided events and repertoires are articulated, the more able the therapist will be to target them as a collective class.

Using the Body Scan as a Clinical Tool

Body-related thoughts are often highly accessible to ED clients and can be used as a way to draw out the system of control and avoidance. A therapist may start this work with a slow, mindful body scan, during which clients are asked to notice and provide very brief verbal responses as to where their mind *lingers* and where it *jumps* (e.g., 'What can you *NOT STOP* thinking about and what can you *NOT* think about').

Conducted in this way, this exercise not only provides important data regarding psychological barriers to behaving effectively and skill deficits in core ACT processes, but also allows for intervention (e.g., development of present moment processes, acceptance, defusion and the cultivation of self-as-context). The body scan involves practice bringing focused, yet flexible, attention to bear in the present moment as the scan moves from one body part to the next. The scan may also provide opportunities for acceptance and defusion as the therapist gently encourages the client to simply imagine breathing difficult thoughts and feelings in and out as if they were air. Finally, as the client is gently directed through an array of thoughts, emotions and bodily sensations, the 'I' that notices, the 'I' that is not those contents, can begin to emerge in awareness.

Assessment within this exercise involves the therapist's session-by-session monitoring of the client's capacity to remain flexibly engaged in the scan. Therapists can expect a shaping process where gains in this capacity will be made over time, with momentary retreats to old patterns in the face of current stressors.

The scan can also provide a means of identifying particularly difficult thoughts, feelings, and bodily sensations. Typically, clients will initially produce ED-specific content (e.g., 'my thighs') and the therapist will have to guide them through the process of unpacking the layers of language attached to directly experienced event. The therapist may ask questions such as, 'What does your mind tell you about the importance or implications of [having fat thighs]?' 'What is [fat] attached to?'

In RFT terms, the therapist is looking for derived equivalence, opposition and If/Then relations that are organizing behavior (i.e., 'If my thighs are fat that means I am undesirable — not just physically, but as a person'). An exercise such as this will result in a list of difficult thoughts and feelings that the ED functions to diminish in some way. It often goes something like this:

When [fat thighs] become psychologically present, I feel unworthy or unlovable. My stomach gets tight and my heart sinks. So I run and run ... then I feel like I am at least addressing the problem. I feel like I am working to make things better.

Unlike some traditional CBT approaches, the ACT therapist will not become engaged in assessing or disputing the validity of these thoughts. Instead, difficult material becomes the target of acceptance and defusion exercises, conducted during the body scan and at a later time. For example, an ACT therapist might ask the client 'Imagine that these thoughts were like air, could you imagine, just for a moment, breathing them in and out, slowly, gently'.

The content that is produced by clients who complete this exercise will be similar in some ways, due to shared sociocultural experience. However, it will also be idiosyncratic and reflect individual learning history. For example, for a client with a sexual abuse history, emaciation might be about avoiding intimacy by literally making their body angular and pointed so that others do not get close.

Further Use of Data Derived From the Body Scan
Once avoided events have been identified, the therapist can work to elucidate avoidance strategies. Clients can typically respond to questions

like 'In what ways have you tried to fix your body in order to fix this problem?' 'How have you tried to change your body [or your intake] in order to change how you feel?' 'What do you do to make this stuff go away?' Initially, responses will consist of ED-specific behaviors (e.g., 'I take laxatives and avoid lunch with friends'). However, this can easily expanded to other behaviors that the client engages in that are aimed at reducing contact with the difficult thoughts/feelings attached to having a particular body size, shape or function (e.g., 'I hide myself away and I work all the time').

It is important that adequate time be allotted to identifying avoided events and avoidant repertoires when working in an ACT model. The functional assessment of avoided events and repertoires provides the foundation for future therapeutic work in ACT, and assessment and intervention are tightly linked. Thus, assessing these domains should be done in a relatively slow, mindful way, interspersing moments where the therapist and client can simply pause and be present when difficult material is uncovered in assessment.

Exploring Workability in the Context of Values

Early in treatment or in refractory cases, clients will often say that their ED strategies have been effective. Further examination, however, indicates that positive effects have been temporary. Clients will report that they have to use strategies sequentially to keep difficult thoughts/feelings away for any real period of time (e.g., restrict all day, then wear baggy clothes, then cancel plans with friends and stay home) or they have to increase the intensity of their current strategies (e.g., lowering caloric intake from 800 to 400 calories in a day, increasing number of hours spent exercising) in order for them to continue to be effective. These strategies should be explicitly explored with the client. For the ACT therapist, the exploration is not merely rational examination, but preferably an experiential exploration using exercises and metaphors.

It is a natural tendency to define the effectiveness of coping strategies in terms of reduction in distress. Indeed, ED clients will often begin therapy with this notion. However, ACT therapists will redefine effective in terms of *movement toward one's values* and form a therapeutic contract focused around what the client values in their life. Therapeutic work will be focused on aligning the client's behavior with their chosen values. The first step of this process, and an important part of motivating behavior change, is to help the client contact experientially the inconsistency between what s/he wants and her/his current behavior.

This often begins with a discussion about how ED behaviors have narrowed the client's life and taken her in a direction they would not freely choose. For example, a client may report that she cares about close connected relationships, yet is spending 40 hours in the gym a week, avoiding any social outing with the possibility of food and not self-disclosing for fear of rejection. All of these behaviors are not conducive to the development of intimacy. For most ED clients, trying to change their body [or intake] in order to change how they feel is not new. They have been engaged in this process in different ways for years. Thus, it may be useful to create a time line of ED behaviors and connect with how, though the topography has changed, their lives have been about body-change efforts (rather than other things they care deeply about). This will set the stage for more extensive values work.

It is useful to bring values into treatment early in order to motivate change. For many ED clients, the eating disorder is *preferred* to the alternative, which is unpredictable, scary and out of control (in the case of AN) or perhaps mundane and empty (more common to BN). Thus, it is absolutely necessary that ED clients connect in a real way to the costs associated with continuing the ED. This is made possible through values clarification.

Values clarification can be extremely difficult with this population (for some of the reasons articulated earlier). On the surface, ED clients seem to be valuing appearance, and the therapist will have to work to identify what about appearance is important. Therapists may ask their clients 'What does thin [or the ED] promise?' The answer is often that which they most desire (e.g., 'It promises connection', 'It promises to allow me live inside my own skin without fear/pain', 'It promises to provide me with a sense of self-worth'). Sometimes what the client most wants will be phrased in an active value; something the therapist and client can build an ACT therapeutic contract around. In this case, the client has typically been treating appearance (e.g., being thin or attractive) as a prerequisite for moving toward that value (e.g., connection with other people). Thus, the work is about *not waiting* until their body is perfected or some other obscure outcome is obtained in order to engage in value-consistent action.

However, often the ED-promise question leads to a 'means' value that is about emotional control (e.g., 'I want to live without fear and pain; being attractive will allow me to do that, or at least make these things easier').

In this case, the question becomes 'What would the absence of fear or pain allow you to do in your life?' 'What would you be doing if you weren't working so hard *to make pain and fear go away?*' In this instance, the value of pain reduction is not merely about pain reduction itself, but about a means to living other values. A contract is then built around living *with* fear and pain (as feelings of a conscious human being, nothing more, nothing less) in a way that embodies their values. Some ED clients will be reluctant to clarify values because they are afraid that if they work toward a value and 'fail', they will feel worse. In this case, the therapist's ability to move flexibly between acceptance and mindfulness-based processes and commitment and behavior change processes will be of the utmost importance. As the therapist works toward clarifying values, she/he must be able to shift to exposure and defusion when the possibility of failure becomes psychologically present and narrows the client's behavior in session (as indicated by changes in the client's tone, pace, and content of speech, or body language).

ED clients seem to benefit significantly from tangible metaphors, and the creation of two-sided cards may be a useful strategy in values work. When using the two-sided card exercise, the client's value is written on one side of the card and the difficult thoughts and feelings that will inevitably show up when they move toward that value are written on the other. This exercise serves a variety of functions. Not only does it function as defusion, allowing the client to step back and observe their private experience, but it also illustrates the inseparability of vulnerabilities and values. The client taking the cards is a physical metaphor for acceptance and willingness. The therapist can also present the card showing the side with the negative thought and ask the client to physically display a posture towards the card. If the client turns away, or presents an outstretched hand to hold the card away, the therapist can explore how much energy that resistance requires. The therapist and client can notice the effect of turning away with respect to the value on the reverse side of that same card. Clients can also be encouraged to try on a different posture, such as gently cradling the card as if it were a treasured object. All of these activities are relatively low threat. Rather than ask directly whether a client can be willing to have a difficult thought, instead the client gets an opportunity to practice acceptance and willingness with these cards that stand in for the thoughts.

Continuing Exposure and Defusion Work

Opportunities to disrupt the system of avoidance and control and work toward the emergence of novel (acceptance-based, values-oriented) behavior are often presented immediately when the client enters a session. Clients will often begin a session by describing experience in almost exclusively ED terms, particularly early in treatment. They will focus on thoughts and feelings about food, eating and the body at the expense of other important aspects of experience. This talk will often have a ruminative quality and lack psychological richness. From an ACT perspective, this limited focus allows the client to avoid or escape other difficult aspects of experience. Thus, the goal is to disrupt this avoidant repertoire so that other relevant thoughts and feelings can emerge. Indeed, when one stops (metaphorically) running, it becomes possible to see aspects of experience that were not seen before. Common themes that emerge as clients slow down and observe their experience are fear of rejection, dominance, imperfection, failure, or vulnerability and intimacy.

Some metaphors may be particularly useful for helping clients make contact with the way in which ED and body concerns mask more central or core difficult thoughts and feelings. For example, the ACT therapist may ask a client to imagine that they are opening a special item or gift that has been wrapped in layers and layers of paper. Each ED thought or feeling can be mentally written on the individual sheets of paper. As layers are shed, the more central issue — the thing that was hiding beneath all the layers of ED talk — is free to emerge. The therapist may then choose to work directly with the content, asking the client to notice or be curious about the item that has been revealed, or to describe how it feels to let it be exposed to the open air. Exposure and defusion should continue to be the focus until the therapist witnesses the client's behavior becoming more broad and flexible in the presence of the difficult psychological content.

Some of the most powerful exposure and defusion sessions with an ED client are about being fully present with another person without hiding physically (under pillows, jackets and book bags) or psychologically (behind defensive walls devoid of affect). This can be extremely hard work and there may be a tendency to underestimate how evocative it can be for this population to sit in an open posture, make eye contact and disclose even benign content. Adequate time should be allotted for such work and therapists should be sensitive and guided by subtle shifts in body language, tone of voice and quality of speech.

Although exposure and defusion work with ED clients may be quite varied, exercises that require clients to experience food or their bodies in new ways may be particularly useful for this population. Such exercises will expand and diversify the psychological functions of food, eating and one's body, and promote broad, flexible action. Clients may be asked to eat mindfully, to take up physical space in the room in a different way (e.g., make body as big or as small as possible), or to write a letter to their body as if it were a friend they are making amends with, an enemy they are waging war against, a teacher, a child or a hidden treasure.

A therapist may also conduct exposures using a food or body hierarchy. This would emulate traditional Exposure and Response Prevention (ERP), but with an additional emphasis on the mindful quality of the ERP and on acceptance, defusion and values. For example, a client may be asked to bring in a feared food from a hierarchy that she then eats with the therapist. During the exercise, the client would be coached on staying fully present with difficult thoughts and feelings as they show up (acceptance-based exposure), without fusing with them or pushing them away (response prevention), and in service of what they care about (values). Therapists might help clients contact the fact that this is their programming (or 'mind') and there is an 'I' independent of their thoughts, feelings and bodily sensations. Clients may be asked to notice the urge to engage in ED behaviors and practice choosing value-consistent behavior in the presence of these difficult private events.

Working with Choice and Committed Action

One of the unique challenges of working with an ED population is that ED behaviors may be viewed passively (e.g., 'I just didn't eat') or mechanistically ('I had to binge'). Rather than seeing behaviors such as restriction as an *active choice* that is either consistent or inconsistent with chosen values, clients will report automaticity to their actions. Thus, commitment and behavior change processes in ACT often necessitate increasing the extent to which behaviors are viewed as choices to be made (i.e., choices that may be more or less compelling depending on current and historical context), of (1) moment-to-moment fluctuations in urges to engage in ED behavior, and (2) thoughts that they are fused with, or feelings that are being avoided by attending to eating, food, or body. Once the skill is in place, therapists have to deal with the challenge of psychological barriers that interfere with clients' willingness to stay fully present to these difficult aspects of their private experience and make a choice about whether to engage in ED behavior.

ACT in Action with ED: Specific Strategies

Below is a clinical excerpt from a therapy session of a client with an eating disorder. She has been working towards more regular food intake. There are a number of potential ACT-consistent responses to the client's statements. Table 4.3 provides a sample of ACT-consistent responses that exemplify the various components of the ACT model.

> Therapist: Based on your food log, it looks like you did not follow your meal plan on Thursday ...
>
> Patient: Yeah ... well, I was drinking my Boost and my stomach started to hurt, so I skipped breakfast and lunch. I don't think that I should be expected to drink Boost and eat breakfast. It's too much. It just felt so out of control ... my stomach felt bloated and fat. It was overwhelming ... to have to drink the Boost. I wasn't even hungry ... and I ate pasta the day before.
>
> Therapist: I hear you. I hear the distress in your voice... out of control, overwhelmed ...

ACT Directions in the Context of a Meal Intervention

The clinical dialogue below is from a 28-year-old female with a history of ED symptoms dating back to her early teens. She was previously diagnosed with ED NOS due to occasional bingeing–purging that did not meet the threshold for BN. She has been restricting and exercising excessively for the past 6 months and is now severely underweight (BMI = 15.5). She has stopped menstruating and, at her last medical appointment, she was bradycardic and orthostatic. She has come to a residential treatment center at the insistence of her husband. She just sat down for dinner.

> Client: I can't do it. I thought I could, but I can't. This is too much ... and I don't need it. I'm not even hungry. I'm fat and gross. They didn't let us

TABLE 4.3
ACT-Consistent Responses to an ED Clinical Excerpt

Potential ACT Directions	
Acceptance	'You've said how hard it is to experience "out of control" ... how you have the urge to push it away. Yet "out of control" keeps coming back. I wonder if you'd be willing to do something different with "out of control" right now. Would you be willing to invite it in ... as an honored guest ...'
Values	'What if *having* "out of control" is necessary for you to move forward in your life? ... When you go to dinner with Susan, you might experience "out of control" ... and you might have an intense desire to leave the restaurant to make that feeling go away (and if you left, it would, at least temporarily). And yet sitting there with Susan and *with* "out of control" may be the very thing that allows your friendship to grow and for you to be closely and intimately connected to her ...'
Defusion	'You're mind was really having a time with this one. Giving you lots of warnings and reasons ... like it always does. This is familiar, isn't it? Old, really. So glad we can count on your mind to do its job, huh? (smile).'
Defusion	'And then came the feeling of "*overwhelmed*". How did it come ... like a blanket? A boulder? ... what was its entrance like? How big was it? Can you see it in your mind's eye now? Does it have a color, a texture ... ?'
Self-as-context	'Let's go back to that place for a moment (eyes closed, slow speech) ... So there you were, sitting at breakfast, and the first thing you notice is sensations in your stomach, and then you have the thought "I shouldn't have to eat this" ... What happens next? [walk through event in detail, labeling thoughts as thoughts, feelings and feelings, bodily sensations as bodily sensations]. And now I am going to ask you to notice who is noticing all of those things, who observed those thoughts, feelings, and bodily sensations coming and going THEN and THERE and who is noticing them HERE and NOW. Now I'm going to ask you to notice that while you HAVE these thoughts and feelings, you are not them ... they come and go and you stay ...'
Present moment	'Something just seemed to shift in the way that you were holding your body. As you talk about this event now, what do you notice? [If it is early in therapy and the client is unable to produce a response independently, the therapist may need to probe with questions such as "Tightness in your chest?" "Heaviness in your stomach?"].'
Commitment/ behavior change	'This is hard work. It's impossible ... and yet I have seen you do amazing things. I have seen you hold "out of control", "overwhelmed", and that difficult stomach tightness close to you ... and chose to eat breakfast, not purge ... I've seen you do the thing that is most difficult for you in that moment. So I guess I am asking ... What will you choose when noon comes and it is time to eat lunch? Will you choose it in the service of [insert value here]?'

exercise yesterday... . I don't think that I will ever be comfortable inside my own body ... I hate this, I hate myself ...

Therapist: This is hard. It sounds like your mind is racing. What else do you notice?

Client: A knot in my stomach. I think it is because I am too full.

Therapist: We anticipated this, didn't we? We knew that this is what your mind would do ... This is what it always does ... and that feeling in your stomach, you know that too, don't you? How old would you say it is?

Client: About 10 years.

Therapist: If that knot could give you advice right now, what would it say?

Client: It would say "Don't eat, whatever you do, don't eat".

Therapist: Yeah ... it's been telling you for a long time ... I wonder if we can take 'fat and gross', that 'knot in your stomach', and 'I hate myself' and place them, carefully and gently, in the chair next to us. Let them have dinner with us. They were coming anyway ... [therapist makes gesture that simulates taking objects from the client and placing them in the chair at the table]

Therapist and Client sit quietly for a moment.

Therapist: You know ... this is what is going to show up when you move in the direction of the life you want ... it couldn't be otherwise ... It is the same thing that happens when you open up to your husband ... feelings of fear and thoughts that you are not good enough — that he will leave — show up ... and threaten to shut you up. And you have to decide ... are you willing to have those thoughts and feelings ... and keep talking and stay present with him in the service of a close, intimate connection with him ...

Client: I keep having the thought that this will be terrible, that I can't stand it, ... that I will become a blimp ... that I will be unlovable and alone.

Therapist: [Pause] Your mind is telling you this is a dangerous situation ... a life-threatening situation in some ways. What does your experience tell you?

Client: That not eating is what has been taking my life ...

Therapist: Good thing your mind doesn't get to decide then ... you do. [Therapist notices client looking down, shoulders dropped, not eating]. Are you buying those warnings of danger right now?

Client: Yes and no. I am able to step back, and then I get pulled back in.

Therapist: That's the dance. This is hard work ... and it may be the very thing that puts you back into your life in a real way. Is there a part of you that can connect to what you'd be willing to do this hard thing for?

Client: Yes ... [pauses]

Therapist: What if it's the case that doing this hard thing will take you one step closer to being with your husband (and in your life) in a real way? ... Would you be willing? Would you be willing to invite the feeling of fear to dinner and eat? ... knowing in a sensed way that although you are experiencing fear, you are separate, distinct and it is you who gets to choose.

TABLE 4.4

Key Clinical Issues for ED Clients and Suggestions for ACT-Consistent Intervention

Key Clinical Issues	Suggested ACT-consistent Approach
Attachment to self-degradation. (ED clients often say that berating themselves helps them stay disciplined and avoid laziness or gluttony, which they fear. Thus, they are sometimes reluctant to let go of self-degradation.)	• Frame as avoidance strategy • Conduct exposure/defusion around client's fear of 'letting go' of negative self-talk • Put 'letting go' in frame of coordination with what they want in their life • Put in contact with the cost of continuing to live as if she is 'not good enough' • *Note: Strategies are not aimed at eliminating negative self-talk, but rather reducing attachment to it
Ego-syntonic symptoms	• Expand identity to decrease attachment to symptoms or 'story' of who they are • Increase experiential contact with the way in which the symptoms have narrowed other areas of life the client cares about • Decrease the utility of the symptoms by helping the client get needs met in another way
Apparent valuing of appearance	• Identify the value that is verbally tied to looking a certain way. May use questions such as 'What does thin [or the ED] promise?'
Perfectionism, exceedingly high standards, feelings of ineffectiveness, low self-esteem, and other features that have been found to characterize ED populations	• Assess the function of these behavioral tendencies • Conduct broad in-session exposure and defusion, around fear of failure, for example.
Client only produces ED-related content in session OR Attends only to one aspect of experience (e.g., somatic correlates of emotion)	• If impoverished content is related to avoidance: Disrupt repertoire with nonconventional questions or responses, therapeutic exercises and an appeal to experiential ways of knowing • If impoverished content appears to be a skill deficit: Train knowing-self or an awareness of full range of experience. May use an ACT-consistent diary card
Body image disturbance	• Disrupt contexts in which body-related thoughts and feelings are associated with ED behaviors (e.g., decrease literality by teaching observation of body-related thoughts) • Increase or diversify associations with the body by having the client experience the body in new ways via experiential (e.g., assume a different posture; 'get big or get small' by taking up as much or as little space in the room as you can) or verbal exercises (e.g., writing a letter to your body as a friend or an enemy)

continued over

TABLE 4.4 (continued)
Key Clinical Issues for ED Clients and Suggestions for ACT-Consistent Intervention

Key Clinical Issues	Suggested ACT-consistent Approach
Inability to identify values (either due to psychological barriers or skill deficits	• If inability is due to psychological barriers (e.g., fear of caring about something): Identify barriers and conduct exposure and defusion • If inability is a skill deficit: Expand client's experience of making choices and determining preferences
Weight gain (or eating in a less restricted way) is not endorsed as goal	• Put weight restoration, health, or letting go of restriction in a frame of coordination with valued events • Conduct exposure and defusion around concerns regarding weight gain or letting go of excessive control over eating
Lack of identity beyond body shape or size	• Diversify conceptualized self • By asking questions about preferences • By setting up systematic self-exploration • By setting up conditions for the client to experiences self in a new way
Excessive attachment to body	• Develop transcendent sense of self (an 'I' independent of body) • Identify what having a particular body promises and examine whether working toward that ideal has been an effective strategy • Grow other valued areas
External vantage point	• Train seeing from one's own eyes For example, a therapist might ask a client to use a mirror to look into her own eyes and practice directing attention from the external image to the internal experience of self
Body shame or phobia	• Conduct exposure and response prevention with body (e.g., mirror exposure to thighs with prevention of body hiding or checking; Exposure to the heaviness of weight or girth by having the client wear a weighted vest or baggy clothes stuffed with balloons; Exposure to the physical sensations of fullness) • Conduct exercises that require clients to experience their body in different ways (changing typical body language or posture, moving body in a way that is novel, yoga or dance, experience body using senses other than sight) • Exposure/defusion of 'shame'
Excessive dietary restraint	• Tie healthy eating behaviors to other valued events • Defuse barriers as the client works towards (1) marking meal times with intake of any kind, (2) increasing the amount of intake at meal times, and (3) improving variety (e.g., including incorporating feared or eliminated foods)

Conclusion

We have provided a conceptual overview of ED from an ACT perspective, along with recommendations for treatment. However, as yet there are not well-controlled data on the application of ACT to ED, meaning clinicians should carefully examine current gold standard treatments and apprise clients of potential well-researched treatment alternatives. To do so is part of any ethical informed consent process. ACT is offered as a basic science-based approach that is a viable alternative for treatment refractory cases, for clients who are not open to approaches offered in gold standard treatments, and finally for research and exploratory purposes. We are not aware of anyone in the ED area who feels satisfied with the current efficacy of treatment. This is especially so for AN clients for whom treatment efficacy is quite low and mortality is quite high.

ACT is one among an array of third-wave treatments that are currently under examination in the treatment of ED. Other treatments with a strong focus on acceptance, mindfulness and values are being studied, protocols are being developed, and we will be seeing clinical trials published in coming years. In addition, there is considerable work ongoing in the area of experimental psychopathology and survey research examining components and processes relevant to these third-wave treatments and their relationship to disordered eating. Given the breadth and depth of this ongoing research program, we anticipate a significant expansion of knowledge in this area over the next decade. It is our hope that this chapter participates in the development of that emerging knowledge base.

References

Agras, W. S., Brandt, H. A., Bulik, C. M., Dolan-Sewell, R., Fairburn, C. G., Halmi, K. A. et al. (2004). Report of the National Institutes of Health Workshop on Overcoming Barriers to Treatment Research in Anorexia Nervosa. *International Journal of Eating Disorders, 35*(4), 509–521.

Alderman, B. L., Arent, S. M., Landers, D. M., & Rogers, T. J. (2007). Aerobic exercise intensity and time of stressor administration influence cardiovascular responses to psychological stress. *Psychophysiology, 44*, 759–766.

Annus, A. M., Smith, G. T., Fischer, S., Hendricks, M., & Williams, S. F. (2007). Associations among family-of-origin food-related experiences, expectancies, and disordered eating. *International Journal of Eating Disorders, 40*(2), 179–186.

Bardone-Cone, A. M. Wonderlich, S. A., Frost, R. O., Bulik, C. M., Mitchell, J. E., Uppala, S., & Simonich, H. (2007). Perfectionism and eating disorders: Current status and future directions. *Clinical Psychology Review, 27*(3), 384–405.

Barnes, D., & Keenan, M. (1993). A transfer of functions through derived arbitrary and non-arbitrary stimulus relations. *Journal of the Experimental Analysis of Behavior, 59*, 61–81.

Berkman, N. D., Lohr, K. N., & Bulik, C. M. (2007). Outcomes of eating disorders: A systematic review of the literature. *International Journal of Eating Disorders, 40,* 293–309.

Birmingham, C. L., Su, J., Hlynsky, J. A., Goldner, E. M., & Gao, M. (2005). The mortality rate of anorexia nervosa. *International Journal of Eating Disorders, 38,* 143–146.

Brownell, C. A., Zerwas, S., & Ramani, G. B. (2007). 'So big': The development of body awareness in toddlers. *Child Development, 78*(5), 1426–1440.

Carr, D., Wilkinson, K. M., Blackman, D., & McIlvane, W. J. (2000). Equivalence classes in individuals with minimal verbal repertoires. *Journal of the Experimental Analysis of Behavior, 74,* 101–115.

Cash, T. F., Fleming, E. C., Alindogan, J., Steadman, L., & Whitehead, A. (2002). Beyond body image as a trait: The development and validation of the Body Image States Scale. *Eating Disorders, 10,* 103–113.

Cassin, S. E., & von Ranson, K. M. (2005). Personality and eating disorders: A decade in review. *Clinical Psychology Review, 25,* 895–916.

Cervera, S., Lahortiga, F., Martinez-Gonzalez, M. A., Gual, P. Irala-Estevez, J., & Alonso, Y. (2003). Neuroticism and low self-esteem as risk factors for incident eating disorders in a prospective cohort study. *International Journal of Eating Disorders, 33*(3), 271–280.

Crow, S. J., Agras, W. S., Halmi, K., Mitchell, J. E., & Kraemer, H. C. (2002). Full syndromal versus subthreshold anorexia nervosa, bulimia nervosa, and binge eating disorder: A multicenter study. *International Journal of Eating Disorders, 32*(3), 309–318.

Davis, R., & Jamieson, J. (2005). Assessing the functional nature of binge eating in eating disorders. *Eating Behaviors, 6*(4), 345–354.

DeGrandpre, R. J., Bickel, W. K., & Higgins, S. T. (1992). Emergent equivalence relations between interoceptive (drug) and exteroceptive (visual) stimuli. *Journal of the Experimental Analysis of Behavior, 58,* 9–18.

Dougher, M. J., Augustson, E., Markham, M. R., Greenway, D. E., & Wulfert, E. (1994). The transfer of respondent eliciting and extinction functions through stimulus equivalence classes. *Journal of the Experimental Analysis of Behavior, 62,* 331–351.

Dymond, S. & Barnes, D. (1994). A transfer of self-discrimination response through equivalence relations. *Journal of the Experimental Analysis of Behavior, 62,* 251–267.

Eisenbarth, G. S., Polonsky, K. S., & Buse, J. B. (2003). Type I diabetes mellitus. In P. R. Larsen, H. M. Kronenberg, S. Melmed & K. S. Polonsky (Eds.), *Williams Textbook of Endocrinology* (10th ed.). Philadelphia: Elsevier Science.

Fairburn, C. G., Cooper, Z., & Shafran, R. (2003). Cognitive behavioural therapy for eating disorders: A 'transdiagnostic' theory and treatment. *Behaviour Research and Therapy, 41,* 509–528.

Fassino, S., Amianto, F., Gramaglia, C., Facchini, F., & Daga, G. (2004). Temperament and character in eating disorders: Ten years of studies. *Eating and Weight Disorders, 9*(2), 81–90.

Fassino, S., Piero, A., Gramaglia, C., & Abbate-Daga, G. (2004). Clinical, psychopathological and personality correlates of interoceptive awareness in anorexia nervosa, bulimia nervosa and obesity. *Psychopathology, 37*(4), 168–174.

Frederick, C. M., & Grow, V. M. (1996). A mediational model of autonomy, self-esteem, and eating disordered attitudes and behaviors. *Psychology of Women Quarterly, 20*(2), 217–228.

Fichter, M. M., & Quadflieg, N. (2007). Long-term stability of eating disorder diagnoses. *International Journal of Eating Disorders, 40*, 561–566.

Franko, D. L., & Keel, P. K. (2006). Suicidality in eating disorders: correlates, and clinical implications. *Clinical Psychology Review, 26*, 769–782.

Garner, D. M., & Garfinkel, P.E. (Ed.). (1997). *Handbook of treatment for eating disorders* (2nd ed.). New York: Guildford Press.

Gillberg, I. C., Rastam, M., & Gillberg, C. (1994). Anorexia nervosa outcome: A six-year controlled longitudinal study of 51 cases including a population cohort. *Journal of the American Academy of Child and Adolescent Psychiatry, 33*(5), 729–739.

Halmi, K.A. (2005). Obsessive–compulsive personality disorder and eating disorders. Eating Disorders: *The Journal of Treatment & Prevention, 13*(1), 85–92.

Haworth-Hoeppner, S. (2000). The critical shapes of body image: The role of culture and family in the production of eating disorders. *Journal of Marriage and Family, 62*(1), 212–227.

Hayes, S. C., Wilson, K. G., & Barnes-Holmes, D. (2001). Derived relational responding as learned behavior. In S. C. Hayes, D. Barnes-Holmes, & B. Roche (Eds.). *Relational frame theory: A post Skinnerian account of human language and cognition.* New York: Kluwer Academic/Plenum Publishers.

Heatherton, T. F., & Baumeister, R. F. (1991). Binge eating as escape from self-awareness. *Psychological Bulletin, 110*(1), 86–108.

Hebebrand, J., Casper, R., Treasure, J., & Schweiger, U. (2004). The need to revise the diagnostic criteria for anorexia nervosa. *Journal of Neural Transmission, 111*(7), 827–840.

Kaplan, A. S., & Garfinkel, P. E. (1999). Difficulties in treating patients with eating disorders: Aa review of patient and clinician variables. *The Canadian Journal of Psychiatry, 44*(7), 665–670.

Keel, P. K., Dorer, D. J., Eddy, K. T., Franko, D., Charatan, D. L., & Herzog, D. B. (2003). Predictors of mortality in eating disorders. *Archives of General Psychiatry, 60*, 179–183.

Keys, A., Brozek, J., Henschel, A., Mickelsen, O., & Taylor, H. L. (1950). *The biology of human starvation.* Minneapolis, MN: University of Minnesota Press.

Kostanski, M., Fischer, A., & Gullone, E. (2004). Current conceptualization of body image dissatisfaction: Have we got it wrong? *Journal of Child Psychology and Psychiatry, and Allied Disciplines, 45*, 1317–1325.

Kostanski, M., & Gullone, E. (1999). Dieting and body image in the child's world: Conceptualization and behavior. *Journal of Genetic Psychology, 160*, 488–499.

Krones, P. G., Stice, E., Batres, C., & Orjada, K. (2005). In vivo social comparison to a thin-ideal peer promotes body dissatisfaction: A randomized experiment. *International Journal of Eating Disorders, 38*(38), 134–142.

Lipkens, R., Hayes, S. C., & Hayes, L. J. (1993). Longitudinal study of derived stimulus relations in an infant. *Journal of the Experimental Child Psychology, 56*, 201–239.

Machado, P. P. P., Machado, B. C., Gonclaves, S., & Hoek, H. W. (2007). The prevalence of eating disorders not otherwise specified. *International Journal of Eating Disorders, 40*, 212–217.

Macht, M. (2008). How emotions affect eating: A five-way model. *Appetite, 50,* 1–11.

Mazzeo, S. E. (1999). Modification of an existing measure of body image preoccupation and its relationship to disordered eating in female college students. *Journal of Counseling Psychology, 46,* 42–50.

McCabe, M. P., & Ricciardelli, L.A. (2004). A longitudinal study of pubertal timing and extreme body change behaviors among adolescent boys and girls. *Adolescence, 39*(153), 145–166.

McIntosh, V. W., Jordan, J., Carter, F. A., McKenzie, J. M., Luty, S. E., Bulik, C. M., et al. (2004). Strict versus lenient weight criterion in anorexia nervosa. *European Eating Disorders Review, 12*(1), 51–60.

Mitchell, J. E., & Crow, S. (2006). Medical complications of anorexia nervosa and bulimia nervosa. *Current Opinion in Psychiatry, 19*(4), 438–443.

Mitchell, J. E., Pomeroy, C., & Adson, D. E. (1997). Managing medical complications. In D. M. Garner & P. E. Garfinkel (Eds.). *Handbook for the treatment of eating disorders* (2nd ed.) (pp. 383–391).The Guilford Press: New York.

Neumarker, K. J. (2000). Mortality rates and causes of death. *European Eating Disorders Review, 8*(2) 181–187.

Neumark-Sztainer, D., Wall, M., Eisenberg, M. E., Story, M., & Hannan, P. J. (2006). Overweight status and weight control behaviors in adolescents: Longitudinal and secular trends from 1999 to 2004. *Preventive Medicine, 43*(1), 52–59.

Polivy, J., & Herman, C. P. (2002). Causes of eating disorders. *Annual Review of Psychology, 53,* 187–213.

Roche, B., & Barnes, D. (1997). A transformation of respondently conditioned stimulus functions in accordance with arbitrarily applicable stimulus relations. *Journal of the Experimental Analysis of Behavior, 67,* 275–302.

Serpell, L., Treasure, J., Teasdale, J., & Sullivan, V. (1999). Anorexia nervosa: Friend or foe? *International Journal of Eating Disorders, 25,* 177–186.

Shelly, G., & Hyde, J. S. (2006). Ethnicity and body dissatisfaction among women in the United States: A meta-analysis. *Psychological Bulletin, 132*(4), 622–640.

Skrzypek, S., Wehmeier, P.M., & Remschmidt, H. (2001). Body image assessment using body size estimation in recent studies on anorexia nervosa. A brief review. *European Child and Adolescent Psychiatry, 10,* 215–221.

Sim, L. & Zeman, J. (2004). Emotion awareness and identification skills in adolescent girls with bulimia nervosa. *Journal of Clinical Child and Adolescent Psychology, 33*(4), 760–771.

Smeets, M. A. M. (1997). The rise and fall of body size estimation research in anorexia nervosa: A review and reconceptualization. *European Eating Disorders Review, 5,* 75–95.

Sodersten, P., Bergh, C., & Zandian, M. (2006). Understanding eating disorders. *Hormones and Behavior, 50,* 572–578.

Spurr, J. M., & Stopa, L. (2002). Self-focused attention in social phobia and social anxiety. *Clinical Psychology Review, 22,* 947–975.

Steiger, H., & Bruce, K. R. (2007). Phenotypes, endophenotypes, and genotypes in bulimia spectrum eating disorders. *The Canadian Journal of Psychiatry, 52*(4), 220–227.

Steiner, H., & Lock, J. (1998). Anorexia and bulimia nervosa in children and adolescents: A review of the past 10 years. *Journal of American Academic Child Adolescent Psychiatry, 37*(4), 352–359.

Stice, E. (2001). A prospective test of the dual-pathway model of bulimic pathology: Mediating effects of dieting and negative affect. *Journal of Abnormal Psychology, 110*(1), 124–135.

Tiggemann, M., & Wilson-Barrett, E. (1998). Children's figure ratings: Relationship to self-esteem and negative stereotyping. *International Journal of Eating Disorders, 23*, 83–88.

Treasure, J., & Schmidt, U. (2001). Ready, willing and able to change: Motivational aspects of the assessment and treatment of eating disorders. *European Eating Disorders Review, 9*, 4–18.

Urbszat, D., Herman, C. P., & Polivy, J. (2002). Eat, drink, and be merry, for tomorrow we diet: Effects of anticipated deprivation on food intake in restrained and unrestrained eaters. *Journal of Abnormal Psychology, 111*(2), 396–401.

Vitousek, K., Watson, S., Wilson, T. G. (1998). Enhancing motivation for change in treatment-resistant eating disorders. *Clinical Psychology Review, 18(*4), 391–420.

Walker, C. D. (2005). Nutritional aspects modulating brain development and responses to stress in early neonatal life. *Progress in Neuro-Psychopharmacology & Biological Psychiatry, 29*, 1249–1263.

Walsh, J. M., Wheat, M. E., & Freund, K. (2000). Detection, evaluation, and treatment of eating disorders the role of the primary care physician. *Journal of General Internal Medicine, 15*(8), 577–590.

Wegner, K. E., Smyth, J. M., Crosby, R. D., Wittrock, D. Wonderlich, S. A., & Mitchell, J. E. (2002). An evaluation of the relationship between mood and binge eating in the natural environment using ecological momentary assessment, *International Journal of Eating Disorders 32*(3), 352–361.

Wulfert, E., Greenway, D. E., Parkas, P., Hayes, S. C., & Dougher, M. J. (1994). Correlation between self-reported rigidity and rule-governed insensitivity to operant contingencies. *Journal of Applied Behavior Analysis, 27*, 659–671.

Zonnevylle-Bender, M. J. S., van Goozen, S. H. M., Cohen-Kettenis, P. T., van Elburg, A., & van Engeland, H. (2004). Emotional functioning in adolescent anorexia nervosa patients: A controlled study. *European Child and Adolescent Psychiatry, 13*(1), 28–34.

chapter five

ACT and Health Conditions

Joanne Dahl

ACT has been found empirically effective in addressing the psychological concerns involved with a variety of health problems, including chronic pain, diabetes, epilepsy and obesity. This chapter will discuss issues and concerns that arise when adapting ACT to health issues, and provide a variety of suggestions and strategies for effectively addressing these issues. In the first part of this chapter, we will look at the differences in the philosophical underpinnings of the medical model versus an ACT model of human suffering. The contribution of the behavior medicine model will be discussed as the first application of behavior analysis of somatic disorders. The final part of the chapter will show how the ACT model can be used to conceptualize and treat two examples of physical disorders: chronic pain and epilepsy.

Models of Human Suffering

Mechanical/Medical Model

A common source of frustration in western cultures may result from the way we attempt to conceptualize physical illness. Our health care system attempts to determine if the patient's symptoms are either somatic (real) or psychogenic (not real). Our health care systems are built on this way of thinking, which stems from the mechanistic scientific tradition. Using the mechanistic tradition, the body is regarded as a collection of biological parts, relations and forces, much the same as any machine. Pathology is conceptualized as defective parts, relations or forces that 'cause' particular signs and symptoms that the physician or the patient is able to detect. Usually the patient detects these 'signs' or symptoms and seeks help to find out the 'cause'. The physician's task is to investigate these symptoms and then scan for the error or underlying pathology in much the same way as a car mechanic would scan for problems in one's car. The strategy is to alleviate the symptom by curing the underlying cause or pathology. Traditional western medicine for chronic illness stems from this tradition (Ogden, 1997).

In many cases, this mechanical conceptualization works fine. However, this simple conceptualization tends to fail with regard to complex and chronic problems. For problems that have multiple forms of physical pathology producing common signs and symptoms, or when behavioral history and context interact with physical pathology to produce signs and symptoms, the mechanistic model is inadequate. When these interactive and multiple determined conditions dominate, there simply is no one-to-one correlation between physical pathology (e.g., damaged tissue) and observed signs and symptoms. As a result, signs and symptoms are no longer a powerful guide to understanding the etiology, function or course of the problem. In most cases for medical problems, there are assumptions already embedded in the diagnostic system. Unfortunately, the assumption that there is a correlation between an underlying simple pathology and symptoms is often not helpful in the conceptualization or the treatment of the disorder. An alternative to the mechanical model based on functional conceptualism was the behavior medicine model where symptoms were conceptualized and treated in context.

Behavior Medicine: Pioneer Applications of Behavior Analysis for Chronic Illness
Behavior medicine, in which arose in the 1970s, was an application of behavior analysis to the treatment of problematic long-term symptoms in (for example) the genitourinary, gastrointestinal, cardiovascular, musculoskeletal, nervous and respiratory systems. Treatments for traditional medical illnesses such as high blood pressure, torticollis, obesity, headache, pain, epilepsy and asthma were developed and evaluated. At the time, these treatment methods were applied as a complement to the traditional medical/pathological model. Behavior therapy interventions were, not surprisingly, executed at the behavioral level, but the purpose of such interventions was still in line with the aims and focus of the medical model: that is control and management of the presenting symptoms.

The first wave of traditional behavior therapy and the second wave cognitive–behavioral therapy (CBT) that followed both adopted the position that psychological suffering is anomalous and that psychological health is inversely related to the number and intensity of psychological complaints. Instead of the intrusion of some biological malfunction, infectious agent or toxic insult, behavior therapists used pathogenic learning histories that generate negative thoughts, emotions, memories, bodily states and behavioral predispositions. These are the behavior equivalents of tumors, viruses and bacteria that must be alleviated in order for good psychological health to return.

This was clearly a step forward from the physical pathological model alone, as demonstrated by the additional treatment options these second-wave therapies offered. While there are certainly physiological factors that predispose human beings to develop symptoms such as pain and epilepsy, our best behavioral and cognitive–behavioral treatments focus on providing the individual with a new learning history that will reduce symptoms. Central in this new learning history is systematic exposure to feared events such as fear of movement or an activity associated with pain or with the epileptic seizure. These applications of behavior medicine are based both on behavioral principles (classical and operant conditioning) and, in more recent times, on cognitive concepts. In the more traditional behavioral approaches, the goal has been to reinforce productive behavior and to stop the negative reinforcement of avoidance behavior, while at the same time reducing the spread and function of stimuli that elicit pain or the seizure through classical conditioning. Exposure-based treatments, for example, used shaping principles to help patients expose themselves to previously avoided situations and movements that were believed to 'cause' the symptom.

While, behavior medicine surely contributed to a contextual understanding of physical symptoms, it still followed the pathology model in much of its conceptualization and aimed at symptom reduction. The ACT model is built on functional contextualism and is an application of behavior analysis. Rather than symptom alleviation, ACT focuses on increasing psychological flexibility, acceptance of that which cannot be changed, and on the creation of larger and larger behavioral repertoires that facilitate valued living.

Acceptance and Commitment Therapy and Chronic Illness

Acceptance and Commitment Therapy (ACT) is a behavior therapy based on a new theory of language and cognition (Relational Frame Theory; Hayes, Barnes-Holmes, & Roche, 2001). A major theme put forward in the ACT model (Hayes, Strosahl, & Wilson, 1999) is that attempts to control negatively valued aspects of experience may, in some contexts, actually increase suffering. In ACT, clients are asked to examine where attempts at control have had beneficial effects over the long term. Instead of alleviating or controlling the 'problem' (usually conceptualized as the presence of aversive private events such as pain, seizures or their perceived threat of occurrence), clients learn in ACT to accept private experiences and focus instead on long-term meaningful goals.

From an ACT perspective, the process of allowing symptoms to 'get into the driver's seat' is both logical and pathological. Popular culture embraces the notion that positive emotions, cognitions and bodily states 'cause' good behavior, and negative emotions, cognitions and bodily states 'cause' bad behavior. We make an enormous effort in our schools and workplaces teaching people to have higher self-esteem, to be more cheerful and optimistic in order to avoid pain or negative feelings. We are taught from childhood that we can and should control negative aspects of experience. We are taught to control, manage and steer clear of stress, pain, symptoms and discomfort of any kind. From an ACT point of view, all of this is quite normal and indeed built into normal human language processes.

Experiential avoidance predicts poorer long-term outcome in a wide variety of psychological problems such as depression (DeGenova, Patton, Jurich, & MacDermid, 1994), the long-term sequelae of child abuse (Polusny & Follette, 1995), alcoholism (Moser & Annis, 1996), to name but a few. The experimental literature is fairly clear that avoidance and suppression of private events tends to increase their frequency and impact in the normal population as well (Purdon, 1999). Wegner, in his studies of thought suppression (Wegner, Schneider, Knutson, & McMahon, 1991), has shown that attempts to suppress thoughts result in immediate decrease in their frequencies, but long-term increases.

Medical conditions such as chronic pain and epilepsy fit readily into an experiential avoidance perspective. Because of some of the special properties of language, we attempt to avoid thoughts of an aversive event such as pain or seizures very much as we attempt to avoid the aversive event itself. Further, any event, thought or activity related to pain, epilepsy or seizures will also begin to be avoided. If pain and seizures are associated with things such as stress, demands, work activities and social situations, all of these will tend to be avoided both in thought and in action. An unwillingness to remain mindful of the pain or seizure symptoms can have serious consequences. Consider all the events that will be associated with these symptoms that will also need to be avoided, such as physical movement, doctors, medication and so forth. In principle, all of the procedures that could be used to manage these symptoms will also be 'contaminated' by the aversive symptoms. We also know that experiential avoidance is one of the most powerful predictors of chronic pain.

In the next two sections, we will illustrate the treatment of two illnesses, chronic pain and epilepsy, and show how they are conceptualized and treated in the medical model, the behavior medicine model and the ACT model.

Chronic Pain

Understanding complex chronic pain illustrates the inadequacy of the mechanistic pathology model and provides an opportunity to use a very different conceptualization and subsequent treatment model. The International Association of Pain (IASP) uses the mechanistic model in the actual diagnostic categories of pain, which from the start sets the stage for mechanistic thinking about symptoms. Pain is classified as nocieceptive, neurogenic or psychogenic, suggesting from the start a specific underlying pathology. Nocieceptive pain is said to be caused by the activation of pain receptors that are in most tissues like the skin, muscles, joints and blood vessels. Pain of this kind includes, for example, scrapes, bumps, bruises, burns and cuts. It can also include most diffuse types of pain such as visceral pain (related to internal organs) or muscular strains. Neurogenic pain is said to be caused by problems in the peripheral and central nervous system. This might include peripheral neuropathy such as seen in people having chronic diabetes or alcoholism (loss of feeling in the feet, for example), or phantom limb pain. In these cases the actual pain does not come from the pain receptors, but rather from the nerve system itself. Psychogenic pain is a category used when no known pathology is found for pain complaints.

In general, these medical classifications may seem logically clear and are, in fact, clear in many cases. However, this type of classification implies that most pain symptoms can be traced back to one of two pathological aspects of the nervous system or, if neither of these can be found, to psychological causes. But in most chronic illness there is, in fact, no simple one-to-one correlation between symptoms and pathology. We can illustrate this in the case of common back pain.

Neck and Back Pain

Pain in the neck and back regions is so common today that it is considered to be a normal part of life. Nearly everyone will experience neck and back pain some time in their lifetime. Back pain is second only to headache as the most common pain symptom reported in the United States (US). Comprehensive reviews of epidemiological studies in Europe and North America (Andersson, 1997; Raspe, 1993; Skekelle, 1997) indicate that back pain is present in about 15–30% of the population, with 19–43% prevalence over a period of 1 month, and that 60–70% of the population will experience significant back pain at some point in their lives. According to the Nuprine Pain Report (Taylor & Curran, 1985), 56% of the US population reported the experience of back pain at least one day during the past year. Similar figures have been shown for the United Kingdom (Papageorgiou, Macfarlane, Thomas, Croft, & Jayson, 1995; Walsh, Cruddas, & Coggon, 1992) and Belgium (Skovron, Szpalski Nordin, Melot, &

Cockier, 1994). The problem is not limited to adults. Prevalence of back pain among children in Sweden is 26% over a year and 9% at the time of interview (Brattier, 1999). Epidemiological studies show that the prevalence of musculoskeletal pain is equally common among men and women, but that women may perceive themselves in worse health and seek help more frequently (Branthaver, Stein, & Mehran, 1995). Only a fraction of persons with chronic back pain will seek professional help and of those who seek help only a few will be put on sick leave. Despite this, chronic back pain is the most common cause of work disability in the United States and the European Union (Waddell, 2000).

Most people seeking help for back pain describe nocieceptive or neurogenic pain symptoms and also show pathological physical findings such as inflammation, fibrosis in the muscles or disc herniation. From the perspective of the biomechanical model, these pathological findings are said to 'cause' the back pain. But here is an example of a major scientific error often found when using the mechanistic model: Herniated discs are commonly found in patients that have no back pain symptoms. As we will see, this lack of correlation between symptom and pathology undermines the medical/pathological model as a useful model for explaining or treating pain.

No Simple One-to-One Correlation Between Symptom and Pathology

Twenty-five years ago investigators found no correlation between positive computed axial tomography (CAT) scans for disc hernia and back pain symptoms. (Weisel, Tsourmas, Feffer, Citrin, & Patronas, 1984). More recently, Boden et al. (1990) found abnormal magnetic resonance scans (MRT) of lumbar spines in patients showing no back pain symptoms. Boos, Wallin, Gbedegbegnon, Aebi and Boesch (1993) showed that disc hernia was a finding just as common among patients with no back pain as those with back pain symptoms. Even clear-cut pathological findings are not consistently related to pain experiences in cases such as spondylosis, degenerative changes caused by osteoporosis with fractures, spinal stenosis and bacterial rheumatoid spondylitis. Even diseases such as ankylosing spondylitis are all semispecific causes of back pain but do not always 'cause' back pain symptoms.

Muscles have long been assumed to play a role in both acute and chronic pain. But here again, extensive research on the topic shows no uniform connection between muscular problems and chronic pain (Hides, Richardson, & Jull, 1995, 1996; Hides, Strokes & Saide, 1994). A common chiropractic theory, for example, is that back pain is 'caused' by locked facet joints between the vertebrae in the spine, which in turn cause the muscle to contract and become spastic. Again, this sounds very logical as a 'cause'. However, anatomic investigations, including the use of biopsies and injections, have not been able to show any correlation between this biological mechanism and back pain (King & Cavanaugh, 1996). In fact, a meta-analysis reviewing these investigations of biological mechanisms in the back over a 50-year period showed no findings of any specific pathology that could explain either acute or chronic pain (Nachemson & Waddell, 2000).

Diagnostic words like 'neurogenic', 'nocieceptive', 'neuropathic', 'psychogenic', 'real', 'muscle' or 'existential pain' draw us into assumptions of structural distinctions that probably do not help us at all to understand or treat the complex problem of pain. Our objection with using this medical–mechanism model of pathology to explain the pain experience is more of a functional than an ontological problem. We are not proposing that pain has no underlying physical pathology. In those cases where pain has a specific pathology, such as with an abscessed tooth, no-one would question that specific medical procedures should be used to address the problem. Future medical research may, in fact, explain complicated pathology that we are unable to detect using today's instruments. But this does not alter the fact that the pain experience is much more complex than mere physical pathology, especially if the pain is chronic. So, even if the physical pathology was clear, it alone would probably never fully explain or lead to a fully satisfying treatment of the pain problem. Human beings are not mere biological machines; they are historical, developmental, thinking creatures interacting in and with their world.

Conservative Medical Treatment of Chronic Pain

Recent meta-analyses investigating the effects of the most common treatments of chronic pain are clear and in agreement. With just a few exceptions, the evidence for our most common medical treatments for pain is limited or nonexistent. These reviews include treatments consisting of analgesic drug therapy, surgery, manipulation, physical therapy, electromyography (EMG) biofeedback, traction, transcutaneous electrical nerve stimulation (TENS), acupuncture, braces, back schools, epidural steroid injections, nonsteroid anti-inflammatory drugs, muscle relaxants/benzodiazepine and antidepressant drugs. Major scholarly reviews of the existing scientific literature by teams of top international experts have provided little support for the most current forms of treatment (Dworkin, et al., 2005).

Behavior Medicine Model of Chronic Pain

Cognitive–behavior therapy-based treatments have been shown to be up to twice as effective in treating the symptoms of chronic pain as single-component programs such as surgery, physical therapy or manipulation alone (Flor, Fydrich, & Turk, 1992).

Within the behavioral paradigm, general goals in the treatment of chronic pain typically involve outcomes such as reduced limping, reduced seizures, walking longer distances and returning to work. Within the cognitive–behavioral paradigm, targets of intervention were expanded to include changing negative feelings and thoughts, along with behavioral goals such as reducing passive coping (pills, resting) and increasing active coping behavior such as exercising. Cognitive restructuring and skills training techniques such as reframing dysfunctional thoughts, mental training for positive thinking, mental distraction, stress management, relaxation training, social skills training, problem solving and activities of daily life training were commonly found in these programs. A large meta-analysis (Linton, 2000) including 28 randomized controlled studies evaluating CBT for chronic pain concluded that patients receiving CBT improved more than control conditions at follow-up.

ACT and Chronic Pain

While behavior therapy addresses the aspects of chronic pain arising through operant and classical conditioning, and CBT additionally attempts to change problematic thoughts and feelings associated with chronic pain, ACT takes a different perspective. From a pathology-oriented perspective, it is the removal of pathology that is supposed to free the patients from symptoms. From an ACT perspective, however, the road to psychological health in the midst of chronic pain involves consistently orienting the client toward living a more valued life, while undercutting client attempts at experiential avoidance. Within the ACT model, there is less focus on pain reduction and a greater focus on increasing the client's ability to more consistently and effectively move in valued directions. The assumption here is that the reduction or avoidance of pain is not required in order to 'start living'. In fact, struggling with pain often intensifies the focus on pain and interferes with living more consistently in line with one's values. ACT aims to help clients let go of this struggle with pain and start living, here and now, in pursuit of valued directions. From basic and applied research we know experiential avoidance to be one of the most powerful predictors of chronic pain. The Acceptance and Action Questionnaire (AAQ; Hayes et al., 2004) was modified for chronic pain (Geiser, 1992) and further developed in a series of studies by McCracken and colleagues (McCracken, 1998; McCracken, Carson, & Eccelston, 2003; McCracken, Vowles, & Eccelston, 2004.). This, together with the Chronic Pain Acceptance Questionnaire (CPAQ), showed that there were two primary aspects of the pain acceptance concept: willingness to experience pain and engaging in valued life activities regardless of the pain. Acceptance of pain is associated with reports of lower pain intensity, less pain-related anxiety and avoidance, less depression, less physical and psychosocial disability, more daily uptime and better work status. These studies also showed that acceptance levels were not simply a function of having less intense pain.

ACT has also been shown to be effective in producing greater behavioral tolerance of acute pain and discomfort. Hayes et al. (1999) showed that a 90-minute training in acceptance produced a greater increase in pain tolerance than either discussion about pain or attempts to control pain, including the types of distraction used in popular CBT pain management programs. These results have been replicated and extended by Gutierrez, Luciano, Rodriguez and Fink (2004). These authors showed that an ACT acceptance and defusion condition produced greater increase in pain tolerance than a closely matched cognitive control-based condition, especially with high levels of pain. In more recent clinical trials, ACT has been shown to be effective in the treatment of pain and stress (Bond & Bunce, 2000; Bond & Hayes, 2002: Dahl, Wilson, & Nilsson, 2004). Recently (Johnston, 2008), a study in New Zealand was performed using an ACT self-help book for chronic pain (Dahl & Lundgren, 2006). This study was a randomized controlled group design using a home intervention over a 6-week period. Half of the participants read the self-help book, completed exercises and received telephone support, while the control group waited for this intervention. Participants completed pre- and postintervention questionnaires for acceptance, values, illness, quality of life, satisfaction with life, depression, anxiety and pain. Initial outcome data were collected for 8 control participants and 6 intervention participants. A total of 11 participants completed pre- and post-intervention measures. Statistically significant improvement in acceptance and quality of life for those who completed the intervention resulted. In order to provide a better understanding of this specific ACT intervention, excerpts from the general treatment introduction letter and a summary of the week 1 readings are provided below (Johnston, 2008).

INTRODUCTION

Enclosed is the material you need to participate in this study. The study will take seven weeks to complete and each week you are required to:

• Read the specified part of the book.

• Do the exercises in that section (the exercises that are in the book are also provided here so you can fill them in — or if you would like extra copies of these please contact me).

• Answer questions to help me evaluate the book during a weekly phone call with me.

The exercises and evaluation questions are attached and are in the order that you are required to complete or look at them.

The research has been designed to allow you to work through the book (Dahl and Lundgren 2007) and complete the exercises at a steady pace. I will phone you once a week to answer any questions and to see how you are going with the book and exercises. The evaluation questions will be discussed on the phone. The questions are to prompt discussion about how you are finding the book. It is not a test!!

The exercises and the questions I will use to evaluate the book are attached.

The weekly time that we have arranged for you to be phoned is:

(Time): _____ on (day):_____

Here is a list of the weekly reading:

Week no.	Start date	Required reading (book chapters)	Tick as complete
1		Intro, 1 & 2	
2		3	
3		4	
4		5	
5		6 and up to page 136 of Chapter 7	
6		From 136 of Chapter 7 and Chapter 8	
7		Final meet with me	

At the last meeting I will need the book returned, but you can keep this handbook.

The agreed date for the final meeting is day: _____ month _____ '07.

FIGURE 5.1
Excerpt from general treatment letter used in an efficacy study (Johnston, 2008) on ACT self-help treatment for chronic pain (Dahl and Luhngren, 2007).

WEEK 1. What is pain? What is ACT?

Reading: Introduction and Chapters 1 and 2.

Introduction

The introduction points out that as pain gets bigger and bigger, life often gets smaller and smaller and becomes about (and becomes only about ...) trying to keep pain at bay. The authors use the 'quicksand' metaphor to illustrate a scenario of struggling against pain but sinking further and further under (preposition at end). The authors suggest changing how you see and deal with your pain — working with it rather than against it. This means that if we apply the ideas in ACT to our lives, pain is not removed; rather, changes are made in our lives.

The aims of the book are:
- To get you out of the quicksand/struggle and to help you live a life you want to live.
- To eliminate suffering.
- To change your perspective on pain.

These sections point out that the main ideas of ACT are:
1. To accept the aspects of your pain that you cannot change, including all the difficult thoughts, feelings, and bodily sensations that come with it.
2. This acceptance then allows you to commit to actions that make you feel vital and energized.

These sections introduce the pain–avoidance–suffering cycle:

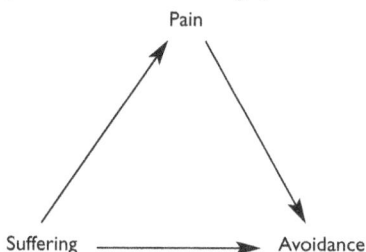

Pain signals to get our attention. In this way pain is helpful. We are conditioned to believe that we must avoid experiences of pain, but in reality avoiding pain creates more pain. Increased pain often leads to us limiting what we do — constraining our lives and leading to situations that are unfulfilling and in which we are unhappy. This pain caused by pain is suffering.

For people with chronic pain, suffering usually follows a sequence of these four steps:

1. Your actual physical pain sensation
2. The way your mind reacts to this pain.
3. Avoidance or escape behaviours based on what your mind says.
4. Long-term choices based on avoidance and escape behaviours.

The authors refer to this as the **pain chain**.

Clean and dirty pain
Clean pain is the simple immediate physical sensation that indicates something is wrong. Dirty pain is our response to the pain—mostly what your mind tells you about your pain. Clean pain cannot really be controlled but dirty pain can. All traditional pain management approaches emphasis controlling clean pain and allowing dirty pain to escalate. ACT is a different way of approaching pain. Eric's story on page 30 illustrates these two types of pain.

Creative hopelessness
Control of pain is not the answer. Creative hopelessness is about letting go of the control and creating a space for new possibilities to change your life. Letting go of control may evoke feelings of grief and emptiness but it might also provide the opportunity for hope. It's not about 'beating' pain or about giving up. Rather, it is about acceptance and looking at alternative solutions.

FIGURE 5.2
Summary of Week 1 readings (Johnston, 2008) from Dahl and Luhngren (2007),

Approaching chronic pain using the ACT model is showing great promise and gaining popularity due to its cost-benefit effects. The ACT treatment models evaluated are far cheaper and perhaps more effective than the traditional CBT based multidisciplinary treatments. In this next section we will look at how epilepsy is conceptualized and treated with respect to these different models.

Epilepsy

Traditional Medical/Mechanistic Model of Epilepsy

Each of the three models for treating the psychological aspects of health conditions discussed above also take markedly different approaches to conceptualizing and treating epilepsy. Epilepsy is defined in traditional medical terms as a symptom of a neurological dysfunction. Epileptic seizures are assumed to be 'caused' by groups of damaged nerve cells in the brain. Seizures are seen as the behavioral manifestation of an underlying temporary aberration of electrical activity. Causes of this organic dysfunction are usually attributed to improper alterations in neurotransmitter function or the dynamics of membrane ionic currents. One-way causation between pathology and symptom(s) is assumed and no consideration to conditioning in terms of precipitory or inhibiting factors is implied. Seizures are classified generally in terms of pathology. If the epileptogenic activity starts all at once over the whole brain, the seizures are classified as generalized. If the epileptogenic activity starts in one part of the brain and spreads to other parts, the seizures are classified as partial or focal seizures. Seizures are assumed to occur randomly. Subsequent anticonvulsant drug treatment aims at reducing nerve cell reactivity and thus reducing the probability of seizure occurrence.

Problems With the Medical/Mechanistic Model of Epilepsy:
Early Documentation of Conditioning Factors

Among the earliest medical documentations of epileptic seizures we find stories of conditioning mechanisms and how they can be used to control seizures. In ancient Greek medicine, Galen describes seizures as a process or predictable chain of behavior that can be interrupted by different stimulation to the body (Temkin, 1945). Much later, the British neurologist Gowers (1881) was the first to classify differing degrees of epilepsy: grand mal, petit mal and hysteroid, and is also notable for publishing case studies where behavioral techniques were applied to successfully stop seizures. Within the medical model, epileptic seizure behavior is carefully documented and treatment interventions entail different ways of stimulating the area around which the seizure starts. Both specific and general stimulation may occur. In one example, a specific stimulus like pressure is put on the hand where the seizure starts and, in other more general types of seizures, strong smells are used to evoke a general arousal contingent upon the start of the seizure. A French physician/physiologist (Brown-Sequard, 1857) presented a review of case studies also demonstrating how seizures can be successfully aborted by the use of stimulation contingent on the onset of seizure. Documentation of these behavioral interventions continued into the 20th century when Jackson (1931) described certain seizures as a 'march' through the body and noted how seizures can be brought to a halt by vigorous rubbing of the affected limb.

From these early studies the principle of competitive recruitment evolves. At this point, based on clinical observations, the assumption is that by localizing hyperexcitable brain areas, competitive recruitment stimulated in relatively normal brain areas will increase normal activity and reduce synchronization and prevent seizures. In other words, if you can identify an early link in the chain of seizure behavior, and either apply stimulation around that area or initiate a 'general arousal', you are likely to stop the seizure.

At the turn of the century, the drug industry developed a chemical solution to stop seizures. This opened the doors to antiepileptic drug treatment (AED), a mode of treatment squarely based on the pathology model. The general principle of AEDs is to generally reduce neuronal brain activity, making the spread of epileptogenic activity less likely. None of the AEDs produced thus far has any specific effect on the epileptogenic neurons causing the seizures, but rather, slows down all brain cell activity. The drugs developed throughout the 20th century do indeed reduce seizure frequency for most people with epilepsy, successfully helping about 67% of persons with epilepsy attain seizure freedom.

However, the relief AEDs can provide from seizures comes at a cost. In a review by Loring and Meador (2001) the effects of AEDs on cognition and overt behavior is significant. They report that the most common AED cognitive effects include psychomotor slowing, reduced vigilance and impairments in memory. Phenobarbital and benzodiazepines showed the most aversive cognitive effects. The most commonly used AEDs — carbamazepine, phenytoin and valproate — showed adverse effects influencing psychomotor speed, memory and mood. The AEDs produced in the last decade like gabapentin, lamotrigine, levetracetam, oxcarbazepine, tiagabine and topiramate may have fewer effects, but no long-term follow-ups have yet been done. Loring and Meador (2001) concluded that patients report their quality of life is more adversely affected by the side effects of the AEDs than by the presence of seizures.

Epileptologists around the world have raised their voices in protest against the oversimplistic pathological model and the sole use of antiepileptic drugs as the treatment of choice. The main argument is that the medical model does not explain the peculiar patterns of seizure behavior, how they are triggered and how they are inhibited. Complaints regarding the antiepileptic drugs concern the new problems they create. In addition, there are considerable theoretical inconsistencies regarding the lack of correlation between the pathology and the presenting symptoms.

In 1968, Rodin criticized the pathological model and the associated medical research as being too simplistic and inadequate:

> The great majority of neurochemical investigations still deal with the epileptic neuron. These are important studies but they are likely to be insufficient in providing the final answer to the problem. One should also ask, what are the factors responsible for the spread of abnormal electrical activity in this particular patient? Even more important would be the question, how does the patient's condition differ on the five days of the week when he is seizure free from the 6th day when he has an attack? (Rodin, 1968, p. 343)

In 1989, Engel made an appeal for alternatives:

> Epileptologists have relied heavily on pharmacological therapy, which is usually nonspecific and associated with disturbing side effects. Both basic and clinical research should focus on improving present alternative therapeutic approaches and finding new ones that may interfere more directly with precipitating and predisposing factors to prevent epileptic seizures without producing additional symptoms. (Engel, 1989)

Theoretical problems with the pathology model show up in the discrepancies pertaining to causal effects. Seizures are proposed to be secondary or 'caused' by repeated abnormal electrical discharges from the neural aggregates in the brain. The behavior of the seizure would, accordingly, be characterized depending on the location of the 'epileptic focus' in the brain as well as the extent of the spread of the neuronal discharges over the cortex. One of the difficulties is that in as many as 70% of cases of epilepsy, the etiology of the seizure symptoms remains unknown (Ross, 1994). In addition, a significant percentage of the 'normal' population with no seizures, display epileptogenic activity on the electroencephalogram (EEG). There are seizures presented with no epileptogenic correlate visible on the EEG. Clearly, the evidence does not support a one-to-one correlation or causal relationship between the pathology of the 'epileptic neuron' and seizure occurrence. The known pathology of the epileptogenic neurons sets the stage for epilepsy but does not cause them to occur. In order to understand eliciting and inhibitory mechanisms of the epileptic seizures, conditioning must be understood.

Conditioning Mechanisms in Epilepsy

The conditioning process of how epileptogenic activity is spread and interrupted was described between 1940 and 1950 by behavioral scientists studying animals (Eriksson, 1940; Gelhorn, 1947; Leao, 1944a,

1944b, 1947; McCulloch, 1949). These studies illustrate how epilepto-genic discharges can be interrupted systematically through the use of contingent stimulation of different sorts.

By 1957, a case study was published by Efron (1956) showing how seizures are arrested using second-order (classical) conditioning of an olfactory stimulus to a bracelet and finally, just thinking about a bracelet to arrest an ongoing seizure. Efron, a behavioral clinician, was treating an internationally known jazz singer who had seizures on stage while performing and was desperate for help to control them. He analyzed the chain of her seizure behavior and saw that seizures were triggered by an increase in cortical activity as she prepared to perform. He introduced the idea of eliciting a competing response, presenting the smell of jasmine, which had a calming effect on the singer, as she prepared to perform. Efron's idea was to break the chain of increased excitation triggering the seizure by introducing a 'calming' competing response. The woman practiced smelling her jasmine scent contingent upon any sign of seizure start, and immediately the seizures subsided. Efron went further and conditioned the smell of jasmine to a bracelet and finally to the thought of a bracelet. Following her training, the singer was able to perform by simply thinking about the smell of jasmine, counteracting any seizure start. This groundbreaking study marked the beginning of the use of classical conditioning procedures in the understanding and treatment of people suffering from epilepsy.

Behavior Medicine

EEG Bio-Feedback: Operant Conditioning of Epileptogenic Activity

The technology of the EEG laboratories enabled new breakthroughs in the understanding of the conditioning mechanisms involved with epileptic seizures. Forster, a neurologist, spent more than 3 decades mapping out the process of conditioning and evaluating the habituating process of reflex seizures using continuous EEGs and video monitoring. Reflex epilepsy is seen as the cleanest form of an unconditioned stimulus (seizure trigger) and unconditioned response (seizure), since the seizure response acts reliably as a reflex to the stimuli. In 1964, Forster and his coworkers (Forster, Ptacek, Peterson, Chun, & Bengzon, 1964) published a study showing that it is possible to alter the seizure threshold through the process of habituation. In his EEG laboratory Forster and his team studied the details of people with reflex epilepsy and were able to discriminate exactly the level and frequency of the seizure trigger stimuli. Through the use of prolonged exposure close to the triggering frequency, Forster was able to demonstrate a habituation effect. This means, for example, that a child suffering from reflex seizures who received such prolonged exposure would no longer be sensitive to the seizure triggering stimuli and thus experiences fewer seizures.

A few years later, another team published a report showing that seizures can actually be extinguished using desensitization and competing responses (Forster, Paulsen, & Baughman, 1969). Based on an individual seizure behavior analysis, young adults with reflex epilepsy were exposed to their identified seizure triggering stimuli using video recordings and, at the same time, were instructed to perform a distraction ritual. These procedures resulted in nearly full seizure control and were verified by significant reductions in the epileptogenic activity on the continuous EEG recordings. By 1977, Forster presented data from over 30 single subject designs of young people with varied forms of reflex epilepsy, using continuous EEG video monitoring, and demonstrated how the desensitization process essentially deconditions all seizure activity and reduces the epileptogenic activity.

Forster's research only dealt with 'reflex' seizures, which constitute only 5% of those suffering from epilepsy, but his work is a major contribution to how we understand the conditioning mechanisms and how they can be used to help people to control seizures with no drugs. The mere name 'reflex epilepsy' implies that the seizure is an unconditioned response. That, in fact, is the definition of a reflex. Every time the seizure trigger is presented — as in a light flicker, sudden sound, reading, laughing, sudden movement and so on — the seizure is elicited 100% of the time. While the response may have initially appeared unconditioned, Forster showed that these so-called 'reflex' seizures responses are, in fact, conditioned responses that can be deconditioned.

At the same time, different groups of behavior researchers showed how operant conditioning mechanisms can be used to develop antiepileptic brain waves and protect against seizure activity. Two larger pockets of research teams developed EEG biofeedback techniques aimed at helping individuals to normalize brain wave activity by learning a state of cerebral activity assumed to elevate seizure threshold. The Sterman group published a number of studies (e.g., Sterman, 1993; Lantz & Sterman, 1988) showing evidence (both in cats and in humans with epilepsy) that a specific rhythm called sensory motor rhythm (SMR) functions in an antiepileptic fashion. This SMR rhythm was shown to have a behavior correlate that we might today called mindfulness, a heightened relaxed state. These studies show seizure frequency reductions between 35% and 50% at a 1-year follow-up when these rhythms were induced in epileptic patients. This mindfulness state is observed to be an active inhibition of peripheral motor activity and mental state described as a concentrated alertness.

Another group led by Birbaumer (Birbaumer, Lutzenberg, Rockstroh, & Elbert, 1992; Rockstroh, Birbaumer, Elbert, & Lutsenberger, 1984) presented evidence of how instrumental conditioning of slow cortical potentials (SCP) reduces epileptogenic activity. Functional analyses were performed on the EEG behavior and these researchers redefined epilepsy as an inability to control cortical excitability. This team presented evidence for a hypothesis of the mechanisms of epilepsy and conditioning that show how behavioral programs can be set up.

Birbaumer and colleagues showed that all organisms have a tendency to go into seizure as cortical activity fluctuates. Normally, feedback mechanisms within the brain control these transitions in excitability. Individuals with epilepsy show overexcitability of cortical tissue due to a failure of these down-regulating mechanisms, which lead to an explosive chain reaction of excitation among the neuronal networks. The sort of seizure symptom that presents itself depends on where and how much of the network is involved. Treatment with SCP biofeedback trains the person with epilepsy to shift his or her cortical excitability and thus reduce the risk of a seizure. This SCP research is built on a functional analysis of behavior as compared to the other biofeedback studies. The SMR studies aimed at teaching one kind of antiepileptic brain rhythm intended to protect the individual in much the same way as drug therapy. The SCP training is built on an awareness of the chain of seizure behavior and requires the individual to generate upward or downward responses of cortical activity, depending on the baseline. For example, upon the first signals of the start of a seizure, a young man was taught to 'correct' his cortical activity using stimulation (upward) or relaxation (downward) in order to stop the seizure. Patients learned to shift cortical activity up or downward depending on what was need to correct the ongoing 'seizure eliciting' ongoing trend.

A Theory of Conditioning and the Epileptic Seizure

Fenwick (1994) presented a theoretical framework as a possible platform for behavioral treatments of epilepsy. Fenwick presented evidence from animal studies that he claims clearly shows the close interrelation between seizure activity and behavior. He went on to say that seizures do not occur in a vacuum and are not merely the result of pathological activity. Fenwick pointed out that, given the animal research available today, the seizure process is significantly influenced by the behavior of the organism.

Fenwick stated that epileptic seizures should not be thought of as arising randomly, but rather act in a predictable manner. He described focal seizures as occurring when pools of neurons surrounding the focus are sufficiently excited, and generalized seizures occurring when the level of cortical excitability has reached a point at which thalamic recruiting volleys generalize and spread. Fenwick not only presented a plausible theory for conditioning, but also described a functional analysis of the chain of seizure behavior and how a behavioral treatment can be created. Fenwick suggested that treating physicians make a detailed clinical history of the 'aura' or start of the seizure, along with details of the characteristic spread of the seizure. Details around how the seizure starts are critical to ask. What are the particular situations, feelings, thoughts and activities (high risk) correlated with the start of a seizure? And what are the particular situations, feelings, thoughts and activities where the client does not (low risk) usually have seizures? Can the client influence the seizure — prevent, postpone or abort a seizure? How aware is the client during a seizure? What kind of learning is going on during a seizure? Have others been able to stop a seizure? In what ways? He advises the medical professionals that this information describes the 'engine' that drives the creation of a countermeasure and is likely to stop the seizures. From his perspective, the functional analysis of the seizure chain is the heart of this behavioral treatment and will define those aspects of behavior that both trigger and inhibit seizure activity. In conclusion, Fenwick stated to the medical community that a complete treatment of epilepsy not only involves medication, but includes teaching the patient about their brain and its functioning and how they can use their feelings, thinking and behavior to control their epilepsy (Fenwick, 1994).

Fenwick based this model on the animal research of Lockard and Ward (1980). This theoretical model is far from the one-way pathology–symptom model. It suggests that pathology, or a set of dysfunctional neurons, only sets the stage for epilepsy but does not cause it to occur. Lockard and Ward call the pathological epileptogenic pacemaker set of neurons 'group 1'. They are clearly the troublemakers, but they cannot cause an epileptic seizure unless they can mobilize recruits among the neighboring 'group 2' neurons, who mostly act in a normal manner. But occasionally, the group 2 neurons either let down their guard, get drowsy or overexcited, and the group 1s are able to recruit them. Once group 2 neurons become involved, the onset of a seizure becomes a real possibility. Lockard and Ward used EEG video recordings to observe how brain-damaged monkeys appeared to notice the spread and how some of them responded by getting active while others did not. One of the significant observations was that, although the monkeys' brains had been damaged in exactly the same place, and all showed abnormal EEGS from the group 1 neurons, only some of them developed epileptic seizures. The conclusion was that while damaged neurons create a predisposition for epilepsy, the behavioral response to the dysfunction is critical. Lockard and Ward speculate that the monkeys who got active at the first signs of the spreading of the dysfunctional signals counteracted and stopped the spread of the 'would-be' seizure. Practically, this means that if an individual can detect the first signs of seizure development, it is possible to 'counter' the seizure by mobilizing the remaining healthy neurons and to stop the seizure from occurring.

A new concept of epilepsy was born, and with it new possibilities for treatment. Epilepsy began to be approached behaviorally as a complex consisting of an organic predisposition to seize and environmental factors that influence the probability of seizure occurrence. Understanding how those factors work to increase or decrease the likelihood of a seizure response fell clearly under the behavior therapist profession.

Recently, Wolf (2005) summarized the rationale for the new paradigm of conditioning:

> Epileptic seizures can be triggered by both nonspecific facilitating factors such as sleep withdrawal, fever or excessive alcohol intake, and specific reflex epileptic mechanisms. These consist of sensory or cognitive inputs activating circumscribed cortical areas or functional anatomic systems that, due to some functional instability, respond with an epileptic discharge. Interruption of seizure activity at the stage of the aura (i.e., locally restricted discharge) also can be achieved by nonspecific (e.g., relaxation or concentration techniques or vagal nerve stimulation) or by specific focus-targeted sensory or cognitive inputs. The latter, again, activate circumscribed cortical areas. Intriguingly, in some patients, the same stimulus can either precipitate or abort a seizure. The response depends on the state of cortical activation: seizure precipitation occurs in the resting condition, and seizure interruption occurs when the epileptic discharge has begun close to the activated area. These relations can be understood on the background of experimental data showing that an intermediate state of neuronal activation is a precondition for the generation of paroxysmal depolarization shifts, whereas a hyperpolarized neuron will remain sub threshold, and a depolarized neuron that already produces action potentials is not recruitable for other activity. Sensory input meeting an intermediately activated pool of potentially epileptic neurons is adequate to produce a seizure. In another condition, the same stimulus can depolarize a neuron pool in the same area sufficiently to block the further propagation of nearby epileptic activity. Understanding these interactions facilitates the development of successful nonpharmaceutical therapeutic interventions for epilepsy. (Wolf, 2005, p. 15)

Wolf describes the paradigm shift from the pathology model to a paradigm that is built on the principles of operant and classical conditioning. Epilepsy is seen here as a predisposition that can be both triggered and inhibited by certain interactions between overt behaviors and cognitions. It is interesting to note that Wolf shows an understanding of the complexity of the behavior analysis in his description that directly follows the slow cortical potential feedback evidence of how to interrupt a seizure. Depending on the baseline of the 'state of cortical excitation', a stimulus can both trigger and inhibit a seizure. Wolf states the importance of gathering careful experimental data in order to generate hypotheses regarding the regarding the contingencies surrounding each seizure.

From Theory to Practice: Behavioral Treatment Guidelines Emerge

Based on behavioral assessment strategies, interventions are tailor-made to help the individual with epilepsy *predict* the seizure response by discrimination of intrinsic and extrinsic factors associated with seizure onset, to *prevent* seizure occurrence by applying exposure procedures to 'high' risk situations or activities associated with seizure occurrence, and to *interrupt* or *counteract* an ongoing seizure response by initiating an appropriate 'correcting', competing response and *reinforce* oneself for doing so. Details for how to do functional analyses and tailored treatment procedures are presented in a handbook for behavioral treatment of epilepsy (Dahl, 1992).

Facilitating the discrimination of high-risk factors and early seizure signs that predict the onset of a seizure is accomplished using seizure dairies, seizure behavior observations and, if possible, using EEG video recordings. Antecedents can be specific factors that enhance excitation and synchronization in discrete areas of the brain uniquely receptive to these particular influences, such as certain frequencies of light, sounds or patterns. However, the triggers may also be nonspecific feelings (such as anticipation, stress, conflict, fear or physical exertion) that also generally enhance shifts in neuronal excitation. The most reliable way to identify seizure antecedents is to check how the individual relates to, and responds to, what they believe to be the trigger.

Another possible antecedent involves the physical sensation at the start of the seizure. Not all seizures have a clear-cut sign. In the case of the simple, partial, and complex partial, it is fairly easy to identify the first sign of the seizure. The seizure response itself would have been experienced or observed a number of times, and may even be on video. In the case of the generalized seizure, antecedents will be found in associated emotional, physical or environmental factors. In a study by Spector and colleagues (Spector, Goldstein, Cull, & Fenwick, 1994) 88% of individuals with epilepsy were able to reliably identify seizure precipitory factors.

A review of studies (e.g., Spector et al., 1994) have shown evidence that fear and stress increase the risk for seizure occurrence and consequently, *preventive* treatment studies have targeted these reactions. A number of studies have evaluated the effect of teaching relaxation techniques (Dahl, Melin, & Lund, 1987; Pushkarich, Whitman, Dell, Hughes, Rosen, & Hermann, 1992; Tan & Bruni, 1986) and yoga (Ramaratnam & Sridharan, 1999) to provide a general protection from the stress response. In nearly all of these studies, the relaxation, breathing or yoga positions are taught generally and not contingent upon the seizure occurrence.

Interrupting an ongoing seizure may seem improbable, but in fact most individuals with epilepsy have at some time already done this either by consciously experimenting or by accident (Antebi & Bird, 1993; Cull, Fowler, & Brown, 1996; Dahl, 1992). Influencing the seizure process can mean (for example) postponing it and then triggering at the safe time and place of your choice, preventing it outright, and/or shortening or lengthening the course of the response. Figures vary, but reports show between 23% (Finkler, Lozar, & Fenwick, 1990) and 53% (Spector et al., 1994) have experienced aborting a seizure. The most common ways individuals do this is simply by increasing or decreasing cortical activity depending on the upward or downward shift of the antecedent (Dahl, 1992; Dahl, Melin, & Leissner, 1988; Spector et al., 1994). A functional analysis would help the individual to determine, in each situation, which direction the countermeasure should aim for. If the trigger is characterized by a high excitation, the countermeasure might be intentional attempts to relax. If the trigger is a drowsy state, the countermeasure would warrant a soft increase in neuronal excitement brought about, for example, by increased activity. In several studies (Dahl, Brorson, & Melin, 1992; Dahl, Melin, Brorson, Schollin, 1985; Wolf, 2005) a menu of tools for changing cortical activity were taught so that the individual could choose appropriate countermeasures depending on the particular situation. Examples of 'up-going' countermeasures used include whistles, strong smells like a raw onion, strong tastes like fresh ginger, singing, shouting, tactile stimulating with massage or pinching oneself, or jumping up and down. Examples of down-going countermeasures used are breathing exercises, inducing muscle relaxation, focusing concentration on a song, a mathematical problem or a calming picture. Betts and colleagues (Betts, 1995; Betts, Fox, & MacCallum, 1995) presented several studies of how aromas are used to stimulate a general arousal contingent on seizure, resulting in an immediate halt to seizure activity. It should be noted that in cases of developmentally disabled individuals with epilepsy, caretakers can help interrupt seizures using countermeasures.

Seizure triggers and seizure response constantly change for individuals with epilepsy. The task for the behavioral therapist involves teaching the individual with epilepsy how to apply behavioral principles swiftly at the start of each seizure and generate an appropriate countermeasure. There is also an obvious difference in 'self-efficacy' with regard to how the individual relates to epilepsy. On the one hand, epilepsy is seen as an uncontrollable illness and seizures threatening and unpredictable, where medication is the only alternative and, on the other, epileptic seizures are viewed as predictable and controllable.

The trickiest part of the behavioral treatment of epilepsy is the analysis and treatment of the *function* of the epilepsy and seizure behavior. At first glance, an epileptic seizure would probably not be viewed as functional. In fact, when medical professionals use the word functional seizures, they mean 'non-epileptic' seizures or pseudoseizures. In the operant way of thinking, all seizures would be called functional since they all 'function' or operate on the environment in some way. To the observer, seizure behavior looks scary, painful, embarrassing and, to say the least, unattractive. Larger seizures are likely to be brain damaging. To the observer, neither the seizures themselves, nor their effects on the environment would seem to have any reinforcing qualities. But like any behavior, the frequency of seizures increases when seizures are reinforced in some way. While parents, caretakers, teachers and physicians may want to get rid of seizures, most children report wanting to keep at least some seizures. Why? Children and young people report positive reinforcement contingent upon the occurrence of seizures, including special privileges, special attention, physical contact, being perceived as someone special, and indeed the stimulating, sometimes euphoric nature of the seizure itself. In fact, Dahl (1992) found that seizure frequency increased in children as social competency decreased, suggesting seizures may function in part to evoke the positive consequences that poor social skills cannot. Dostoyevsky describes his seizure experience as follows:

> ... the air was filled with a big noise and I tried to move. I felt the heaven was going down upon the earth and that it had engulfed me. I have really touched God. He came into me myself. Yes, God exists. I cried, and I don't remember anything else. You all, healthy people ... can't imagine the happiness we epileptics feel during the second before our fit ... I don't know if this felicity lasts for seconds, hours, or months but believe me, for all the joys that life may bring, I would not exchange this one. (Alajouanine, 1963, p. 214)

Young people and adults also report seizures leading to negative reinforcement such as a means of escaping undesirable situations or reducing anxiety and tension (Dahl, 1992).

This collage of possible functions of a seizure shows how complicated and sophisticated a functional analysis of epileptic seizures must be. If the individual's seizures function to receive desirable consequences or effectively reduce something undesirable, no treatment is going to stop the seizures. The job of the behavior therapist is to find out the nature of the function and to help find better alternatives to serve these functions.

Behavior Medicine Clinical Trials Treating Epilepsy

More evidence about conditioning comes from clinical and the laboratories during the 1970s and 1980s. A clinical study published by Zlutnick, Mayville and Moffat (1975) found plausible seizure antecedents for the subjects involved and, in each individual case, showed how establishing a competing response interrupts the chain of seizure behavior. The study showed how individuals suffering from frequent drug refractory seizures of several different kinds, become essentially seizure free.

The Contribution of the Acceptance and Commitment Therapy Coupled With Behavior Technology in Seizure Control

Recently, an ACT protocol that incorporates the behavioral approach to seizure management just discussed was created and evaluated for groups of individuals with refractory epileptic seizures in India and in South Africa. These countries were chosen due to the primary author's chairmanship of a commission for development of psychological treatment of epilepsy in the International Bureau of Epilepsy working in cooperation with the World Health Organization. In these countries, the majority of people with epilepsy do not have access to anticonvulsant drugs, and it is essential to develop inexpensive and accessible alternative treatments. The results of these studies will not be presented here, but rather a summary description of the treatment protocol will be provided.

Participants in both studies included persons between the age of 15 and 60 years with verified refractory and frequent epileptic seizures. Treatment entailed only four sessions in the following order: one individual session, two group sessions, and one final individual session, for a total of 9 therapy hours.

The primary components of the ACT approach include acceptance, defusion, contact with present moment, self-as-context, values and committed action. These concepts are discussed extensively in the ACT literature (e.g., Hayes & Strosahl, 2005). As applied to epilepsy, *acceptance* as a concept involves accepting the parts of having epilepsy that one cannot change, and at the same time learning how to change what you are able to change. In this ACT protocol, the clients learned to accept the predisposition, or tendency to seize, and all the fears and negative thoughts and emotions associated with epilepsy, rather than struggling against them. The terms 'clean' and 'dirty' epilepsy were used with clients to help convey what constitutes an accepting stance toward epilepsy. Whereas clean epilepsy is the tendency to seize when conditioned thoughts and reactions occur, dirty epilepsy involves the struggle against everything conditioned to epilepsy. Preventing, avoiding or interrupting the seizures itself is a skillful and desirable thing to do, but avoiding everything associated with epilepsy is not, as the first may save your life and the second may handicap you for life. Clients in the ACT conditions were taught that learning how to control seizures is a life skill and makes having a seizure a choice, while fighting against all aspects of the epilepsy is a war that cannot be won. Additionally, clients were taught that learning how to accept the risk of having seizures and live life fully together with that risk is also a life skill. An example of the power of acceptance and its effect on seizures, and one which many with epilepsy have experienced, is demonstrated by what happens in EEG examinations. Both the client and the neurologist prefer to see a seizure with EEG correlates to verify the diagnosis of epilepsy. In this situation, most clients 'try' to have seizures and it is exactly this 'trying' or acceptance that usually leads to no seizures, even among those with very frequent seizures.

Defusion as applied to epilepsy involves learning to see thoughts as an ongoing process rather than a commentary on reality. Thoughts, stigmatization and rules about epilepsy and seizures are looked *at* rather than looked *from*. The clients learned to subscribe to their thoughts when it was helpful and just notice them when they were not. Defusion strategies used in this protocol were virtually identical to the ones normally used in ACT interventions, but were brought to bear especially to problematic thoughts about each client's seizures and their consequences.

Contact with the present moment involved helping the clients get present with positive reinforcement occurring right here and now. A common problem is that individuals struggling with epilepsy believe that they need to get somewhere else other than here to begin to live. Learning how to contact the here and now gives individuals a way to let go of the struggle with one's private experiences and start creating the life they want. The most important part of these processes in ACT may be *values,* since values provide the motivation to step up to difficulties and make changes. The common problem is that the more an individual struggles and organizes life around prevention, avoidance and control of the seizures, the less he or she is involved in valued life activities. As the avoidance agenda grows, life quality diminishes. Contacting constant valued directions provides a way forward toward a meaningful and vital life and shows the individual how far off course avoiding seizures has taken them.

The Treatment Protocol

Treatment in the ACT condition consisted of four sessions, entailing one individual, two group sessions, and followed by one individual session. Session 1 focused on establishing the client's 'life compass' (for a description of how this is done, see Dahl, et al., 2005), finding discrepancies between how the client wants to live (valued directions) and how he or she is actually living now, examining what symptoms or problems are presented as barriers to moving toward valued directions, examining control strategies for reducing those barriers and finally, examining the client's experience of how these control strategies actually function. The chain of seizure behavior was also examined, along with what the individual believes 'triggers' the seizures and if and how he or she is able to control them. Associations and 'rules' about the seizures were also mapped out. Typical rules presented were: 'I would like to study, but I have epilepsy'; 'I would like to have a partner and have a family but no one wants someone with seizures'.

Sessions 2 and 3 took place in group sessions consisting of six to eight individuals during a 3-hour period. The aim of the group sessions was to help the clients to: understand, experience, and practice the concepts of taking steps in valued directions together with obstacles; see thoughts as thoughts and not truths; receive repeated exposure to fears and experience the difference between clean and dirty epilepsy; and to learn and practice seizure control strategies and making public commitments towards creating the vital life of their choosing. The principle used in each group session involved role-playing how each key ACT concept pertained to the clients' experiences of epilepsy, so that they understood these points with their intellect but also experienced them through practice. The group also practiced doing functional analyses on each other's seizures and brain-stormed possible seizure interruption methods.

The aim of the final individual session was to summarize and evaluate how the participant was applying the treatment components: taking steps in valued directions, defusion of less useful mind chatter and using seizure control techniques. New commitments to steps in valued life directions were made.

Measurements of Treatment Effect

Dependent variables used to measure the effects of this treatment model were seizure frequency and duration, life quality, vitality and experiential avoidance with regard to epilepsy. Seizure frequency and duration were measured by the Seizure Index, used previously in several behavioral studies (Dahl et al., 1985; Dahl et al., 1992). Three standardized life quality measures were used to evaluate the larger context of many aspects of life: the World Health Organization Quality Of Life (WHOQOL-brief) question-naire (World Health Organization Geneva, 1996), the Subjective Wellbeing Life Scale (SWLS; Diener, Emmons, Larsen, & Griffin, 1985), and the Personal Wellbeing index (PWI; Cummins 1991; Deiner et al., 1985). The new instruments developed for this study included a variation of the AAQ called the AAEPQ (Acceptance and Action Questionnaire for Epilepsy) and the Bulls-eye, an instrument assessing individual values and degree of successful movement toward them.

The AAEPQ is a 12-item instrument developed to measure acceptance and emotional avoidance related to epilepsy. The participant answers how well they agree with the statement on a Likert scale (between 1 = *never true* and 7 = *always true*). The Bulls-Eye is a functional measure that was created for this study to measure consistency with vital valued areas in life and persistency in taking action in chosen important areas, even in the face of difficulties. The Bulls-Eye measurement consists of four dartboards. For the first three dartboards, the client is asked to choose one valued direction per dartboard that he or she would like to develop/improve/have that they do not have today. The bulls-eye of the dartboard represents 100% consistency with a defined vital valued direction. Using the first three dartboards the subjects are asked to mark how close he/she is living in the defined vital direction in that chosen value. On the last dartboard the client is asked to describe the barriers of living as he or she values them, then to rate how often he or she generally follows valued life directions in the face of the described difficulties and barriers. On the first three dartboards, scores are computed by taking the distance between the X placed by the subject and the bulls-eye. Measurements from these three dartboards are summed and averaged into an index. The last dartboard is measured the same way as the first three, but is presented by as a single measure.

Results

The results of both studies have recently been published. From the South African study, at the 1-year follow-up almost all of the participants from the ACT condition are free of seizures as compared to only a couple of those in the control condition (Lundgren, Dahl, Melin, & Kies, 2006). Overall, the ACT intervention produced a greater than 90% reduction in total amount of time in seizures from baseline to the 1-year follow-up. The quality of life also significantly improved for the ACT participants, using the World Health Organization measure, which taps into psychological health, physical health, environmental health and quality of social relationships. Interestingly, that improvement was not significant at posttreatment, but was at a 6-month follow-up and by the 1-year follow-up; the effect size was very large (Cohen's $d = 1.57$). Not only was the outcome positive but also the model itself was supported. For example, the postscore on the Epilepsy AAQ, the combined values attainment Bulls-Eyes, and the persistence in the face of barriers Bulls-Eye all showed a very large effect in favor of the ACT condition, with effect sizes between 1.95 and 3.23, depending on the measure. These processes fully mediated the effect seen 1 year later both in seizures and (more impressively since these changes emerged only over time) quality of life. For example, the three process scores at posttreatment accounted for between 43% and 53% of the variance in quality of life outcomes seen a year later, depending on the specific process examined (Lundgren, Dahl, & Hayes, 2008). The Indian study (Lundgren, Dahl, Yardi, & Melin, 2008) showed that both ACT and yoga significantly reduced the seizure index and increased quality of life over time. The ACT group showed significant reduction in seizure frequency as compared to the yoga group. Participants in both the ACT and the yoga group improved their quality of life significantly in one of two life quality instruments, with the ACT group increasing the quality of life significantly as compared to the yoga group on the WHOQOL-Brief, and the yoga group increasing their quality of life significantly as compared to the ACT group on the SWLS.

Summary

Psychological and medical problems are typically viewed through the lens of a mechanistic/pathological paradigm. Our popular culture maintains the idea that the cause of human suffering is something defective that can be fixed. This would lead us to thinking that greater access to more physicians, investigations and drugs would lead to better health. Most of these factors, along with better working environments, have dramatically improved over the last 50 years, but human suffering has not decreased. Why individuals see themselves as sick and why they seek health care are complicated issues. This chapter has presented the medical and functional contextual models of human suffering, along with subsequent applications using chronic pain and epilepsy. The research presented here may be a stepping stone towards a paradigm shift necessary for the conceptualization and treatment of complicated human suffering.

References

Alajouanine, F. (1963). Dostoyevski's epilepsy, *Brain*, 86, 214–218.

Andersson, G. (1997), The epidemiology of spinal disorders. In J. Frymoyer (Ed.), *The adult spine, principles and practice* (2nd ed., pp. 93–141). New York: Raven Press.

Antebi, D., & Bird, J. (1993). The facilitation and evocation of seizures. A questionnaire study of awareness and control. *British Journal of Psychiatry, 162,* 759–764.

Betts, T. (1995). An olfactory countermeasures treatment for epileptic seizures using a conditioned arousal response to specific aromatherapy oils. *Epilepsia, 36,* (Suppl. 3), 130–131.

Betts, T., Fox, C., & MacCallum, R. (1995). Assessment of countermeasures used by people to attempt control their own seizures, *Epilepsia,* 36, (Suppl. 3), 130.

Birbaumer, N., Lutzenberg, W., Rockstroh, B. (1992). Area-specific self-regulation of slow cortical potential on the sagittal midline and its effects on behavior. *Electroencephalogy Clinical Neurophysiology, 84,* 353–361.

Boden, S. D., McCowin, P. R., Davis, D. O., Dina, T. S., Mark, A. S., & Wiesel, S. (1990). Abnormal magnetic-resonance scans of the cervical spine in asymptomatic *subjects. A prospective investigation. Journal Bone Joint Surgery (Am),* 72, 1178–1184.

Bond, F. W., & Bunce, D. (2000). Mediators of change in emotion-focused and problem-focused worksite stress management interventions. *Journal of Occupational Health Psychology, 5,* 156–163.

Bond, F., & Hayes, S. C. (2002). ACT at work. In F. Bond & W. Dryden (Eds.), *Handbook of brief cognitive behaviour therapy* (pp. 117–140). Chichester, England: Wiley.

Boos, N., Wallin, A., Gbedegbegnon, T., Aebi, M., & Boesch, C. (1993). Quantitative MR imaging of lumbar intervertebral disks and vertebral bodies: Influence of diurnal water content variations. *Radiology, 188,* 351–354.

Branthaver, B., Stein, G. F., & Mehran, A. (1995). Impact of a medical back care program on utilization of services and primary care physician satisfaction in a large, multispecialty group practice health maintenance organization. *Spine, 20,* 1165–1169.

Brown-Sequard, C. (1857). *Researches on epilepsy: Its artificial production in animals, and its etiology, nature and treatment in man.* Boston: Clapp.

Cull, C., Fowler, M., & Brown, S. (1996). Perceived self-control of seizures in young people with epilepsy. *Seizure, 5,* 131–138.

Cummins, R. A. (1991). The comprehensive quality of life scale — Intellectual disability: An initial report. *Australia and New Zealand Journal of Developmental Disabilities, 17,* 259–264.

Dahl, J. (1992). *Epilepsy: A behavior medicine approach to assessment and treatment in children.* Göttingen, Germany: Hogref & Huber.

Dahl, J., & Lundgren, T. (2006). *Living beyond your pain.* Oakland, New Harbinger Publications, Inc.

Dahl, J. A. Melin, L., & Leissner, P. (1988). Effects of a behavioral intervention on epileptic seizure behavior and paroxysmal activity: A systematic replication of three cases of children with intractable epilepsy. *Epilepsia, 29*(2), 172–83.

Dahl, J. Brorson, L-O., & Melin, L. (1992). Effects of a broad-spectrum behavioral medicine treatment program on children with refractory epileptic seizures: An 8-year follow-up. *Epilepsia, 33*(1), 98–102.

Dahl, J., Melin, L., & Lund, L. (1987). Effects of a contingent relaxation treatment program on adults with refractory epileptic seizures. *Epilepsia, 28*(2), 125–32.

Dahl, J., Melin, L., Brorson, L-O., & Schollin, J. (1985). Effects of a broad-spectrum behavior modification treatment program on children with refractory epileptic seizures. *Epilepsia, 26*(4), 303–309.

Dahl, J., Wilson, K., & Luciano, C. (2005). *Acceptance and commitment therapy for chronic pain.* Reno, NV: Context Press.

Dahl, J., Wilson, K. G., & Nilsson, A. (2004). Acceptance and commitment therapy and the treatment of persons at risk for long-term disability resulting from sress and pain symptoms: A preliminary randomized trial. *Behaviour Therapy, 35,* 785-801.

DeGenova, M., Patton, D., Jurich, J., & MacDermid, S. (1994). Ways of coping among HIV-infected individuals. *Journal of Social Psychology, 134,* 655–663.

Diener, E., Emmons, R. A., Larsen, R. J., & Griffin, S. (1985). The Satisfaction With Life Scale. *Journal of Personality and Social Psychology, 49,* 71–75.

Dworkin, R. H., Turk, D. C., Farrar, J. T., Haythornthwaite, J. A., Jensen, M. P., Katz, N. P., et al. (2005). Core outcome measures for chronic pain clinical trials: IMMPACT recommendations. *Pain, 113,* 9–19.

Efron, R. (1956). Effect of olfactory stimuli in uncinate fits. *Brain, 79,* 267–281.

Engel, J. (1989). *Seizures and epilepsy.* Philadelphia: Davis Publishing Co.

Eriksson, T. (1940). Jacksonian march. *Archives of Neurology and Psychiatry, 43,* 429.

Fenwick, P. (1994). The behavioral treatment of epilepsy generation and inhibition of seizures. *Neurological Clinics, 12,* 175–202.

Flor, H., Fydrich, T., & Turk, D. C. (1992). Efficacy of multidisciplinary pain treatment centers: A meta-analytic review. *Pain, 149,* 221–230.

Forster, F., Ptacek, L., Peterson, W., Chun, R., & Bengzon, A. (1964). Stroboscopic-induced seizures altered by extinction techniques. *Transactions of the American Neurological Association, 89,* 136.

Geiser, D. (1992). A comparison of acceptance-focused and control-focused psychological treatments in a chronic pain treatment center. Unpublished doctoral dissertation, University of Nevada, Reno. *Dissertation Abstracts International*, B 54/02, 1096.

Gelhorn, E. (1947). Effects of afferent impulses on cortical suppression areas. *Journal of Neurophysiology*, *10*, 125–138.

Gowers, W. (1881). *Epilepsy and other chronic convulsive diseases*. London: J. & A. Churchill.

Guiterrez, O., Luciano, C., Rodríguez, M., & Fink, B. C. (2004). Comparison between an acceptance-based and a cognitive-control-based protocol for coping with pain. *Behavior Therapy*, *35*, 767–783.

Hayes, S. C., Barnes-Holmes, D., & Roche, B. (2001). *Relational frame theory: A post-Skinnerian account of human language and cognition*. New York: Kluwer

Hayes, S. C., Bissett, R., Korn, Z., Zettle, R. D., Rosenfarb, I., Cooper, L., & Grundt, A. (1999). The impact of acceptance versus control rationales on pain tolerance. *The Psychological Record*, *49*, 33–47.

Hayes, S., Bisset, R., Stroshal, K., Follette, W., Polusny, M., Pistorello, J., et al. (2002). Psychometric properties of the Acceptance and Action Questionnaire (AAQ). New York: Academic/Plenum Publishers.

Hayes, S. C., & Strosahl, K. D. (Eds.). (2005). *A practical guide to acceptance and commitment therapy*. New York: Springer-Verlag.

Hayes, S. C., Stroshal, K. D. & Wilson, K. G. (1999). *Acceptance and commitment therapy – An experiential approach to behaviour change*. New York: The Guilford Press.

Hides, J., Richardsson, C., & Jull, G. (1995) Magnetic resonance imaging and ultrasonography of the lumbar multifidus muscle: Comparison of two different modalities. *Spine*, *20*, 54–58.

Hides, J., Richardsson, C., & Jull, G. (1996) Multifidus muscle recovery is not automatic after resolution of acute, first-episode low back pain. *Spine*, *21*(23), 2763–2769.

Hides, J. Stokes, M, & Saide, M. (1994) Evidence of lumbar multifidus muscle wasting ipsilateral to symptoms in patients with acute/subacute low back pain. *Spine*, *19*, 165–172.

Jackson, J. H. (Ed.) (1931). *Selected writings on epilepsy and epileptiform convulsions*. London: Hodder and Stoughton.

Johnston, M. (2008). Acceptance and commitment therapy for chronic pain: An evaluation of the self-help book, *Living beyond your pain*. Unpublished thesis for the degree of Masters and Social Sciences of Psychology, The University of Waikato, New Zealand.

King, A., & Cavanaugh, J. (1996). Neurophysiologic basis of low back pain. In S. Wiesel, J., Weinstien, H. Herkowitz, J. Dvorak, & G. Bell (Eds.), *The lumbar spine* (2nd ed., pp, 74–85) Philadelphia: Saunders.

Lantz, D., & Sterman, M. (1988). Neuropsychological assessment of subjects with uncontrolled epilepsy: Effects of EEG feedback training. *Epilepsia*, 29, 163–171.

Leao, A. (1944a). Spreading depression of activity in the cerebral cortex. *Journal of Neurophysiology*, *7*, 359–390.

Leao, A. (1944b). Pial circulation and spreading depression of activity in cerebral cortex. *Journal of Neurophysiology*, *10*, 409–414.

Leao, A. (1947). Further observations on spreading depression of activity in cerebral cortex. *Journal of Neurophysiology*, *10*, 409–414.

Linton, S. (2000). *Psykologiska faktorers betydelse. In Ont I ryggen, ont I nacken* [The Swedish Council on Technology Assessment in Health Care] (Vol. 1, pp. 117–155). Stockholm, Sweden: The Swedish Council on Technology Assessment in Health Care.

Lockard, J. S., & Ward, A. (1980). (Eds.). *Epilepsy: A window to brain mechanism*s. New York: Raven Press.

Loring, D., & Meador, K. (2001). Cognitive and behavioral effects of epilepsy treatment, *Epilepsia, 42*, (Suppl. 8), 24–32.

Lundgren, T., Dahl, J., & Hayes, S. (2008) Evaluation of mediators of change in the treatment of epilepsy with acceptance and commitment therapy. *Journal of Behavior Medicine, 31*(3), 225–235.

Lundgren, T., Dahl, J., Melin, L., & Kies, B. (2006). Evaluation of acceptance and commitment therapy for drug refractory epilepsy: A RCT trial in South Africa.— A pilot study. *Epilepsia, 47*(12), 2173–2179.

Lundgren, T., Dahl, J., Yardi, N., & Melin, L. (2008). Acceptance and commitment therapy and yoga for drug refractory epilepsy: A randomized controlled trial. *Epilepsy and Behavior, 13*(1), 102–108.

McCracken, L. M. (1998). Learning to live with pain: Acceptance of pain predicts adjustment in persons with chronic pain. *Pain, 74*, 21–27.

McCracken, L. M., Carson, J. W., & Eccleston, C. (2003). Coping or acceptance: What to do about chronic pain. *Pain, 105*, 197–204.

McCracken, L. M., Vowles, K. E., & Eccleston, C. (2005). Acceptance-based treatment for persons with complex, longstanding, chronic pain: A preliminary analysis of treatment outcome in comparison to a waiting phase. *Behaviour Research and Therapy, 43*, 1335–1346.

McCulloch, W. (1949). Mechanism for the spread of epileptic activation of the brain. *Electroencephalography and Clinical Neurophysiology, 1*, 19–27.

Moser, A. E., & Annis, H. M. (1996). The role of coping in relapse crisis outcome: A prospective study of treated alcoholics. *Addiction, 91*, 1101–1114.

Nachemson, A., & Waddell, H.(2000). Prevalence of pain in neck and low back. In *Pain in back, pain in neck* (pp. 311–389). Stockholm: SBU.

Ogden, J. (1997) The rhetoric and reality of psychosocial theories of health. *Journal of Health Psychology, 2*, 21–29.

Papageorgiou, A. C., Macfarlane, G. J., Thomas, E., Croft, P. R., Jayson, M. I. V., & Silman, A. J. (1997). Psychosocial factors in the workplace — Do they predict new episodes of low back pain? Evidence from the south Manchester back pain study. *Spine, 22*, 1137–1142.

Polusny, M., & Follette, V. (1995). Long-term correlates of child sexual abuse: Theory and review of the empirical litterature. *Applied and Preventive Psychology, 4*, 143–166.

Purdon, C. (1999). Thought suppression and psychopathology. *Behavior Research and Therapy, 37*, 1029–1054.

Pushkarich, C., Whitman, S., Dell, J., Hughes, J., Rosen, A., & Hermann, B. (1992). Controlled examination of effects of progressive relaxation training on seizure reduction. *Epilepsia, 3*(4), 675–680.

Ramaratnam, S., & Sridharan, K. (1999). *Yoga for epilepsy.* Cochrane Database of Systematic Reviews 1999, Issue 2. Art. No.: CD001524. DOI: 10.1002/14651858. CD001524.

Rasp, H. (1993) Back pain. In A. Silman & M. C. Hoch (Eds.), *Epidemiology of the rheumatic diseases* (pp. 330–374). Oxford: Oxford University Press.

Rockstroh, B., Birbaumer, N., Elbert, T., & Lutsenberger, W. (1984). Operant control of EEG, event related and slow potentials. *Biofeedback & Self Regulation, 9,* 139–160.

Rodin, E. (1968). *The prognosis of patients with epilepsy.* Springfield, ILL: Charles C. Thomas.

Ross, E. (1994). Childhood epilepsies: A measure of concern, *Seizure, 3,* (Suppl. A), 5–9.

Skekelle, P. (1997) The epidemiology of low back pain. In L. Giles & K. Singer (Eds.), *Clinical anatomy and mangement of low back pain* (pp. 18–34). Boston: Butterworth, Heinemann.

Skovron, M. L., Szpalski, M., Nordin, M., Melot, C., & Cukier, D. (1994). Sociocultural factors and back pain: A population-based study in Belgian adults. *Spine, 19,* 129–137.

Spector, S. Goldstein, L., Cull, C., & Fenwick, P. (1994). *Precipitating and inhibiting epileptic seizures: A survey of adults with poorly controlled epilepsy.* London: International League against Epilepsy.

Sterman, M. (1993). Sensiorimotor EEG feedback training in the study and treatment of epilepsy. In D.I. Mostofsky & Y. Loyning (Eds.), *The neurobehavioral treatment of epilepsy.* Hillsdale, NJ: Lawrence Erlbaum.

Tan, S., & Bruni, J. (1986). Cognitive-behavior therapy with adult patients with epilepsy: A controlled outcome study. *Epilepsia, 27,* 255–263.

Taylor, H., & Curran, N. (1985). *The Nuprin pain report.* New York: Louis Harns and Associates.

Temkin, O. (1945). *The falling illness.* Baltimore, MA: The Johns Hopkins Press.

Waddell, G,. & Norlund, A. (2000). System for health insurance: An international comparison. In *Pain in back, pain in neck,* (pp. 311–389). Stockholm: SBU.

Walsh, K., Cruddas, M., & Coggon, D. (1992). Low back pain in eight areas of Britain. *Journal of Epidiology and Community Health, 46,* 227–230.

Wegner, D., Schneider, D., Knutson, B., & McMahon, S. (1991). Polluting the stream of consciousness: The effect of thought suppression on the mind's environment. *Cognitive Therapy and Research, 15,* 141–152.

Wolf, P. (2005). From precipitation to inhibition of seizures: rationale of a therapeutic paradigm. *Epilepsia, 46,* (Suppl. 1), 15–6.

World Health Organization. (1996). WHOQOL-BREF *Introduction, Administration and Generic Version of the Assesment. Programme on Mental Health.* Geneva: Author.

Zlutnick, S., Mayville, W., & Moffat, S. (1975). Behavioral control of seizure behavior of seizure disorder. In R.C. Katz & Zlutnick (Eds.), *Behavior therapy and health care* (pp. 317–336). New York: Pergamon Press.

chapter six

ACT With Depression: The Role of Forgiving

Robert D. Zettle, Stacy L. Barner and Suzanne Gird

Issues of forgiveness are likely to have been part of the fabric of human interpersonal relationships ever since the evolution of language by *homo sapiens*. The ability to derive arbitrary relationships among events as one of the defining properties of language (Hayes, Barnes-Holmes, & Roche, 2001) created the capacity to evaluate our interpersonal interactions along a number of qualitative dimensions, such as those encompassing justice, fairness and equality. Reviewing how we had been wronged by others ensured that we would not 'forgive and forget' and thereby possibly prevented further mistreatment, but at the cost of prolonging the emotional pain that comes with interpersonal transgressions.

This chapter is about how human suffering that is linked to issues of forgiveness may be alleviated in conducting acceptance and commitment therapy (ACT; Hayes, Strosahl, & Wilson, 1999) with clients who struggle with depression. We are not suggesting, nor do we wish to suggest, that struggles with forgiveness are unique to depression, or that ACT is the only approach for possibly alleviating such difficulties. Indeed, as we will discuss, religious and other psychotherapeutic approaches to forgiveness have predated ACT. Nor do we wish to imply that withholding forgiveness or continuing to 'hold a grudge' is inevitably dysfunctional. As with any behavior, it is most useful to evaluate such actions by their impact upon psychological flexibility and the capacity of clients to lead full and valued lives. We have, however, been struck by how often depressed clients appear to be stuck in life when fused with reports of victimization and mistreatment by significant figures within the life stories they tell.

We have also noted the favorable response from other mental health professionals during ACT workshops on depression when we have discussed how to address issues with traumatized clients. This chapter is informed by our own work in this area, as well as suggestions and insights offered by workshop attendees who have shared their related clinical experiences. As such, it encompasses one set of practical suggestions and guidelines from an ACT perspective for responding to depressed clients for whom forgiveness is a central issue, and supplements previous coverage this topic has already received within the ACT literature.

Forgiveness as a form of willingness first received some explicit, albeit limited, discussion in the original ACT book (Hayes et al., 1999, pp. 257–258). Strosahl (2004, pp. 240–241) subsequently extended this approach to the clinical management of multi-problem clients, and Walser and Westrup (2007, pp. 170–174) to the reduction of trauma-related suffering. While Zettle (2007, pp. 213–216) more recently addressed forgiveness issues as they specifically relate to ACT with depression, this chapter both expands upon this coverage and provides a broader context within which to situate this work. In particular, we will first discuss various ways in which forgiveness itself may be conceptualized. Next, we will consider how forgiveness has more specifically and typically been regarded within several major religious traditions and review how psychotherapeutic approaches, in general, and those from a cognitive–behavioral perspective, in particular, have addressed forgiveness before concluding with a presentation of the unique way that ACT seeks to promote it. Apart from a consideration of self-forgiveness from an acceptance and commitment perspective, our primary focus will be upon forgiveness that may be offered by those who have been transgressed against. A discussion of the array of unique and intriguing issues involved when the offending party is the one seeking forgiveness from those who have been wronged is, unfortunately, beyond the scope of this chapter.

Conceptualization of Forgiveness

Even a cursory review of the forgiveness literature reveals a lack of consensus about how to conceptualize it. While most dictionary definitions include synonyms such as 'excuse' or 'pardon', many contemporary authors (e.g., McCullough, Pargament, & Thoresen, 2000) specifically exclude these terms in their exploration of what forgiveness is *not*. From a philosophical perspective, the following 'ingredients' have been suggested as being necessary for forgiveness: (a) a moral agency is invoked, (b) a 'real' (as opposed to perceived or imagined) wrong must have occurred, (c) negative feelings, that are a result of the harm, must be present, and (d) an effortful attitudinal change must be accomplished (Yandell, 1998).

In their recent review of the forgiveness literature, Legaree, Turner and Lollis (2007) found that a common thread in the disparate conceptualizations of forgiveness is the cessation of feelings of resentment toward another person who has inflicted harm. However, according to North (1998) — and echoed by Enright, Freedman and Rique (1998) — the mere eradication of resentment or anger is not sufficient to constitute 'forgiveness' because the former process lacks the moral quality of bestowing an undeserved gift to the offender.

In the original ACT book (Hayes et al., 1999) an etymological definition of forgiveness is offered. Viewing 'forgive' as a compound word, the authors suggest that the first part of the word conveys the sense of 'before', while the second part means 'to give'. Thus, to forgive is to 'give what went before'. Similarly, Recine, Werner and Recine (2007) offer a linguistic definition that links the first part of 'forgiveness' to a sense of 'away'. Hence to forgive is to 'give away'. While both of these etymologies are based on 'forgive' being a result of compounding, Ayto (1990) defines the term as a calque, in which the literal translation of the separate parts of a foreign compound word are recombined into a new word. According to this source, then, the compound parts of 'forgive' convey a sense of 'giving wholeheartedly'. A combination of these etymologies, 'giving wholeheartedly that which came before', underscores the ACT view of forgiving as a form of willingness and committed action.

Religious Approaches to Forgiveness

Forgiveness is a central concept within major world religions. In this section, we summarize the findings of a survey conducted by Rye and colleagues (2000) of scholars from a variety of religious traditions.

Judaism

In Judaism, forgiveness is defined as the total expunging of an offense or debt, and is largely contingent on the offender performing the process of *teshuvah*, or return. This involves eight clearly defined steps, two of which include public acknowledgement of the offense and a promise that the transgression will not be repeated. Forgiveness is a required response of the victim, both as a matter of theology and of law; failing to forgive after return has been performed casts the original victim as a transgressor. While forgiveness may be offered as a matter of expediency without *teshuvah* having been performed by the transgressor, freely offered forgiveness is discouraged, as this may imply that the transgressor is free to commit the same offense without fear of consequence. Receiving God's forgiveness on the high holy day *Yom Kippur*, the Day of Atonement, is contingent on petitioners having been forgiven by those they have wronged. Reconciliation is a separate process from forgiveness and, while encouraged, may be denied even if forgiveness is given, or may be offered even if forgiveness is not. The overarching theological basis for forgiveness is the all-forgiving nature of God that humans are charged to imitate.

Islam
In Islam, forgiveness refers to 'closing an account of offense against God or any of his creation' (Rye et al., 2000, p. 21) with sincerity. Repentance is encouraged, though not required, of the offender; however, one must repent in order to be forgiven by Allah. Revenge is permitted in equal measure to the offense, but as it is sometimes easy to ask for recompense in excess of the damage, engaging in forgiveness protects the victim from becoming the transgressor. Similar to Judaism, Islam teaches that forgiveness ultimately comes from God, and that those who seek forgiveness must be willing to bestow it on others.

Hinduism and Buddhism
Both Hinduism and Buddhism draw from a number of different traditions. Hinduism, like the Abrahamic religions, has exemplars of forgiveness in the acts of various divinities. Additionally, those who wish to follow the path of *dharma* (righteousness) must engage in moral practices such as compassion, duty, patience and forgiveness. In both theistic and nontheistic Hindu traditions, *karma*, the natural law of cause and effect, ensures that contingencies of actions in life must be faced in future reincarnations. As a nontheistic tradition, Buddhism teaches that if one is wronged and holds onto resentment or hatred, that person is likely to be hated by others in the future, through the law of karma. Buddhism has no concept directly analogous to 'forgiveness', but it is contained within the twin virtues of forbearance and compassion. From the Buddhist perspective, forbearance involves both enduring a wrong and the renouncement of resentment. Compassion involves an attitudinal shift wherein a transgressor is viewed as the one who is suffering, and a consequential effort to ease the suffering of the other. By practicing forbearance, one seeks to keep from causing additional suffering, to oneself or to another.

Christianity
Forgiveness is at the heart of Christianity. References to forgiveness pervade the Gospels, and some of the most recognizable Biblical quotes and stories extol forgiveness and its related concepts of mercy and compassion. Jesus entreats God to forgive his crucifiers from the cross. In the Lord's Prayer, God is asked to 'forgive us our debts, as we forgive our debtors'. Ultimately, Jesus was born and died to forgive the sins of all who are willing to accept this fact. God offered this gift, not because humans are 'deserving' by virtue

of their acts, but because of his own compassion for humankind. As is the case in other theistic traditions, God is the exemplar of forgiveness, and humans strive to emulate this model.

Psychotherapeutic Approaches to Forgiveness

As McCullough, Pargament and Thoresen (2000) discuss, the concept of forgiveness has been largely ignored within psychotherapy until recently, even by major theorists in the field. According to them, some modest attention to the concept was paid between 1932 and 1980 in the fields of social and developmental psychology and in the work of Milton Rokeach (1973) investigating human values. During this same period, forgiveness was addressed in a counseling context primarily by pastoral counselors or other professionals acting from a religious perspective. In the period since 1980, counseling and clinical psychologists have followed the lead of earlier pastoral counseling traditions in examining forgiveness as a potential path toward increased mental health.

In essays drawn from personal and case experiences, Brandsma (1982), Hope (1987), and Pingleton (1989) suggest forgiveness as a psychotherapeutic goal, using a psychodynamic model and tying forgiveness to Christian theology. These authors speak to the debilitating effects of resentment and anger and the healing effects of forgiveness. Hope frames a state of unforgiveness in psychodynamic terms which evokes a sense of karma: '... if persons condemn others, they may be expected to have a harsh and punitive superego monitoring their own behavior' (p. 242). These authors also address both the interpersonal and intrapersonal aspects of forgiveness, giving equal weight to forgiveness of others and self. Pingleton proposed a tripartite model designed to demonstrate an integration of the theological and psychological aspects of forgiveness: '... (a) forgiveness can only be received from God if given by others, (b) forgiveness can only be given to others if received from self, and (c) forgiveness can only be given to self if received from God' (pp. 33–34).

Denton and Martin (1998) surveyed clinicians to determine if professionals who were regularly engaged in the process of treating clients agreed with a specific definition of forgiveness. The authors operationally defined forgiveness as:

> ... involving two people, one of whom has received a deep and long-lasting injury that is either psychological, emotional, physical, or moral in nature; as an inner process by which the person who has been injured is released from the anger, resentment, and fear and does not wish for revenge; as slow in coming; and as not necessarily eradicating all the painful memories. (p. 284)

While at least 80% of their respondents agreed with four of these six criteria, one-half of the sample disagreed with or were neutral regarding the interpersonal requirement (i.e., 'involving two people'), and a majority of respondents either disagreed with or were neutral regarding the nature of the offense (long-lasting, psychological, and so on). Similarly, Konstam et al. (2000) found that a majority of practitioners also did not emphasize the interpersonal aspects of forgiveness, and concluded that this majority appears 'to view forgiveness as a gift primarily to the self alone, in contrast to a gift to the offending person as well as the self' (p. 265).

The above findings are in contrast to the conceptualization of forgiveness by North (1998) and Enright, Freedman and Rique (1998). According to North, 'Forgiveness is not something that we do for ourselves alone, but something that we give or offer to another. The forgiving response is outward-looking and other-directed ...' (p. 19). Enright and colleagues also argue that 'the essential quality of forgiveness' is lost if 'the response of goodness toward the offending person' is eliminated (p. 50). Moreover, according to these authors, '... equating forgiveness with a generalized acceptance brings the construct away from the moral qualities of generosity and/or moral love' (p. 51).

Kaminer, Stein, Mbanga and Zungu-Dirwayi (2000) identified several models of forgiveness based on prominent personality and psychopathology theories, including psychoanalytic, Jungian, object relations and existential approaches. Similarly, in their review of the forgiveness literature from 1990–2005, Lagaree et al. (2007) concluded that a number of prominent authors evidently adopted assumptions from psychodynamic theory supporting the conceptualization of forgiveness as a 'discovery' that occurs over time. The primary component in these therapies is a commitment to 'working through' emotional difficulties that are a result of past hurts. Forgiveness, which can be construed as an emotional state, consequently can emerge within the therapeutic environment, even if not suggested or directed by the therapist.

However, Lagaree and colleagues (2007) found that the majority of authors stress a position of intentionality in the forgiveness process. Intentionality is most often described as a cognitive change or shift. Lagaree et al. place the position of DiBlasio (2000) clearly at the 'decision' end of their 'intentionality' continuum, and cite his '... transparent ... alignment with cognitive–behavioral theory' (p. 202). Enright et al. (1998) state that their model has elements of 'Freudian, psychodynamic, Eriksonian, cognitive developmental, [and] behavioristic' theories (p. 57). However, Yandell (1998) casts Enright et al. (1998) squarely in a cognitively oriented camp:

> The cognitively oriented psychologies will be concerned with the need for forgiveness of real, as opposed to imaginary, wrongs, and this will require a thorough examination of the beliefs and assumptions the victim holds about

his or her attacker. Any theory of forgiveness that emphasizes 'reframing' on the part of the victim, as the Enright-North view does, is obviously cognitively oriented. (p. 39)

Cognitive–Behavioral Approaches to Forgiveness

Cognitive–behavioral approaches to psychotherapy propose that distorted thoughts lead to unhealthy negative emotional states (Burns, 1999). According to this perspective, clients must identify and challenge these cognitive distortions and develop more positive, realistic thought patterns in order to alleviate negative emotional states, including depression and resentment. For our purposes, we define a cognitive–behavioral approach to forgiveness as one that seeks to reduce negative thoughts, feelings and behaviors toward offenders through the process of cognitive restructuring.

The current state of the cognitive–behavioral literature on forgiveness appears to be rather fragmentary and disconnected in nature. It appears as though several theorists — each of which we will discuss separately — have developed their own approach to forgiveness, without attempting to build upon the work of others. Although four prominent cognitive–behavioral approaches to forgiveness have been developed within the past decade (DiBlasio, 2000; Enright & Fitzgibbons, 2000; Gordon & Baucom, 1998; Wade & Worthington, 2005), these models contain many different steps through which clients must progress in order to attain forgiveness.

At the same time, there are also several common elements among these approaches. For instance, all suggest that clients must make a cognitive decision to forgive the offender in order for feelings of injury and betrayal to be resolved. In order to resolve negative feelings toward the transgressor and decrease the desire for revenge, the client is encouraged to give the transgression some type of meaning. This may involve exploring aspects of the relationship with the offender, and a consideration of environmental stressors and the life history of the offender in order to gain a better understanding of why the transgression occurred. This process is thought to result in an increase in empathy and compassion for the offender. Following this increase in positive emotions, the client is then encouraged to reconcile with the offender when it is safe and reasonable to do so.

Worthington and Wade's Emotional Dissonance Model

Similar to the approaches of Brandsma (1982), Hope (1987) and Pingleton (1989), Worthington and Wade (1999) define unforgiveness as the negative emotional state that occurs when an offended individual experiences bitterness and anger toward a transgressor. The transgression in question must be an objective event that external observers would agree inflicts psychological or physical pain or injury on the client. Forgiveness is regarded as an emotional process in which an individual chooses to abandon unforgiveness and seeks to reconcile with the offender when it is safe and possible to do so. By choosing to forgive, the individual begins to experience empathy, love and other positive emotions that compete with the cold emotional state associated with unforgiveness. Therefore, choosing to forgive the transgressor is one way in which an individual may transform feelings of unforgiveness to those of forgiveness.

For example, in marital infidelity, the first step toward forgiveness would be to encourage the offended partner to experience events or thoughts that are incongruent with unforgiveness. This may involve requesting that the offender provide the offended partner with a reasonable explanation for the infidelity (e.g., dissatisfaction with the relationship), sharing of good memories, or expressing love toward the offended partner (e.g., 'We've shared many good memories. We can work through this obstacle in order to rebuild our relationship').

The incongruence between the cold affective state associated with unforgiveness and positive thoughts toward the unfaithful partner produce a state referred to by Worthington and Wade (1999) as emotional dissonance. Emotional dissonance can then be resolved by rejecting or accepting the positive emotional state produced by positive thoughts about the unfaithful partner. Clients may choose to accept the positive affect by changing their perceptions of the transgression. For example, the offended partner can explore and gain a better understanding of why the offender decided to have an affair. Alternatively, clients may choose to reject the positive affect by ruminating about the original pain produced by the unfaithful act. For instance, the client may choose to hold onto anger, resentment and bitterness toward the offender (e.g., 'I'll never be able to trust my partner again. He ruined my life!'). The former would allow the client to move away from unforgiveness and toward forgiveness. The latter would be resolved by moving back toward unforgiveness.

DiBlasio's Decisional Model

DiBlasio (2000) conceptualizes forgiveness as a decision-based process in which an individual makes a cognitive decision to let go of negative emotional states (e.g., anger, bitterness, resentment) associated with a perceived transgression. Once clients decide to forgive, they take steps to move forward, despite feelings of hurt. This model involves a step-by-step process in which clients make a decision to forgive the transgressor, identify with the offender's hurt and engage in a ceremonial act that represents the forgiveness of the offender.

In the example of marital infidelity, the first step toward forgiveness would involve defining forgiveness and identifying some of the key components within the process, explaining that forgiveness is a decision to let go of the negative emotional state associated with the transgression. The therapist also explains that it is possible to have emotional pain while controlling negative thoughts (e.g., thoughts of revenge) and that forgiveness can lead to positive emotional states. In the second step of the decision-based model, both partners have an opportunity to seek forgiveness for any actions for which they wish to be forgiven.

Once the couple has moved through the first two stages, the forgiveness intervention is introduced. Both partners take turns working through the forgiveness intervention separately. Each states the offense for which they are asking forgiveness and provides an explanation for the transgression. Subsequent to the explanation, the nonparticipating partner is allowed an opportunity to raise questions about the offense. The therapist helps the couple discern which details are appropriate and helpful and which details may be harmful. Next, the offended partner gives emotional reactions to the transgression by expressing hurt, anger, anguish and other emotional reactions to the offending partner. After the offended partner has had an opportunity to express the emotions associated with the affair, the offender provides empathy for the hurt caused to the victim and develops a plan to stop or prevent the harmful behavior.

In the next step of the forgiveness process, the offended partner identifies with the offender's hurt. Then, emphasis is placed on the choice of letting go of the negative emotional state associated with ruminating about the transgression. In this step, the client can choose to forgive or not to forgive. In the subsequent step, the offender makes a formal request for forgiveness. According to DiBlasio, the offender must extend a request for forgiveness before the offense can be forgiven. Once each partner has gone through the forgiveness process, a ceremonial act occurs as an expression that the offense has been forgiven. For instance, in the case of marital infidelity, a couple may choose to renew their vows as a ceremonial act.

Gordon and Baucom's Synthesized Model

According to Gordon and Baucom (1998), forgiveness consists of three components: (a) a realistic view of the relationship, (b) a release from negative affect toward the offender, and (c) a decreased desire to punish the offender. Forgiveness is conceptualized as a step-by-step process in which clients recognize and assess the need to forgive, begin to understand why the event happened and eventually attain a decrease in distorted cognitions about themselves and the offender.

In instances of marital infidelity, the first step toward forgiveness is to recognize and assess the need to forgive the unfaithful partner. Once clients become aware of the transgression, they feel that the unfaithful partner has treated them in an unjust manner and that such a violation may occur again in the future. This leads to uncertainty, confusion and negative cognitions about their partners (e.g., 'My partner is not capable of fidelity' or 'My partner was unfaithful because he is selfish'), as clients may not be able to predict the occurrence of future unfaithful actions or other transgressions.

Within this stage of therapy, the therapist explains the process of recovery and that it may take as long as necessary for clients to change their assumptions about the offense and their relationship with their partner. The therapist also allows offended partners to express the impact of the infidelity on themselves and their views of the relationship, with a main goal of helping the couple solve current problems and set boundaries on 'lashing-out' behaviors and interrogations about the infidelity.

The second step involves giving the infidelity some type of meaning and helping the client realize why the infidelity occurred. The therapist helps clients explore several factors surrounding the infidelity, including relationship issues, outside influences, and the life histories of both partners in order to challenge the initial attributions made toward offenders during the first stage of the forgiveness process. Recognizing the role that various factors may have played in the infidelity does not excuse the offending partner, but offers clients important information about the context in which the offense occurred, and thus helps reduce negative affect.

The client is also allowed to express anger and other negative emotions toward the offending partner in order to legitimize such emotional states. During this stage, an apology is often necessary in order to promote healing by giving clients a sense of power over their partners. The couple is encouraged to think about ways in which their behaviors may be contributing to or hindering the process of forgiveness. For example, clients may be punishing their partners by waiting for an opportunity to engage in an action that may 'pay them back' by offending them. Alternatively, the couple may choose to focus on behaviors that may be beneficial to the relationship, such as ending the likelihood that the unfaithful partner will have contact with the other participant in the affair.

In the final step of successful therapy, clients achieve a decrease in cognitive distortions surrounding themselves, their partners and their relationship. Through cognitive restructuring, clients experience a reduction in anger and desire to punish their partners. Clients are encouraged to view their partners as individuals with both positive and negative qualities, rather than continually seeking information that would justify withholding trust. Additionally, clients are encouraged to create realistic expectations and assumptions about the behavior of their partner, rather than idealizing them or the relationship. This new understanding of the unfaithful partner allows clients to reduce their anger regarding the unfaithful act and minimizes the likelihood of retaliatory actions. At this point, the couple must decide whether to recommit to their relationship based on a more rational, realistic understanding of it formulated throughout the process of forgiveness. The partners can decide to terminate the relationship and still gain the beneficial effects received through the process of forgiveness.

Enright and Fitzgibbons' Phasic Model

Enright and Fitzgibbons (2000) define forgiveness as a process in which clients relinquish resentment and replace associated, negative emotional states with compassion and generosity. Throughout the forgiveness therapy process, both the clients and therapist examine the ways in which they were treated unfairly to help clients understand the offender and learn how to replace anger with a positive response of goodness toward the transgressor. This model involves a step-by-step process in which clients become aware of their pain (uncovering phase), decide to forgive the offender (decision phase), shift their view of the offender (work phase) and notice any personal benefits that result from the forgiveness process (outcome phase).

In cases of marital infidelity, the therapist in the uncovering phase helps clients better understand how the affair has impacted their psychological health. Throughout this phase, clients are encouraged to explore negative emotional states associated with the infidelity. For instance, clients are encouraged to confront and release anger rather than harboring it. Clients are also encouraged to become aware of the amount of time that is spent ruminating over the infidelity by asking them to keep a journal in which they note each time they think about the offender.

In the uncovering phase, clients also become aware of ways in which their world view has changed. Before the infidelity, clients likely saw the world as a place in which others attempt to act fairly. However, following the pain associated with the affair, their world view often changes to where they now believe that others are not to be trusted. The therapist may ask clients how their world view has changed because of the infidelity.

In the decision phase, clients are asked to judge how well they are coping with the current situation. By analyzing patterns uncovered in the previous phase, most clients begin to see that the ways in which they are responding to the infidelity are not working and that changes must be made. At this point, clients are given the opportunity to choose or reject forgiveness as an alternative way in which to respond to the infidelity.

In the work phase, the therapist asks clients questions designed to challenge views of their partner. For example, to attain 'cognitive insight', the therapist might instruct clients to examine their partner's childhood and the events surrounding the infidelity. After doing so, clients are asked to examine the emergence of empathy and compassion for the offender. If they are unable to express empathy for their partner, the therapeutic process moves back to the cognitive insight stage and further cognitive restructuring is attempted.

Enright and Fitzgibbons (2000) note that compassion appears to emerge as part of the forgiveness process, and no particular exercises or techniques are used in this stage to foster its development. Clients are asked to bear the pain as a part of their life history prior to seeking justice in ways other than those that may occur when they are angry or upset. The next step in the process involves giving a 'gift' to the unfaithful partner, such as preparing a nice meal as an extension of beneficence.

In the outcome phase, the first step is to give the suffering some type of meaning. In doing this, the therapist may ask clients what good might come from suffering or whether the suffering might benefit others. Clients are also encouraged to think about a time they wronged another person and if forgiveness was offered. This helps clients understand the process of forgiveness from another's point of view and allows them to let go of the idea that it is wrong to forgive their partner.

Forgiveness as the Acceptance and Commitment Therapist Views It

Unlike other perspectives on the matter, forgiveness within ACT is critically regarded as a behavior rather than as an affective state, emotional condition or array of thoughts and feelings. In this respect, the gerund 'forgiving' rather than 'forgiveness' is a more useful way of speaking. Forgiveness is not viewed as a noun or thing that is felt or passively experienced, but as an act of willingness and commitment that is freely chosen. As such, forgiving is under the control and choice of depressed clients, while the resentment, desire for vengeance, memory of how they have been 'wronged' and related private events that serve as barriers to forgiveness of others are not. Forgiving is not dependent upon forgetting a wrong that has been inflicted, as failing to remember a transgression would render forgiveness of it moot. Moreover, forgiving can be freely chosen, even if the client does not feel like offering it or believe that it is warranted or deserved.

Forgiving, like many behaviors, is not a single one-time event, but can occur to varying degrees in a gradual step-like fashion. This does not mean, however, that forgiving inevitably unfolds within a fluid process. It may be offered on one occasion, only to be withheld later. This applies to both types of forgiving that we will now consider in greater detail — that which involves relationships with others and that which also entails self-forgiveness.

Forgiving Others

Certainly, not all depressed clients will display nonforgiveness of others to a level that requires that it be addressed in therapy. The first indication that it may be an issue usually comes in listening to the life story of clients. We recommend that clients, fairly early on in ACT — often within the first session — relate their life story with depression. The purpose in doing so is not to take what the clients have to say literally, but instead to initially gauge the degree to which explanations offered for depression are held onto rigidly. Spontaneous client comments like 'Anyone who was mistreated as badly as I have been would be depressed', or 'I have every right to be depressed given how often I've been lied to' reveal a level of investment in and fusion with a verbal construction that is likely to be problematic.

Whether or not fusion with a traumatic life story is problematic ultimately depends upon the degree to which rigid attachment to such a narrative serves as a barrier to valued living. In essence, clients who are highly invested in an abused life story see themselves stuck in their own depression as an inevitable outcome of the mistreatment they have borne. Because time only moves in one direction and past events cannot be altered, living a valued life becomes permanently blocked by the solidified psychological distress that results from causally relating depression to transgressions at the hands of others. The extent to which fusion with an abused life story prevents valued living can be further assessed by asking the following hypothetical questions: 'If you had not been mistreated the way that you have, how would your life be different? What would your life look like and what might you be doing differently?'

Client answers may not only help gauge the degree of psychological rigidity surrounding the life story, but perhaps equally, if not more importantly, tell a great deal about what they value. This information can then be used as a focal point in organizing and directing the rest of therapy, in general, and any subsequent forgiveness work, in particular. For example, a client who indicates that she would have a more rewarding career can be asked if working towards this would be a worthy therapeutic goal and, if so, whether forgiving her transgressors would move her closer to or further away from it.

Rewriting the Life Story

One way of beginning to loosen the grip of the life story and thereby facilitate the process of forgiveness is to ask clients to reconstruct it. In doing so, ACT is similar to narrative therapy (White & Epston, 1990) in its view that changing their life story may have a liberating impact upon clients (Zimmerman & Dickerson, 1994). Before discussing in greater detail how to accomplish this objective, a few cautionary and advisory comments are in order. It is not uncommon for clients to feel threatened by the possibility that their life story could be anything other than what it is. Indeed, such client reactions are likely to occur in direct proportion with their degree of fusion with and attachment to the life narrative — questioning their story about depression is functionally equivalent to challenging their personal integrity. As a consequence, be sensitive to how clients may react to the suggestion to rewrite the life story and be prepared to respond to such reactions with further defusion and acceptance work if necessary. In particular, it is useful to emphasize the fact that a client was mistreated is not being called into question by a request to rewrite the life story. The critical issue is not what happened or did not happen in the past, but how whatever happened continues to impact the client in the present.

The potential costs and risks associated with encouraging clients to rewrite their life story are typically offset by the possible benefits that may be derived from doing so. One such instance was cited by Zettle (2007, p. 104) of a client who found it difficult to forgive herself for a failed marriage. Her initial life story presented her as being solely responsible for the divorce. When the client protested upon being asked to rewrite the story with a new conclusion that did not end in her depression, she was asked to approach it as a creative writer might. Her second narrative 'uncovered' new facts about how her husband's behavior now contributed to the divorce. Still, two more reconstructions of the narrative in which additional external, historical facts were incorporated into it were necessary to create enough defusion from the life story for the client to forgive herself and begin to move her life in a valued direction.

The rewriting of the life story can occur within-session, though we recommend structuring it as a series of homework assignments. The first step asks clients to put their life story in writing so that facts within it can be underlined. Clients are then instructed to take those same facts and formulate a narrative with an alternative ending that does not culminate in depression. As seen in the case just summarized, it may be necessary to request that clients construct several versions of the life story to create sufficient separation from the original version. For some clients, rewriting the life story may be all that is needed to initiate and maintain forgiveness. For the majority of clients, however, the goal is to simply clear out enough psychological space for subsequent forgiveness work to gain some traction. This additional work can involve committed action, mindfulness and enhancing the contextual self (both which will be discussed later in this chapter within the context of self-forgiveness), and the defusion and acceptance of further experiential barriers to forgiveness.

Forgiving as Committed Action

In our experience, most clients are not accustomed to seeing forgiving as a freely chosen action. Rather, it is more commonly viewed not as a change in overt behavior, but as an alteration in their judgment or evaluation of what happened to them. Moreover, forgiveness is commonly construed as something that is verbally offered, even if done so grudgingly, to the transgressor provided certain conditions are met. For example, many clients withhold forgiveness unless the transgressor apologizes for any wrongdoing and specifically requests forgiveness of it. Accordingly, it is usually necessary to assist clients in reframing forgiving as committed action if defusion from the life story is not sufficient to initiate it.

Explicitly framing forgiving as value-directed behavior underscores that it is undertaken for the benefit of the client and not for the perpetrator of the wrongdoing. As with any committed action within ACT, forgiveness itself is important only insofar as it moves the client's life in a valued direction. Some additional values identification and clarification may be necessary following the telling and rewriting of the life story if it is still unclear how a lack of client forgiveness may be sapping life of its vitality and helping to perpetuate depression. Both indirect means (Zettle, 2007, pp. 119–122) — such as the 'what do you want your life to stand for?' (Hayes et al., 1999, pp. 215–217) and epitaph exercises (Hayes et al, 1999, pp. 217–218) — as well as direct means, employing values questionnaires (Blackledge & Ciarrochi, 2005; Wilson & Groom, 2002), can be used in further clarifying client valuing.

As suggested earlier, the occurrence of forgiving as a committed action frequently unfolds in a discontinuous fashion. Forgiveness may be offered on one occasion, only to be later taken back. In addition, while forgiving happens in all-or-nothing fashion whenever it does occur, the amount of wrongdoing that it encompasses may vary from occasion to occasion. A useful metaphor within ACT is to liken forgiving as a form of committed action to jumping (Hayes et al., 1999, pp. 240–241). Like jumping, forgiving can not occur partially — a jump cannot occur 'just a little'. However, the height from which a jump is made can be freely chosen, just as clients can determine how much wrongdoing to encompass in a single act of forgiveness. A sequence of jumps that start out small, but graduate to greater heights, may be undertaken in attaining the goal of jumping from a predetermined terminal height; for example, jumping off a series of progressively higher diving boards may work up to taking a plunge off the high dive. Similarly, it may be useful with clients who have compiled a fairly extensive list of mistreatment to support forgiveness as a series of small, incremental steps where relatively minor transgressions are forgiven before major instances are targeted. For example, clients can be asked questions such as: 'Of all the wrongdoings that you say have been inflicted upon you, which ones would you like to forgive first? Which ones would be the easiest for you to forgive and which ones would be the most difficult for you?'

As is the case in supporting any committed action within ACT, it may be both necessary and useful to clarify with clients several other critical dimensions of forgiving. Of perhaps greatest importance is holding for-giveness as a choice that is freely made by clients for their benefit. Forgiving as committed action is made neither to nor for the therapist or the wrong-doer, but to and for the client who chooses it. If forgiving is not chosen, but is made as a decision, it remains impacted by thoughts and feelings that arose from the mistreatment — wanting revenge, feeling resentment, believing that the wrongdoer does not deserve to be forgiven and so on. It may also require potential actions on the part of the transgressor. For example, clients may claim that forgiveness cannot be offered unless the perpetrator apologizes, makes amends, displays remorse and asks for forgiveness. Such preconditions for forgiving are compounded even further if the whereabouts of transgressors are unknown or if they are deceased. Like any other committed action from the perspective of ACT, it is useful to regard forgiving as being freely chosen *with* reasons, rather than as an action that is decided upon *because of* reasons. We will have a bit more to say about how private events of the client that may function as barriers to/reasons against forgiving can be approached with additional defusion and acceptance work shortly.

Included among the reasons present when forgiveness is chosen can be the personal costs associated with fusion with the life story. It is useful to review with depressed clients two sets of costs that accrue with continuing to play the 'right versus wrong' game. One set of costs constitutes the 'pain of presence' (Hayes & Smith, 2005, p. 15) and includes the resentment, anger, depression and possible sense of betrayal and violation that clients have struggled with following their mistreatment by others. Another set of costs that may be even of relatively greater importance are those that come from the loss of life's vitality. Termed as the 'pain of absence' (Hayes & Smith, 2005, p. 15), such costs include how much valued living has already been compromised and sacrificed while clients remain mired in depression and stuck within the role of victim. In extreme instances, clients may even be willing to pay the ultimate cost with their own lives to validate their mistreatment and/or extract revenge from their transgressors. In effect, to prove that a grievous crime has been committed, clients produce their own corpse as the evidence (Hayes et al., 1999, p. 253; Zettle, 2007, p. 217). An accompanying and related motive may be revenge against transgressors, particularly if the suicide is carried out in such a way that they discover the body. In less dramatic instances, remaining chronically depressed may serve the same function. The client is not literally dead but has psychologically ceased to live.

The purpose in reviewing with depressed clients the personal costs they pay in withholding forgiveness is not to transform forgiving into a decision for which a persuasive list of supportive reasons can be compiled. Instead, doing so explicitly situates the act of choosing to forgive or not to forgive within the context of valuing. If anything, such a move makes it very clear to both you as the therapist and to your client what is at stake. It is nonetheless not unusual for clients at this point to comment that they will *try* to forgive as a means of shirking the response-ability of choosing. If and when this occurs, forgiving can again be likened to jumping. Trying to do either is not an option and neither requires any effort. Jumping is not hard to do and is merely what happens when we choose to put our body in a space where gravity does what it does. Likewise, the act of forgiving does not require strength, but rather willingness and commitment. Once it occurs, experiential gravity does the rest. The distinction between 'trying to forgive' and the act of forgiving can also be addressed further, if necessary, with a trying versus doing exercise (Zettle, 2007, p. 129) in which clients are asked to *try* to pick up an object such as a pen. Clients find that they can pick up the pen or let it lie, but that they cannot successfully *try* to pick it up, thus underscoring the words of Yoda: 'No! Try not. Do. Or do not. There is no try' (Yoda quotes, n.d.)

Enacting Forgiveness

There are at least two means that can be used within sessions through which clients can symbolically, or as Diblasio (2000) has termed it, 'ceremonially' enact forgiveness. Unfortunately, we know of no data attesting to their collective efficacy nor of any research that has directly compared their relative therapeutic benefits. The two procedures are accordingly being discussed and recommended primarily because they seem to make sense clinically and have been fairly useful in our experience. One is the empty-chair technique (originally borrowed from the Gestalt tradition, but described in an ACT context in Hayes et al., 1999, p. 257; Walser & Westrup, 2007, pp. 173–174; Zettle, 2007, p. 214) and the other letter-writing (Zettle, 2007, p. 214). Clients are able to offer forgiveness to their transgressors using both methods, without the perpetrators being present, having asked for forgiveness or having met any other preconditions for forgiveness on their part. One possible relative advantage to letter-writing is that it may be possible to send what has been composed to the wrong-doers still living and whose whereabouts are known. Regardless of which means of forgiveness enactment is used, its ultimate utility must be gauged by the impact they have in moving clients from being bogged down in depression to resuming an active and valued life.

Weakening Barriers to Forgiving: Acceptance and Defusion

Numerous thoughts, feelings, memories, bodily sensations, impulses and other psychological experiences related to having been victimized may stand in the way of forgiving. Especially when it comes to thinking about forgiveness and the events it may encompass, single thoughts as well as more complex networks of relational framing at a molar level, such as reason giving and the life story, can function as barriers to forgiving as committed action. We focus here on lessening further barriers to forgiving, such as specific thoughts, that occur at a more molecular level of experience.

The full range of defusion and acceptance techniques and procedures within ACT can be applied to supporting forgiving as an act of willingness. Because of obvious space limitations, our coverage of these tactics here will be limited to a few examples that share the strategic goal of establishing the conditions under which clients can learn the discrimination between responding to experiential barriers to forgiving in an avoidant versus accepting manner. We have found the 'tug-of-war with a monster' metaphor (Hayes et al., 1999, p. 109) and a variation on 'carrying your depression' exercise (Zettle, 2007, pp. 110–111) to be particularly useful in conducting this experiential discrimination training with clients stuck in unforgiveness.

Specific thoughts (e.g., 'What happened to me wasn't right', 'My offender doesn't deserve to be forgiven', and so on) and feelings (anger, resentment, betrayal, desire for revenge, and so on) can either be individually or collectively likened to a monster with which the client is engaged in a tug-of-war. If the client were to win the struggle, the emotional pain and psychological fallout from having been wronged could be eliminated forever as the monster is pulled into the abyss lying between it and the client. However, most clients will experientially acknowledge that they, rather than the monster, are being pulled ever closer to the bottomless pit. Many of these same clients, though, do not experientially realize that another way of responding to this struggle is to simply drop the rope. The discrimination between pulling on the rope versus dropping it can be magnified by enacting the metaphor physically between you and your clients. Produce a rope, towel, or belt that both of you can pull on. Ask the client to pull as hard as possible and to notice the difference between that experience and that of dropping the rope. Further, ask the client to consider the possibility that her struggle to forget or get over the hurt of having been wronged is like engaging in an unwinnable tug-of-war with a monster.

Because forgiving, as mentioned, is not a one-time event, it is quite common for clients to drop, pick up and pull on the rope numerous times. These occurrences can be viewed as constituting the multiple trials required for successful discrimination training. Each time a client appears to be experientially avoiding and/or escaping from private events related to an interpersonal transgression is an opportunity to ask him if he is, at that moment, in the process of pulling on the rope or dropping it.

It is useful to regard acceptance or willingness as not the mere absence of experiential avoidance. Accordingly, simply disengaging clients from experiential control exemplified by dropping the rope is not tantamount to accepting the 'unforgiveness monsters' against which they struggle. As alluded to earlier, we have found it useful in promoting acceptance and willingness to supplement the tug-of-war metaphor and exercise with a 'carrying' exercise. Unwanted thoughts, feelings, bodily sensations, impulses and other private events surrounding the transgression can be likened to a trash can that clients, because of their mistreatment, have no choice but to carry with them throughout the rest of their life. They are free, however, to choose how they carry it. In particular, we ask clients to first walk around carrying the trash can as far away from themselves as possible. They are then asked to walk similarly, but this time while cradling the trash can as they would cuddle a baby. The differing degrees of physical discomfort clients experience underscore the discrimination between the clean pain of acceptance versus the dirty pain of unwillingness.

Acceptance can also be facilitated by defusion from specific thoughts or beliefs that stand in the way of forgiving. We will only elaborate on two specific defusion methods here although, as mentioned earlier, the full array of defusion and acceptance strategies and techniques within ACT can be used in your work with unforgiving clients stuck in depression. One method is a variation on the 'Milk, milk, milk' exercise (Hayes et al., 1999, pp. 154–156). Clients can be asked to rapidly say aloud key words or phrases (such as 'unfair', 'backstabber' or 'liar') contained within thoughts about the transgression with which they remain fused.

A second defusion procedure uses an adaptation of the 'bad cup' metaphor (Hayes et al., 1999, p. 169; Zettle, 2007, pp. 100–101) to differentiate evaluations from descriptions. Unforgiving clients commonly hold their evaluation of what happened to them (e.g., 'It was wrong', 'It was unfair', 'I didn't deserve it', and so on) as psychologically equivalent to a description of the mistreatment ('My husband had an affair', 'I was lied to', 'My best friend betrayed me', and so on). For this reason, it is often useful to use additional discrimination training to magnify the distinction between the two. A physical object such as a cup or chair can be used as a referent in this process. Multiple examples of both evaluations (e.g., 'It's a good cup', 'That's an ugly chair') and descriptions (e.g., 'The cup is white', The chair is made of wood') can be offered and contrasted against each other before the same process is extended to client thoughts about their mistreatment and the offender.

Forgiving Oneself

Issues of forgiveness involving others and oneself are not mutually exclusive. Some depressed clients will struggle with both, while others may be solely blocked by unpardonable sins of omission or commission that have been committed against others or oneself. Still there are other clients for whom either form of forgiving is inconsequential. As with our coverage of forgiving others, we do not wish to imply that withholding forgiveness toward oneself is inevitably dysfunctional. This must be determined by assessing the degree to which guilt and not letting oneself 'off the hook' contribute to psychological rigidity and compromise valued living.

Three Senses of 'Self'

ACT has found it useful to speak of three different aspects of the self (Hayes et al., 1999, pp. 181–187; Zettle, 2007, pp. 68–70): (a) self as process, (b) self as concept, and (c) self as context. Briefly stated, self as process, or our ability to be aware of our ongoing stream of experience as it unfolds, is implicated in mindfulness and exercises that enhance it (Kabat-Zinn, 1994). Self as concept refers to a verbally constructed network about who we are (i.e., 'I am married', 'I cheated on my spouse', and so on), while self as context is that part of us that is aware of what we are aware of. Self as context can be regarded as the sense of 'I-ness', or what is referred to in ACT as the 'observer' or 'observing self' (Hayes et al., 1999, p. 184), that transcends experience.

The various strategies and techniques within ACT to promote forgiving of others that have already been discussed can also be extended to issues of self-forgiveness. In what follows we will discuss a few additional procedures that, while also applicable to forgiving others, appear to be particularly relevant in helping depressed clients free themselves from guilt. Specifically, exercises for enhancing mindfulness and the observer self can be used to further solidify self as context and differentiate it from the self as concept. Placing clients in contact with a transcendent and spiritual dimension of self (Hayes, 1984) may be useful, if not necessary, for them to freely choose to extend forgiveness to the transgressing conceptual self (Zettle, 2007).

Acquiring Mindfulness

Mindfulness has been defined as 'paying attention in a particular way: on purpose, in the present moment, nonjudgmentally' (Kabat-Zinn, 1994, p. 4). Mindfulness can be usefully regarded as a skill that can be experientially acquired and shaped by a series of exercises that initially focus on eating and drinking and progress to 'just noticing' depressing thoughts and other troublesome private events (Zettle, 2007). It is beyond the scope of this chapter to present any of these exercises that have been detailed by Kabat-Zinn and adapted into mindfulness and acceptance-based approaches to the prevention (Segal, Williams, & Teasdale, 2002; Williams, Teasdale, Segal, & Kabat-Zinn, 2007) and treatment of unipolar depression (Zettle, 2007). While the primary purpose of mindfulness training is to strengthen self as process, it also provides clients with the opportunity to observe their experiences from the same invariant perspective. In doing so, mindfulness exercises also indirectly promote self as context as the vantage point from which clients can forgive the conceptual self.

Enhancing Self as Context

The perspective of self as context can also be enhanced by the presentation of several exercises common to ACT more broadly. In particular, the chessboard metaphor (Hayes, 1987, pp. 359–360) and observer exercise (Hayes, 1987, pp. 360–361; Hayes et al., 1999, pp. 193–195) can be adapted to be somewhat more responsive to the experiences of clients who struggle with depression (Zettle, 2007, pp. 148–155). Due to space limitations, neither will be presented here; the interested reader is encouraged to consult the cited references. While these techniques can be introduced separately and independently of each other, our general recommendation is to precede their implementation with a series of mindfulness exercises. It also seems preferable to introduce the chessboard metaphor prior to the observer exercise if both are presented.

Summary and Conclusions

In this chapter we have presented one approach to addressing forgiveness with depressed clients that we believe is consistent with the model upon which ACT itself is based. As such, it is not the only approach as others that are also ACT-consistent are certainly also possible. Until further research is conducted, the approach and guidelines that we have presented here cannot be favored over other possible ACT-based alternatives based upon empirical guidelines. For that matter, what we have offered cannot be recommended on empirical grounds over other cognitive–behavioral, broader psychotherapeutic or even religious approaches to forgiveness.

In closing, we would also like to acknowledge that this chapter has not addressed instances in which asking for or seeking forgiveness by others may play a central role in liberating clients from depression. Further conceptual, clinical and empirical work is obviously needed if we are to make further progress in alleviating emotional suffering that is perpetuated by the withholding of forgiveness of others and/or oneself.

References

Ayto, J. (1990). *Dictionary of word origins*. New York: Arcard Publishing, Inc.

Blackledge, J. T., & Ciarrochi, J. (2005). *Initial validation of the Personal Values Questionnaire*. Unpublished manuscript, University of Wollongong, New South Wales, Australia.

Brandsma, J. M. (1982). Forgiveness: A dynamic, theological and therapeutic analysis. *Pastoral Psychology, 31,* 40–50.

Burns, D. D. (1999). *The feeling good handbook*. New York: Plume.

Denton, R. T., & Martin, M.W. (1998). Defining forgiveness: An empirical exploration of process and role. *The American Journal of Family Therapy, 26,* 281–292.

DiBlasio, F. A. (2000). Decision-based forgiveness treatment in cases of marital infidelity. *Psychotherapy: Theory, Research, Practice, Training, 37,* 149–158.

Enright, R. D., & Fitzgibbons, R. P. (2000). *Helping clients forgive: An empirical guide for resolving anger and restoring hope.* Washington, DC: American Psychological Association.

Enright, R. D., Freedman, S., & Rique, J. (1998). The psychology of interpersonal forgiveness. In R. D. Enright & J. North (Eds.), *Exploring forgiveness* (pp. 46–62). Madison: University of Wisconsin Press.

Gordon, K. C., & Baucom, D. H. (1998). Understanding betrayals in marriage: A synthesized model of forgiveness. *Family Process, 37,* 425–449.

Hayes, S. C. (1984). Making sense of spirituality. *Behaviorism, 12,* 99–110.

Hayes, S. C. (1987). A contextual approach to therapeutic change. In N. S. Jacobson (Ed.), *Psychotherapists in clinical practice: Cognitive and behavioral perspectives* (pp. 327–387). New York: Guilford.

Hayes, S. C., Barnes-Holmes, D., & Roche, B. (2001). *Relational frame theory: A post-Skinnerian account of human language and cognition.* New York: Plenum.

Hayes, S.C., & Smith, S. (2005). *Get out of your mind and into your life.* Oakland, CA: New Harbinger.

Hayes, S. C., Strosahl, K. D., & Wilson, K. G. (1999). *Acceptance and commitment therapy: An experiential approach to behavior change.* New York: Guilford.

Hope, D. (1987). The healing paradox of forgiveness. *Psychotherapy: Theory, Research, Practice, Training, 24,* 240–244.

Kabat-Zinn, J. (1994). *Wherever you go, there you are: Mindfulness meditation in everyday life.* New York: Hyperion.

Kaminer, D., Stein, D. J., Mbanga, I., & Zungu-Dirwayi, N. (2000). Forgiveness: Toward an integration of theoretical models. *Psychiatry: Interpersonal and Biological Processes, 63,* 344–357.

Konstam, V., Marx, F., Schurer, J., Harrington, A., Lombardo, N. E., & Deveney, S. (2000). Forgiving: What mental health counselors are telling us. *Journal of Mental Health Counseling, 22,* 253–267.

Lagaree, T., Turner, J., & Lollis, S. (2007). Forgiveness and therapy: A critical review of conceptualizations, practices, and values found in the literature. *Journal of Marital and Family Therapy, 33,* 192–213.

McCullough, M. E., Pargament, K. I., & Thoresen, C .E. (2000). The psychology of forgiveness: History, conceptual issues, and overview. In M. E. McCullough, K .I. Pargament, & C. E. Thoresen (Eds.), *Forgiveness: Theory, research, and practice* (pp. 1–16). New York: Guilford Press.

North, J. (1998). The 'ideal' of forgiveness: A philosopher's exploration. In R. D. Enright & J. North (Eds.), *Exploring forgiveness* (pp. 35–45). Madison: University of Wisconsin Press.

Pingleton, J. P. (1989). The role and function of forgiveness in the psychotherapeutic process. *Journal of Psychology and Theology, 17,* 27–35.

Recine, A. G., Werner, J. S., & Recine, L. (2007). Concept analysis of forgiveness with a multi-cultural emphasis. *Journal of Advanced Nursing, 59,* 308–316.

Rokeach, M. (1973). *The nature of human values.* New York: Free Press.

Rye, M. S., Pargament, K. I., Ali, M. A., Beck, G. L., Dorff, E. N., Hallisay, C., et al. (2000). Religious perspectives on forgiveness. In M. E. McCullough, K. I.

Pargament, & C .E. Thoresen (Eds.), *Forgiveness: Theory, research, and practice* (pp. 17–40). New York: Guilford.

Segal, Z. V., Williams, J. M. G., & Teasdale, J. D. (2002). *Mindfulness-based cognitive therapy for depression: A new approach to preventing relapse*. New York: Guilford.

Strosahl, K. D. (2004). ACT with the multi-problem patient. In S. C. Hayes & K. D. Strosahl (Eds.), *A practical guide to acceptance and commitment therapy* (pp. 209–245) New York: Springer.

Wade, N. G., & Worthington, E. L., Jr. (2005). In search of a common core: A content analysis of interventions to promote forgiveness. *Psychotherapy: Theory, Research, Practice, Training, 42*, 160–177.

Walser, R. D., & Westrup, D. (2007). *Acceptance and commitment therapy for the treatment of post-traumatic stress disorder and trauma-related problems: A practitioner's guide to using mindfulness and acceptance strategies*. Oakland, CA: New Harbinger.

White, M., & Epston, D. (1990). *Narrative means to therapeutic ends*. New York: W. W. Norton & Company.

Williams, M., Teasdale, J., Segal, Z., & Kabat-Zinn, J. (2007). *The mindful way through depression: Freeing yourself from chronic unhappiness*. New York: Guilford.

Wilson, K. G., & Groom, J. (2002). *The Valued Living Questionnaire*. Unpublished manuscript, University of Mississippi, Oxford.

Worthington, E. L., Jr., & Wade, N. G. (1999). The psychology of unforgiveness and forgiveness and implications for clinical practice. *Journal of Social and Clinical Psychology, 18*, 385–418.

Yandell, K. (1998). The metaphysics and morality of forgiveness. In R. D. Enright & J. North (Eds.), *Exploring forgiveness* (pp. 35–45). Madison: University of Wisconsin Press.

Yoda quotes. (n.d.). Retrieved October 6, 2006, from http://en.thinkexist.com/quotes/yoda/

Zettle, R. D. (2007). *ACT for depression: A clinician's guide to using acceptance and commitment therapy in treating depression*. Oakland, CA: New Harbinger.

Zimmerman, J. L., & Dickerson, V. C. (1994). Using a narrative metaphor: Implications for theory and clinical practice. *Family Process, 33*, 233–245.

chapter seven

Brief Group ACT for Anxiety

Natalie M. Glaser, John T. Blackledge, Louise M. Shepherd and Frank P. Deane

CBT and ACT Intervention Research for Anxiety Problems

This chapter outlines the use of ACT as a brief group treatment for anxiety problems. To date, the treatment of choice for anxiety problems is cognitive–behavior therapy (CBT; Butler, Chapman, Forman, & Beck, 2006), which emphasizes controlling and diminishing anxiety symptoms. An abundance of evidence suggests that CBT is effective for anxiety problems such as generalized anxiety disorder (GAD; Borkovec & Ruscio, 2001), obsessive compulsive disorder (OCD; Eddy, Dutra, Bradley, & Westen, 2004), panic disorder (Gould, Otto, & Pollack 1995) and posttraumatic stress disorder (PTSD; Bradley, Greene, Russ, Dutra, & Westen, 2005). However, not everyone benefits from CBT treatments for anxiety (Barlow, Allen, & Choate, 2004; Eifert & Forsyth, 2005a). A meta-analysis of 19 studies treating panic disorder found that cognitive–behavioral approaches were effective (mean effect size 0.68) but that 26% of participants still experienced some panic attacks at the end of treatment (Gould, Otto, & Pollack, 1995). A review of treatments for social phobia found the mean dropout rate across seven trials using cognitive restructuring was 11.6%. The mean dropout rate across 21 trials using exposure plus cognitive restructuring was 18.6% (Fedoroff & Taylor, 2001). A meta-analysis of CBT for pathological worry among clients with GAD found large overall effect sizes when compared to control groups (mean $ES = -1.15$) but benefits were much greater for younger adults than older adults (Covin, Ouimet, Seeds, & Dozois, 2008). One explanation for differences between younger and older adults related to the observation that most of the CBT studies for older adults used group versus individual modes of delivery. The authors suggested that 'group

CBT for GAD may be less effective than its counterpart' (Covin et al., 2008, p. 114). The mean dropout rate for CBT conditions across the seven studies reviewed was 15.7%, but there was higher attrition among the older adults. Overall, the number of studies assessing the effects of CBT for GAD are small (Butler et al., 2006) and thus the ability to clarify such differential effects is limited. Together, these reviews indicate that although CBT for anxiety disorders appears effective and leads to sustained changes in symptoms, there is also considerable room for improvement. Acceptance-based approaches have also shown early promise in the treatment of anxiety disorders and ACT has the potential to extend outcomes beyond just symptom amelioration. In fact, Craske and Hazlett-Stephens (2002) suggest that experiential avoidance 'may be a hallmark feature and contributor' (p. 71) of anxiety problems and acceptance-based approaches may therefore be appropriate for all types of anxiety.

ACT and acceptance-based treatments have been shown to yield significant improvements for anxious sufferers. In a study using acceptance-based behavior therapy with people with GAD results indicated significant reductions in clinician-rated severity of GAD, anxiety and depression and improvements in quality of life at posttreatment and 3-month follow-up (Roemer & Orsillo, 2007).

Evidence suggests that ACT has been helpful for anxiety problems such as OCD (Hayes, 1987; Twohig, Hayes, & Masuda, 2006), PTSD (Batten & Hayes, 2005), agoraphobia and panic attacks (Carrascoso Lopez, 2000; Hayes, 1987), social phobia (Block, 2002; Dalrymple, 2006; Hayes 1987; Ossman, Wilson, Storaasli, & McNeill, 2006), workplace stress management (Bond & Bunce, 2000) and maths anxiety (Zettle, 2003).

An example of the effectiveness of ACT with anxiety problems was an 8-session ACT intervention for OCD that produced reductions in self-reported compulsions, standard measures of OCD, anxiety and depression as well as reductions in experiential avoidance and believability of obsessions (Twohig et al., 2006). Similarly, in case studies of people with panic attacks and agoraphobia ACT was found to reduce anxiety symptoms and avoidance (Carrascoso Lopez, 2000; Hayes, 1987). In studies of social anxiety, a 12-session individual treatment protocol resulted in significant improvement in self-reported and clinician-rated symptoms, observer-rated social skills and quality of life (Dalrymple, 2006). In another study of a 10-session group treatment for social phobia, posttreatment and follow-up data showed significant decreases on the social phobia and experiential avoidance measures (Ossman et al., 2006). Ratings of effectiveness in living significantly increased at follow-up.

The available data comparing ACT with CBT is limited. A small randomized control trial assigned people with social anxiety to either an

ACT condition, a cognitive–behavioral group therapy condition or a no-treatment control condition (Block, 2002). People in the ACT condition reported a significant increase in willingness to experience anxiety and decreases in avoidance and anxiety during a public speaking task compared with the control group. More recently, large and similar levels of improvement in anxiety, depression and quality of life were found in ACT and cognitive therapy groups for people with anxiety and depression (Forman, Herbert, Moitra, Yeomans, & Geller, 2007). A multi-site study funded by the National Institute of Health in the United States that compares individual ACT and individual CBT for anxiety disorders is currently underway (J. Forsyth, personal communication, November, 2006).

Preliminary evidence suggests that more can be done to enhance treatment for anxiety. ACT incorporates elements that may meet some of the challenges faced by CBT treatment for anxiety. First, ACT involves in vivo and imaginal exposure embedded within an acceptance-based framework. Research suggests that people who had high levels of anxiety sensitivity and who were exposed to carbon dioxide enriched air reported less intense fear, cognitive symptoms and behavioral avoidance if they were trained in an acceptance condition, compared to people trained in a control or no instruction condition (Eifert & Heffner, 2003). McMullen and colleagues (2008) found that people trained in an acceptance condition were more likely to continue with a task and report lower levels of pain when exposed to a shock, than people in a distraction condition. Such findings suggest that exposure within an acceptance context may be more palatable for people than exposure in a control context. Second, ACT emphasizes exposure for the purposes of living a meaningful life. That is, ACT links exposure to deeply meaningful values. These elements may increase treatment acceptability and reduce attrition. Third, ACT views symptoms across a wide range of problems to be a function of experiential avoidance and cognitive fusion. Therefore, ACT may be an appropriate treatment for people who might be considered poor candidates for traditional CBT because of problem comorbidity (Orsillo, Roemer, Block-Lerner, LeJeune, & Herbert, 2004).

ACT Conceptualisation of Anxiety

ACT theory of psychopathology suggests that experiential avoidance and cognitive fusion contribute to the development and maintenance of many forms of psychopathology, including anxiety disorders (Hayes, Strosahl, & Wilson, 1999). Experiential avoidance can be defined as 'mental and behavioural strategies aimed at changing the form or frequency of one's current internal experience' (e.g., thoughts, emotions, images, physiological sensations; Orsillo, Roemer, & Holowka, 2005, p. 11). Cognitive fusion refers to 'fusing with or attaching to the literal content of private experiences whereby we respond to a thought or feeling not just as a thought or feeling but as the actual event it describes' (Eifert & Forsyth, 2005a, p. 88). ACT theory of psychopathology suggests that the processes of experiential avoidance and cognitive fusion are not harmful in and of themselves. However, they become destructive when they become a rigid way of operating and are related to avoidance of important and meaningful activities, goals and values (Hayes et al., 1999). For example, the experience of fear and anxiety is normal and, in and of itself, is not a problem. When one feels fear and anxiety we experience a range of physiological and psychological reactions such as heart rate rising, muscle tension, sweating, shaking, nausea, apprehension, worry and the urge to escape. When these reactions occur we are programmed to look out for danger so our attention narrows and we search for threat. One of the purposes of this is to avoid danger by detecting it early and removing ourselves from the threatening situation. These responses, under most circumstances, are adaptive and have helped humans survive for thousands of years. They are not, in and of themselves, 'disordered'. Anxiety and worry can be protective when they help us plan and problem solve for some future threat (e.g., planning for the loss of a job or impending financial difficulty). Therefore, some anxiety is natural and some is brought on by our own attempts to control it (i.e., when we engage in experiential avoidance and cognitive fusion).

Rationale for Using a Group ACT Approach to Treating Mixed Anxiety Problems
Prolonged individual psychotherapy is often not viable in applied settings due to limited resources in publicly funded treatment clinics and the costs of prolonged therapy for the consumer. ACT delivered in a brief individual and group format has so far yielded promising results for some difficult-to-treat problems, including sick leave and medical utilization associated with chronic pain (Dahl, Wilson, & Nilsson, 2004) and psychosis (Bach & Hayes, 2002; Gaudiano & Herbert, 2006). In the studies with patients who have psychosis, ACT was found to be significantly more effective than treatment as usual (TAU), with participants in the ACT condition receiving TAU plus 4 hours of individual therapy. In the chronic pain study, ACT was found to be useful with only 4 hours of group treatment (Dahl et al., 2004). Thus, it is possible that brief group ACT therapy may also be effective with various forms of anxiety.

ACT may be particularly suited to treating a variety of 'forms' of anxiety (e.g., different diagnoses) in a single group, because the overriding focus of ACT is on psychological processes (e.g., experiential avoidance and cognitive fusion) that are likely to play critical roles across many diagnostic boundaries. In other words, ACT may be well suited to the group treatment of mixed anxiety disorders because it views the mechanisms underlying these 'different' disorders as being largely similar, and its techniques are thus designed to be broadly applicable. In fact, Eifert and Forsyth (2005a) suggest that 'there is increasing empirical support for the notion that the powerful and self-defeating impact of avoiding negative affect is the core pathological process that fuels all anxiety disorders' (p. 26). If a common mechanism underlies all varieties of anxiety disorders, then group treatments of mixed anxiety diagnoses may be a viable treatment option.

A mixed-group treatment modality for anxiety would provide a number of benefits for clinicians and consumers. First, group treatment would maximize psychologist resources, which are often scarce, thus enabling more people to be seen in shorter amounts of time. Group treatment would increase accessibility for low income earners. While this poses less of an issue in countries where psychological treatment is largely subsidized, it poses a major issue in countries where insurance for treatment is not readily forthcoming.

A study is currently being undertaken at the University of New South Wales Counselling Service where a 6-session ACT group treatment program is being compared to a 6-session group CBT program delivered to students experiencing mild to severe mixed anxiety problems (Glaser, Blackledge, & Deane, 2008). Preliminary data suggest that the ACT and the CBT groups are equally efficacious at posttreatment, with the ACT group experiencing fewer anxiety symptoms than the CBT group at 12-month follow-up. This treatment format appears to have been well accepted by the majority of participants. The protocol, along with tips and recommendations for running ACT groups for anxiety, are discussed in the remainder of this chapter.

How to Apply ACT Treatment of Anxiety in Group Settings

Unlike traditional CBT, ACT therapy does not have symptom reduction or amelioration as its main goal. The main goal of ACT is to help people observe unwanted anxious thoughts, feelings and sensations while being able to do what is important to them (Orsillo et al., 2004). Paradoxically, research suggests that when less control is exerted over anxious symptoms one is likely to feel more in control and report fewer symptoms of anxiety (Eifert & Forsyth, 2005a). Therefore, if anxiety symptom reduction does occur during ACT therapy it is seen as a welcome byproduct of the real therapeutic goal, which is living a meaningful life. Eifert and Forsyth (2005a) have suggested that the core treatment components of ACT for anxiety are as follows.

Psychoeducation and treatment orientation. The purpose of this phase of treatment is to provide the client with a general understanding of the nature and purpose of anxiety and the processes that lead to the development and maintenance of anxiety disorders. Treatment orientation involves introducing the client to the experiential nature of treatment and the emphasis on living a rich and meaningful life rather than symptom reduction.

Developing acceptance and willingness. The development of acceptance and willingness is considered 'an ongoing process in ACT' (Eifert & Forsyth, 2005a, p. 100). It involves eliciting the clients' anxiety control and avoidance agenda and helping them recognize that it is unworkable. Thus, the clients' experiential control is undermined and this provides motivation for willingness to choose living in accordance with one's values, rather than control and avoidance of anxious symptoms. Developing acceptance and willingness also involves undermining cognitive fusion. This is accomplished by clients experiencing defusion exercises, mindfulness exercises, metaphors and behavioral tasks to detach from the literal content of private experiences, to be able to discriminate actual experience from conceptualized experience and to teach the ability to detect cognitive fusion that keeps them stuck.

Developing an observer self. This involves clients using mindfulness and experiential exercises to separate the self from the self-evaluations that the mind generates. The client learns to make contact with the 'observer self' and to experience self-evaluations as transient.

Getting in contact with the present moment. This involves the use of mindfulness exercises to help clients notice thoughts, feelings, sensations and memories without evaluating and judging. The aim is to bring these perceptions into present awareness rather than the past or future.

Choosing valued life directions. This involves helping clients clarify how they wish to live their lives by working out what is important to them.

Taking action. This involves the therapist helping the client build an action plan based on articulated values. Exposure exercises are implemented to help clients take action with unwanted anxiety responses. Exposure in ACT differs to CBT in that the goal is not to reduce or eliminate anxiety, it is to provide clients with more flexible ways of responding when experiencing anxiety.

The Group Protocol

In addition to general treatment parameters for ACT with anxiety disorders, Eifert and Forsyth (2005a) provided a detailed individual treatment protocol, which served as the initial template for the current outcome study. However, brief group treatment requires a substantially different approach to individual therapy and the modified group protocol is described below. Eifert and Forsyth's ACT for anxiety disorders protocol includes 12 sessions delivered individually. The group protocol involved six 2-hour sessions. The group protocol retains the most important therapeutic elements of the individual program and uses exercises that translate well to groups and make best use of group process. The following session-by-session outline does not describe all of the exercises in full, but instead refers the reader to the original sources where a more detailed description is available. Revisions in delivery for a group format are outlined as necessary.

SESSION 1: CREATIVE HOPELESSNESS

Materials required for each session: PowerPoint slides, whiteboard, whiteboard markers

Materials required for session 1: 'Living in Full' (LIFE) self-monitoring form, ACT daily diary

GOALS

- to establish rapport and develop connections between participants
- to normalize human suffering
- to introduce the experiential nature of the treatment
- to explore the workability (i.e. costs and benefits) of previous attempts to control or reduce anxiety
- to experience the unworkability of a rigid control agenda.

SESSION OUTLINE

1. Introductions and setting the therapeutic frame
Welcome participants. Normalize their experience of anxiety about being at the group. Create a context of acceptance from the outset by telling participants that any emotion, thought, or sensation that they have in the group is completely acceptable. Introduce the participants to the experiential nature of treatment.

2. Introduction to the nature of treatment
Establish group rules. Remind the group that it is a 6-week program and each session is 2 hours with a 10-minute break in the middle. Discuss the limits of confidentiality. Clarify that the goal of treatment is to live a more meaningful life rather than anxiety reduction by referring back to the personal values questionnaire participants filled out before the group started. To normalize the participant's experiences of anxiety it can be useful to explore the universality of human suffering by discussing the prevalence of anxiety disorders.

3. *Developing creative hopelessness*

When group members discuss their control strategies and what the strategies have cost them it creates a sense of cohesion and understanding among group members. It also highlights the futility of the struggle against anxiety when the discussion elicits sadness, frustration and often anger from group members when they reflect on having spent so much energy struggling and yet they are attending a group to reduce anxiety. Coming into contact with the futility of the struggle with anxiety provides group members with motivation to try new approaches.

- Ask group members to give you examples of thoughts, feelings, sensations, memories, that they would rather not have, that they have tried to change, control, reduce or get rid of? Write these strategies up on one side of a whiteboard.
- Discuss patterns and costs of avoidance and write these on the other side of the whiteboard.
- Ask the group members how these methods have worked?
- Identify the costs of avoidance and control. It is important for participants to experience the costs of their control efforts at an emotional level as well as intellectually.

4. *Between-session activities*

Between-session activities (homework) are a very important part of the treatment program. The purpose of the activities is firstly for self-monitoring and secondly to generalize the skills learned in the groups to the participant's real world. It is important to provide the participant with a rationale for completing the exercises and give written instructions (Twohig, Pierson, & Hayes, 2007).

Rationale for LIFE exercises:

- Worksheets to monitor contexts where anxiety and fear show up; associated thoughts feelings sensations and behaviors; willingness to have those experiences and how reactions to them are interfering with values and goals.
- LIFE exercises (Eifert & Forsyth, 2005a, p. 128) and Daily ACT Ratings (Eifert & Forsyth, 2005a, p. 129, instructions for exercises on pages 126–127).

5. *Finish the session with any questions or concerns the participants may have.*

SESSION 2: CONTROL IS THE PROBLEM AND INTRODUCTION TO THE WHY AND HOW OF WILLINGNESS

Materials required for Session 2: Centering Exercise, Acceptance of Thoughts and Feelings Exercise, Chinese Finger Traps

GOALS

* to give the struggle a name — 'control'
* to help clients differentiate what they can control and what they cannot control in their lives
* to experience mindfulness and acceptance as a skill to enable willingness
* to build understanding of the nature and function of anxiety.

SESSION OUTLINE

1. *Centering exercise (Eifert & Forsyth, 2005a, p. 125)*

Tell group members that each session will begin with a mindfulness exercise if they are willing to do it. Introduce this exercise as a way of enabling group members to leave the outside world outside and to bring their awareness into the room and to the purpose of attending the group.

2. *Review of in-between session activities: LIFE exercises and daily ACT ratings*

Ask group members to give examples of when fear and anxiety 'showed up' for them over the week, what they did (if anything) to control it and, what effect these efforts had on their behavior. At this stage of treatment it is important to pay particular attention to the workability of control efforts. The self-monitoring provides evidence and builds a case for the unworkability of control as well as motivation for participants to try something fundamentally different.

3. *Control is the problem*

This section of the treatment program builds on the discussion of the costs and unworkability of experiential avoidance. This session also helps clients develop an understanding of how experiential avoidance is a learned behavior and they are not at fault, broken or stupid for using control strategies.

* Link introduction of 'Control is the problem' to LIFE exercises and discussions in Session 1 about what strategies participants had tried in order to control unwanted internal experiences.

- Use the 'Feeding the Anxiety Tiger' metaphor (Eifert & Forsyth, 2005a, pp. 138–139). This metaphor illustrates the cost of control efforts.
- Ask participants how we develop a control agenda. Make sure you include discussion of modeling and the role of the 'mind', that is, control is a logical rational thing to do in the world outside our skin because if we do not like something we get rid of it (give examples).
- Discuss research that control of thoughts and feelings can be counterproductive.
- Use Polygraph metaphor (Eifert & Forsyth, 2005a, pp. 167–169) and Do Not Think of a Pink Elephant exercise (ask participants to try to not think of a pink elephant). These metaphors illustrate how difficult it is to control thoughts and feelings.

4. *Nature and function of normal fear and anxiety*

Introduce this section by linking it to participant's experience that it is difficult to control anxiety and that some anxiety is actually useful. See Eifert and Forsyth (2005a, pp. 115–129) for comprehensive psychoeducational material.

5. *Willingness as an alternative to control*

The concept of willingness is more effectively learned experientially than discussed verbally. Therefore, the following exercises are 'acted' out with participants to enable them to experience the difference between control and willingness.

- The Chinese Finger Trap exercise (Eifert & Forsyth, 2005a, p. 147). Provide participants with actual finger traps. These can be purchased on the Internet at such sites as eBay or at novelty stores.
- Tug of War with an Anxiety Monster (Eifert & Forsyth, 2005a, pp. 149–151)
- Willingness Dial (Eifert & Forsyth, 2005a, pp. 195–196)
- The exercises can be combined with a brief discussion of willingness — what it is and what it is not (Eifert & Forsyth, 2005a, p. 194).
- Learning to accept thoughts and feelings with mindfulness

Discuss the benefits of mindfulness and how mindfulness is related to willingness and acceptance. The following excerpt is taken from Russ Harris's (2008) 'ACT mindfully website':

Practicing mindfulness helps you

- to be fully present, here and now
- to experience unpleasant thoughts and feelings safely
- to become aware of what you're avoiding
- to become more connected to yourself, to others and to the world around you
- to become less judgmental
- to increase self-awareness
- to become less disturbed by and less reactive to unpleasant experiences
- to learn the distinction between you and your thoughts
- to have more direct contact with the world, rather than living through your thoughts
- to learn that everything changes; that thoughts and feelings come and go like the weather
- to have more balance, less emotional volatility
- to experience more calm and peacefulness
- to develop self-acceptance and self-compassion. (Harris, 2008)

- Acceptance of Thoughts and Feelings exercise (Eifert & Forsyth, 2005a, pp. 139–143)
- Process Acceptance of Thoughts and Feelings exercise.

6. *Homework*

Practice Acceptance of Thoughts and Feelings exercise and monitor practice.

SESSION 3: BUILDING ACCEPTANCE BY DEFUSING LANGUAGE AND INTRODUCTION TO VALUES.

Materials required for Session 3: Acceptance of Anxiety Exercise, Life Compass

GOALS

- to introduce value-driven action as the primary goal of treatment
- to introduce willingness for the purpose of living a meaningful life
- to clarify client values
- to continue to develop the skills of mindfulness and acceptance
- to experience the limits of language and develop defusion skills.

SESSION OUTLINE

1. *Exercise — Being Willing to Be Out of Breath (Hayes & Smith, 2005).*
This involves asking participants to time themselves as they take a deep breath and to hold it for as long as they can and to then write down how long they held it for.

2. *Review of Practice of Acceptance of Thoughts and Feelings exercise.*
Encourage participants to discuss their experiences practicing mindfulness and willingness with thoughts and feelings. Ask if participants have any problems or concerns about the exercise.

3. *Acceptance of Anxiety Exercise (Eifert & Forsyth, 2005a, pp. 163–166).*
This exercise, as with the Acceptance of Thoughts and Feelings exercise, is an interoceptive exposure exercise. The aim of this exercise is for participants to practice mindfulness and willingness of unwanted anxious thoughts, feelings and sensations.

4. *Undermining the power of language*
Like willingness, defusion is best learned experientially not verbally. Therefore, the following exercises are most useful when experienced rather than taking participants through a discussion of defusion.

- Very briefly discuss the limits of language (Hayes et al., 1999; Eifert & Forsyth, 2005a, pp. 78–79 & 229–230) — relate to participants experience with anxiety.
- Finding a Place to Sit metaphor (Hayes et al., 1999, pp. 152–153)
- Milk Milk Milk exercise (repeat with relevant thought — e.g., 'too anxious', Hayes et al., 1999, pp. 154–156)

- Leaves on a Stream or Soldiers on Parade exercise (Hayes et al., 1999, pp. 158–162).
- 'But-and' exercise (Hayes et al, 1999, pp. 166–168).

5. *Values dignify willingness and make the hard work worthwhile*
This section of the program encourages participants to think about what they want their life to be about. This is very important because thus far participant's behavior may have been in the service of avoiding anxiety rather than living a meaningful life. Articulating and clarifying values serves as motivation for willingness to accept uncomfortable anxious thoughts and feelings.

- Corridor and Hammer metaphor (Eifert & Forsyth, 2005a, p. 153).
- The Epitaph Exercise — what do you want your life to stand for (Eifert & Forsyth, 2005a, pp. 154–155). Ask clients to fill in two epitaphs — one for life in the service of managing anxiety and the other for a life well lived.

6. *Making a commitment*
Making a verbal commitment in front of the group serves as motivation to adhere to the particular goal and enhances group cohesion.

- Discuss a value identified in the epitaph exercise.
- Chose a goal related to a value they want to work on in the remainder of the program (i.e., over the next 3 weeks).
- Make a commitment to a chosen value and goal they will achieve over the next week.

7. *Discussion of homework — LIFE Compass worksheet (Eifert & Forsyth, 2005a, p. 189)*

- Instructions for the Life Compass worksheet can be found in Eifert and Forsyth (2005a, pp. 186–187).
- Practice of Acceptance of thoughts and feelings exercise

8. *Being Willing to Be Out of Breath exercise (Hayes & Smith, 2005)*
- Repeat the exercise from the beginning of the session, but this time using skills of mindfulness, acceptance and defusion to practice willingness to be out of breath. Compare experience with the exercise from the beginning of the session.

SESSION 4: BUILDING ACCEPTANCE BY DEVELOPING SELF
AS CONTEXT AND VALUE-GUIDED EXPOSURE

Materials required: Short observer exercise, FEEL Sensation record.

GOALS

- to develop self as context
- to continue clarifying values and barriers impeding movement towards values
- to practice mindful observation and defusion in exposure tasks
- to create broader and more flexible patterns of behavior when experiencing anxiety
- to increase psychological and experiential flexibility to enable movement toward values.

SESSION OUTLINE

1. *Thinking Self Versus Observing Self Exercise*

The purpose of this exercise is to develop the observer self. This exercise is taken from *The Happiness Trap* (Harris, 2007) and is based on the Observer exercise (Hayes et al., 1999).

Close your eyes, and simply notice what your mind does. Stay on the lookout for any thoughts or images, as if you're a wildlife photographer, waiting for an exotic animal to appear from the undergrowth. If no thoughts or images appear, keep watching; sooner or later one will.

Notice (a) where your thoughts seem to be located: out in front of you, above you, behind you, to one side of you, or within you. (b) whether they're moving or still (c) if they are moving, what direction, and how fast?

As you do this notice there are two separate processes: thinking and observing. One part of you is thinking, generating a stream of thoughts, while another part of you is observing those thoughts.

Do this again. Step back and observe your thoughts: where are they located? moving or still?, what direction and speed?

As you do this, your observing self is observing your thinking self. (Harris, 2007, p. 79)

2. *Review acceptance of anxiety exercise*

Encourage participants to discuss their experiences practicing mindfulness and willingness with anxious thoughts and feelings, whether their behavior changed and any problems or concerns they have about the exercise.

3. *Review Life Compass and Commitment*
- Identify discrepancies between intentions and behavior.
- Identify barriers to pursuing valued directions in areas that clients have rated as high importance.
- Use 'thought' barriers to inform the next exercise.

4. *Building awareness of self as context*
- Introduce the exercise by discussing the 'concept' of observer self as difficult to grasp.
- Chessboard metaphor (Eifert & Forsyth, 2005a, pp. 182–184). Eifert and Forsyth suggest using a real chessboard for this exercise. Another alternative is using the floor as a chessboard and crumpled pieces of paper as thoughts and feelings. Ask the participant to give examples of anxious thoughts and feelings. Crumple pieces of paper and throw them on a side of the board (floor) telling the participant that these thoughts and feelings are the black chess pieces. Ask the participant what thoughts show up after these initial thoughts. The participant will often then say thoughts that try and combat and change or control the anxious thoughts and feelings. Crumple more pieces of paper and throw these on the other side of the board (floor) telling the participant that these are the white pieces. Continue this process with each thought and feeling the participant volunteers. This provides an effective visual representation of the struggle between the thoughts and feelings the client experiences, the idea that the struggle is useless because it is ultimately against oneself and the possibility to develop an observer perspective (Walser, 2004).

5. *Interoceptive Exposure exercises (Eifert & Forsyth, 2005a, pp. 200–209)*
- Discussion of rationale, procedure and anticipated costs and benefits of exposure exercises.
- Link the rationale with anxiety related barriers to values using worksheet and life compass.
- Determine appropriate interoceptive exposure exercises.
- Instruction — Participants are instructed to mindfully observe their internal experience of the exercise, (e.g. 'I'm noticing light-headedness', 'I'm having the thought that what if I collapse').
- Model interoceptive exposure exercise
- Conduct interoceptive exposure exercise
- Process exercise.

6. *Discussion of homework*

- Encourage practice of at least one interoceptive exposure exercise each day.
- Discussion of goal achievement record.
- Select activities based on life compass (Eifert & Forsyth, 2005a, p. 226).
- Can the client commit to one activity?

SESSION 5: VALUE-GUIDED BEHAVIOR IN THE REAL WORLD

Materials required: FEEL imagery record form.

GOALS

- to practice mindfulness and acceptance of anxiety provoking images
- to practice mindfulness, acceptance and defusion of anxiety related barriers to value-guided behavior.

SESSION OUTLINE

1. *Centering exercise (Eifert & Forsyth, 2005a, p. 125).*
2. *Review of interoceptive exposure exercises and value-guided activities.*
- Include discussion of images of the worst case scenario as perceived barriers to goal achievement.

3. *Imaginal exposure exercises (Eifert & Forsyth, 2005a, pp. 211–214).*
- Client to choose one fear-provoking image based on worst case scenario.
- Rate willingness to have image.
- Mindfulness of Image exercise — use FEEL imagery record.
- Re-rate willingness to have image.

4. *Mindfulness and acceptance of perceived anxiety barriers to goal achievement.*
- Discuss barriers to goal achievement on goal achievement record.
- Participants act out 'Monsters on the bus' (Eifert & Forsyth, 2005a, p. 197) or
- Take Your Mind for a Walk exercise. This exercise can be done in pairs. Ask participants to write down thoughts that are barriers to goal achievement. Tell them they will be sharing the thoughts with a partner in an exercise. Pair up participants. One participant chooses a direction they want to walk. The other participant acts as the persons mind and follow them around repeating the thoughts on the card and trying to put them off course by saying things like, 'turn left, right, stop, straight ahead'. The person is instructed to use skills of mindfulness, defusion and acceptance to stay on course despite the 'mind chatter' (Walser, 2004).

5. *Discussion of homework — Encourage practice of at least one interoceptive or imagery exercise each day and pursuit of a goal from the goal achievement record.*

SESSION 6: STAYING COMMITTED TO VALUE-GUIDED BEHAVIOR

Materials required: Where to From Here? handout.

GOALS

- to reinforce commitment to value guided behavior in the real world
- to practice mindfulness, acceptance and defusion of anxiety related barriers to value-guided behavior
- to prepare participants for the end of treatment
- to equip participants with strategies for relapse prevention
- to administer post treatment evaluations (if relevant).

SESSION OUTLINE

1. *Mindfulness exercise of facilitator's choosing*

2. *Review of goal-achievement homework*
- Focus on any particular concerns or questions clients have about continuing progress.
- Use these concerns to inform the next exercise.

3. *Mindfulness and acceptance of anxiety barriers to goal achievement*
- Discuss barriers to goal achievement.
- Cards on Lap exercise (Eifert & Forsyth, 2005a, p. 215).
- Anxiety news radio (Eifert & Forsyth 2005a, p. 184–186).

4. *Treatment summary*
- Provide a brief summary of the treatment program.
- Include the ACT acronym (**A**ccept thoughts and feelings, **C**hoose Directions and **T**ake Action).

5. *Maintaining process and learning*
- Continue to practice mindfulness and acceptance exercises.
- Continue to set short term goals.
- Make personal commitments.
- Prepare for relapse and setbacks.
- Identify high-risk situations.

6. *Wrap up*
- Give out posttreatment evaluation.
- Feedback.
- Final discussion.
- 'Joe the bum' metaphor (Hayes et al., 1999, p. 239–240).

Assessment Strategies

The assessments undertaken for the outcome study were for the purposes of collecting clinical information and measuring treatment processes and treatment outcomes. The mood and anxiety disorders sections of the Structured Clinical Interview for the DSM–IV–TR (SCID-CV; First, Spitzer, Gibbon, & Williams, 1996) were used to determine if group members had an anxiety or mood disorder, or experienced anxiety in the subclinical range. Self-report questionnaires were administered to measure change in the common features of anxiety or related disorders and change in movement toward values. Although ACT therapy is not directly focused on reducing anxious symptoms, clients often report symptom reduction. If symptom reduction does occur it is generally a function of reductions in experiential avoidance, cognitive fusion and behavioral avoidance (i.e., clients have started doing what is important to them and have lessened the control of their thoughts and feelings). Therefore, the study included the Beck Anxiety Inventory (BAI; Beck & Steer, 1990) that measures common symptoms of anxiety and the Symptom Checklist-90-Revised (SCL-90-R; Derogatis, 1983) that measures symptoms across nine symptom dimensions.

Assessment of values and change in movement towards values is crucial as this is the ultimate goal of ACT. The values assessment undertaken in the current study was by means of the Personal Values Questionnaire (Blackledge & Ciarrochi, 2006), which assesses the importance of, and activity in nine areas of living.

The study also included questionnaires that measured changes in ACT-specific processes and outcomes. The Acceptance and Action Questionnaire (AAQ-II; Bond et al., 2008) was used to assess willingness to accept undesirable thoughts and feelings and action in accordance with one's values. The Believability of Anxious Thoughts and Feelings Scale (BAFT; Eifert & Forsyth, 2005b) assesses levels of fusion and defusion. The questionnaire asks for believability ratings on a 7-point Likert scale from, *Not at all believable* to *Completely believable*. Higher scores indicate higher levels of fusion. The Mindfulness Attention Awareness Scale (MAAS; Brown & Ryan, 2003) is a 15-item scale that measures mindfulness across cognitive, emotional, physical, interpersonal and general domains (Eifert & Forsyth, 2005a).

Group Composition

From an ACT perspective, the core processes (e.g., experiential avoidance and cognitive fusion) that underlie all anxiety disorders are the same (Eifert & Forsyth, 2005a). Therefore, the inclusion criterion in the current study was that participants could have mild to severe anxiety problems of mixed types. Comorbidity is often present in people with anxiety problems (Eifert & Forsyth, 2005a) and it has been suggested that 'in general individuals exhibiting pervasive and costly experiential avoidance and cognitive fusion, particularly those in close contact with their pain are excellent candidates for ACT group work' (Walser & Pistorello, 2004, p. 353). Therefore, the exclusion criteria for the current study was limited to people with very severe depression and people who were actively suicidal, self-harming or experiencing a manic or psychotic episode. The exclusion criteria also included those who were concurrently receiving psychological treatment for an anxiety problem (not including medication).

Group Structure and Format

In the group protocol each session built on the previous session, therefore it was necessary to run closed groups. Seventeen groups with a minimum of 6 and a maximum of 19 participants were run as part of the current study. The experiential nature of the group made it particularly important to encourage and reinforce group members' commitment to attending each session. If participants missed a session it was disruptive to group process because they would have missed the group exercises from the previous session. Catch-up on experiential exercises in a subsequent group session was difficult. So, while time consuming, the group facilitator met individually with the person who missed the session to work through the exercises. Although the protocol is outlined in this chapter there is room for flexibility when using metaphors and exercises in group ACT for anxiety. In the groups run for the current study it was more powerful and effective to use a metaphor or exercise based on what emerged in the group at a particular time, rather than adhere rigidly to a set protocol. However, it was also important to adequately address each of the core ACT processes throughout the duration of the groups (i.e., acceptance, defusion, contact with the present moment, self as context, values, and building patterns of committed action). In our experience, participants found the 2-hour length of the group to be acceptable and it would be challenging to cover all of the material if sessions were less than two hours.

Process Issues in Running ACT Groups for Anxiety

Individual ACT treatment for anxiety translated very well to group format. There appeared to be several advantages of applying ACT for anxiety in a group setting. First, a lot of the ACT metaphors work very well in groups where they can be experienced physically rather than simply spoken. For example, metaphors such as the 'Tug of war with a monster' (Eifert & Forsyth, 2005a), 'Cards on lap' (Hayes et al., 1999), and the 'Chessboard' metaphor (Eifert & Forsyth, 2005a) are very effective when acted out by a participant with a group. Acting out these and other metaphors enables the participant and the facilitator to work with the present moment experience that 'shows up' during the exercise. Working with immediate thoughts, feelings and sensations is crucial to ACT group work as participants 'need to experience ACT, not to understand it' (Walser & Pistorello, 2004, p. 358).

In the 'Tug of war with a monster' exercise the facilitator played the role of 'monster', provoking the volunteer using language that they were familiar with when anxious. To begin, the facilitator and participant face each other and hold a rope (or belt/towel). The experience is likened to the struggle the client engages in against his anxiety and the facilitator/monster is likened to the anxiety struggled against. The participant is asked to continue to engage in an actual tug of war with the facilitator while she/he voices some of the actual thoughts and worries that emerge when the client is anxious. For example, someone with social anxiety in groups might have been told, 'if you go to the party you will make a fool of yourself and people will laugh at you'. A struggle continues back and worth until the participant realizes that they could simply drop the rope rather than struggle. In a group situation one of the benefits is that if the person volunteering for the exercise does not have an insight there will be others in the room that do. Once the rope is dropped the 'monster' continues to taunt and remind the participant that they are not going anywhere. Hence the message that you can stop the struggle with anxiety but this does not mean that anxiety disappears from your life.

In the 'Cards in lap' exercise the facilitator works with a volunteer with material that is personally relevant, possibly their present experience in the group (e.g., 'I feel silly doing this exercise'). The facilitator takes a pile of cards, approximately 10 cm by 15 cm, and writes the various thoughts, feelings and physical sensations that the client describes. The facilitator takes time to understand the flow of thoughts and other internal experiences for the volunteer; for instance, by inquiring with 'And then what happens?' Once a series of thoughts has been identified the facilitator instructs the volunteer that their task is to make 100% sure that none of the cards touches his or her lap. One by one the facilitator attempts to flip the cards towards the volunteer's lap while he or she tries to push them away. Then the volunteer is asked if they would be willing to try something different and allow the cards to land in their lap, just noticing them as they do so. Slowly the cards are placed in the participant's lap. Once this has been done the person is asked to describe their experience. Often they will speak of the amount of effort and stress in trying to not have the cards. Again, if the volunteer does not seem to develop insight that it is easier to allow the cards to be there, someone else in the group will have noticed this and share it with the rest. See also Hayes et al. (1999, p. 162) for a description of this exercise.

A further advantage of ACT group work is that participants often feel anxious about judgment from others during experiential exercises. This provides a good opportunity to practice the core skills of ACT (willingness, defusion and acceptance) with anxiety responses in vivo. Groups also provide a context where change may occur more quickly than would be the case in individual therapy. This is likely because the groups are longer than individual sessions (i.e., 2 hours per week rather than 1 hour per week) and participants learn from the experiences of others and witness change in others.

Groups also provide an opportunity to detect and work with a wide variety of examples of experiential avoidance. This can be very informative for people who lack the insight to detect their own variations of experiential avoidance. As with any group process some group members take to the material more quickly than others. Therefore, it is not uncommon for group members to support each other or provide feedback and guidance to other group members as described in the exercises above.

Groups also provide opportunities for participants to learn from the experience of others and reinforce the idea of the universality of human suffering. As the groups consist of people with mixed anxiety problems people learn that not all experiences of suffering are the same, but everyone experiences suffering. In fact, one of the most common pieces of feedback the authors have received when running ACT groups for anxiety is that the groups help people feel like they are not alone, stupid or broken because they experience anxiety. People learn that they are normal and that anxiety does not have to be a barrier to living a meaningful life.

Group Composition and Diversity

During the course of the study, some specific issues arose in working with university students. A high proportion of group participants were international students from a range of non-English-speaking countries who had very recently moved to Australia. A key issue that was identified, particularly in the preassessment interviews, was a fear of embarrassment when speaking English. Some of these students reported a long-standing social anxiety or a tendency to worry, but others noted that their anxiety levels were far higher since moving to a new country and trying to assimilate socially. These students faced anxiety-provoking issues that most native Australians would not be burdened with, including homesickness, having to continue to meet visa requirements and being a great distance away when family crises arose in their home country. The facilitators also noticed the great sense of anxiety about disappointing families given the high expense of attending university in another country. While the *content* or topography of these students' anxieties was different from the anxieties expressed by the native Australians in the group, they were treated *functionally* the same. This exemplifies one of the strengths of the ACT model, that is, regardless of what problematic thoughts showed up and where anxiety was encountered, these thoughts and feelings were still dealt with (via acceptance and defusion techniques) in the same way. Thus a 'mixed group', in this case involving foreigners anxious about being in a new country, and Australian citizens anxious about very different things, was not at all problematic.

Another related issue was the cultural composition of the group. Certain metaphors that are commonly used in ACT may not be culturally relevant to some group members. For example, talking about quicksand or being caught in a rip (or riptide), may be culturally appropriate for many American (in the former case) or Australian participants (in the latter case), but may be unfamiliar to people from other cultures. The Chinese finger trap seemed to be one example that translated well across a range of participants, perhaps because it is quite concrete and not so culturally bound.

Another potential issue to consider is the age of participants. In this university setting, many of the participants were young adults. There are possibly advantages in this, as it is likely that they are not yet as entrenched in long-standing habits of experiential avoidance as older individuals. One disadvantage was that some students did not practice exercises and would turn up late or miss groups altogether. This is likely to reflect factors other than age, but it would seem to be an issue that may need to be addressed in future programs with a predominantly young sample. Additionally, it is possible that a free service may adversely affect motivation to participate and practice exercises outside of group meeting times. Email or telephone contact may be useful to follow up with participants who do not attend, but changes to the group structure may also be necessary. For example, one strategy to increase motivation of participants may be to introduce the values component of treatment early on.

Occasionally, issues arose that needed to be addressed outside the group, given the personal nature of the issue. For example, one student was facing issues with immigration and another student was struggling with the demands of university and caring for a young child. While participants were welcome to discuss such issues in a group setting, some appeared to feel awkward or embarrassed to do so. It is important that there be an avenue to allow further support to address such circumstances, whether through telephone, email or brief contact with facilitators before or after the group if necessary.

Conclusion

The current evidence for the use of ACT with anxiety and the use of brief ACT interventions provides an excellent basis to apply ACT for mixed anxiety problems delivered in a brief group format. This chapter outlines the protocol for a six-session ACT intervention for mixed anxiety problems. Currently, a comparison of this ACT group with a six-session CBT group is being undertaken at the University of New South Wales Counselling Service. Preliminary findings suggest the ACT group leads to reductions in anxiety but pending analyses will determine whether it has differential effects on believability, acceptance, mindfulness and values-related outcomes compared to the CBT condition.

Acknowledgments

The authors would like to sincerely thank Annie Andrews (Director, UNSW Counselling Service) for her willingness, support and encouragement to undertake the study discussed in this chapter. Annie's open mind, flexibility and creativity made it possible to conduct the study with very limited resources. The authors would also like to thank the staff at the UNSW Counselling Service for their support and willingness to be involved in the study and their hard work that made the study a success.

References

Bach, P., & Hayes, S. C. (2002). The use of acceptance and commitment therapy to prevent the rehospitalization of psychotic patients: A randomized controlled trial. *Journal of Consulting and Clinical Psychology, 70*(5), 1129–1139.

Barlow, D. H., Allen, L. B., & Choate, M., L. (2004). Toward a unified treatment for emotional disorders. *Behavior Therapy, 35*, 205–230.

Batten, S. V., & Hayes, S. C. (2005). Acceptance and commitment therapy in the treatment of co-morbid substance abuse and post-traumatic stress disorder: A case study. *Clinical Case Studies, 4(3)*, 246–262.

Beck, A. T., & Steer, R. A. (1990). *Beck Anxiety Inventory Manual*. San Antonio, TX: The Psychological Corporation.

Blackledge, J., T., & Ciarrochi, J. (2006). *The Personal Values Questionnaire*. Wollongong, Australia: University of Wollongong.

Block, J. A. (2002). *Acceptance or change of private experiences: A comparative analysis in college students with public speaking anxiety*. Doctoral dissertation, University at Albany, State University of New York.

Bond, F. W., & Bunce, D. (2000). Mediators of change in emotion-focused and problem-focused worksite stress management interventions. *Journal of Occupational Health Psychology, 5*, 156–163.

Bond, F. W., Hayes, S. C., Baer, R. A., Carpenter, K. M., Orcutt, H. K., Waltz, T. et al. (2008). *Preliminary psychometric properties of the Acceptance and Action Questionnaire—II: A revised measure of psychological flexibility and acceptance*. Manuscript submitted for publication.

Brown, K. W., & Ryan, R. M. (2003). The benefits of being present: Mindfulness and its role in psychological well-being. *Journal of Personality and Social Psychology, 84(4)*, 822–848.

Borkovec, T. D., & Ruscio, A. M. (2001). Psychotherapy for generalized anxiety disorder. *Journal of Clinical Psychiatry, 62*, 37–42.

Bradley, R., Greene, J., Russ, E., Dutra, L., & Westen, D. (2005). A multidimensional meta-analysis of psychotherapy for PTSD. *American Journal of Psychiatry, 162*, 214–227.

Butler, A. C., Chapman, J. E., Forman, E. M., & Beck, A. T. (2006). The empirical status of cognitive behavioral therapy: A review of meta-analyses. *Clinical Psychology Review, 26*, 17–31.

Carrascoso Lopez, F. J. (2000). Acceptance and commitment therapy (ACT) in panic disorder with agoraphobia: A case study. *Psychology in Spain, 4*(1), 120–128.

Covin, R., Ouimet, A. J., Seeds, P. M., & Dozois, D. J. A. (2008). A meta-analysis of CBT for pathological worry among clients with GAD. *Journal of Anxiety Disorders, 22*, 108–116.

Craske, M., & Hazlett-Stephens, H. (2002). Facilitating symptom reduction and behavior change in GAD: The issue of control. *Clinical Psychology: Science and Practice, 9*, 69–75.

Dahl, J., Wilson, K. G., & Nilsson, A. (2004). Acceptance and commitment therapy and the treatment for persons at risk for long-term disability resulting from stress and pain symptoms: A preliminary randomised trial. *Behavior Therapy, 35*(4), 785–801.

Dalrymple, K., L. (2006). Acceptance and commitment therapy for generalized social anxiety disorder: A pilot study. *Dissertation Abstracts International: Section B: The Sciences and Engineering, 66*, 6267.

Derogatis, L. R. (1983). *SCL-90-R, Administration, scoring and procedures manual II.* Baltimore, MD: Clinical Psychometric Research.

Eddy, K. T., Dutra, L., Bradley, R., & Westen, D. (2004). A multidimensional meta-analysis of psychotherapy and pharmacotherapy for obsessive–compulsive disorder. *Clinical Psychology Review, 24*(8), 1011–1030.

Eifert, G. H., & Forsyth, J. P. (2005a). *Acceptance and commitment therapy for anxiety disorders.* Oakland, CA: New Harbinger Publications.

Eifert, G. H., & Forsyth, J. P. (2005b). *Believability of Anxious Feelings and Thoughts (BAFT) Scale.* Orange, CA: Authors.

Eifert, G. H., & Heffner, M. (2003). The effects of acceptance versus control contexts on avoidance of panic-related symptoms. *Journal of Behavior Therapy and Experimental Psychiatry, 34*, 293–312.

Fedoroff, I., & Taylor, S. (2001). Psychological and pharmacological treatments of social phobia: A meta-analysis. *Journal of Clinical Psychopharmacology, 21*, 311–324.

First, M. B., Spitzer, R. L., Gibbon M., & Williams, J. B. W. (1996). *Structured Clinical Interview for DSM-IV Axis I Disorders, Clinician Version (SCID-CV).* Washington, DC: American Psychiatric Press.

Forman, E. M., Herbert, J. D., Moitra, E., Yeomans, P. D., & Geller, P. A. (2007). A randomized controlled effectiveness trial of acceptance and commitment therapy and cognitive therapy for anxiety and depression. *Behavior Modification, 31*(6):772–799.

Glaser, N., Blackledge, J. T., & Deane, F. P. (2008). *The effectiveness of brief group acceptance and commitment therapy (ACT) and cognitive–behavioral therapy (CBT) for people with anxiety.* Manuscript in preparation.

Gaudiano, B. A., & Herbert, J. D. (2006). Acute treatment of inpatients with psychotic symptoms using Acceptance and Commitment Therapy: Pilot results. *Behaviour Research & Therapy, 44*(3), 415–437.

Gould, R. A., Otto, M. W., & Pollack, M. H. (1995). A meta analysis of treatment outcome for panic disorder. *Clinical Psychology Review, 15,* 819–844.

Harris, R. (2007). *The happiness trap.* Wollombi, Australia: Exisle Publishing.

Harris, R. (2008). *ACT mindfully website.* Retrieved March 10, 2008, from http://www.actmindfully.com.au/mindfulness

Hayes, S. C. (1987). A contextual approach to therapeutic change. In N. S. Jacobson (Ed.), *Psychotherapists in clinical practice. Cognitive and behavioral perspectives* (pp. 327–387). New York: Guilford Press.

Hayes, S. C., Barnes-Holmes, D., & Roche, B. (Eds.). (2001). *Relational frame theory: A post-Skinnerian account of human language and cognition.* New York: Plenum Press.

Hayes, S., & Smith, S. (2005). *Get out of your mind and into your life. The new acceptance and commitment therapy.* Oakland, CA, New Harbinger.

Hayes, S. C., Strosahl, K., & Wilson, K. G. (1999). *Acceptance and commitment therapy: An experiential approach to behavior change.* New York: Guilford.

McMullen, J., Barnes-Holmes, D., Barnes-Holmes, Y., Stewart, I., Luciano, M. C., & Cochrane, A. (2008). Acceptance versus distraction: Brief instructions, metaphors and exercises in increasing tolerance for self-delivered electric shocks. *Behaviour Research and Therapy, 46,* 122–129.

Orsillo, S. M., Roemer, L., Block-Lerner, J., LeJeune, C., & Herbert, J. D. (2004). ACT with anxiety disorders. In S. Hayes & K. Strosahl (Eds.), *A practical guide to acceptance and commitment therapy* (pp. 103—132). New York: Springer.

Orsillo, S. M., Roemer, L., & Holowka, D. W. (2005). Acceptance-based behavioural therapies for anxiety. Using acceptance and mindfulness to enhance traditional cognitive–behavioural approaches. In S. M. Orsillo & L. Roemer (Eds.), *Acceptance and mindfulness-based approaches to anxiety: Conceptualization and treatment* (pp. 3–37). New York: Springer.

Ossman, W. A., Wilson, K. G., Storaasli, R. D., & McNeill, J. W. (2006). A preliminary investigation of the use of acceptance and commitment therapy in group treatment for social phobia. *International Journal of Psychological Therapy, 6,* 397–416.

Twohig, M. P., Hayes, S. C., & Masuda, A. (2006). Increasing willingness to experience obsessions: Acceptance and commitment therapy as a treatment for obsessive–compulsive disorder. *Behavior Therapy, 37*(1), 3–13.

Twohig, M. P., Pierson, H. M., & Hayes, S. (2007). Acceptance and commitment therapy. In N. Kazantzis & L. L'Abate (Eds.), *Handbook of homework assignments in psychotherapy: research, practice, and prevention* (pp. 113–132). New York: Springer.

Walser, R. (2004). *Clinical skills training workshop* in Adelaide, Australia.

Walser, R., & Pistorello, J. (2004). ACT in groups. In S. Hayes & K. Strosahl (Eds.), *A practical guide to acceptance and commitment therapy* (pp. 3–29). New York: Springer.

Zettle, R. D. (2003). Acceptance and commitment therapy (ACT) versus systematic desensitization in treatment of mathematics anxiety. *The Psychological Record, 53,* 197–215.

chapter eight

Self-Destructive Behavior, ACT and Functional Analysis

Tobias Lundgren

This chapter introduces an ACT approach in the treatment of self-destructive behavior. Using case examples, metaphors and theoretical discussions the key elements in an ACT treatment for self-destructive behavior are highlighted. Case examples will be given from sessions with adolescent clients. The chapter outlines ways of working with clients using functional analysis of behavior strategies, specific ACT processes and instruments such as the Bulls-Eye diary and the presence report. Furthermore, a value-based therapeutic relationship based on a functional analysis is the foundation on which the ACT therapy is built. Creating a therapeutic environment, where creativity is fostered and where the clients dare to challenge vicious cycles and take new valued steps in life, is a necessary element of therapy. The chapter starts by focusing on self-destructive behavior and how it is described in the literature. It continues by discussing how self-destructive behavior can be analyzed with functional analytic thinking and the therapeutic relationship.

Self-Destructive Behavior

Self-destructive behaviors seem to have increased in frequency during the last decades (Hawton, Fagg, Simkin, Bale, & Bond, 2000; Gratz, 2001; Lundh, Karim, & Quilisch, 2007). A study conduced by Gratz (2001) showed that 35% of 150 students (mean age of 23) had self-harmed at least once during their lifetime. Furthermore, in a Swedish study, about 65% of the participating high school students reported that they had harmed themselves deliberately (Lundh et al., 2007). A study examining the general and clinical population suggests that 4% of the general population and 21% of a clinical population had either deliberately burnt or cut themselves without attempting to commit suicide (Briere & Gil, 1998). Despite the recent increase in attention to the area of self-harm there is not a satisfying definition of self-harming behavior. When defined broadly, self-harming behavior can be stated as a deliberate and direct attempt to destroy or alter bodily tissues without trying to commit suicide (Favazza, 1998; Winchel & Stanley, 1991). However, the aim of this chapter is not to debate the definitions of self-harming behavior or to speak about self-harm as a category. Instead, the chapter discusses self-destructive behaviour from a clinical ACT perspective that is clearly based on a functional analysis of behaviors in certain contexts. From this perspective both the analysis and intervention view behaviors as less categorical and more dimensional.

There are a number of studies that describe similarities, background variables and maintenance factors of self-destructive behaviors (Gratz, 2001). The topography (e.g., traits, diagnosis) of self-harming behavior differs between populations. The most common self-harming behavior reported is overdose. Thirty per cent or more of those who commit suicide have a medically documented history of self-harming behavior (Hawton & Fagg, 1992). The literature suggests a number of overrepresented background variables for those who self-harm including sexual abuse, troublesome home environment, neglect, loss of significant other, and early injury that needs medical attention, to name a few (Chapman, Gratz & Brown, 2006; Hawton, Fagg & Simkin, 1996). In describing integration of topographical and functional assessments, it has been suggested that '... behavior topography may serve as a useful starting point for the identification of relevant target behaviors and that topographical assessment should then give way to the identification of the more functional properties of clinically relevant behavior' (Farmer & Nelson-Gray, 2005, p. 133).

Functional Analysis of Self-Destructive Behavior

Chapman and colleagues (2006) state that there is a lack of a unifying, evidence-based, theoretical framework within which to understand the factors that control deliberate self-harm (DSH). They suggest a model for understanding how DSH is controlled called the Experiential Avoidance Model (EAM). Experiential avoidance has been conceptualized as a functional response class. That is, it represents 'a group of behaviors that, although possibly different in form, are alike to the extent that they produce the same or similar outcomes' (Farmer & Nelson-Gray, 2005, p. 104). Experiential avoidance occurs when humans not only avoid situational dangers but also thoughts, emotions and memories related to unpleasant events. The EAM has been based on an integration of research on emotions,

DSH and experiential avoidance. The model is built on research findings that indicate that DSH is primarily controlled by negative reinforcement and concludes that emotional regulation is a key element of DSH (Chapman et al., 2006). Even though negative reinforcement is the most common described maintenance factor for DSH, positive reinforcement is also a contributing process. Thus, DSH is developed and maintained by multiple processes, and although one of the key functions appears to be emotional regulation, the specific manifestation of these relationships in individual cases, requires analysis.

Dialectic Behavior Therapy and ACT are two models built on functional analysis that have been evaluated in the treatment of self-harm, both on its own and in combination with other problems. The models aim to decrease experiential avoidance and increase behaviors that will help the client in directions that they consider meaningful and important (Linehan, Armstrong, Suarez, Allmon, & Heard, 1991; Gratz & Gundersson, 2006; Swedish Council on Technology Assessment in Health Care, 2005). Both DBT and ACT therapists continuously conduct functional analyses of behaviors as they relate within sessions and outside of sessions. The following chapter examines an acceptance, values and mindfulness inter-vention, developed through a functional analysis of self-destructive behaviors.

The base of any ACT therapy is the functional analysis of behavior in a certain context. Context refers to behaviors that can be observed by one or more persons, and the situation in which the behaviors occur. Using a functional approach on behavior implies that it is not the topography of behavior that we as therapist are interested in, but the function of the behavior. The functional stance toward behavior in an ACT model suggests that self-destructive behaviors are only self-destructive if the function of the behavior is not effective in building a more value-based, vital life. Consider the following example of a broad and general analysis of how self-destructive behavior for adolescents may develop. Note that an analysis of behavior can be done on different levels and that this is a broad and general analysis. The focus that follows is mainly on an individual and interpersonal level.

Case Analysis

Linda is a 14-year-old adolescent who has grown up in a home where alcohol and fighting has been very common. Linda tried different ways to get her parents' attention during her early years, but most of the time she was neglected. She tried to talk to them but was not listened to; she tried to help out at home but did not get any feedback except when she had not done the dishes or taken care of her sister and her brother. She tried to talk to her teachers at school but they saw her as a troublemaker and did not know what to do. In the classroom she was rowdy and disturbed the class in different ways. Linda's teachers tried to control and discipline her by sending her out of the classroom, yelling at her, imposing strict rules, and placing her in a smaller class. Nothing seemed to work; her destructive behavior escalated and she dropped out of school. Finally, the Social Service department conducted an evaluation about the ability of Linda's parents to care for her needs. Consequently Linda was removed from her home and placed in a centre for self-destructive adolescents who self-harm. Figure 1 depicts the vicious cycle Linda was stuck in before she was removed from her family and placed at the treatment centre.

Linda's basic human need for attention and care was neglected at home and in school. Teachers and adults around Linda tried to discipline her using rules and punishment that led to more resistance, self-harm and a rigid behavior pattern, which led to more out-of-control behavior. On the surface, this might not seem like functional behavior from Linda's point of view. However, on second viewing, her attention needs were met, she was removed from a family where she was neglected, and people started to listen to her and care about her family situation. Important human functions were met for Linda in both the short term and long term.

Nock and Prinstein (2004) target four types of functions that maintain self-destructive behavior:

• *automatic negative reinforcement,* where self-destructive behavior is used to reduce negative affect

• *automatic positive reinforcement* where self-destructive behavior is used to create arousal, elation or a feeling of being relaxed

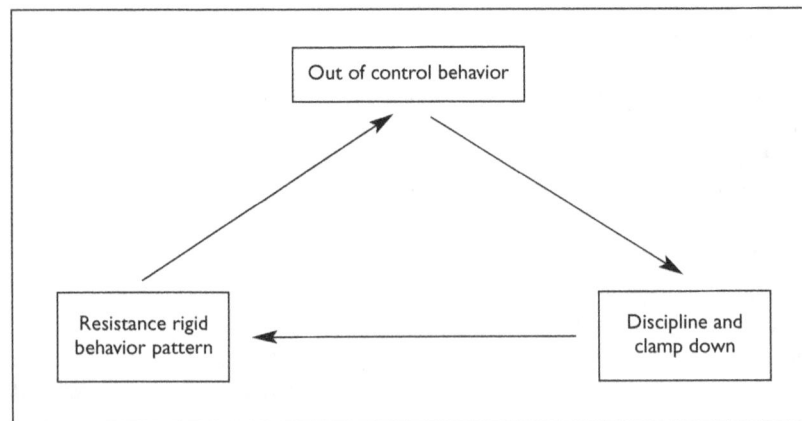

FIGURE 8.1
Linda's vicious cycle.

- *social negative reinforcement* with the function of escaping unpleasant situations

- *social positive reinforcement* which functions to create important attention from persons in his/her surrounding.

Obviously, the understanding of maintenance factors is of the utmost importance in treating a person with self-destructive behavior with an ACT approach.

Breaking the Cycle

The first step in therapy is to analyze the behavioral cycle and create a hypothesis about how to respond to Linda's behavior differently in order to stimulate new learning experiences. The analysis should include triggering factors, behaviors, maintenance factors, and the context in which the behavior occurs. The analysis will provide a guide during treatment. A treatment hypothesis is developed and evaluated, and the analysis and treatment hypothesis may need to be reviewed and revised to best help Linda. Linda's environment has not encouraged the development of commonly accepted behaviors. She has developed rowdy behavior and self-harm as a way of expressing herself and to help her gain both situational and emotional control (emotional control is discussed later in the chapter). Her behavior repertoire seems rigid. She is not behaving in a way that makes people around her want to care for her and spend time with her. Discipline and rules have not been helped Linda at school, but have led to more resistance and out-of-control behavior. In her context, being rowdy and self-harming have been functional, and it can be assumed she will continue to behave in that way if the response (discipline, rules and control) to her behaviors continues in the same way. This vicious cycle needs to be broken and help provided to Linda to build a broader behavior repertoire so that she can choose behaviors, rather than reacting to sensations and emotions. A key factor in behavior change is to create a space where an interaction between the client and the therapist can take place. In the following treatment sequence, the therapist responds to out-of-control behavior with acceptance and interest in order to break the destructive behavior cycle and make room for new learning experiences.

The aim of the treatment is to help Linda choose behaviors controlled by what she wants her life to be about, instead of being controlled by emotions, fears, memories, sensations and thoughts. Instead of reacting to out-of-control behavior and responding with increased discipline, rules and control, an alternative is to respond with values-based acceptance in order to make room for increased interaction, communication and new learning experiences. Discipline, rules and control are dysfunctional ther-

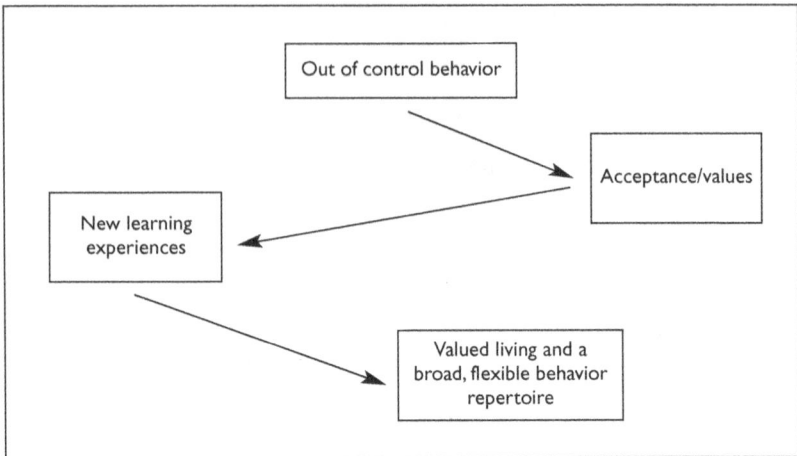

FIGURE 8.2
Example of treatment sequence.

apeutic behaviors in this context because the function of the responses is that Linda has continued to apply self-harming behaviors. It is not that discipline, control and rules are bad per se, it is simply recognizing that, according to our analysis, the function of the behaviors people around Linda have applied to her have functioned as reinforcers of self-harm. For Linda, although those behaviors may have had an important function, at this stage of her life they may no longer be necessary. The aim is to help Linda develop a broader behavior repertoire in her own valued direction. This will emerge from establishing of a relationship where Linda listens her therapist. The therapeutic space between Linda and the therapist is an important element in successful therapy. It is partly developed through an accepting and respectful stance between clients and therapists. Acceptance involves not only accepting Linda's and the therapist's feelings in session but also accepting feelings from both Linda and the therapist when they seek to understand what Linda cares deeply about. Metaphorically speaking, the role of the therapist is to be the 'advocate' of Linda's personally stated values. The therapist validates the suffering and gently acts as an advocate of values. In Linda's case this approach is likely to be radically different from anything she has previously experienced. Her behavior has either been met with frustration, neglect, punishment or full discipline, which have not helped her develop into a person living a valued, vital life.

Below is an example of a values- and acceptance-based introduction between Linda and her therapist in the initial phase of the treatment. Prior to this conversation Linda had cut herself and she was obviously expecting the therapist to tell her that she has to stop doing that.

T: Hi Linda, I am glad to see you.

L: Hmm, sure you are ... I have cut myself and I don't care what you say, it felt great!

T: Ok ... well Linda, I am here to get to know you and find out in what way I can be of help for you in your life and where we are right now. Even though it may sound strange to you, I am here because one important part of my life is being here for you and other girls, to find out a way to live life that is based on what you want, what gives you strength, fun and meaning in life. I am here for you and your life, not your cutting. I can't make you stop your cutting and I don't want to force you into anything. You will probably cut yourself as long as it works for you and until you have something that is more important and an alternative. If you ever want to try other things in life and other ways of relating to life I would like to do that with you. How does that sound?

In this initial phase of therapy the therapist wants to establish a values- and acceptance-based context. The aim of this relationship is to help the client to develop her behavior repertoire and contact new learning experiences. Ultimately, we want the client to get in touch with natural contingencies that help her choose valued behaviors, search for meaningfulness and not be a 'slave' to aversive stimuli. The therapist states his value of being a therapist and does not get into any discussions about right or wrong, good or bad. The functional approach is established and consistently flows through the whole treatment. Wherever possible, every response in the therapeutic relationship should be based on functional thinking.

Note that the therapist in this conversation stated that he was not especially interested in her cutting behavior; he was interested in what she wanted to be about, what she was afraid of and how he could be of help to her in life. The aim of that response is to help the client and the therapist not to get stuck in discussions about the pros and cons related to cutting, but to be about 'life' and 'something else', even if that 'life' and 'something else' is not defined yet in their relationship. What the therapist wants is to get in contact with other possible behaviors that would reinforce and develop another way of communicating. Furthermore, telling Linda (and many other self-cutting girls) to stop cutting herself is something others have tried to do and that has not worked, in the sense that she is still cutting herself and she is not developing and making her behavior repertoire more flexible. This approach states that Linda will cut herself as long as cutting works for her. This statement is informed by several concepts. First, the therapist does not want to get stuck in arguments with Linda about what she should or should not do. Arguments may make Linda distance herself from the therapist or engage in pliant behavior and that is not the aim of therapy. Second, the therapist wants Linda to develop a behavior repertoire based 'in' her life, in contact with her natural contingencies. Third, the therapist wants to introduce a functional base in their communication for when they discuss behaviors. Fourth, the therapist wants to weaken the verbal and emotional links between this therapy and Linda's prior experiences of therapy and therapist. Adolescents like Linda may have often had negative prior experiences with therapists and 'helpers'. This therapy is meant to be about a fresh start based in the here and now, with the aim of increasing Linda's flexibility and valued behavior.

Therapist as a Stimulus, Responder and Reinforcer

As a therapist you are the stimulus, responder and possible reinforcer for behavior. Reflecting on your behavior as a therapist from a base of learning principles can affect the therapy session and the treatment of self-harming behavior. Applying learning principles in-session can broaden your behavior repertoire as a therapist and give you an opportunity to reinforce and stimulate behaviors that lead to a more valued life for the client, contingent on behavior. Functional analytic psychotherapy (FAP; Kohlenberg & Tsai, 1991) applies learning theory inside the therapeutic relationship and states that effective interpersonal behaviors can be trained in session. With a 'FAP stance' in ACT, problematic behaviors are evoked and blocked, and effective behavior is stimulated and reinforced. Ideas from FAP may be helpful in the treatment of self-destructive behavior, especially when interpersonal problematic behaviors are evident (which they often are). Interpersonal problems often co-occur with self-harming behaviors and this is found particularly in those diagnosed with borderline personality disorder.

The literature evaluating the etiology of self-cutting suggests that sexual abuse and other physical harm that require hospital care are positively correlated with self-harm (Weierich & Nock, 2008). Furthermore, lack of emotional closeness and neglect from caregivers during the child's upbringing is a common factor for those who self-harm (Briere & Gil, 1998; Favazza, 1989). Neglect occurs in an interpersonal relationship and influences the child's future behavior in relationships. The neglected child may not acquire the commonly accepted interpersonal skills, but instead develops behaviors to survive in a specific environment. The behaviors can be different, but share the same function of providing attention, feelings of security and so forth. The learning history in interpersonal relations affects the adolescent's future interpersonal skills and will be given special attention in this section of the chapter. A functional approach is used to reflect upon how neglect can affect behavior and how the developed behavior may be dealt with in the therapy room.

The interpersonal behavior repertoire for a person who has been neglected and for whom the needs of attention and care have not been met may be affected in numerous ways. Consider this example: a child seeks reassurance and comfort from her caregiver because she is sad. She has been hurt when she played with friends on the street and runs inside for comfort. When she gets inside and seeks comfort her caregiver ignores her most of the time, which in this case has the function of a punisher or blocker. A punished or blocked behavior will decrease in frequency when the punisher (the caregiver) is present. Running inside to seek comfort is something that the child will do less frequently. If the behavior class of seeking comfort is punished in different situations it is likely that the child will develop a rule saying that 'seeking comfort is bad and not something I should do'. The child may also develop a rule saying, 'I should not tell people what I feel or show them I am sad'. A clinical reflection is that the child will probably, through relational framing, mix two responses that could be called closeness and pain. Closeness refers to the warm, secure, safe and comforting experience a child/person has when he/she is taken care of when hurt. Pain refers to the experience a child/person might feel when he/she has been punished, hurt, traumatized or neglected. The caregiver who initially may have been associated with a safe haven, someone who has given comfort and someone to trust, has added punishment, hurt, ignorance and suffering functions to her/his appearance. This leads to uncertainty in relations and affects future relations in important ways. Intertwining pain and closeness has important implications for treatment planning.

Through transformation of stimulus functions it is likely that a therapist who wants to help evokes the same functions as the caregivers, earlier therapists, teachers and other persons in the health and social service agencies. The new therapist acquires both the 'good' and 'bad' functions. Seeking and receiving care and being vulnerable in relations are in a relation frame with pain and suffering. When the therapist applies a warm, caring therapeutic stance he or she may evoke both emotions and experience that trigger destructive behaviors. Consider the following therapeutic conversation between a therapist and a self-destructive adolescent with a history of being neglected and abused by her caregivers. The therapist uses a functional approach in session and is very sensitive to the client's body language, positioning and overall behavior in session. The conversation takes place during the start of therapy. The client has started to be a little engaged in session and they start to get a more relaxed contact.

T: Welcome back Linda, how glad I am to see you!

L: Sure you are … I am sure that you say that to everyone!

T: What is so hard about me saying that I am glad to see you?

L: Just because ... (Linda looks away and starts to scratch her scars)

T: Linda, I don't want to hurt you, I notice that you are getting anxious. I am curious to understand why your body reacts and evokes so much feeling and you get so anxious when I say that I am glad to see you and that I care about you.

L: You are not the first and you will leave me just like everyone else! I hate you!

T: OK, Linda (with a soft voice), I see a lot of emotions and memories popping up ... do I understand you correctly, that people you have been close have left you and that has been really painful for you?

L: Sort of ...

T: So, when I say I am glad to see you and we are getting to know each other, painful memories of when people close to you, have abandoned you and emotions connected to those memories pop up, here and now, and makes our connection painful ... am I correct?

L: Yes, that is what happens, I get very anxious and angry!

T: Would it be important for you to be able to develop relations where people can care about you without you pushing them away because your emotions and memories say that it is dangerous?

L: Yes, that would be nice but people leave me. That is how it is ...

T: Is it OK if I suggest something?

L: Yes, I really don't want to get anxious around people I care about all the time, I want to be able to make friends, have fun and trust others.

T: In order to help you to be able to let people care about you, I suggest that we start in here with our relationship, you and me. When you react to me or to things I say you can just tell me that and we can stop and reflect on it together in order to learn more about you and what you need. No reaction or thought is wrong or bad, they are what they are. OK?

L: OK, a bit scary, but OK.

This conversation shows a range of different aspects of the analysis and treatment of self-destructive behavior. All of them are important, summarized and discussed below.

The beginning of the interaction between Linda and her therapist shows how Linda's memories are brought into the present and trigger an aggressive behavior. Linda is not reacting on natural contingencies but instead she reacts to the relation between stimuli in the outer and inner context, which is a verbally derived process. Her therapist states that he is happy to see her and that he cares about her. That triggers memories, emotions and sensations that remind her about being left behind and punished. This stimulates aggressive behavior and pushing people away. People around Linda have probably reinforced the aggressive behavior by letting her be alone or becoming angry with her when she has behaved aggressively. Being on her own might be easier in the short run because Linda might think that at least she will not get hurt. The therapist presents this hypothesis to Linda and she supports it by stating that persons have left her and that she is afraid that the therapist will do the same. Nothing in the present moment suggests that he would do that, except Linda's memories and her related experiences.

The therapist acknowledges and validates Linda's feelings and says that he can see that Linda is strongly affected by her emotions. However, he does not let himself be drawn into a discussion about right versus wrong, pros and cons, nor does he get drawn into arguing about whether he is going to leave her or not. Instead he takes a functional approach toward the content she is presenting. He reflects on why the emotions are evoked in this context and how this can be brought into an analysis of Linda's behavior and treatment. He evaluates the possible contextual factors triggering her behavior and he reflects on the maintenance factors for Linda's behavior in their interaction. The therapist takes a functional stance toward Linda, both in their therapeutic relationship and toward the content she is presenting.

After acknowledging, validating and helping Linda to reflect functionally on her reactions the therapist takes the next step in the treatment by asking Linda about her values in this situation. The therapist introduces values early in the treatment to create a reference point. The reference point — metaphorically the 'lighthouse', the compass or the Bulls-Eye — will become a guide for the client, the therapist and their time together. The reference point will also function as the measure of whether Linda is on her preferred track. Values have important functions in a successful therapy. In addition to being a reference point and a guide for behavior, values work may broaden Linda's behavior repertoire and stimulate behaviors toward her valued directions. She would be able to build a relationship with the therapist based on what she wants and needs in therapy and not her negative emotions. Therapy can help Linda take steps to create the life she values, instead of getting rid of negative emotions. Furthermore, values work can highlight the discrepancy between how Linda is living and what she wants to be about. The experience of the discrepancy creates a psychological space that can stimulate value-driven actions.

The reference point is established and the therapist asks for a commitment to the chosen direction. What the therapist suggests is built on the analysis he has conducted in the first two or three interactions. He validates Linda by summarizing what she has said in the analysis and asks if he understands her correctly. Furthermore, he suggests that they start to act according to her valued direction inside their therapeutic relationship. He suggests that Linda practice being as she values being in their relationship and make room for all the emotions, memories and reactions in the service of learning more about her reactions. The aim of this intervention is to help Linda be more able to choose actions, instead of reacting to emotions and memories. Linda agrees with the suggestion and commits to the work. A treatment hypothesis is created and built on a functional analysis. As in all behavior therapeutic the treatment hypothesis is tested, evaluated, and changed if the results dictate.

Avoiding Emotions, Thoughts and Sensations Instead of Natural Dangers

Aspects of how therapists can think about self-destructive behavior and self-harm from a functional analytic perspective have been discussed. An example was provided describing how functional analysis can be conducted relatively quickly and early in the session to create a treatment hypothesis and to develop direction in therapy. The following section of the chapter describes how to continue the treatment from the initial analysis. Limited space does not permit presentation of a full protocol but key processes and ways to work with these processes are presented. Initially, emotional avoidance is examined and related to self-destructive behavior. The discussion about emotional avoidance and how to relate to that leads to values clarification and how to use the Bulls-Eye diary in the treatment of self-harm.

Experiential avoidance has been shown to be a core process in psychopathology (Hayes et al., 2006). Experiential avoidance is the process where a person avoids thoughts, feelings and emotions related to a painful event and not the painful event per se. A review of information about Linda will help explain the concept of experiential avoidance.

Linda had one place were she could go when her parents fought in a way that she could not stand and that was to her grandparents. The grandparents did not live far from Linda's family. She could easily jump on her bike and go to them when she needed. At her grandparents Linda could rest and eat properly. She felt safe and in harmony with her grandparents. With them she could be a little girl who played with dolls and sat by the kitchen table drawing for hours. One day, just after Linda turned 12 her grandfather sexually abused her. The abuse did not stop until Linda was removed from her home by the Social Service. In therapy, Linda was a high experiential avoider, and much of her behavior was aimed at avoiding experiences that were likely to be related to that abuse. She tried to avoid almost all emotions, especially emotions related to possible important and vital relationships. She avoided thoughts about her grandparents and did not want to talk about her family. Her grandparents were related to pain as well as warmth, which probably made Linda try to avoid almost all emotions. Linda's emotional life was very chaotic due to her verbally derived network between her different experiences of warmth/security on the one hand and abuse on the other hand. 'Good' and 'bad' feelings were mixed and created emotional chaos.

When Linda felt emotions she automatically, almost reflexively, did something to diminish that emotion. She developed a behavioral repertoire that worked in the short run (symptom reduction) but with her valued life as a reference many of her behaviors were not effective. Her avoidance behaviors might have had important functions earlier in her life but not at the centre (new contexts often requires new behaviors) and probably not in her future life. Furthermore, her avoidance behavior made her less receptive to natural contingencies; instead she was under aversive control and acted on her thoughts and feelings about the world instead of what it is that actually happens in the situations she is in. Metaphorically speaking, it is not Linda who makes choices, rather it is her emotions, thoughts and feelings. Our aim is to help Linda be free and not a slave to her experiences; not free in the sense that she will be rid of her experiences, but in the sense that she can have emotions, sensations, and thoughts, and choose her behavior according to what she wants her life to be about. The aim is to help Linda get in touch with her 'potential' in any situation. For example, imagine that a valued area for Linda is friendship. Friendship for Linda includes being able to laugh and have fun as well as cry and be vulnerable in relationships. Therapy aims to help Linda be able to choose that direction. At the beginning of therapy Linda is fused and stuck with experiences that occur in situations here and now and control her behavior. This fusion and 'stuckness' with experiences creates a rigid behavior repertoire and a 'values illness'. Consider the following conversation, where the therapist tries to help Linda get present with natural contingencies and not be stuck in the past or the future. The aim of the session is to create a space for emotions in the service of making Linda more able to create relations outside the therapy room with all her emotions. The therapist will introduce a home assignment for Linda with the aim of being more in the present moment.

Linda: This is so hard, I cannot have a relationship with anyone I am hopeless (whispering, looking down).

Therapist: Hmm, you are sitting here struggling with a lot of thoughts and emotions.

L: Hmm

T: What does this lead to right now?

L: I don't know ... nothing good I guess

T: Does it take us closer or further apart?

L: Further apart I guess.

T: OK, so when you are sitting there struggling with emotions and thoughts it doesn't help you to live the life you want, is that so?

L: Yes, that is right (looking up).

T: Hmm, and now you are more here with me, are you?

L: Yes, it loosens up in my chest a bit.

T: Let's sit with this for a moment ... with your emotions at the same time as you are connecting with me, looking me in the eyes.

(After about 30 seconds of silence.)

L: Sometimes I am here and sometimes I wander off.

T: OK, so by looking up and getting in contact with the things around you, where you are and what you are set to do, loosens your chest a bit. Struggling doesn't seem to help you ... Does this often happen to you? That you are getting stuck in experiences like emotions and thoughts instead of what is really happening in the actual situation?

L: Yes, it happens quite often, especially at school where there are a lot of people.

T: OK, I have an idea that you can try if you want to work with being here and now and do what you are set to do. I call it the Presence Report.

L: Sure, let's try it.

At the beginning of this conversation Linda is struggling with emotions and thoughts, instead of being in contact with the situation here and now. Linda is not in contact with what it is that happens between her and her therapist. Her focus is on her own emotions and thoughts. In this conversation the therapist is helping her to shift perspective and let the focus instead be on Linda's values (being present with others and her therapist). The therapist is asking about the function of her behavior in a values context. Furthermore, the therapist is reinforcing behaviors that seem to help her to be more in contact with natural contingencies, that is, her conversation and connection with her therapist. In the middle and the end of the conversation Linda is encouraged to be in the moment, in contact with her values and in contact with the moment. At the end of the conversation a home assignment is introduced and Linda shows a willingness to work on her ability to be more present in situations and relations.

The Presence Report (see Appendix A) was developed to function as a discrimination-training tool, an instrument to measure presence in life, a pedagogical tool and a way to measure outcome in therapy. It is also possible to ask the client to rate how she felt during different actions and to evaluate the correlation between being present and how they feel. In the example below, the client is given a diary to use with the Presence Report. On the second page the client is encouraged to write notes about how she felt and the differences between being present and not present. Furthermore, she is encouraged to develop her own thoughts about this exercise on the 'reflection page'. Doing this every evening aims to help the client to become more aware of thoughts, emotions and sensations that are controlling her behavior and encouraging her to willingly embrace these experiences. Below is an example of Monday's reflection section from a self-destructive adolescent.

> Today was a pretty good day. I ate breakfast and usually I feel present when I do that, even calm. Maybe I should start eating breakfast more often, I think it gives me more energy during the days ... At about 11 am I took the bus to the gym. There were some others on the bus but I didn't hide behind my hood as I usually do. I noticed them and that my pulse aroused a bit and continued to read my book. I went to school after the gym and it was OK. I was there to 3.00 pm. Got on the bus around 3:30 and went to the centre. When I arrived there were two girls fighting which made me scared and I almost dissociated. Fighting makes me so scared! It is even worse when I like the ones involved. Anna, who is a friend of mine, was one of the girls fighting. At 6.00 pm I had a meeting with the Social Service and I was just thinking about other things, I hate those meetings! I am not present at all! It didn't feel good because we talk about budget and that is important for me. Have to practice more on that! During the evening I sat by the computer watching movies, it was OK but I think I did that on autopilot.

Using the presence diary helps the client practice being present in everyday life. Furthermore, it encourages the client to reflect on her behavior and may help her to do her own analysis on triggers for fear and avoidance. In session, the Presence Report and reflection diary can be used to support functional analysis in difficult situations and when experiencing difficult bodily sensations and thoughts. The aim is to help the client to decrease experiential avoidance and increase psychological flexibility. Creating a psychological space for sensations and emotions also creates space for values and commitment work. Being present and in contact with natural contingencies is important, both in everyday life and in the therapy session. Without a functional contact between the therapist and the client therapy will not be of help to increase valued living.

Increase Valued Living, Avoid Values Pitfalls and How to Use the Bulls-Eye Living Instrument

Valued living is the goal of therapy for self-destructive clients, just as it is for all clients when using an ACT approach. The use of mindfulness training and the decrease of experiential avoidance increases the possibility of adding new learning experiences. Practicing mindfulness might, for many clients, be a new experience in itself. However, the aim of that training is to increase valued living and contact with natural contingencies. Choosing a new direction in life and broadening the behavior repertoire can be a tough task for self-destructive adolescents. Discussions about values need to be conducted in a way that helps the client become willing to embrace what they consider important in life.

Closely linked with values is pain. Values work has been incorporated in the chapter so far because it is closely intertwined with all the other processes. Contacting your feelings and being present with your friends can be an important value. Being present in therapy and in the therapeutic relationship can be a value. Being present with family members and your body can be a value. A key aspect of the therapeutic flow is the analysis. This will guide you about which processes to work with. Another way to work with values for self-destructive adolescents is the Bulls-Eye diary.

The Bulls-Eye diary is often presented to adolescents after work to decrease experiential avoidance to increase their willingness to explore what they want life to be about. Questions about what adolescents want their life to be about often need a base in psychological flexibility and a strong therapeutic relationship. Furthermore, work with values, psychological flexibility and the therapeutic relationship are intertwined and one does not necessarily come before the other. Again, what is done in therapy should be suggested by your functional analysis.

Working with values and what is important in life for adolescents needs careful attention. Values work contains dangerous pitfalls for the therapist. Possible pitfalls are described below, with a statement and an example from a conversation, followed by possible thoughts from the therapist's perspective.

Pitfall 1

Beware of your own values of what you consider to be an important and meaningful life.

Example from a therapeutic conversation:

T: What do you want your life to be about from now on, Linda?

L: I have given that quite a lot of thought. I want to move home to Mum and just be with her helping her with my brothers, clean and wash.

Possible therapist thoughts:

She's going to do what! She has the ability to do so much more! Move home, clean and take care of her brothers! Hmm, how can I make her choose school instead? I absolutely think that she is meant for something more than that!

It is quite possible that if you have worked with clients you recognize these types of thoughts. You want something different and something more, because of your own programming of what a good life is like. You care about your client and you might have had the thought that she is worth something else. Being a therapist does not mean that you are right about life; who are we to decide what a good life is? That is not our job as ACT therapists. An ACT therapist's job is to help our clients be able to live their chosen valued lives inside of the limits of the law. It is important that therapists working with self-destructive clients have access to supervision where they can discuss and reflect on their own reactions in therapy. Furthermore, videotaping and letting colleagues in a supervision group comment on it might help the therapist get perspective on their therapeutic stance. It can also be a help to write a therapeutic diary reflecting on both the work and the reactions you might have as a therapists.

Pitfall 2

That action cannot be a value driven action because of the form of it!

> T: Hi Linda, I am very curious to hear about your values work during the week.

> L: I have taken steps! I contacted a guy over the Internet and met him. He wanted to have sex, he was ugly, but I had sex with him anyway. It was not very good but I really want to be able to have physical intimacy and closeness to others.

Possible therapist thoughts:

> My God! She sold herself on the Internet! That was not a valued step, that was prostitution! You have to tell her to meet other guys!

As discussed earlier in the chapter, ACT work is built on a functional analysis. An ACT therapist is more interested in function than form and topography. All countries have laws that set limits on what we can and cannot do. It is important to make room for your own thoughts. However, in this case it is possible that it was a valued step. We can as therapists help adolescents to broaden their behavior repertoire and help them to reflect on the function of behavior in both the short and long term. An ACT therapist should avoid to get caught up in right or wrong or good or bad. An ACT therapist is only interested if it is workable or not with values as a reference.

The Bulls-Eye Living Diary

Using the Bulls-Eye in a diary form may encourage the client to work with values every day. The aim of the Bulls-Eye diary is to help clients get in contact with their valued directions and stimulate activity in those chosen directions. In this exercise we want the adolescents to ask themselves what they want their life to be about, every morning when they get up. We encourage them to choose a direction and choose a step that will coincide with that direction. When they get back to their diary in the evening they evaluate their steps using the Bulls-Eye dartboard. See Appendix B for an example of the Bulls-Eye diary for adolescents.

Clients are encouraged to write down what they are choosing to value during the day. If friendship is the area, we encourage them to describe the quality of friendship. Describing the quality and not only saying the word can strengthen the reinforcing qualities of the described value. Furthermore, after choosing the area to value they are asked to choose a step that they are willing to take to honor that value. Remember that it is not the form or the topography of the step, but rather the function we are interested in. We encourage clients to challenge themselves, but at the same time not 'force' themselves into doing things. Forcing behavior can never be a valued action in ACT. If friendship is the value, sending an SMS to an old friend they lost contact with and asking them out for a cup of tea can be a valued action. They choose what they think is important. In the evening he/she marks an X on the dartboard describing how close he/she was to living in a valued direction during the day. An X in the Bulls-Eye of the dartboard represents that the action, sending an SMS to a friend and the area of friendship, were congruent with the valued direction and vital. An X far from the Bulls-Eye represents that the client was far from living in valued direction. The client and therapist evaluate the work in session.

The form and the layout of the Bulls-Eye diary may influence the effectiveness of the diary. The dartboard is attached on one page of the book. The other page is used as a space for reflection, as with the Presence Report exercise. Clients are asked to write down anything related to the exercise. Reflecting on the difference between living in the Bulls-Eye and not living in the Bulls-Eye is important for discrimination training purposes.

Summary

In this chapter important components in an ACT approach for self-destructive behavior have been discussed. The content is mainly clinical and built on clinical experiences with self-destructive adolescents. ACT applies a functional approach toward behavior. The chapter started with a general analysis of self-destructive behavior and continued with a discussion of treatment processes such as values, experiential avoidance and building a value-based therapeutic relationship. Using case examples, metaphors and transcribed sessions, protocols, experiential avoidance, values and being present were described. At the end of the chapter specific tools and possible home assignments were provided.

References

Briere, J., & Gil, E. (1998). Self mutilation in clinical samples: Prevalence, correlates, and functions. *American Journal of Orthopsychiatry, 68,* 609–620.

Chapman, L. C., Gratz, K. L., & Brown, M. Z. (2006) Solving the puzzle of deliberate self-harm: The experiential avoidance model. *Behaviour Research and Therapy.* 44 (2006) 371–394.

Farmer, R. F., & Nelson-Gray, R. O. (2005). *Personality guided behavior therapy.* Washington, D.C.: American Psychological Association.

Favazza, A. R. (1989). Why patients mutilate themselves. *Hospital and Community Psychiatry, 40,* 137–145.

Favazza, A. R. (1998). The coming of age of self-mutilation. *Journal of Nervous and Mental Diseases, 186,* 259–268.

Gratz, K. L. (2001). Measurement of deliberate self-harm: Preliminary data on the Deliberate Self-Harm Inventory. *Journal of Psychopathology and Behavioral Assessment, 23*, 253–263.

Gratz, K. L., & Gundersson, J. G. (2006). Preliminary data on an acceptance-based emotion regulation group intervention for deliberate self-harm among women with borderline personality disorder. *Behavior Therapy, 37*(1), 25–35.

Hawton, K., & Fagg, J. (1992). Deliberate self-poisoning and self-injury in adolescents: A study of characteristics and trends in Oxford, 1976–1989. *British Journal of Psychiatry, 161*, 816–823.

Hawton, K., Fagg, J., Simkin, S,. Bale, E., & Bond, A. (2000). Deliberate self-harm in adolescents in Oxford, 1985–1995. *Journal of Adolescence, 23*, 47–55.

Hawton, K., Fagg, J., & Simkin, S. (1996). Deliberate self-poisoning and self-injury in children and adolescents under 16 years of age in Oxford, 1976–1993. *British Journal of Psychiatry, 169*, 202–208.

Hayes, S. C., Luoma, J., Bond, F., Masuda, A., & Lillis, J. (2006). acceptance and commitment therapy: Model, processes, and outcomes. *Behaviour Research and Therapy, 44*, 1–25.

Kohlenberg, R. J., & Tsai, M. (1991). *Functional analytic psychotherapy: Creating and curative therapeutic relationships.* New York: Plenum.

Linehan, M. M., Armstrong, H. E., Suarez, A., Allmon, D., & Heard, H. L. (1991). Cognitive–behavioral treatment of chronically parasuicidal borderline patients. *Archives of General Psychiatry, 48*, 1060–1064.

Lundh, L. G., Karim, J., & Quilisch, E. (2007). Deliberate self-harm in 15-year-old adolescents. A pilot study with a modified version of the Deliberate Self-Harm Inventory. *Scandinavian Journal of Psychology, 48*, 33–41.

Nock, M. K., & Prinstein, M. J. (2004). A function approach to the assessment of self-mutilative behavior. *Journal of Consulting and Clinical Psychology, 72*, 885–890.

Swedish Council on Technology Assessment in Health Care. (2005). *Dialectic behavior therapy for borderline disorders.* SBU alert report NO; 2005–07, www.sbu.se/alert

Winchel, R. M., & Stanley, M. (1991). Self-injurious behavior: A review of the behavior and biology of self-mutilation. *American Journal of Psychiatry, 148*, 306–316.

Weierich, M. R., & Nock, M. K. (2008). Posttraumatic stress syndrome mediates the relationship between childhood sexual abuse and nonsuicidal self-injury. *Journal of Consulting and Clinical Psychology, 76*, 39–44.

APPENDIX A
The Presence Report

Name_____ Week_____

Time of day	Monday	Tuesday	Wednesday	Thursday	Friday	Saturday	Sunday
8–9	~/X	Z	Z	€	Z	Z	Z
9–10	X	Z	€	€	Z	~	Z
10–11	~	Z	€	€	Z	€	Z
11–12	~	€	~	~	~	~	Z
12–13	X	€	X	~	~	€	Z
13–14	X	€	~	€	€	€	~
14–15	X	~	~	~	€	~	~
15–16	€	€	~	~	€	€	~
16–17	€	~	~	€	~	€	€
17–18	€	~	€	~	~	~	~
18–19	~	~	~	~	€	~	€
19–20	~	~	€	€	~	€	~
20–21	~	~	€	~	~	~	~
21–22	~	€	€	Z	~	~	€
22–23	~	~	€	Z	€	~	~
23–00	€	~	~	Z	€	~	~
00–01	Z	~	~	Z	~	€	€
01–02	Z	~	~	Z	€	€	~
02–03	Z	~0	€	Z	~	Z	€

Use the symbols below to describe your level of presence during the day. Use your dairy to reflect on your day. Here are some questions that may stimulate your thinking. What was the difference between being present and not being present? How did that feel? What type of situations was it easy or respectively difficult to be present? Is there a pattern in your presence diary, when you are present and when you are not?

Note: € = Not present

~ = Present and not present

X = Present

Z = Sleeping

APPENDIX B
The Bulls-Eye Living Diary

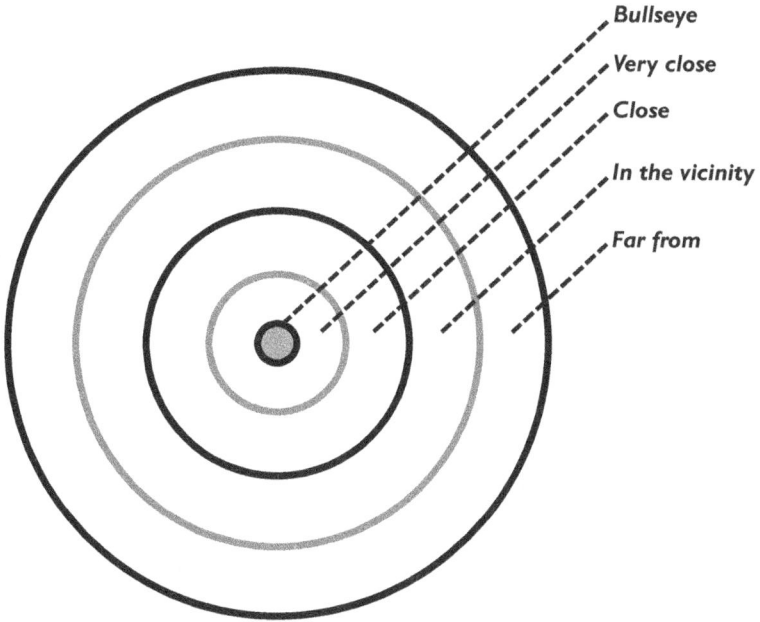

Part A. What direction would you like to develop in today? Write the direction on the lines below.

_____
_____
_____

Part B. What can be a step in that direction?

_____
_____
_____

chapter nine

Acceptance and Commitment Therapy Training for Work Stress and Burnout in Mental Health Direct Care Providers

J. Scott Bethay, Kelly G. Wilson and Katherine H. Moyer

Robert, age 19, has been working for the past year as a direct care worker in a public residential facility for children with intellectual disabilities. Initially, he was very dedicated and enthusiastic about this work because it allowed him to do things that he valued highly — helping others less fortunate than him and making a difference in the lives of young people. The children loved him and he was liked and respected by his fellow employees. He had even contemplated taking some night classes toward a degree in special education. Yet just this past week, Robert decided to quit his job.

In the beginning he was sure his efforts would pay off, but lately it seems that, despite all his hard work, the children never really improve. To make matters worse, he has come to believe that the psychologists and other 'experts' brought in to help them manage the children's behavior really don't know what they are talking about and are unwilling to listen to the direct care staff. Often, the interventions that they suggest actually seem to make the clients' behavior worse, and he has become increasingly cynical about the 'team' approach extolled by his organization. When things aren't up to standard it always seems that he, as the 'lowest on the food chain', catches the blame. He reasoned that he certainly wasn't being paid enough to put up with this sort of thing.

This altogether common scenario plays out among direct care staff across the globe. This chapter addresses work stress and burnout among such staff, and is aimed at helping them to face the many challenges with which they are presented each day. A large percentage of this workforce lacks formal qualifications, and many of them are young and relatively inexperienced (Hatton & Lobban, 2007; Savicki, 2002). Further, the work itself can be quite daunting, as it may involve providing services to individuals who exhibit high rates of challenging behaviors such as self-injury, aggression and property destruction. This may be particularly true for staff working in psychiatric hospitals and other inpatient settings, because the move toward community placement has concentrated the more challenging clients in those types of facilities (Duff, Readhead, Paxton, Iceton, & Rochester, 2006).

Work-related stress appears to be prevalent among mental health direct care staff. Survey studies conducted in the United Kingdom (UK) have indicated that as many as 30% of intellectual disabilities staff report a clinically significant level of general psychological distress, in comparison to a rate of 18% among other employed adults (Hatton & Lobban, 2007). Staff stress appears to be related to high rates of turnover and absenteeism, which tend to have detrimental effects on the continuity and quality of care (Hastings, Horne, & Mitchell, 2004). Further, staff who are under relatively high levels of stress have been shown to interact less frequently with clients and to engage in fewer positive interactions with them (Lawson & O'Brien, 1994; Rose, Jones, & Fletcher, 1998).

Burnout and its Correlates

It is important to reduce chronic work-related stress, and one step in doing so is to develop ways of speaking that capture its behavioral and affective consequences. One such concept is *burnout*, which is a syndrome that may emerge over time as work demands exceed an employee's personal resources, resulting in dysphoria and impaired performance (Hastings et al., 2004; Lawson & O'Brien, 1994).

Researchers have conceptualized burnout as consisting of three components: *emotional exhaustion, depersonalization* and a *lack of personal accomplishment* (Maslach, Jackson, & Leiter, 1996). Emotional exhaustion refers to feelings of being emotionally depleted, such that workers are no longer able to give of themselves and be psychologically present to clients' distress. A related construct, depersonalization, is the development of callous or impersonal attitudes towards clients. Finally, the third component is a lack of feelings of personal accomplishment, characterized by negative evaluations of one's competence and feeling that one's work has little positive influence (Maslach et al., 1996).

Burnout has been positively correlated with a number of factors, including staff perception of greater investment than return from their organizations and their interactions with clients (Van Dierendonck, Schaufeli, & Buunk, 1996; Van Yperen, 1995), perception of lack of support from management (Blumenthal, Lavender, & Hewson, 1998; Chung,

Corbett, & Cumella, 1998), and a lack of clarity concerning job roles (Blumenthal, Lavender, & Hewson, 1998). Further, positive correlations have been consistently observed between negative emotional reactions to challenging client behaviors and work-related stress measured as burnout (Mitchell & Hastings, 1998; Rose, Horne, Rose, & Hastings, 2004). Tentative evidence links these negative emotional reactions to direct observations of undesirable staff behaviors such as inappropriate restraint and avoidance of clients (Bailey, Hare, Hatton, & Limb, 2006).

Relationships Between Attributions, Emotions, Staff Behavior and Burnout

Significant research attention has been devoted to links between burnout, attributions, emotions and staff behavior toward clients (Dagnan, Trower, & Smith, 1998; Hastings, 2005; Stanley & Standen, 2000). In particular, cognitive–emotional theorists (e.g., Weiner, 1986), have proposed that causal attributions work in concert with emotional reactions to determine behavioral responses. One implication of such cognitive models is that staff experiencing burnout may be more likely to make negative and blaming attributions in response to client behavior (Rose & Rose, 2005). These negative attributions may lead to negative emotional reactions such as anger. When this occurs, staff are less likely to help and more likely to avoid clients (Rose & Rose, 2005). Such post-hoc predictive models may work reasonably well, because past behaviors — even internal ones, such as attributions — predict future behaviors (Stewart, Barnes-Holmes, Barnes-Holmes, Bond, & Hayes, 2006) in similar contexts. However, when the conditions that maintain the relationship between staff attributions and their overt responses are not known, it is difficult to predict and influence staff behavior.

An Alternative View

Given the tendency for stressed staff to avoid client contact, it is reasonable to assume that challenging client behaviors may elicit negative emotional reactions that are aversive to staff (Hastings, 2002). These challenging behaviors would then serve as establishing operations for escape or avoidance behavior (Hastings & Remington, 1994). Paradoxically, this avoidance behavior may take the form of attending to challenging clients. For example, Hall and Oliver (1992) observed staff interactions with an intellectually disabled client who engaged in self-injurious behavior (SIB). Data indicated that the probability of staff attending to the client prior to his exhibiting SIB was very low; however, this probability greatly increased during long bouts of self-injury and was at its highest immediately after the bout ceased. When the client stopped exhibiting SIB, staff attending declined to the previous level. Thus it appeared that SIB functioned as an establishing operation for staff attending behavior, and that attending behavior was negatively reinforced by the termination of SIB. Lack of staff attention served as an establishing operation for the client's SIB, which was positively reinforced by attention from staff, beginning the cycle again.

Continued cycles of aversive control in staff–client interactions may cultivate *emotional exhaustion*. For example, staff who are inadvertently reinforcing challenging client behavior by attending to it may have the impression that no matter how much they attend to the client's needs, the client still wants more. They may abstract an attitude such as 'working with clients is a real strain' (c.f., Stewart et al., 2006), a belief that correlates with the emotional exhaustion component of burnout (Maslach et al., 1996). Such a formulation also effectively coordinates 'clients' with 'strain' (c.f., Hayes, Barnes-Holmes, & Roche, 2001). Since strain is generally regarded as something to be avoided, such beliefs may promote avoidance of clients in general. This is possible because sometimes staff may be responding to contingencies described in their attitudes and beliefs rather than direct experience. Thus, the observed correlations between burnout or stress and avoidance of client contact (Lawson & O'Brien, 1994; Rose et al., 1998) may be due, in part, to the behavior regulatory functions of verbal stimuli such as attitudes or beliefs.

Mutual reinforcement processes (Oliver, 1995) between challenging client behavior and avoidant staff behavior lead to a greater probability of challenging behavior on the part of the client, which in turn leads to more negative emotional reactions from staff that then may contribute over time to emotional exhaustion and depersonalizing attitudes (Hastings, 2002). As such, an important factor in determining burnout may be the extent to which staff members are able to respond to challenging behaviors in a manner that will decrease the probability of their occurrence, rather than in a manner that will necessarily allow staff to escape their aversive reactions to these behaviors.

Finally, the detrimental effects of the avoidance of aversive work experiences may extend to situations other than staff–client interactions per se. For example, Rose (1999) found that a measure of 'support' from professionals was positively correlated with a measure of anxiety in staff. Further, Rose, Ahuja and Jones (2006) found that higher levels of general stress in care staff were associated with more negative attitudes toward interactions with professionals. It is possible that when such attitudes regulate behavior, staff might avoid contact with professionals and perceive a general lack of support (Blumenthal et al., 1998; Chung et al., 1998), and lack of feelings of personal accomplishment that has been associated with burnout.

Cognitive Fusion and Experiential Avoidance

This unhealthy dominance of certain verbal processes over other forms of behavior regulation has been referred to as 'cognitive fusion' (Hayes, Luoma, Bond, Masuda, & Lillis, 2006, p. 6). Specifically, Hayes (Hayes et al., 2006) describes cognitive fusion as 'the excessive or improper regulation of behavior by verbal processes, such as rules and derived relational networks' (p. 6). Cognitive fusion is believed to support 'experiential avoidance' (Hayes et al., 2004b, p. 554), which is defined as:

> the phenomenon that occurs when a person is unwilling to remain in contact with particular private experiences (e.g., bodily sensations, emotions, thoughts, memories, images, behavioral predispositions) and takes steps to alter the form or frequency of these experiences or the contexts that occasion them, even when doing so causes behavioral harm. (Hayes et al., 2004b, p. 554)

Paradoxically, these attempts to regulate internal experiences often intensify suffering and inhibit the pursuit of valued action (Hayes et al., 2006), such as the behaviors necessary to perform well at work.

In the current context, it appears to be the case that experiential avoidance of the private events associated with challenging client behaviors often leads to actions that cause 'behavioral harm', in that these actions often reinforce the client behaviors that are associated with staff stress (Hastings, 2002, 2005). Since the termination of these aversive experiences appears to be a powerful reinforcer, staff tend to persist in their patterns of avoidant or escape behaviors. However, if staff are able to remain in contact with these aversive stimuli without having to control the stimuli or allowing the stimuli to determine their actions, then extinction of these avoidant or escape responses may occur. This would lead to greater variability in responding, which might set the stage for learning more effective responses to challenging clients and other work stressors (c.f., Bond, Hayes, & Barnes-Holmes, 2006).

Acceptance and Psychological Flexibility

The willingness to experience emotions, thoughts, bodily sensations and other private events without attempting to control them or allowing them to control one's actions has been referred to as 'acceptance' (Bond & Bunce, 2003, p. 1057). Acceptance is a component of 'psychological flexibility' (Hayes et al., 2006), which can be defined as the ability to fully experience whatever internal or external events are present in or elicited by the current environment while persisting with or changing one's behavior in a manner consistent with one's values (Bond & Flaxman, 2006).

Correlational Studies of Acceptance and Psychological Flexibility

Although the effects of acceptance and psychological flexibility have not been studied as predictors of mental health and performance outcomes in mental health direct care staff, related work has been done. For instance, Lloyd and Hastings (2008) examined acceptance as a predictor of distress in mothers of autistic children. Cross-sectionally, acceptance was significantly negatively associated with measures of maternal anxiety, depression and stress. Longitudinally, mothers whose acceptance scores increased over an interval of 18 months exhibited less stress, anxiety and depression. Increasing anxiety, stress and depression were related to lower levels of acceptance.

Further, studies examining the influence of psychological flexibility on work-related stress and performance outcomes have indicated that flexibility is an important factor. In one such investigation, Bond and Bunce (2003) examined the ability of psychological flexibility and job control (i.e., the amount of control workers have over how they do their jobs) to predict mental health, job satisfaction and an objective measure of performance in customer service center workers. The authors found that level of psychological flexibility was positively correlated with mental health and job performance one year later, over and above the effects of job control, negative affect and locus of control (Bond & Bunce, 2003). Bond and Flaxman (2006) replicated these findings and extended them by showing that the synergistic interaction of job control and psychological flexibility predicted customer service workers' ability to learn a new computer software program, in addition to improving general mental health and job performance.

Taken together, these studies suggest that, in addition to promoting decreased stress and improved performance (Bond & Bunce, 2003), the increased flexibility in responding afforded by acceptance of difficult private events enhances employees' ability to learn new job skills (Bond & Flaxman, 2006). Further, Lloyd and Hastings' (2008) study suggests that acceptance may buffer the long-term effects of the stress associated with caring for individuals with special needs.

These findings suggest important avenues for intervention to address burnout in mental health direct care staff. First, interventions to increase levels of acceptance and flexibility may help to decrease levels of stress and burnout in staff. Second, when psychological flexibility is thus enhanced, staff may benefit more from training to enhance their behavior management skills and, because they are less experientially avoidant, they may be better equipped to put these skills into practice. As a result of increased psychological flexibility and improved behavior management skills, staff may experience fewer incidents of challenging behavior in their interactions with clients, thus ameliorating a potentially significant source of stress. Acceptance and Commitment Therapy (ACT; Hayes, Strosahl, & Wilson, 1999) is one such intervention aimed at improving psychological flexibility that has also shown promise in reducing work-related stress (Bond & Bunce, 2000) and burnout (Hayes et al., 2004b), and in fostering the learning of new therapeutic skills (Bond et al., 2006).

ACT and its Core Processes

In contexts where behavior is likely to be regulated by rules or derived relational networks (e.g., thoughts, attitudes, etc.), individuals may be more likely to respond in accordance with these verbal processes rather than the contingencies available to them in the present environment that might lead to more effective behavior. From an ACT perspective, it is not the content of thoughts that is important. Rather, the focus is on the behavior regulatory impact of those thoughts and the contexts that support cognitive fusion and experiential avoidance (Hayes et al., 2006).

ACT seeks to bring these relational behaviors under appropriate contextual control so that individuals can live their lives according to their values, rather than have their actions dictated by efforts to avoid or control unpleasant thoughts and emotions (Hayes, et al., 1999). To this end, ACT seeks to undermine the contexts that give rise to cognitive fusion, to foster acceptance of difficult thoughts and emotions in the service of valued ends and to encourage and build patterns of commitment to individual values.

Such interventions can be incorporated into group in-service trainings for mental health direct care staff. Many of the commonly used ACT techniques are adaptable to group formats and there are a number of studies that report positive outcomes from ACT trainings that have been delivered in group workshops (e.g., Blackledge & Hayes, 2006; Bond & Bunce, 2000; Hayes et al., 2004a). These trainings make use of six interrelated core processes (cognitive defusion, acceptance, present-moment focus, self as context, values and committed action), which will now be discussed in turn.

Cognitive Defusion

Cognitive defusion techniques attempt to alter the functional contexts in which cognitive fusion occurs. One such context is the 'context of literality' (Hayes et al., 2006, p. 7), in which one treats verbal representations (the thought, 'this is a dead-end job') as if they were literally true (i.e., my job truly is a dead-end). A 'context of reason-giving' (Hayes et al., 2006, p. 7) is supported by a history of reinforcement for being able to verbalize 'causes' for one's behavior (e.g., 'I can't do my job when I am anxious or uncomfortable'). Frequently, these causes consist of conditioned private events (e.g., emotions and thoughts) over which the individual has little actual control. When emotions and thoughts are regarded as reasons for behavior, individuals turn increasingly inward in a needless effort to regulate their internal experiences (Hayes et al., 2006), and their attention is drawn away from opportunities for learning in the present moment (Bond et al., 2006) that might lead to more effective behavior.

Defusion techniques attempt to alter the impact of thoughts and other internal events, rather than their content, by attempting to change the ways individuals relate to them (Hayes et al., 2006). For example, thoughts can be observed objectively or repeated out loud until they lose their meaning (c.f., Hayes et al., 1999, pp. 154–156), and language conventions can be employed to encourage distancing from one's cognitions (e.g., 'I don't get the credit I deserve for my work' vs. 'I am having the thought that I don't get the credit I deserve for my work').

Additionally, trainers may make use of metaphor to encourage experiential contact with defusion processes. One such technique is the 'Thoughts on Cards' exercise (Hayes et al., 1999, p. 162), which may be done with a volunteer from the training group who is willing to publicly discuss his or her reactions to a difficult client. Recall Robert from the beginning of this chapter. If he were to volunteer to take part in this exercise, it might unfold as follows:

Trainer: (The two of them are seated directly across from each other, in front of the group. The trainer should maintain a slow, steady pace and pitch in voice throughout the exercise. If the client speeds up, the trainer should gently coach them to slow the pace.) OK, Robert, if you are willing, I'd like for you to close your eyes and simply follow your breathing for a few moments. Just take some time to get centered. (The trainer coaches Robert through a mindfulness exercise for about 30 seconds.) Good. Now, I'd like for you to remember a recent incident when you were with one of your most difficult clients. See if you can really be there in your mind's eye, and really put yourself in the room with that person. Let me know when you can do that.

Robert: OK, I've got it.

Trainer: Good. OK, now take just a second and see if you can let yourself look around that room and just breathe gently in and out. Please tell what you see there, what's going on?

Robert: I'm on the unit in the day room. Bradley is at it again … he's started to slap himself in the head. If I say something to him he will stop for a little while, but I will have to keep doing that over and over again. If I don't say something to him, it will get worse … he'll fall to the floor and start banging his head on the ground, maybe to the point he actually draws blood. If that happens, then I might get written up for letting him hurt himself. It never ends.

Trainer: I see, and now notice yourself in that moment. What are you feeling in that moment?

Robert: Angry. Angry and very tired … and then just sort of sad.

Trainer: And, breathe, gently, gently. What sorts of thoughts are you having?

Robert: I don't know what to do. I think that Bradley knows what he is doing, that he does this on purpose to get a rise out of people. Then I give in to it and give in to what he wants … attention. But on a bad day, he can never get enough of that. Really, I just want to get away from him. I ask for help from the supervisors and psychologists, but they don't get it. They aren't the ones that are there every day. They tell me to ignore the bad behavior and attend to the good. Well, like I have already said, if I do that then he will hurt himself and I don't want that, nor do I want to be blamed for it. It seems like people around here don't really take action until someone gets hurt, and I am tired of it. (As Robert is talking, the trainer writes each troublesome thought and emotion on a separate notecard. He then places the cards on the floor between himself and Robert.)

Trainer: OK, I'd like for you to bring you attention back to the present now, and when you have done that, please open your eyes. Good. OK, here in this pile between us are some cards. On each of them, I've written one of the difficult thoughts or feelings that you just told me about. Notice how if I were Bradley these things would be between us, like the pile of cards is now.

Robert: OK, I get it.

Trainer: Good. So, if it's okay with you, I'd like to read some of these cards.

Robert: Go ahead.

Trainer: OK, here's one: 'Angry'. And another: 'Sad'. 'It never ends.' 'He's doing it on purpose.' 'I'll be blamed if he hurts himself.' 'I don't know what to do.' 'They don't get it.' 'No one does anything until someone gets hurt.' 'I'm tired.' 'I just want to get away from him'… They all seem pretty negative, like problems that need to be solved. Do you like these cards? (The trainer should retain the slow steady pitch and pace, especially while reading each thought and emotion.)

Robert: Of course not!

Trainer: I don't blame you. I certainly wouldn't like them either. (To the other group members: Can any of you relate to this? Does it remind you of your own experiences with difficult clients?) It's like we really need to get rid of these thoughts and feelings … to fight them off. If you're willing Robert, I'd like to act this out in way that others can see.

Robert: OK.

Trainer: Good. So now here's what we're going to do: I am going to toss each of these cards at you and try to make them land on your lap. Your job is to do whatever you can … short of punching me … to keep that from happening. Ready?

Robert: (Laughs) … alright, go ahead.

Trainer: OK here it comes. (The trainer reads off each card, then tosses it at Robert, who bats them away or makes whatever evasive maneuver necessary). Whew! So what was that like?

Robert: It felt pretty silly, like I was some sort of half-assed Jackie Chan or something!

Trainer: Laughs … OK, fair enough. Now, if you're willing I'd like to try one more thing.

Robert: Sure, why not?

Trainer: OK. This time I am just going to read off the cards and then hand them to you, and I want you to simply accept them from me without any sort of resistance. Just take them and let them sit cradled in your hands. OK? Here goes. (Trainer reads each card and hands it to Robert, who quietly accepts them.) Now, compared to the first time when you were trying to keep the cards away, what is different?

Robert: Well, it seems a little calmer I suppose. More peaceful and less effort.

Trainer: Do you like holding the cards or having these thoughts and feelings now?

Robert: No, I still don't want them. I think they are bad, and there are still problems for me.

Trainer: Yes, and it seems like either way, with fighting or without, you still have the cards. It's just that when we fight, then we have the troublesome thoughts and feelings in addition to our struggle not to have them. Or maybe we could give up altogether and tell ourselves we don't care, but I don't think that's the case here. I think you do care — otherwise, this stuff wouldn't bother you. I wonder if it is possible for you to really show up to working with Bradley, while still having these thoughts and feelings?

Robert: Show up? I don't know … I suppose that may be possible. I mean it matters to me, or I wouldn't have hung around here as long as I have. I 'show up' all the time, but after a while it seems I am putting into it more than I get out.

Trainer: Yes, I understand that you have those thoughts, and please realize that I am not saying they are untrue. I realize that Bradley exhibits some really difficult behaviors, and those are things that you all are going to have to work together to address. I am not suggesting that you give up trying to improve the circumstances you are in at work, or that you stop trying to help Bradley. What I am suggesting is that we work at developing a more open stance toward the thoughts and feelings that inevitably come about when you do this work that you care about.

In addition to experiential exercises like the one described above, trainees are taught defusion techniques that take the form of meditative practices. For instance, the 'Just Noticing/Leaves on a Stream' (Bond & Hayes, 2002, pp. 126–127) exercise can be particularly useful for encouraging healthy distancing from and nonjudgmental awareness of thoughts, emotions and other internal stimuli. An example of this technique follows:

I'd like for you all to get seated in a comfortable position and close your eyes. Now, I am going to ask you to simply notice various things that go on inside your body and mind. The point of this exercise is to "just notice" these things without trying to change them, as if you are watching a show on TV. You don't have the remote, so you can't change the channel on the TV. Nor can you decide what the show is about. Your job is simply to notice what is happening.

Now, I'd like for you to notice your breathing. Notice how the air comes in and flows down your windpipe, and how it fills your chest and makes a little pressure or fullness there, and then notice how it flows back out. Notice the cool air coming in and the warm air going out. No breath is too short or too long, so don't try to change it. Just notice how you do it. (The observation of the breath should continue for about 2–3 minutes. Periodically, the trainer should say something like, 'You may find yourself thinking about other things. If that happens, just gently bring your attention back to your breathing.')

Now, I'd like you to bring your attention to a sensation that you may be feeling in your body right now. Perhaps you feel a sense of warmth, or a sense of pressure where your body rests in the chair. Or you may feel a tingle, or a cramp or an itch. It might be in your hands, feet, arms, legs, shoulders, back or neck. Please focus now on that bodily sensation, without deliberately trying to alter it or to make it stop. Notice if the sensation changes in any way. If it doesn't change, simply notice that as well. (The observation of the body should continue for about 2–3 minutes. As is the case with the breath, periodically remind trainees to simply bring their attention back to the bodily sensation if they find themselves distracted with other things.)

Now, I'd like you to imagine that you are walking through a beautiful, green valley. The sun is bright and pleasantly warm and there is a soft breeze. As you walk, you notice that there is a clear, gentle stream running through the valley. You go over to look at it, and you find the perfect spot and sit down there by the stream. Now that you are closer to the water, you see that there is a trail of fallen leaves floating gently by. Imagine now that you can place any thoughts that you are having on those leaves. As each thought occurs to you, simply place it one of the leaves and watch as the water carries it down the stream.

(The observation of the 'stream' should continue for about 5 minutes. The trainer should intermittently make comments like 'If you find this really hard to do or you are wondering if you are doing it right, that is OK. Just put the thought 'This is hard!' on a leaf and watch as it floats down the stream. Also, the trainer should periodically remind the trainees that if they find themselves thinking of other things, they should gently turn their attention back to the stream. After approximately 5 minutes has passed, the trainer should have the trainees imagine themselves sitting, as they are now, back in the room, and instruct them to open their eyes when they are ready.)

When debriefing this exercise, the trainer should emphasize how it relates to the difficulties that trainees may face in their work. Particular emphasis should be placed on how the technique begins to teach them to notice their thoughts and feelings without necessarily acting on them or taking them literally. The trainer should also note that this exercise is particularly useful as a technique that participants can practice between training sessions.

Acceptance

Defusion techniques support acceptance, which can be regarded as an alternative to experiential avoidance (Hayes et al., 2006). Acceptance techniques allow individuals to experience and observe uncomfortable emotional content without needlessly engaging in escape or avoidance behaviors (Bond et al., 2006), so that valued action can be taken. This is probably best accomplished through experiential techniques because the actual behavioral repertoire that comprises acceptance is not easily communicated via direct instruction. The 'Face-to-Face' (Bond & Hayes, 2002, p. 128) exercise taps these processes, and is applicable to a group format. It may be conducted as follows:

> Trainer: This exercise will involve simply looking at another person for about 3 minutes. What I would like for you to do, if you are willing, is to pull a couple of chairs together so that you and your partner can sit facing each other. Your 'goal' is simply to notice what it is like to be there, making eye contact with that person. You don't have to say or do anything. Many of you will notice that your mind is giving you all sorts of reasons why you can't do this. You may have the thought that this is really weird, or you may worry that you are not doing it right. You may have the urge to laugh or to look away. Your job is to simply notice how all these things sort of come and go while you are here with this person, focusing on them. Go ahead and sit facing one another, making eye contact. Ready ... begin. (Periodically, the trainer should say some thing like, 'See if you can stay with what it feels like to be here looking at another person who is looking at you'. Towards the end of the exercise, the trainer should say something like, 'See if you can get in touch with the fact that this person sitting across from you is someone who cares deeply about their work with people with special needs. Notice that they, like you, often feel confused or frustrated by the work that they do. See if you can get in touch with that. Now imagine what this person here might be feeling. If you were them and they were you, what would you be feeling?... . If you were them and they were you, what would they be feeling?')

In debriefing this exercise, trainers should focus the dialogue on how the exercise is relevant to the difficulties that trainees face in their work. The following is an example of such a dialogue with Robert after he has just completed the Face-to-Face exercise:

> Trainer: What was that last exercise like for you?
>
> Robert: Well, to begin with it was hard. Like you said, I wanted to laugh or maybe just look away. Really, I wanted to do pretty much anything except sit there and stare at Jimmy.
>
> Trainer: But you were able to do it?

Robert: Yeah, I was able to do it for the most part. It's like even though I was there looking at him my mind kept going away and then turning back. I kept wondering what he was thinking about me. And then I kept wondering when it would be over because it made me nervous.

Trainer: So it made you uncomfortable. It was like all these thoughts and feelings ... like 'I wonder what he's thinking about me' or 'This is weird' or being nervous ... were coming up. All those things were there and it sort of made you want to look away.

Robert: Yes.

Trainer: Well that's interesting. I wonder if what you just experienced was something like what you face every day with your hard clients. I mean it's like, you were simply making eye contact there for a couple of minutes, but all those things came up for you. I wonder how much more comes up when you are dealing with some of the hard cases back on the unit?

Robert: Sometimes a lot more! But when you said that last part it was different.

Trainer: The last part?

Robert: Yes, about how they might be feeling like me. It makes me wonder just how the clients feel. And more than that, it makes me wonder about the people that I work with ... like the supervisors that I think don't listen. Could they be confused and just doing the best they can, like I am?

Trainer: Well, it's possible they may be. It is also possible that they may not listen. We all have all kinds of thoughts about the people around us — about our clients and coworkers. But let me ask you this: What if you could choose the stance you take toward all those thoughts? What if we could respond with compassion and integrity, regardless of our circumstances? What if we could make the assumption that everyone really is doing the best they know how to do right now? I am not asking you to believe this in the sense that you should try and prove or disprove what I am telling you. I am asking you to try it out and see what your experience tells you in terms of the sense of engagement and purpose you feel in your work.

There are a number of other ACT exercises that feature significant acceptance components and that are adaptable to a group experiential format. One such exercise is the 'Tin Can Monster' (Hayes et al., 1999, pp. 171–174), which makes use of guided imagery and metaphor to encourage exposure to aversive stimuli that are associated with stressful experiences. For example, trainees might be taken through a brief relaxation procedure, after which they may be asked to remember an interaction with a client that made them feel uncomfortable. Once this image is in place, trainees would then be asked to attend to particular bodily sensations that they feel in response to this memory, and are encouraged to simply observe these experiences as they unfold as opposed to attempting to alter their form or intensity. This process is then repeated for associated thoughts and behavioral predispositions, such that the 'monster' which the experience represents is gradually dismantled. As is the case with the aforementioned 'leaves on a stream' exercise, it may be helpful to encourage trainees to practice these exercises on their own between sessions, instructing them to use various memories of troublesome work situations as content. When trainees have sufficient practice with acceptance and defusion skills, the stage is then set for more mindful attention to the direct contingencies available in the present moment.

Present-Moment Focus

Acceptance and defusion encourages nonjudgmental contact with the present environment and whatever stimuli it entails. 'Present-moment focus' enables individuals to note and describe events as they unfold, without becoming entangled in judgments and evaluations of these events (Hayes et al., 2006). When this occurs, individuals have more resources to bring to bear on effectively interacting with their environment, thus their behavior is more under control of direct versus verbally-mediated contingencies.

Present-moment focus is a common thread in many of the ACT processes, thus it is implicit in many ACT techniques. Further, it may be cultivated by daily 'mindfulness practice' which can be incorporated with trainees' work routines. An example of one such mindfulness practice exercise follows (adapted from Singh et al., 2006):

Example of a Mindfulness Exercise

Being in the Present Moment

1. This exercise will help you to empty your mind so that you can focus entirely on the present moment.

2. Choose a task that you perform with one of your clients every day. It should be a task that you can perform automatically, almost without thinking.

3. Before you begin this task, decide that today you will note exactly what you are doing when you perform this task. For example, if you are teaching a client how to use a washing machine, you might keep up an internal dialogue on each step that you take. To help you focus, you may use the word 'now' to describe each step. For example, you may begin this way: 'I am now showing Katherine how to wash her clothes. I am now helping her separate the dark from the light colored-clothes. Now I am getting the detergent and measuring cup from the shelf. I am now measuring out half a cup ...' and so forth, until the task is done.

4. At your next break, find a quiet spot and think about the effect that providing yourself with a commentary had on you. Did you see and experience things that you had not noticed before? Did you see the little changes in Katherine's facial expressions or posture when you showed her

the different steps of the task? Did Katherine ask questions or say anything when you were teaching her? How was this experience different from other times you have done this task automatically, almost without noticing what you were doing? Try to visualize each action that you took to teach Katherine. What sorts of emotional reactions did you have during the task?

5. Each day pick a different activity at work and repeat this exercise.

6. To enhance mindfulness at home, each day choose a task that you engage in at home and provide yourself with an internal commentary until you reach the point that you are fully present in each moment.

Self as Context

Skinner posits that the verbal community shapes our sense of self-awareness by 'arranging the conditions under which a person describes the public or private world in which he lives' (1974, p. 31). This requires a consistent locus from which we perceive our own behavior and the behavior of others (Hayes, 1984). One byproduct of human relational abilities is this transcendent sense of self that allows us to observe our own perceptions and verbal behaviors without actively engaging in them, thus setting a context for the extinction of responding to self-talk as if it were literally true (Hayes, 1984). In short, the self is the context in which thoughts, emotions and other private events exist. Developing this stable sense of perspective is what allows trainees to dispassionately observe the flow of experience, thus fostering defusion and acceptance (Hayes et al., 2006). Like present-moment focus, this process is implicit in many ACT interventions. For instance, any time someone labels a thought as a 'thought' or an emotion as an 'emotion', a sense of perspective or context is implied. However, one exercise that more precisely targets these processes is the 'Observer' exercise (Bond & Hayes, 2002, pp. 131–132). An example of this technique follows:

> Trainer: Now, if you all are willing, I'd like for you to close your eyes and follow the sound of my voice. Relax, and picture yourself in this room. Now, just notice your body and any sensations that you may be having. Notice any emotions that you are having. Notice any thoughts. I'd like for you to get in touch with the part of you that noticed these thoughts, emotions and sensations. This is the you-yourself, the part that I will call 'the observer'. From that perspective, hear what I am saying to you now.

> Your body is constantly changing. Once you were a little baby, and then you grew into a child, and then that child grew into the man or woman you are now. Your body may become fat or thin, strong or weak. Sometimes your body may be sick or hurt. You may have developed an illness or injured yourself in some way. Over time, these hurts have either healed or, perhaps they are with you even now. Notice these things, but also notice that there is a

'you' that was there all along. Even though your body has changed, the person that is you — the observer — was there all along.

Now, I'd like you to notice your roles. You have many of them. You are constantly playing a role. There is the role you play here at work. Perhaps you have other jobs as well, and you play different roles at those different jobs. At home, you may play the role of a spouse or a parent. You play the role of a son or a daughter. You play the role of someone who is of a certain race, or age, or religion or nationality. Your roles are constantly changing and you change in and out of them like they were suits of clothes. Even now you are playing the role of a trainee. If you were to try to not play a role, then you would be in the role of someone who does not play a role. Allow yourself to notice this as a fact that you have experienced: I have many roles, but they are not me. You are there all along, observing these many roles.

Now, notice that you have many emotions. They are constantly changing. There may be things that you liked at one time, that you do not like now. Or there may be things that you did not like at one time, that you now like. Sometimes you may have more than one emotion at the same time. Sometimes these emotions contradict themselves. Even now you are experiencing emotions, but they are not you. You have been there all along, observing these many emotions. The emotions are like waves, but you are like the ocean. Allow yourself to experience this as a fact: You have many emotions, but these emotions are not you.

Now, notice that you have many thoughts. Your thoughts are constantly changing. You have learned new things, and have had different experiences from which you have gotten new knowledge and new ideas. Perhaps there are some things that you once believed were true, that you now know to be false. Or the opposite may also be true, that there are things that you once thought were false that you now know to be true. Sometimes your thoughts may make little sense to you. At other times, they may seem to pop into your head for no apparent reason. You have many thoughts, but they are not you. You have been there, observing your thoughts all along.

Notice that you are not your body, your roles, your emotions or your thoughts. These things are all part of your experience, yet they are not you. When you notice this, see if you can create a sense of distance between you and the things that you may be struggling with that cause you stress. Note that you may have been trying to change some of these thoughts, emotions or roles. Perhaps you have been trying to get rid of the 'bad' thoughts or feelings, but as you do so you may find that you are caught up in them, and you do not notice the you that is separate from them. See if you can experience this fact: There is a you-yourself, an observer you, that has been there all along. You encompass all of these things and are bigger than these things. And you can choose a direction for your life and follow it independent of what all these other things may tell you.

Now, picture yourself back in the room, and when you are ready to come back to the room you may open your eyes.

Values

Values are chosen patterns of action that can be worked toward but cannot be achieved definitively (e.g., being a good employee, being a loving parent). From an ACT perspective, the degree of consistency with personally held values is what determines the effectiveness of behavior. When behavior is inconsistent with values, it tends to be dominated by pliance, avoidance or seeking primary reinforcers when doing so does not serve one's interests over the long term (Bond et al, 2006).

Values interventions in ACT are aimed at enhancing psychological contact with these intrinsic sources of reinforcement. Doing so places work in a context of valued action as opposed to a context of literally held beliefs about 'unjust' and 'impossible' work conditions (Bond et al., 2006). Further, behavior consistent with values may ameliorate some of the effects of work-related stress or burnout, such as emotional exhaustion and a perceived lack of personal accomplishment (Wilson, Sandoz, Kitchens, & Roberts, 2008).

ACT employs techniques that attempt to clarify and prioritize personal values in order to make individuals more aware of such sources of reinforcement. In doing so, trainers should avoid the tendency to engage language processes that might lead to fusion, in the sense that trainees become overly attached to notions of what they 'should' value. We want staff to contact the contingencies in their work that 'work' for them, in that these experiences are sources of reinforcement in their own right. One way to do this is to illustrate the difference between 'choices' and 'decisions' (Hayes et al., 1999, p. 212), as described in the following dialogue.

> Trainer: Acceptance (or willingness) is important because it enables us to do more of the things that we value. By value, I mean the things that have meaning for us. A value is like a direction or purpose that you choose for your work. It's a choice you make. Let's try an example to see if I can get my point across here. Which do you all like better, Coke or Pepsi?
>
> Trainee: Pepsi.
>
> Trainer: Why Pepsi?
>
> Trainee: Because I like the way it tastes better.
>
> Trainer: Yes but why do you like the way it tastes better than you do Coke?
>
> Trainee: I don't know. I just do.
>
> Trainer: Fair enough. Could you find a reason why not to pick that one?
>
> Trainee: Well maybe. Like if the Coke was cheaper.
>
> Trainer: Good. That's a good reason to pick the other. You could also decide to pick the Pepsi anyway because you like the way it tastes better. You decide things *for* reasons. You can come up with reasons for the choice you made,

regardless of what choice that is. But you can also make a choice independent of those reasons, because the reasons are sort of after the fact anyway. That is the difference between a choice and a decision.

Trainee: Huh?

Trainer: Let me try another example from my own experience. I once worked with this client who was autistic. You know how they can get fixated on a certain routine? Well this guy got in the habit of having a quarter-pounder with cheese and a medium Dr. Pepper every Thursday. Maybe all this talk about soda is what reminded me of him! Anyway, for a while it was part of his behavior plan to get his special lunch on Thursdays if he had earned it, and I was the one who went and got it for him. Sometimes he didn't earn it, and on those days it was like I lost out too! I couldn't really tell you why. I enjoyed being with him most times. But at others, he just made a terrible mess. Still, I felt this sense of commitment or purpose in being with him, in doing this small act for somebody who appreciated it. It seems silly, but it mattered. I could come up with all sorts of noble-sounding reasons for why I 'wanted to be of service to others less fortunate than myself', or some other such guff as that. The fact of the matter is much simpler: I did it because that is who I chose to be.

Robert: Yeah, I know what you mean. We do stuff like that all the time. It's like when we take the guys in wheelchairs out for walks during our own break time. Or playing catch with the clients during their recess. You know, no one even knows we do these things and there's not really anything we stand to gain. Well, not other than what we gain by simply doing them.

Trainer: Right. Those are things you *choose*. That's why I think we should try and stay focused on what's happening in the present — in the here and now. Because if we get caught up in what's going on in our heads — like 'I'm not getting what I deserve from this!' — then we may miss all these other small, but important things.

ACT also employs experiential techniques to clarify and prioritize personal values. One such exercise is the 'Retirement Party Meditation' (Luoma, Pistorello, Hayes, & Kohlenberg, 2007). An adapted version of this exercise follows:

Guide trainees through a brief relaxation or 'centering' exercise, such as having them follow their breathing. Next, say something like: 'There are many possible directions that your life may take, but for now, I'd like you to imagine just one of those directions. I'd like you to fast-forward into the future, and to imagine that you are at the point where you are retiring from your work as a care provider for people with special needs. Imagine now that many people have gathered for a retirement party in your honor. There are coworkers, supervisors, clients, and clients' families. See if you can imagine all the sights, sounds, and smells. See if you can really feel what it is like to be there. Take a moment to walk around the party and notice all the familiar faces (give trainees about 30 seconds to do this). Now comes the time in the party when people get up and talk about what they remember most about you. See if you can see them all there. Imagine now that one of your long-time coworkers is getting up to speak. Since it is your imagination, have them say what you would want them to say, rather than what you think they might actually say. In other words, have them say what you would want them to say if you could choose it. How would you want them to remember you? Just take a moment now and listen to them (allow about 30 seconds for this) ... Now one of your former supervisors is getting up to talk. What would you want her/him to say, if you could have then say anything you want? What kind of employee were you? What was it like to work with you? Take a moment to listen ... Now, imagine that one of your clients is getting up to speak. If your client is someone who is not able to talk, you may imagine that they can now speak, or, you may imagine that one of their family members is getting up to speak for them. What would you have them say about you? What kind of care did you provide? What will they take from all the time that you have spent together?... . Take a moment to listen'.

This process may be repeated as many times as is desired for coworkers, family members, etc.

When done, have the trainees gradually refocus their attention on the present. During debriefing, it may be useful to have trainees note any discrepancies between what they would like to be remembered for and their current behavior, which may provide targets for committed action. Also, it will be useful to have the trainees list and possibly prioritize any values that they identify.

Committed Action

ACT encourages the expansion of patterns of committed action in accordance with values. This is accomplished through the formation of values-consistent goals and the development of behavior change strategies related to those goals (Hayes et al., 2006). Further, ACT encourages individuals to make public commitments to pursue valued actions, with the understanding that commitment itself is a process rather than an outcome. This means that 'relapses' into old behavior patterns are opportunities to recommit to pursuing valued actions in the workplace, rather than triggers for further maladaptive behaviors. In anticipating these difficulties, it is useful to have trainees identify possible barriers to committed action. To the extent that these barriers consist of internal events, it is also useful to have trainees make commitments to give up their struggle with these internal stimuli in order to more effectively pursue their values. Acceptance, defusion, present-moment focus and perspective-taking skills can be brought to bear when troublesome thoughts, emotions or circumstances create barriers to effective committed action.

Integration of ACT With Applied Behavioral Analysis (ABA)

Given that behavioral knowledge and perceived self-efficacy in dealing with challenging behaviors have been correlated with decreased negative emotional reactions to challenging behaviors (Hastings & Brown, 2002), it would seem that training in applied behavior analysis would provide staff with tools to better their interactions with clients and thus attenuate work stress. Although lengthy programs of instruction in applied behavior analysis for staff have been shown to facilitate the development of effective behavior modification programs (McClean et al., 2005), and to increase causal attributions that are consistent with behavioral principles (Berryman, Evans, & Kalbag, 1994), there is no evidence as yet that would suggest that such training positively affects staff stress or burnout levels. Further, there is as yet little evidence that manipulating these attributions has any direct effect that would lead to more habilitative staff behavior (Grey, Hastings, & McClean, 2007).

That being said, it may be the case that augmenting behavioral training with other forms of interventions, such as ACT, that are aimed at altering staff members' relationships with clients may prove beneficial. In one such study, Singh and colleagues (Singh et al., 2006) examined the effect of augmenting behavior analysis training for staff with mindfulness training. Mindfulness training involves using meditative practices to cultivate focus on the present moment and a nonjudgmental awareness of both internal and external events. As such, it overlaps to a large extent with many ACT techniques. Results indicated that although there was some decrease in client aggression and increase in the number of learning objectives mastered by clients after staff received behavioral training, the decreases in aggression were more substantial and the increases in learning were larger and more consistent after staff received mindfulness training. Thus Singh et al. (2006) concluded that the addition of mindfulness training considerably enhanced staff's ability to manage aggression and foster learning among clients.

It may be the case that staff who have practiced skills such as defusion and acceptance are better equipped to bring focused, compassionate awareness to their work with difficult clients. Such awareness might prove especially beneficial because staff who are more focused on the direct contingencies available in the present moment may be more able to apply behavioral knowledge by recognizing and appropriately reinforcing adaptive behaviors in clients, while refraining from actions that might perpetuate challenging client behaviors. These skills are likely to be particularly beneficial when implementing behavior change programs based on differential reinforcement procedures, as these techniques require staff to recognize two or more different client responses while acting in ways that reinforce some of these client behaviors while extinguishing others.

Conclusion

Mental health direct care staff face many challenges. Although changes in the structure of treatment settings, such as hiring better-trained staff, improving compensation of workers or altering the level of control workers exert over their work environments would be beneficial, such interventions are often impractical for financial and structural reasons. However, we can readily provide in-service trainings to these staff, and ACT shows unique promise in this regard. By altering the contexts in which staff experience troublesome thoughts and emotional reactions, ACT provides staff with a measure of freedom to respond more effectively to the demands of their work. When combined with values-based action, this flexibility in responding may set the stage for a treatment milieu that encourages adaptive behavior in both clients and staff, and which may lessen the impact of stressful conditions by imparting a sense of dignity and value to those who do this difficult work.

References

Bailey, B. A., Hare, D. J., Hatton, C., & Limb, K. (2006). The response to challenging behavior by care staff: Emotional responses, attributions of cause, and observations of practice. *Journal of Intellectual Disability Research, 50,* 199–211.

Berryman, J., Evans, I. M., & Kalbag, A. (1994). The effects of training in non-aversive behavior management on the attitudes and understanding of direct-care staff. *Journal of Behavior Therapy and Experimental Psychiatry, 25,* 241–250.

Blackledge, J. T., & Hayes, S. C. (2006). Using acceptance and commitment training in the support of parents of children diagnosed with autism. *Child & Family Behavior Therapy, 28*(1), 1–18.

Blumenthal, S., Lavender, T., & Hewson, S. (1998). Role clarity, perception of the organization and burnout amongst support workers in residential homes for people with intellectual disability: A comparison between a national health services trust and a charitable company. *Journal of Intellectual Disability Research, 42,* 409–417.

Bond, F. W., & Bunce, D. (2000). Mediators of change in emotion-focused and problem-focused worksite stress management interventions. *Journal of Occupational Health Psychology, 5(1),* 156–163.

Bond, F. W., & Bunce, D. (2003). The role of acceptance and job control in mental health, job satisfaction, and work performance. *Journal of Applied Psychology, 88*(6), 1057–1067.

Bond, F.W., & Flaxman, P. E. (2006). The ability of psychological flexibility and job control to predict learning, job performance, and mental health. *Journal of Organizational Behavior Management, 26*(1/2), 113–130.

Bond, F. W., & Hayes, S. C. (2002). ACT at work. In F.W. Bond & W. Dryden (Eds.), *Handbook of brief cognitive behavior therapy* (pp. 117–139). New York: Wiley.

Bond, F. W., Hayes, S. C., & Barnes-Holmes, D. (2006). Psychological flexibility, ACT, and organizational behavior. *Journal of Organizational Behavior Management, 26*(1/2), 25–54.

Chung, M. C., Corbett, J., & Cumella, S. (1998). Relating staff burnout to clients with challenging behavior in people with learning difficulty: Pilot study 2. *European Journal of Psychiatry, 10,* 155–165.

Dagnan, D., Trower, P., & Smith, R. (1998). Care staff responses to people with learning disabilities and challenging behavior: A cognitive-emotional analysis. *British Journal of Clinical Psychology, 37*, 59–68.

Duff, E., Readhead, A., Paxton, R., Iceton, J., & Rochester, J. (2006). Challenging behaviour in Mental Health Services: Combining psychological perspectives. *Journal of Mental Health, 15*(4), 475–490.

Grey, I. M., Hastings, R .P., & McClean, B. (2007). Staff training and challenging behaviour. *Journal of Applied Research in Intellectual Disabilities, 20*, 1–5.

Hall, S., & Oliver, C. (1992). Differential effects of self-injurious behavior on the behavior of others. *Behavioral Psychotherapy, 20*, 355–366.

Hastings, R. P. (2002). Do challenging behaviors affect staff psychological well-being? Issues of causality and mechanism. *American Journal on Mental Retardation, 107*(6). 455–467.

Hastings, R. P. (2005). Staff in special education settings and behavior problems: Towards a framework for research and practice. *Educational Psychology, 25*(2–3), 207–221.

Hastings, R. P., & Brown, T. (2002). Behavioral knowledge, causal beliefs, and self-efficacy as predictors of special educators' emotional reactions to challenging behaviors. *Journal of Intellectual Disability Research, 46*(2), 144–150.

Hastings, R. P., Horne, S., & Mitchell, G. (2004). Burnout in direct care staff in intellectual disability services: a factor analytic study of the Maslach Burnout Inventory. *Journal of Intellectual Disability Research, 48*(3), 268–273.

Hastings, R. P., & Remington, B. (1994). Rules of engagement: Toward an analysis of staff responses to challenging behavior. *Research in Developmental Disabilities, 15*, 279–298.

Hatton, C., & Lobban, F. (2007). Staff supporting people with intellectual disabilities and mental health problems. In N. Bouras & G. Holt (Eds.), *Psychiatric and behavioral disorders in intellectual and developmental disabilities*. New York: Cambridge.

Hayes, S. C. (1984). Making sense of spirituality. *Behaviorism, 12*, 99–110.

Hayes, S. C., Barnes-Holmes, D., & Roche, B. (2001). *Relational frame theory: A post-Skinnerian account of human language and cognition*. Reno, NV: Context Press.

Hayes, S. C., Bissett, R., Roget, N., Padilla, M., Kohlenberg, B. S., Fisher, G., et al., (2004a). The impact of acceptance and commitment training and multicultural training on the stigmatizing attitudes and professional burnout of substance abuse counselors. *Behavior Therapy, 35*, 821–835.

Hayes, S. C., Luoma, J. B., Bond, F. W., Masuda, A., & Lillis, J. (2006). Acceptance and commitment therapy: Model, processes and outcomes. *Behavior Research and Therapy, 44*, 1–25.

Hayes, S. C., Strosahl, K., & Wilson, K. G. (1999). *Acceptance and commitment therapy: An experiential approach to behavior change*. New York: Guilford Press.

Hayes, S. C., Strosahl, K. D., Wilson, K. G., Bissett, R. T., Pistorello, J., Toarmino, D., Polusny, M. A., et al. (2004b). Measuring experiential avoidance: A preliminary test of a working model. *The Psychological Record, (54)*, 553–570.

Lawson, D. A., & O'Brien, R. M. (1994). Behavioral and self-report measures of burnout in developmental disabilities. *Journal of Organizational Behavior Management, 14*, 37–54.

Lloyd, T., & Hastings, R. P. (2008). Psychological variables as correlates of adjustment in mothers of children with intellectual disabilities: Cross-sectional and longitudinal relationships. *Journal of Intellectual Disability Research, 52*(1), 37–48.

Luoma, J., Pistorello, J., Hayes, S. C., & Kohlenberg, B. (2007). *Acceptance and commitment therapy workshop manual on overcoming barriers to engagement with difficult clients.* Unpublished treatment manual, University of Nevada at Reno, NV.

McClean, B., Dench, C., Grey, I., Hendler, J., Fitsimmons, E., & Corrigan, M. (2005). Outcomes of person-focused planning: A model for delivering behavior supports to individuals with challenging behaviors. *Journal of Intellectual Disabilities Research, 49*(5), 340–353.

Maslach, C., Jackson, S. E., & Leiter, M. P. (1996). *The Maslach Burnout Inventory manual* (3rd ed.). Palo Alto, CA: Consulting Psychologists Press.

Mitchell, G., & Hastings, R. P. (1998). Learning disability care staff's emotional reactions to aggressive challenging behaviors: Development of a measurement tool. *British Journal of Clinical Psychology, 37,* 441–449.

Oliver, C. (1995). Self-injurious behavior in children with learning disabilities: Recent advances in assessment and intervention. *Journal of Child Psychology and Psychiatry, 36,* 909–927.

Rose, J. (1999). Stress and residential staff who work with people who have an intellectual disability: A factor analytic study. *Journal of Intellectual Disability Research, 4*(4), 268–278.

Rose, J., Ahuja, A. K., & Jones, C. (2006). Attitudes of direct care staff towards external professionals, team climate, and psychological well-being: A pilot study. *Journal of Intellectual Disabilities, 10*(2), 105–120.

Rose, D., Horne, S., Rose, J., & Hastings, R. P. (2004). Negative emotional reactions to challenging behavior and staff burnout: Two replication studies. *Journal of Applied Research in Intellectual Disabilities, 17,* 219–223.

Rose, J., Jones, F., & Fletcher, C. B. (1998). Investigating the relationship between stress and worker behavior. *Journal of Intellectual Disability Research, 42,* 163–172.

Rose, D., & Rose, J. (2005). Staff in services for people with intellectual disabilities: The impact of stress on attributions of challenging behavior. *Journal of Intellectual Disability Research, 49*(2), 827–838.

Savicki, V. (2002). *Burnout across thirteen cultures: Stress and coping in child and youth care workers.* Westport, CT: Praeger Publishers/Greenwood Publishing Group.

Singh, N., Lancioni, G. E., Winton, A., Curtis, W. J., Wahler, R. G., Sabaawi, M., et al. (2006). Mindful staff increase learning and reduce aggression in adults with developmental disabilities. *Research in Developmental Disabilities, 27,* 545–558.

Skinner, B. F. (1974). *About behaviorism.* New York: Knopf.

Stanley, B., & Standen, P. J. (2000). Carers' attributions for challenging behavior. *British Journal of Clinical Psychology, 39,* 157–168.

Stewart, I., Barnes-Holmes, D., Barnes-Holmes, Y., Bond, F. W., & Hayes, S. C. (2006). Relational Frame Theory and industrial/organizational psychology. *Journal of Organizational Behavior Management, 26*(1/2), 55–90.

Van Dierendonck, D., Schaufeli, W. B., & Buunk, B. P. (1996). Inequality among human service professionals: Measurement and relation to burnout. *Basic and Applied Social Psychology, 18,* 429–451.

Van Yperen, N. W. (1995). Communal orientation and the burnout syndrome among nurses: A replication and extension. *Journal of Applied Social Psychology, 26,* 338–354.

Weiner, B. (1986). *An attributional theory of motivation and emotion.* Springer: New York.

Wilson, K G., Sandoz, E. K., Kitchens, J., & Roberts, M. E. (2008). *The Valued Living Questionnaire: Defining and measuring valued action within a behavioral framework.* Manuscript submitted for publication.

chapter ten

Promoting Social Intelligence Using the Experiential Role-Play Method

Linda L. Bilich and Joseph Ciarrochi

Why do humans have such difficulty getting along? We are capable of behaving badly towards each other even without any observable threats, provocation or external adversity. For example, between 25% and 50% of Australians have reported experiencing workplace bullying (Barron, 1998; Jetson, 2005; McAvoy & Murtagh, 2003). Bullying forms one part of what could be labeled *aversive interpersonal behavior*, along with other behaviors such as abuse (physical, emotional, and so on), gossiping, manipulation and lying. This behavior is particularly problematic in organizations as it can result in potential legal costs, lost time, reduced morale and motivation, and increases in staff turnover and recruitment (Barron, 1998; McAvoy & Murtagh, 2003; Salin, 2003).

In this chapter, we present a theoretically driven intervention that is designed to promote social harmony and effectiveness in the workplace. We will outline the theoretical basis and practical application of the program as was conducted with members of the New South Wales (NSW) Police organization. The program involved helping officers to develop effective interpersonal behavior in line with their values and related goals, especially in the context of distressing emotions and thoughts. The training program was a form of acceptance and commitment therapy (Hayes, Strosahl, & Wilson, 1999), which will be outlined below. This program was quite different from existing programs that seek to modify dysfunctional attitudes and explicitly teach social skills.

Acceptance and Commitment Therapy (ACT)

Our culture teaches us that positive thoughts and feelings are good, and negative thoughts and feelings are bad and ought to be removed or minimized. According to ACT theorists, humans can get caught in the cycle of trying to eliminate negative internal experiences (thoughts, memories, emotions, body sensations), in order to replace them with positive experiences. Unfortunately, our emotion control strategies may be a major source of our suffering (Wilson & Murrell, 2003). That is, our attempts to get rid of our feelings may paradoxically increase the extent that we experience those feelings (Wenzlaff & Luxton, 2003; Wenzlaff & Wegner, 2000).

The purpose of ACT is to help clients remove themselves from the cycle of emotional control and unhelpful beliefs, not by challenging or changing the thoughts, but by learning to react more mindfully to such thoughts. The goal of ACT is to help clients consistently choose to act effectively (concrete behavior in alignment with their values) in the presence of difficult private events.

ACT is based on a philosophy of functional contextualism (Hayes, 2004; Hayes et al., 1999; Hayes, Wilson, Gifford, Follette, & Strosahl, 1996), and a theory of language called relational frame theory (RFT; Hayes, Barnes-Holmes, & Roche, 2001). For the purposes of this chapter, we will not go into detail about this, and readers are encouraged to refer to the above referenced texts for further information. We will now briefly review ACT research.

ACT (Hayes et al., 1999) is referred to as a cognitive therapy that forms part of the third wave of cognitive–behavior therapies, such as dialectical behavior therapy (DBT; Linehan, 1993) and mindfulness-based cognitive therapy (MBCT; Segal, Williams, & Teasdale, 2001). ACT has been used effectively to treat numerous clinical disorders (e.g., depression) and health-related problems (e.g., pain; see Bach & Hayes, 2002; Dahl, Wilson, Luciano, & Hayes, 2005; Eifert & Forsyth, 2005; Lundgren, Dahl, Melin, & Kies, 2006; Zettle & Hayes, 1986; Zettle & Hayes, 2002; Zettle & Raines, 1989). ACT has also been used with nonclinical populations, particularly in relation to work-related stress. There are several empirical studies that support the use of ACT for worksite stress and the reduction of long-term sick leave (Bond & Bunce, 2000, 2003; Bond & Hayes, 2002; Dahl, Wilson, & Nilsson, 2004; Flaxman, 2006).

ACT seeks to increase psychological flexibility, or the ability to contact the present moment fully as a conscious human being, and to change or persist in behavior when doing so serves valued ends (Hayes et al., 1999). Psychological flexibility is established through six core ACT processes.

I. Acceptance. This process involves developing and increasing an individual's willingness to have and accept their private experiences. Individuals are encouraged to let go of emotional control and avoidance, when doing so promotes valued living. A common phrase often used in ACT is 'control is the problem, not the solution' (Hayes et al., 1999, p. 115).

2. Defusion. Fusion, the opposite of defusion, refers to when an individual's behavior is excessively controlled by their verbal content. For example, in a context that supports fusion, one's behavior might be excessively influenced by evaluations (e.g., 'I'm not good enough') or rules (e.g., 'I must be loved by everybody'). When fused with a thought, one can lose contact with other direct and indirect psychological functions (Strosahl, Hayes, Wilson, & Gifford, 2004). Defusion is a process that involves undermining the verbal processes that promote fusion (Strosahl et al., 2004). Defusion involves teaching individuals to see thoughts for what they are and not what they say they are (Hayes et al., 1999). Defusion essentially undermines the power of words to act as barriers to effective action.

3. Getting in contact with the present moment. This process is equivalent to mindfulness. It involves individuals connecting with and being fully open to what is happening in the present moment, including difficult and negative private experiences, and connecting with one's values and living. According to Strosahl et al. (2004), the qualities that reflect this process are vitality, spontaneity, connection and creativity.

4. Self-as-context. In this process, individuals work on decreasing their attachment or fusion with a conceptualized self (i.e., I am boring; I am unlovable; I am hopeless) and increase their experiential contact with a transcendent sense of self, or self-as-context. People learn to see that they are not the same as their thoughts, feelings and physical pain. There is a self that observes all experience. This self is experienced as constant and stable, while feelings and evaluations come and go. The key phrase often used in this process is, 'you are not just your thoughts, emotions, memories, roles … These things are the content of your life, whereas you are the context … the space in which they unfold' (Hayes et al., 1999, p. 195). Once people context the self-as-context, they are presumably more willing to let go of unhelpful self-evaluations, or unhelpful cognitive content (Pierson & Hayes, 2007). People learn that giving up an unhelpful self-concept is not the same as giving up one's sense of self.

5. Values. Values refer to directions in life that individuals choose that result in enrichment, vitality and authenticity. An individual's behavior is guided by values. In this sense, values are never actually achieved, or obtained as concrete objects, yet they are always present every time an individual chooses them (Hayes et al., 1999; Pierson & Hayes, 2007). When an individual is stuck, and fusion and experiential avoidance dominate, it is easy for individuals to get 'off track' and engage in behaviors that are inconsistent with their values. For example, an individual may value meeting people and engaging socially with others. However, they avoid this situation because of the significant amount of anxiety they experience when they think about it. Helping individuals to let go of the struggle with negative private events allows them to regain their sense of direction and work on engaging in behavior that is consistent with their values. Willingness and acceptance of unpleasant private experiences, which are part of being human, are important processes that assist the individual in pursuing values and engaging in valued behavior (Strosahl et al., 2004).

6. Committed Action. Living according to our values often produces distress and the temptation to engage in experiential avoidance. Committed action involves engaging in behavior, in spite of difficult private experiences that may 'show up'. There will be failures, and we do not always live up to our commitments from day to day. Commitment involves helping people return to their valued direction again and again.

There is no correct order for addressing these processes and not all individuals need work in each of the domains (Strosahl et al., 2004). To summarize, the ACT model purports that the normal verbal processes that influence psychological inflexibility make it difficult for humans to learn effectively from experience and to take advantage of opportunities afforded by situations (Pierson & Hayes, 2007). This translates to behavioral ineffectiveness in pursuing one's values in a range of areas, such as connecting in relationships and being effective at work. Behavioral ineffectiveness can result when individuals engage in avoidance behavior, instead of living their values. Applying the ACT model may lead to an increase in an individual's psychological flexibility, sensitivity to the current social situation and effectiveness in engaging in valued living.

ACT and Aversive Interpersonal Relationships

In this section, the therapeutic model of ACT will be expanded to a social–emotional training program that has been used with the NSW police. The aim of the program is to increase participants' effectiveness in interpersonal situations. The training mostly involved participants ranging from sergeants and above, and there are plans to provide training to officers across the board (i.e., recruits to Commanders).

Recently, much attention has been focused on leadership and what it means to be a good leader within workplaces and organizations (e.g., see Austin, 2007; Kaiser, Hogan, & Craig, 2008; Leskiw & Parbudyal, 2007; Walz, 2007). Leadership is a quality that is also considered essential within the NSW police, particularly as there is a section within this organization that is focused on developing leaders. Forster (2005) summarizes several important skills that are required for effective leadership, including enhancing and improving employees' performance through identifying and working towards common values and goals, making important changes that will enable their staff to be effective, and being concerned about the relationships that are developed with and among employees, which is particularly important for resolving conflict. 'The most effective leaders are very aware of the simple but powerful idea that effective leadership, like communication, is a two-way process ... leadership and followership is a dynamic relationship, based on the situations that people are facing' (Forster, 2005, pp. 24–25).

The training program that is described here supports and promotes the development of participants' leadership skills. The workshop aims to develop participants' ability to participate in a two-way process with fellow employees, which will be described shortly. For example, it has long been recognized that identifying and setting goals can have a 'powerful influence on the motivation and performance levels of individual employees and work groups' (Forster, 2005, p. 177). The ability of leaders to enlist their employees as 'change agents' in the identification, design and planning of common and self-determined goals can reduce employees' resistance, negativity and opposition to change (Toch, 2008). The goal is to help participants return to their workplaces with skills that influence cohesive teamwork, and with clear communication and awareness of one's own and other individuals' responses to situations.

The key is to help them to apply the skills in situations with high levels of stress. For example, difficulties arise because of overarching organizational systems, such as the hierarchical system in the police force, organizational change and restructures, and problems getting along with other individuals. These situations are likely to produce a great deal of distress among police officers. ACT helps officers to accept the distress that naturally occurs and to stay committed to their social values, even when distress seems to be pushing them in the wrong direction.

As mentioned previously, this training program has many of the same general goals as 'social skills training' as used in many CBT interventions, However, there are important differences.

Teaching Social Skills Via Experiential Feedback Versus Verbal Suggestions
Social skills training programs are used to develop and improve such things as communication and assertiveness skills, social problem solving, negotiation, and team and organisation development (Baldwin, 1992; Taylor, 1990). Social skills training programs have been used with a wide range of populations, including clinical and nonclinical populations, and with a range of clinical and behavioral problems such as anxiety, schizophrenia,

excessive anger and parenting issues (see Deffenbacher, Oetting, Huff, & Thwaites, 1995; Deffenbacher, Thwaites, Wallace, & Oetting, 1994; Grizenko et al., 2000; Rosenfarb, Hayes, & Linehan, 1989; Taylor, 1990).

Studies have identified a number of problems with some social skills training programs, including failure of generalization of acquired skills across different events and over time, limited evidence supporting the long-term benefits of social skills training and the questionable effectiveness of measures that are used to assess social skills (Baldwin, 1992; Deffenbacher et al., 1994; Grizenko et al., 2000; Rosenfarb et al., 1989). It has been hypothesized that past interventions have not been maximally effective because they encourage excessive rule and instruction following and do not provide sufficient experiential contact with the context in which the behavior occurs (Follette & Callaghan, 1995; Hayes, Brownstein, Zettle, Rosenfarb, & Korn, 1986; Luoma et al., in press; Rosenfarb et al., 1989).

According to Follette and Callaghan (1995), there are several problems with teaching complex social behaviors using a strictly rule- and instruction-giving approach. First, it is difficult to know what rules to teach. For example, there are many different social rules that relate to nonverbal communication, assertiveness, making complaints, teaching people, and so forth. So which social rules are most important and need to be taught first? Second, situations and events can be unique; therefore this implies that they require their own set of 'unique rules'. Third, not all people will use or follow the same rules. Fourth, rules can often be quite complex to teach, as social situations can be filled with subtle and changing contingencies. Finally, social skills are more likely to be learned and shaped by the natural contingencies that occur during a social interaction, in the actual experience. The natural contingencies in an interaction are likely to become lost when rules dominate the learning experience (Follette & Callaghan, 1995, p. 414).

What does this all mean? It might be best to learn social skills via experience (Cherniss, 2000; Rosenfarb et al., 1989). One way to do this is to have people role-play social situations they find difficult (Rosenfarb et al., 1989). Then, the role-play partner can give some simple feedback (e.g., 'that was good'; 'I give that a 7 on a 1 to 10 scale'). The key is to maximize the extent that experience, rather than language, is shaping behavior. In support of this idea, Rosenfarb et al. (1989) found that experiential feedback was better than direct instruction in improving social skills deficits in adults.

The Three Levels of Social Training in ACT

The ACT social–emotional training program includes all the key ACT processes, as described earlier, and it does this by combining them all in social exercises. The program is based on a recent ACT model that has been applied to the therapeutic relationship between therapists and clients

(Pierson & Hayes, 2007). We will outline the model by Pierson and Hayes, and then show how this model can be adapted for social skills training.

In the ACT therapeutic relationship model, three levels have been identified that can assist with the therapeutic relationship (Pierson & Hayes, 2007). The first level concerns the 'psychological stance' of the therapist. That is, the therapist needs to be aware of their own psychological events, or private experiences, that are 'likely to show up' during the 'moment-to-moment' interaction of the therapist and client (Pierson & Hayes, 2007, p. 11). Therapists need to bring their ACT-relevant psychological skills (including acceptance, defusion and flexibility) to the therapeutic relationship.

The second level relates to the therapeutic process; in other words, the qualities of the therapeutic relationship that are empowering and enhance flexibility. The third level refers to the psychological process of the client (see Eifert & Forsyth, 2005; Hayes & Smith, 2005; Hayes & Strosahl, 2004; Hayes et al., 1999). All three levels can vary in terms of levels of acceptance, mindfulness, defusion, self-as-context, values and commitment. For example, I can accept my own emotions in the moment (level 1), the client can accept their emotions (level 3), and the relationship interaction can involve acceptance-related behavior (level 2).

Our social skills intervention used experiential role-plays to target all three of these levels. We first targeted the psychological stance of the participant, including their level of acceptance and willingness to experience difficult private experience, their ability to use defusion and mindfulness skills, and their connectedness with values and goals. This level could also be referred to as 'intrapersonal' training.

The second level concerns the ability of the participant to put into play the relevant ACT processes during a social interaction. For example, participants might practice being fully present to the other person, accepting and/or observably value-driven. The final level concerns the participant's attempts to increase ACT processes, such as acceptance in the other person. This level is particularly relevant to people who manage others. We help managers to help others engage in value-congruent behavior, accept the feelings they cannot change, be mindful of what they are doing, and so on.

The Experiential Role-Play Method in Practice
During the course of the workshops that were conducted with the police, participants identified several social situations that they found difficult to resolve, or that ended very badly. We decided that the experiential role-plays would be more useful if they closely resembled what the participants dealt with in everyday life. The exercise was done in a series of steps.

Step 1: Elicit the details of the situation. Participants are asked to identify a work-related interpersonal situation that they are struggling with, such as bullying at work, difficulty communicating with supervisor, or having to give a colleague negative feedback. Participants are asked to write the details of the situation, including the difficult private experiences that show up, the avoidance strategies that may be used and the value they would like to put into play (see 'My Struggle' worksheet in Appendix A). By writing about their private experiences, they are engaged in defusion as it involves them looking *at* the content of thinking, rather than *through* it.

Part of this exercise also requires that participants identify difficult behavioral patterns in themselves and others. If participants have difficulty identifying behavior patterns, we provide them with a table that lists several different types of behavior patterns, such as a 'clam' (e.g., behavior involves either brief or no response to questions), 'sniper' (e.g., behavior that is passive–aggressive, that is intended to tease or hurt the other person), or 'bull' (e.g., behavior that seeks to aggressively dominate a person). While we use these labels, we also encourage participants to not take them too seriously, and we help them to notice that no person is the same as a label.

Step 2: The role play. The facilitator asks if any of the participants would like to describe their difficult social situation to the group. Willing participants are also asked to role-play the situation. In most cases, the facilitator usually participates in the first role-play and will either 'act' out the behavior of the participant or the 'other' individual.

Step 3: Identify willingness, defusion and values. The facilitator asks the participant engaged in the role-play to identify their private experiences and to notice what happens during the interaction. They are also asked to identify their value in that situation, as well as the value of the other person involved in the situation.

Finally, they are asked the fundamental question: 'Are you willing to have all the difficult private experiences that arise, particularly when trying to behave consistently with your value?' For example, if the social situation involves giving negative feedback to a colleague, they are asked, 'Are you willing to have anxiety show up in yourself, and sit with the anger of the other person, in order to do what you value?' If they answer 'yes', then we move on to step 4 of this exercise. If the participant says 'no', then the facilitator engages them in some defusion work around the difficult feelings and thoughts, and/or talks about using a different behavioral approach, or putting a different value in play.

The 'Fundamental Question Worksheet; (see Appendix B) provides some structure to what has been described above. The worksheet can be completed by the client, or it can be completed on a whiteboard by the facilitator.

Step 4: Experiment and provide experiential feedback. In this last phase of the exercise, the participant and facilitator may role-play the difficult social situation several times, each time trying a different approach. The role-play can continue for several minutes. After each role-play the facilitator and workshop participants should give the participant some simple feedback. People can rate the behavior on a 1 (*very ineffective*) to 9 (*highly effective*) scale and do not need to elaborate on their rating. The format follows that of Rosenfarb et al. (1989) where the rating is mainly based on a person's 'gut-level' and the facilitator does not specify what discrete behaviors the rating was based on. Participants are then encouraged to engage in their own role-plays in order to practice giving and receiving experiential feedback, as well as working on their own willingness, defusion, identifying values and choosing effective behavior in certain social situations.

There are two goals for this exercise. The first goal is for participants to discover what works for them via experiential feedback, as opposed to learning new rules or social skills. Second, participants are encouraged to use their acceptance and willingness skills in order to make room for unpleasant thoughts and emotions, and still engage in effective value-driven behavior. Ideally, in each of the steps of this exercise, the facilitator and participants are putting all of the ACT ingredients into play (i.e., mindfulness, acceptance, defusion, valued behavior, etc.).

The exercise also encourages participants to engage in social perspective. Through this exercise participants contact an observer-self who can watch the social situation unfold and notice how they and others are reacting. Participants learn to notice that the observer remains constant during the entire role-play and is not equivalent to their difficult thoughts and feelings. The observer helps them to step back from the situation, take a breath and choose an effective course of action in line with their values.

Finally, the exercise gives people a chance at improving the nature of their social interactions. For example, they are encouraged to be mindful and accepting during the role-play. After a practice interaction, they are asked what it felt like to be mindful. The interaction partner is also asked how it felt to interact with someone who was fully present to him or her.

Expansion of Experiential Role-play
The role-play forms an extensive part of the ACT social training workshop, and from this one-on-one role-play we have also developed a group role-play exercise. This role-play follows the same format as the experiential role-play, except that more participants are involved and the standard scenario that is used is a meeting. Participants are given the Fundamental Question

Worksheet and are asked to choose and work with one other individual in the role-play to practice identifying their values and private experiences that may arise during a difficult social situation. In this exercise, the facilitators encourage participants to engage in discussion about their behavior and reactions during the role-play based on what they have written on the worksheet, with particular attention focused on the ACT processes engaged in by participants.

Social Interaction Metaphors

The facilitators also use several ACT metaphors that highlight the struggles that we get caught in when social situations become difficult. Some of these metaphors can be found in the original ACT book (see Hayes et al., 1999) such as 'Joe the Bum Metaphor', 'Fish on the Hook Metaphor', and a group version of the 'Passengers on the Bus Metaphor'. The 'Tar Baby Metaphor', as we have called it, has proven to be particularly useful. This metaphor is used to emphasize the problem of using ineffective control strategies repeatedly to control another person's behavior, and the way that these control strategies may further entangle you in a destructive relationship with the other.

Tar Baby Metaphor (adapted from Harris, 1881)

Br'er Fox had enough of Br'er Rabbits tricks and of not being able to catch Br'er Rabbit. So one day, Br'er Fox comes up with a solution so that he can finally catch Br'er Rabbit. He creates a tar baby out of a lump of tar and dresses it up in some clothes, and hides behind a bush to see what happens to Br'er Rabbit when he passes by. Br'er Rabbit comes along, sees Tar Baby, and stops and says 'Good morning', and tries to engage in a conversation with Tar Baby. Of course, Br'er Rabbit receives no response. Br'er Rabbit becomes increasingly frustrated by Tar Baby's lack of manners and decides that he's going to 'beat' some manners into Tar Baby. He punches Tar Baby, and his fist becomes stuck. Br'er Rabbit again assumes Tar Baby is being rude so he punches it again to try and free himself, and his other hand became stuck. Br'er Rabbit again demands Tar Baby let go of him or he'll kick him. Tar Baby does not respond so Br'er Rabbit kicks him … now, one of his feet is stuck. Eventually Br'er Rabbit's hands, feet and even head are stuck in Tar Baby.

So the fox seems to have won. Now with Br'er Rabbit stuck, Br'er Fox ponders the way he will dispose of Br'er Rabbit. This is when Br'er Rabbit quickly pays attention to the situation and figures out what to do. Br'er Rabbit pleads with Br'er Fox: 'Please, whatever, you do, don't throw me in the Br'er patch'. Of course, the fox, who wanted to harm Br'er Rabbit as much as possible, throws him in the Br'er patch. That's when Br'er Rabbit escapes — rabbits are at home in briar patches or thickets.

The metaphor illustrates the idea that often, the more you seek to control a 'difficult person', the more you often get stuck to them and intertwined in their lives. It is as if you are making this person and the problem more and more important to your life, as opposed to living a valued life. In this metaphor, all of the ACT processes are reflected.

For example, the struggle that people find themselves in when they are 'stuck' in a difficult social situation corresponds to the ACT process of acceptance, more specifically 'control is the problem'. In a social situation, an individual who continues to use ineffective social behavior is like Br'er Rabbit. They end up getting stuck and 'nothing works'. Acceptance of one's own and the other person's private experiences, the situation and 'being stuck', may lead to psychological flexibility. Increased flexibility may enable the person to let go of having to 'control' their own private experiences and the other person's behavior. Psychological flexibility helps us to reconnect with our values, which leads to more effective and value-driven behavior. This whole process also involves being present and being aware of the context of the situation and doing 'what works', as opposed to being fused with private experiences. The value of 'living' for Br'er Rabbit helped him survive, in spite of being stuck in Tar Baby!

Conclusion

Why is it that we have such difficulty getting along? We have argued that our attempts to control our emotions become one part of the problem that leads to aversive interpersonal relationships. In the workplace this can prove to be costly (emotionally, financially and socially) not only to the individual, but also to other work colleagues, the employer and the business/organisation as a whole.

This chapter outlined an approach to reducing individual suffering and providing individuals with social skills in order to improve and empower interpersonal relationships. The approach is based on ACT and identifies the way in which the six core ACT processes can be used to reduce aversive interpersonal interactions in the workplace. An important part of this program is the use of experiential feedback to improve social skills. Experiential feedback enables an individual to become more aware of environmental contingencies, or the context of a situation, and so orient their behavior to what may be most effective in that situation — what works.

Employee motivation and performance is likely to be enhanced by a manager or coworker that encourages value-congruent behavior, and improves relationship quality. Getting along can be hard at times, yet if individuals are willing to accept and be mindful of the difficult emotions that show up in social relationships, they might be less likely to suffer. They may then be able to model and engage in effective behavior that will possibly lead to better relationships.

References

Austin, A. (2007). Review of the quest for a general theory of leadership. *Leadership & Organization Development Journal, 28*(8), 786–788.

Bach, P., & Hayes, S. C. (2002). The use of acceptance and commitment therapy to prevent the rehospitalization of psychotic patients: A randomized controlled trial. *Journal of Consulting and Clinical Psychology, 70*(5), 1129–1139.

Baldwin, T. T. (1992). Effects of alternative modeling strategies on outcomes of interpersonal-skills training. *Journal of Applied Psychology, 77*(2), 147–154.

Barron, O. (1998). Bullying at work: The distinction between workplace bullying and workplace violence and the ramification for OHS. *Journal of Occupational Health and Safety, Australia and New Zealand, 14*(6), 575–580.

Bond, F. W., & Bunce, D. (2000). Mediators of change in emotion-focused and problem-focused worksite stress management interventions. *Journal of Occupational Health Psychology, 5*(1), 156–163.

Bond, F. W., & Bunce, D. (2003). The role of acceptance and job control in mental health, job satisfaction and work performance. *Journal of Applied Psychology, 88*(6), 1057–1067.

Bond, F. W., & Hayes, S. C. (2002). ACT at work. In F. W. Bond & W. Dryden (Eds.), *Handbook of brief cognitive behaviour therapy* (pp. 117–139). Chichester, England: John Wiley & Sons.

Cherniss, C. (2000). Social and emotional competence in the workplace. In R. Bar-on & J. D. A. Parker (Eds.), *The handbook of emotional intelligence: Theory, development, assessment and application at home, school and in the workplace* (pp. 433–458). San Francisco: Jossey-Bass.

Dahl, J. C., Wilson, K. G., Luciano, C., & Hayes, S. C. (2005). *Acceptance and commitment therapy for chronic pain.* Reno, NV: Context Press.

Dahl, J. C., Wilson, K. G., & Nilsson, A. (2004). Acceptance and commitment therapy and the treatment of persons at risk for long-term disability resulting from stress and pain symptoms: A preliminary randomized trial. *Behavior Therapy, 35,* 785–801.

Deffenbacher, J. L., Oetting, E. R., Huff, M. E., & Thwaites, G. A. (1995). Fifteen-month follow-up of social skills and cognitive-relaxation approaches to general anger reduction. *Journal of Counseling Psychology, 42*(3), 400–405.

Deffenbacher, J. L., Thwaites, G. A., Wallace, T. L., & Oetting, E. R. (1994). Social skills and cognitive-relaxation approaches to general anger reduction. *Journal of Counseling Psychology, 41*(3), 386–396.

Eifert, G. H., & Forsyth, J. P. (2005). *Acceptance and commitment therapy for anxiety disorders.* Oakland, CA: New Harbinger Publications, Inc.

Flaxman, P. E. (2006). *Acceptance-based and traditional cognitive–behavioural stress management in the workplace: Investigating the mediators and moderators of change.* Unpublished doctoral dissertation, Goldsmiths College, University of London.

Follette, W. C., & Callaghan, G. M. (1995). Do as I do, not as I say: A behavior-analytic approach to supervision. *Professional Psychology: Research and Practice, 26*(4), 413–421.

Forster, N. (2005). *Maximum performance: A practical guide to leading and managing people at work.* Cheltenham, England: Edward Elgar.

Grizenko, N., Zappitelli, M., Langevin, J., Hrychko, S., El-Messidi, A., Kaminester, D., et al. (2000). Effectiveness of a social skills training program using self/other perspective-taking: A nine-month follow-up. *American Journal of Orthopsychiatry, 70*(4), 501–509.

Harris, J. C. (1881). *Uncle Remus: His songs and sayings*. New York: Appleton.

Hayes, S. C. (2004). Acceptance and commitment therapy, relational frame theory, and the third wave of behavioral and cognitive therapies. *Behavior Therapy, 35,* 639–665.

Hayes, S. C., Barnes-Holmes, D., & Roche, B. (Eds.). (2001). *Relational frame theory: A post-Skinnerian account of human language and cognition*. New York: Plenum Press.

Hayes, S. C., Brownstein, A. J., Zettle, R. D., Rosenfarb, I. S., & Korn, Z. (1986). Rule-governed behavior and sensitivity to changing consequences of responding. *Journal of the Experimental Analysis of Behavior, 45,* 237–256.

Hayes, S. C., & Smith, S. (2005). *Get out of your mind and into your life: The new acceptance and commitment therapy*. Oakland, CA: New Harbinger Publications, Inc.

Hayes, S. C., & Strosahl, K. (Eds.). (2004). *A practical guide to acceptance and commitment therapy*. New York: Springer.

Hayes, S. C., Strosahl, K., & Wilson, K. G. (1999). *Acceptance and commitment therapy: An experiential approach to behavior change*. New York: The Guilford Press.

Hayes, S. C., Wilson, K. G., Gifford, E. V., Follette, V. M., & Strosahl, K. (1996). Experiential avoidance and behavioral disorders: A functional dimensional approach to diagnosis and treatment. *Journal of Consulting and Clinical Psychology, 64*(6), 1152–1168.

Jetson, S. (2005). *Workplace bullying*. Retrieved July 3, 2007, from http://www.jetson. net.au/SJA%20pdfs/SJA%20Bullying%202005.pdf

Kaiser, R. B., Hogan, R., & Craig, S. B. (2008). Leadership and the fate of organizations. *American Psychologist, 63*(2), 96–110.

Leskiw, S., & Parbudyal, S. (2007). Leadership development: Learning from best practices. *Leadership & Organization Development Journal, 28*(5), 444–464.

Linehan, M. M. (1993). *Cognitive–behavioral treatment of borderline personality disorder*. New York: Guilford Press.

Lundgren, T., Dahl, J. C., Melin, L., & Kies, B. (2006). Evaluation of acceptance and commitment therapy for drug refractory epilepsy: A randomized controlled trial in South Africa: A pilot study. *Epilepsia, 47*(12), 2173–2179.

Luoma, J. B., Hayes, S. C., Roget, N., Fisher, G., Padilla, M., Bissett, R., et al. (In press). Augmenting continuing education with psychologically-focused group consultation: Effects on adoption of group drug counseling. *Psychotherapy Theory, Research, Practice, Training*.

McAvoy, B. R., & Murtagh, J. (2003). Workplace bullying. *British Medical Journal 326,* 776–777.

Pierson, H., & Hayes, S. C. (2007). Using acceptance and commitment therapy to empower the therapeutic relationship. In P. Gilbert & R. Leahy (Eds.), *The therapeutic relationship in cognitive–behavior therapy* (pp. 205–228). London: Routledge.

Rosenfarb, I. S., Hayes, S. C., & Linehan, M. M. (1989). Instructions and experiential feedback in the treatment of social skills deficits in adults. *Psychotherapy, 26*(2), 242–251.

Salin, D. (2003). Ways of explaining workplace bullying: A review of enabling, motivating and precipitating structures and processes in the work environment. *Human Relations, 56*(10), 1213–1232.

Segal, Z. V., Williams, J. M. G., & Teasdale, J. D. (2001). *Mindfulness-based cognitive therapy for depression: A new approach to preventing relapse*. New York: The Guilford Press.

Strosahl, K., Hayes, S. C., Wilson, K. G., & Gifford, E. V. (2004). An ACT primer: Core therapy processes, intervention strategies, and therapist competencies. In S. C. Hayes & K. Strosahl (Eds.), *A practical guide to acceptance and commitment therapy* (pp. 31–58). New York: Springer.

Taylor, E. H. (1990). The assessment of social intelligence. *Psychotherapy, 27*(3), 445–457.

Toch, H. (2008). Police officers as change agents in police reform. *Policing & Society, 18*(1), 60–71.

Walz, J. T. (2007). Review of Leadership for leaders. *Leadership & Organization Development Journal, 28*(3), 288–289.

Wenzlaff, R. M., & Luxton, D. D. (2003). The role of thought suppression in depressive rumination. *Cognitive Therapy and Research, 27*(3), 293–308.

Wenzlaff, R. M., & Wegner, D. M. (2000). Thought suppression. *Annual Review of Psychology, 51*, 59–91.

Wilson, K. G., & Murrell, A. R. (2003). Values-centered interventions: Setting a course for behavioral treatment. In S. C. Hayes, V. M. Follette & M. Linehan (Eds.), *The new behavior therapies: Expanding the cognitive–behavioral tradition*. New York: Guilford Press.

Xavier. (2008). *The wonderful Tar Baby: Rewritten text of the original Brer Fox, Brer Rabbit and the Briar Patch 'Uncle Remus' Story by Joel Chandler Harris*. Retrieved March 4, 2008, from http://www.abelard.org/brer_fox_brer_rabbit_briar_patch.php

Zettle, R. D., & Hayes, S. C. (1986). Dysfunctional control by client verbal behavior: The context of reason giving. *The Analysis of Verbal Behavior, 4*, 30–38.

Zettle, R. D., & Hayes, S. C. (2002). Brief ACT treatment for depression. In F. W. Bond & W. Dryden (Eds.), *Handbook of brief cognitive–behaviour therapy* (pp. 35–54). Chichester, England: John Wiley & Sons.

Zettle, R. D., & Raines, J. C. (1989). Group cognitive and contextual therapies in treatment of depression. *Journal of Clinical Psychology, 45*, 438–445.

APPENDIX A
My Struggle Worksheet

My Struggle: Work-Related Interpersonal Situation

Identify a work-related interpersonal situation that you are struggling with (i.e., bullying, communication problems, giving a colleague negative feedback). What value / goal were you trying to put into play? Write about this situation in the lines below:

_____
_____
_____
_____
_____
_____
_____

Write about the difficult emotions and thoughts that showed up during this interaction

_____
_____
_____
_____

What was the outcome of this situation, or is it unresolved? What behaviour did you engage in?

_____
_____
_____
_____

What control strategies did you engage in? How did you try to make yourself feel better? Examples include: Playing big, avoiding the person, playing small, and making a sarcastic comment towards the other person.

_____
_____
_____
_____
_____

Reflection question: How successful were these control strategies?

_____
_____
_____
_____

APPENDIX B
Fundamental Question Worksheet

The fundamental question: Willingness, values, and commitment

Value: What value would you like to put into play?

_____
_____
_____
_____
_____
_____

Other's value: What value is the other person trying to put into play?

_____
_____
_____
_____
_____
_____

Internal 'bullies': What private experiences sometimes 'push' you around and seem to get in the way of your valued action?

_____
_____

Thoughts/evaluations

_____
_____
_____

Emotions

_____
_____
_____

Other's internal bullies: What are likely to be the other person's 'internal bullies'

_____
_____

Thoughts/evaluations

_____
_____
_____

Emotions

_____
_____
_____

Willingness: Are you willing to make room for these private experiences, in order to do what you value?

Yes: Go to the next step and commit to valued behavior. Carry your thoughts and feelings with you, like keys.

No: You may need to choose another value to put into play.

Commitment: What concrete actions would you like to commit to, that will put your values into play

_____
_____
_____
_____
_____
_____
_____

Other's actions: What behavior would I like the other person to engage in? Can I connect this behavior to their values?

_____
_____
_____
_____
_____
_____
_____

chapter eleven

ACT and CBT for Psychosis: Comparisons and Contrasts

Hamish J. McLeod

Cognitive–behavior therapy (CBT) is now a widely recognised and empirically supported treatment for psychosis (Wykes, Steel, Everitt, & Tarrier, 2008). However, its development lagged substantially behind that of CBT for anxiety and depressive disorders. Literally decades passed before the techniques and therapy models of CBT for nonpsychotic disorders were systematically applied to the understanding and treatment of symptoms such as hallucinations and delusions (see Lowe & Chadwick, 1990, for an early case study). This delay may have arisen because of assumptions that meaningful participation in CBT requires 'rationality' that is lacking in psychosis or that diagnostic categories such as schizophrenia represent a distinct class of mental disorders that are too severe to be treated with psychological techniques (Bellack, 1986).

In contrast, the application of acceptance and commitment therapy (ACT) to psychotic symptoms has occurred much more rapidly. The first trial to apply ACT to psychosis (Bach & Hayes, 2002) was published only 3 years after the main ACT therapy manual (Hayes, Strosahl, & Wilson, 1999) and an attempted replication was published 4 years later (Gaudiano & Herbert, 2006a). This reflects the view that ACT as a therapy package and relational frame theory (RFT) as an underlying theoretical framework should have therapeutic utility for all humans who use language (Hayes, Luoma, Bond, Masuda, & Lillis, 2006). ACT is meant to be applicable irrespective of the nature of the private mental events that are causing distress, because emphasis is placed on the individual's relationship to those experiences, rather than the content of them. Hence, in psychosis, the presence of bizarre or unusual private mental events has, theoretically, little relevance to the question of whether ACT would be a suitable treatment.

It is this universality of the RFT model that has encouraged the use of ACT with a wide range of psychological problems and disorders. However, the most effective ways to treat psychosis are far from resolved. People with psychotic disorders such as schizophrenia are overrepresented in suicide statistics (Birchwood, Iqbal, Chadwick, & Trower, 2000) and the cost to society of treating people with psychotic disorders far exceeds that of treating other mental health problems (Carr, Lewin, Neil, Halpin, & Holmes, 2004). While favorable outcomes from psychosocial treatments such as CBT are encouraging, there is scope for further refinement. The application of ACT and other mindfulness-based approaches (Chadwick, Newman Taylor, & Abba, 2005) to psychosis provides an opportunity to identify innovations of case conceptualization, therapeutic technique and therapy delivery models that may expand the range of options that can be offered to people with psychotic disorders. This chapter will examine the ACT approach to treating psychosis and compare and contrast it with CBT approaches. It will identify innovations that can be applied to clinical practice now and suggest areas for further investigation and development.

Minding, Ps and Qs

Most of us assume that we have a personal mind that is separate from that of others and is situated within our skin (Frith, 2004). Hence, we tacitly treat the mind as a thing that we can 'have' and, therefore, can 'lose'. This conception of the mind is evident when we examine the experience of psychosis. For many people, psychosis is synonymous with 'losing one's mind' and implies a state of being that is discontinuous with 'normality'. ACT and other mindfulness-based psychological therapies take an explicitly different stance toward the mind. In ACT, the mind is viewed not as a thing that can be lost, but instead is conceptualized as a 'repertoire of public and private verbal activities' (Hayes et al., 1999, p. 49). Hayes et al. suggest that the term 'minding' is a more accurate but cumbersome description of the process of interacting with these verbal constructions. Problems arise when 'minding' entails the treatment of mental content as truth and so '[d]isentangling people from their minds is one of the main goals of ACT' (Hayes et al., 1999, p. 69).

This disentangling often involves helping people take an observer perspective toward their mind so that they learn to separate the self from unhelpful verbally-mediated mental content. In fact, ACT therapists will often encourage the patient to treat their mind as a separate entity from the self and refer to it as such. But, the person with psychotic experiences such as auditory hallucinations or delusions of control presents a difficult challenge; they already experience aspects of their mental content as separate from self even though their friends, family and therapist would argue that it is a product of processes from within them. As discussed below, this is not an insurmountable barrier to effective therapy, but it does highlight that treatment of psychotic disorders involves idiosyncrasies of technique and case conceptualization that differentiates it from the treatment of other conditions.

The unique challenges of psychosis have led to theorists adding a 'p' to the standard CBT acronym when the techniques are applied to the experience of psychotic symptoms. Hence, CBTp involves some assumptions, techniques and therapy processes that are different from those used in CBT for other forms of suffering (Startup, Jackson, & Pearce, 2002). In particular, the goals of CBTp are contrary to the oft-cited claim that CBT emphasizes the elimination of irrational thoughts and feelings. From the start, CBTp has emphasized that psychotic experiences are dysfunctional when they interfere with living, not because of their mere presence, and so the elimination of symptoms has not been a primary focus (Fowler, Garety, & Kuipers, 1995; Nelson, 2005).

It remains to be determined whether ACT for psychotic symptoms differs from ACT for other disorders enough to warrant a 'p' suffix. But, some features of the published ACT for psychosis trials are different from ACT for other problems, so for this chapter, the abbreviation ACTp will be used to refer to the ACT studies that specifically focused on psychotic symptoms.

Before progressing, it is also necessary to precisely specify which 'ps' are the focus of ACTp and CBTp. There is a widespread tendency to associate psychosis with schizophrenia and by far the majority of participants in CBTp trials have attracted that diagnosis (Wykes et al., 2008). However, it is more accurate to say that most of the published intervention trials have focused on reducing the adverse consequences of delusional beliefs and auditory verbal hallucinations ('voices') irrespective of psychiatric diagnosis. Other psychotic symptoms such as thought disorder tend not to be a focus of intervention. This is certainly the case in the ACTp trials where the critical inclusion criteria were the presence of hallucinations and/or delusions irrespective of primary psychiatric diagnosis (Bach & Hayes, 2002; Gaudiano & Herbert, 2006a). Hence, delusions and hallucinations will be the main focus of the discussion here.

All that remains is to specify some questions. For example, what are the similarities and differences in the CBTp and ACTp models and how do they impact on our understanding of the most effective ways to understand and treat psychosis? Are the models of therapy delivery and case conceptualization incompatible? And, finally, what future directions might be explored to enhance the humane and efficient treatment of people whose lives are severely disrupted by psychosis?

Empirical Evidence for ACTp

Two randomized controlled trials provide the current empirical evidence for the efficacy of ACTp. Bach and Hayes (2002) compared a four-session ACT intervention to treatment as usual (TAU) in a sample of mixed diagnosis hospitalized patients with chronic psychotic symptoms. The rehospitalization rate for the ACTp treated group was half that of the TAU group over 4 months' follow-up. The ACTp treated patients also showed significant reductions in the 'believability' of their symptoms but were more likely than TAU patients to report the presence of symptoms. This was particularly evident for participants who presented primarily with hallucinations and the authors interpreted this as a direct result of the acceptance emphasis of ACT. Although the TAU group also showed a reduction in the believability of symptoms over the follow-up period, this was not as great as that shown by the ACTp group.

The second trial was an attempted replication and extension of Bach and Hayes' (2002) original study. Gaudiano and Herbert (2006a) compared an abbreviated ACT protocol with enhanced treatment as usual (ETAU) delivered to 40 inpatients with various affective and nonaffective psychoses. The treatment sessions were designed to 'stand alone' and most participants received three sessions (range 1–5 sessions). The methodological enhancements in this study included the use of structured psychiatric symptom rating scales, attempts to check the fidelity of the intervention and analyses to determine clinically significant improvement. More participants in the ACTp than the ETAU group demonstrated clinically significant levels of improvement in psychopathology ratings. The ACTp group also showed greater reduction in observer-rated affective symptoms, lower self-reported distress related to hallucinations and reduced believability of hallucinations following treatment. However, Bach and Hayes' significant reduction in rehospitalization rates at four-month follow-up and the tendency for ACTp treated participants to more readily report symptoms was not replicated.

Overall, these two studies suggest that relatively brief ACT-based interventions can have a significant impact on the believability of auditory hallucinations in patients with affective and nonaffective psychotic disorders. The impact on negative symptoms, delusional thinking and the durability of the treatment effects are less clear. For example, the ACT emphasis on value-consistent action could conceivably reduce negative symptoms by increasing behaviors in the service of values. But, so far, changes in negative symptoms have not been observed in ACTp trials (Gaudiano & Herbert, 2006a).

These are promising but preliminary studies with some methodological limitations (Ost, 2008). Gaudiano and Herbert (2006a) included a number of methodological improvements over the original Bach and Hayes (2002) study but showed less impressive results. This is an issue that has been confronted in the CBTp literature as it has evolved. A recent meta-analysis of 34 trials involving 1964 patients shows the general pattern that studies of higher methodological rigor have yielded lower effect sizes (Wykes et al., 2008). As both of the existing ACTp trials have been subject to independent criticism on methodological grounds (Ost, 2008; Wykes et al., 2008), there is a need for further empirical investigation before strong recommendations can be made about the widespread use of ACTp.

However, scientific caution should not dampen enthusiasm for the development of ACTp. It is clear that CBTp is not an optimized treatment that requires no further development and evidence from non-ACT researchers has highlighted that adapted mindfulness techniques may benefit people with psychotic symptoms (Abba, Chadwick, & Stevenson, 2008; Chadwick et al., 2005). The following section describes and contrasts the ACTp and CBTp models with a view to identifying possible points of future therapy development.

ACT and CBT Models of Psychosis

Models of psychopathology are usually posed to explain the origin and maintenance of the target problem(s) and to determine the mechanisms by which therapeutic improvement can be achieved. The next section compares and contrasts the models used in ACTp and CBTp. A major difference between these approaches is that there is no specific ACT model of psychotic symptoms. Instead, the principles codified in the ACT 'hexaflex' model (Hayes et al., 2006) are viewed as equally applicable to psychotic symptoms as to other forms of suffering. In contrast, the CBT literature has been influenced by several multifactorial accounts of psychotic disorders (Garety, Bebbington, Fowler, Freeman, & Kuipers, 2007; van der Gaag, 2006) and models of specific symptoms (Beck & Rector, 2003; Bentall, Corcoran, Howard, Blackwood, & Kinderman, 2001; Gilleen & David, 2005).

General Principles: Psychosis and Suffering

Both the ACTp and CBTp view the presence of psychotic symptoms such as delusions and hallucinations as insufficient to cause distress. It is the functional consequences of these experiences that determine whether they may become a target of intervention. Private events such as delusional thoughts or auditory hallucinations are only a problem when they play a controlling role in blocking the person's adaptive functioning. One of the core assumptions of ACT is that language can make us insensitive to contingencies in the immediate environment and instead we can respond to a verbally-mediated analogue of the world. This ability to deploy symbolic representations underpins numerous functional behaviors such as predicting events and extrapolating from prior experience to novel problems in the present. Put another way, *derived relational responding* (Blackledge, 2003) allows humans to develop predictive models of the world that have been learned via language forms rather than via direct conditioning. The cost of this facility is that symbols such as words and other mentally experienced events (e.g., images) can stimulate emotional states and behavioral responses that thwart adaptive functioning or bear little resemblance to the observable environment outside our heads. In this way, language-based constructions of self-concept can predominate even when there is little 'objective' evidence to support these constructions. In psychotic states, these constructions can seem entirely nonsensical to others but are treated as completely plausible by the patient.

Suffering in psychosis can emerge in several ways. The transformation of stimulus functions means that verbal constructions of the world such as 'I am the subject of an alien experiment' acquire the same properties as actually being experimented on and influences the behaviors that are emitted (e.g., spending hours each day inspecting oneself in the mirror to identify scars where the probes were inserted). Hence, the person experiences distress because they are entangled in the literal content of their thoughts (Pankey & Hayes, 2003) or they suffer because their preoccupation with psychotic thoughts blocks participation in more rewarding behaviors. A second source of suffering in psychosis is experiential avoidance (Bach & Hayes, 2002). In particular, attempts to avoid hallucinations will increase the functional importance of the experience and may raise the actual rate of voice hearing. Finally, suffering in psychosis may arise from low self-acceptance strategies aimed at eliminating past psychotic experiences from the person's self-concept. The problem for the patient is that they may be unaware that their attempts to 'act normal' may perpetuate the process of negative self-evaluation (Bach, Gaudiano, Pankey, Herbert, & Hayes, 2006).

Modeling the Causes of Psychosis

The ACT approach to the causes of human suffering differs markedly from the CBT approach. The ACT view is that attempting to identify the literal causes of current suffering by trying to unravel the myriad of past learning episodes perpetuates unhelpful 'reason giving' and entanglement in language processes Not that learning history is unimportant; it is simply that trying to identify a historical reason for current suffering may perpetuate inaction in the present (Hayes et al., 1999). The current ACT position on the etiology of psychosis is descriptive one: ' ... the core of psychosis seems to rest in the odd cognitions and more specifically, the individual's *relationship* to those cognitions' (Pankey & Hayes, 2003, p. 313 [italics in original]). A corollary is that by changing aspects of that relationship (e.g., by undermining a tendency to evaluate mental experiences as true or false) the 'pathology' is removed. Identifying additional historical causal factors is only relevant if those factors are manipulable in the present (Hayes et al., 1999).

Unlike ACT, CBTp did not emerge directly from a single model of cognition. Instead, the models used to explain the onset and maintenance of psychosis have developed in parallel to the therapy techniques and include reference to neurobiological and social factors, rather than exclusively psychological processes (Garety et al., 2007; van der Gaag, 2006). This might reflect the historical dominance of medical treatments and the disease model of schizophrenia, which emphasizes the need to pin psychological phenomena to a biological substrate. However, it has also proven to be the most realistic descriptive account of how psychosis emerges. Currently, there is considerable epidemiological evidence that genetic and biological factors (e.g., cannabis abuse) combined with psychosocial stressors (e.g., sexual trauma, social defeat) contribute to the odds of developing a psychotic disorder (Broome et al., 2005). Although many of these factors may not be directly manipulable, attempting to elucidate the distal causes of psychosis has drawn attention to the importance of psychological processes and the relevance of psychological treatments (Birchwood & Trower, 2006). This approach has also led to more refined explanations of how learning history may be expressed in the present in the form of self-schemas and how these might interact with different types of psychotic symptoms (Fowler et al., 2006).

The Maintenance of Psychotic Symptoms

The ACT position regarding the maintenance of psychotic symptoms is clear: cognitive fusion and experiential avoidance will maintain problems with hallucinations and delusions (Bach & Hayes, 2002). The corresponding proposition in the CBTp models is that the appraisal of anomalous experiences determines whether or not those experiences lead to dysfunction (Garety et al., 2007) and general beliefs about dangerousness and uncontrollability of one's thoughts sets up control efforts that lead to more mental intrusions (van der Gaag, 2006).

At a broad level, the two accounts share the view that hearing voices or having 'unusual' ideas is not the problem; it is the response to these experiences that confers dysfunction (Nelson, 2005). However, the details regarding the maintenance of delusions and hallucinations do differ across the models.

Hallucinations

The most common hallucination is in the form of 'voices' experienced as if they emanate from an external source. A growing literature from cognitive and neuroimaging studies suggests that deficits in the monitoring of willed intentions and a functional disturbance of the neural structures involved in inner speech production underpin the proclivity to hear voices (Hunter et al., 2003; Jones & Fernyhough, 2007). Hence, while the capacity to experience voices is on a continuum in the general population, some people are more susceptible. There does not appear to be an ACT or RFT account of how the phenomenological experience of voices arises; instead, voices are treated in the same way as other mental content. In contrast, the normalizing component of CBTp often includes reference to explanatory models of how voices can be generated within the brain but experienced as emanating from an external source (Nelson, 2005).

Several dimensions of the hallucinatory experience can be distressing. Appraising the content of voices as true may elicit distress (e.g., critical comments may provoke anger or sadness) or stimulate the patient to act in a way that is detrimental to their well-being (e.g., command hallucinations telling the patient to harm themselves). Beliefs about the identity, source and intentions of the voice have also been shown to modulate affective and behavioral responses (van der Gaag, 2006). For example, appraising voices as malevolent elicits anger and resistance, while benevolent voices provoke positive affect and engagement (Birchwood & Chadwick, 1997).

In the CBTp literature, the Beliefs About Voices Questionnaire-Revised (BAVQ-R; Chadwick, Lees, & Birchwood, 2000) has been widely used to assess appraisals relating to voice benevolence, malevolence, omnipotence and the response patterns of engagement and resistance. In contrast, the ACTp approach places more explicit emphasis on the role of acceptance in coping with voices and this has stimulated the development of the Voices Acceptance and Action Scale (VAAS; Shawyer et al., 2007). This scale assesses acceptance (willingness to experience voices in a nonavoidant detached way) and autonomous action (self-directed, rather than voice-directed behavior) and has shown promise as a robust measure of ACT-relevant processes that is stable over time and internally consistent (Shawyer et al., 2007).

The inclusion of acceptance and autonomous action in the scale struc-ture of the VAAS resonates with the ACT view that experiential avoidance and cognitive fusion will maintain problems with hallucinations. In this context, experiential avoidance entails an unwillingness to have the voices and the taking of steps to alter their form or frequency (Hayes, Wilson, Gifford, Follette, & Strosahl, 1996). This avoidance may have the para-doxical effect of increasing voice frequency because excluding voices from consciousness requires thinking about them. Put another way, making an ongoing effort to not have a mental experience actually refreshes that experience in consciousness.

The possibility that trying to avoid having voices may be detrimental has been addressed in a trial comparing CBT-based distraction versus focusing interventions (Haddock, Slade, Bentall, Reid, & Faragher, 1998). Haddock et al. found no difference in symptom severity ratings at two-year follow-up, but participants in the focusing intervention were more likely to view the voices as being their own thoughts. One possible interpretation of this is that being willing to experience voices provides the opportunity to notice features of them that indicate that they are internally generated. Thus, acceptance rather than distraction provides an opportunity to learn to appraise voices differently.

Appraising voices differently should reduce believability (or cognitive fusion) (Bach & Hayes, 2002; Gaudiano & Herbert, 2006a). This raises the question of what is meant by 'believability'. In the published studies to date, the concept of believability is defined somewhat ambiguously as an appraisal of the degree that 'auditory hallucinations that actually occurred corresponded to reality' (Bach & Hayes, 2002, p. 1134). This leaves open the question of whether it is the comments offered by the voices that is being judged to be believable or not, versus judgments about whether the voice originates from within or outside of the person's head. Examination of the rating scale used in the clinical trials does not clarify this issue (i.e., 'On a scale from 0 to 10, how much do you believe that when you experience [specific hallucination] that it is real? Zero means that you are certain it is not real or true, and 10 means you are absolutely certain that it is real or true' (Gaudiano & Herbert, 2006b, p. 420). One possibility is that ACTp techniques can change beliefs about the nature of the voice (e.g., it is not truly the devil talking to me) and/or its content (e.g., those critical comments are just words) by instilling the general principle that our mind can create illusions that we can choose to question or not.

While the CBTp approach shares the view that modifying patients' relationship with their voices is the key to improved functioning, there is a greater emphasis on gathering evidence to demonstrate this. For example, reducing the believability of the idea that a voice is literally coming from Elvis Presley may involve examining logical inconsistencies in voice content or reality tests in order to substantiate the alternative that the voice was made by the patient's mind or could be false (see Nelson, 2005). This is distinct from the ACTp approach that would frame such attempts at evidence gathering and disputation as a perpetuation of an unhelpful struggle with mental content.

Delusions

While the ACT model views hallucinations as stimuli that may elicit avoidance, delusions are seen as a form of avoidance that prevents feelings of failure and anxiety from being attended to (Bach & Hayes, 2002). The argument seems to be that directing attention toward delusional ideas reduces the experience of unwanted negative thoughts and feelings. This is a variant of the 'delusions as defense' hypothesis which proposes that delusions protect the individual from experiencing noxious affect (Bentall et al., 2001; Freeman & Garety, 2003; Kinderman, Kaney, Morley, & Bentall, 1992; Zigler & Glick, 1988). An implication of this model is that reduced delusional thinking may lead to an increase in the avoided mental content (such as thoughts of low self-worth) because it is no longer being suppressed. This is not supported by evidence from CBTp trials that have demonstrated an improvement in depression and low self-esteem following a reduction in delusional ideation (Freeman & Garety, 2003; Smith et al., 2006).

An alternative view is that delusions arise from normal attempts to make sense of aberrant sensations (Maher, 1992). In CBTp models, the source of aberrant sensations is ascribed to biological factors. Specifically, dysregulation of the mesolimbic dopamine pathway in people with schizophrenia leads to stimuli that would normally be inconsequential capturing attention and being experienced as highly salient (Kapur, 2003). Hence, the patient feels a profound sense of great personal significance that requires explanation (van der Gaag, 2006). The explanations are secondary delusions that are maintained because they reduce ambiguity about the state of the world but at the cost of establishing unhelpful patterns of preoccupation and delusional interference with day-to-day life. Taking the experiential avoidance view, it may be that delusions facilitate avoidance of a noxious feeling of uncertainty and that fusion with unhelpful explanations that interfere with valued activity (Hayes et al., 1999).

This type of proposition has been examined in a study of 187 delusional people who were assessed with the Need for Closure Scale (Freeman et al., 2006). This scale has two main dimensions: a preference for decisive answers (e.g., 'I usually make important decisions quickly and confidently') and a desire for simple structure. Freeman et al. failed to demonstrate a direct association between delusional thinking and need for closure. In fact, the delusional participants rated themselves as indecisive. At present it would seem that the 'delusions as a means of experiential avoidance' requires further investigation.

Factors and Processes Implicated in Therapeutic Change

Different processes have been invoked to explain therapeutic change in ACTp and CBTp. The six core processes, or positive psychological skills, identified as underpinning change in ACT are: acceptance, defusion, contact with the present moment, values, committed action and self as context (Hayes et al., 2006). This situates the change processes largely within the individual, although the stimuli for change occur in the context of the therapeutic interaction. In contrast, attempts to account for CBTp effects have specified features of the therapist–patient dyad as well as intraindividual factors. For example, the establishment of a working alliance, learning of new coping skills, normalizing and destigmatizing, and cognitive reframing all show some influence in predicting a favorable CBTp outcome (Lecomte & Lecomte, 2002; Tarrier & Wykes, 2004). However, as several of these factors and processes are not unique to CBT, a more refined analysis is needed.

It has been argued that changes in appraisal are critical to a positive outcome in CBTp (van der Gaag, 2006). In particular, experiences that were attributed to an external cause are reascribed to an internal source. But appraisal of stimuli is not a unitary function in the brain (van der Gaag, 2006). Two circuits have been identified, a fast subcortical route and a slower cortical pathway. The proposition is that patients with schizophrenia are particularly liable to respond to appraisals generated by the faster 'better-safe-than-sorry' subcortical pathway and this manifests in a jumping-to-conclusions decision-making style (Garety, 1991). CBTp may produce therapeutic benefit by reducing reliance on the rapid subcortical pathway and increasing the use of slower, more deliberate and consciously accessible reasoning processes mediated by cortical structures (Nelson, 2005).

This general principle of slowing the response to compelling mental experiences applies equally to delusional thoughts and auditory hallucinations. Rapidly deployed safety behaviors may become ingrained in patients' repertoire of responses to psychotic experiences and so there is little opportunity to learn that the 'solution' is ineffective (Freeman, Garety, & Kuipers, 2001). Shaping up a slower response to the psychotic experience creates the opportunity to appraise that experience differently and try out alternative response patterns (van der Gaag, 2006). This slowing down of responding and decreasing the use of the same unhelpful interpretations of events has some similarity to the state targeted in ACTp and mindfulness interventions for psychosis (Abba et al., 2008; Chadwick et al., 2005). There are also parallels with the ACT change process of 'being present' as opposed to letting verbal descriptions of events obscure the actual contingencies in operation. However, the difference in CBTp is that there is greater emphasis on exploring new appraisals of experience rather than learning to observe the experiences in a nonjudgmental, mindful manner.

As a final comment on the change processes in CBTp and ACTp, there appears to be a parallel between the concept of psychological flexibility in

ACT and the narrower notion of cognitive flexibility in CBTp (Garety et al., 1997). In ACT, the six core processes noted above are targeted with the goal of increasing 'the ability to contact the present moment more fully as a conscious human being, and to change or persist in behavior when doing so serves valued ends' (Hayes et al., 2006, p. 7). This is a broader concept than that used in CBTp where cognitive flexibility is closely linked to 'reaction to hypothetical contradiction' (RTHC; Brett-Jones, Garety, & Hemsley, 1987). RTHC is used as an index of how readily a person would modify their delusion in the face of contradictory evidence. This is cognitive flexibility in the sense of willingness to entertain alternative views of the world and sensitivity to the implications of new information that bears on a particular belief. RTHC has proven to be a pretreatment predictor of response to CBTp (Garety et al., 1997) and may be a critical change process in CBTp (Lecomte & Lecomte, 2002).

Comparison of Therapy Process and Structure: CBTp and ACTp
Both ACTp and CBTp take a 'workability' approach to the treatment of psychosis. The overriding aim is to improve functioning and reduce unnecessary distress, rather than eliminate the experience of delusions and hallucinations (Nelson, 2005; Tarrier et al., 1993). However ACTp can be distinguished by its strong primary emphasis on two key issues: building acceptance of unavoidable private events and the clarification and day-to-day application of values (Bach & Hayes, 2002; Bach et al., 2006; Gaudiano & Herbert, 2006a). This conception of goal setting is much broader than the concept as it is applied in CBTp where the emphasis is often on identifying a circumscribed 'goal' belief that may replace unhelpful delusion (Nelson, 2005).

The published ACTp trials differ substantially from CBTp in the structure of the treatment package. Examination of both ACTp trials suggests the following elements characterize the current package: (1) psychoeducation regarding psychosis; (2) inculcation into the ACT model; (3) introduction of mindfulness and acceptance as an alternative to struggling with symptoms; (4) identification of values, goals and barriers; (5) normalization of psychosis; and (6) homework and other in vivo practice (Bach & Hayes, 2002; Gaudiano & Herbert, 2006a). But most strikingly, the 'dosage' is delivered over 3–5 sessions of about 50 minutes contact. This is discrepant with the UK National Institute for Clinical Excellence (NICE; 2003) guidelines for CBTp ,which recommend a minimum of 10 sessions spaced over 6 months. One reason for the longer CBTp protocols is the perceived need to establish a strong therapeutic alliance before challenging delusions or hallucinations (Nelson, 2005; Turkington, Kingdon, & Weiden, 2006). But, an abbreviated protocol appears feasible in ACTp because there is no explicit belief disputation and the emphasis on delivery in inpatient settings allows little time for establishing a therapeutic relationship (Gaudiano & Herbert, 2006a).

Conclusions and Future Directions

There is preliminary evidence that ACT and other mindfulness-based interventions are viable treatments for people experiencing psychotic symptoms, particularly auditory hallucinations. The exciting prospect is that these benefits may be achieved following relatively brief treatment protocols of three to five sessions. However, there is a need for development in a number of domains. A direct comparison of ACTp and CBTp under randomized conditions will help to tease out the role that acceptance versus disputation processes play in determining change in psychosis. There is also a need to clarify whether differential effects are seen for different symptoms. The existing ACTp interventions appear to have influenced responses to voices but have had less impact on delusions. The phenomenological differences of each experience may be of importance and it remains for future studies to determine whether acceptance strategies may be particularly efficacious for the treatment of voice hearing while, in contrast, the treatment of delusions may require longer therapy contact and greater use of disputation methods. Additionally, ACTp appears to show promise as a treatment for negative symptoms via its impact on engagement in values-consistent behaviors. But, the only data available to date (Gaudiano & Herbert, 2006a) did not show any effect of ACT on anergia as measured with the Brief Psychiatric Rating Scale (BPRS). Given that negative symptoms are among the most disabling symptoms of schizophrenia, there may be substantial benefit to be gained from developing a treatment package that addresses these problems explicitly.

Some basic conceptual points may also benefit from focused experimental research and refinement of terms and definitions. In particular, the notions of contact with the present moment and self-as-context require attention. The justification for this is that one of the disturbances of neurocognition in people with schizophrenia is that there is a failure of 'stored regularities' to guide current processing (Gray, Feldon, Rawlins, Hemsley, & Smith, 1991; Hemsley, 2005). This is a disturbance of context processing in that past learning does not adequately regulate ongoing moment-to-moment processing. This is evident in basic behavioral paradigms, such as the latent inhibition task and the Kamin blocking paradigm, where psychotic subjects are shown to be *more* sensitive to changes in reinforcement contingencies because their learning is less influenced by prior trials (Gray, 1998). In essence, psychotic subjects fail to learn what stimuli are redundant and can be ignored. Therefore, they are able to detect changes in contingencies more quickly than healthy control subjects because they have not learned to ignore aspects of the stimulus field. Hence, this type of greater contact with the present moment does not appear to lead to adaptive functioning in people with schizophrenia. Specification of an ACT/RFT account of how delusions and hallucinations emerge and are maintained should help to address this anomaly.

Further refinement of the theoretical understanding of psychotic symptoms from an ACT perspective should also improve the ability of therapists to apply the techniques in a flexible but coherent and theoretically justifiable manner. This also points to the need to conduct studies to determine the trainability of the ACTp techniques and case conceptualization skills. Finally, there is an ongoing need for the development of specialized instrumentation to measure the key processes of interest so that the mechanisms of change can be elucidated. The development of the VAAS (Shawyer et al., 2007) represents a good example of how the ACT approach is stimulating innovation and theoretical refinements in psychosis research. Hopefully, the relatively rapid application of ACT to psychosis bodes well for a continued refinement of interventions that decrease suffering and improve meaningful functioning in people with psychosis.

References

Abba, N., Chadwick, P., & Stevenson, C. (2008). Responding mindfully to distressing psychosis: A grounded theory analysis. *Psychotherapy Research, 18*(1), 77–87.

Bach, P., & Hayes, S. C. (2002). The use of acceptance and commitment therapy to prevent the rehospitalization of psychotic patients: a randomized controlled trial. *Journal of Consulting and Clinical Psychology, 70*(5), 1129–1139.

Bach, P. A., Gaudiano, B. A., Pankey, J., Herbert, J. D., & Hayes, S. C. (2006). Acceptance, mindfulness, values, and psychosis: applying acceptance and commitment therapy (ACT) to the chronically mentally ill. In R. A. Baer (Ed.), *Mindfulness-based treatment approaches. Clinician's guide to evidence base and applications* (pp. 93–116). San Diego: Elsevier.

Beck, A. T., & Rector, N. A. (2003). A cognitive model of hallucinations. *Cognitive Therapy and Research, 27*(1), 19–52.

Bellack, A. S. (1986). Schizophrenia: Behavior therapy's forgotten child. *Behavior Therapy, 17*, 199–214.

Bentall, R. P., Corcoran, R., Howard, R., Blackwood, N., & Kinderman, P. (2001). Persecutory delusions: a review and theoretical integration. *Clinical Psychology Review, 21*, 1143–1192.

Birchwood, M., & Chadwick, P. (1997). The omnipotence of voices: testing the validity of a cognitive model. *Psychological Medicine, 27*, 1345–1353.

Birchwood, M., Iqbal, Z., Chadwick, P., & Trower, P. (2000). Cognitive approaches to depression and suicidal thinking in psychosis. I. Ontongeny of post-psychotic depression. *British Journal of Psychiatry, 177*, 516–521.

Birchwood, M., & Trower, P. (2006). The future of cognitive–behavioural therapy for psychosis: not a quasi-neuroleptic. *British Journal of Psychiatry, 188*, 107–108.

Blackledge, J. T. (2003). An introduction to relational frame theory: Basics and applications. *The Behavior Analyst Today, 3*(4), 421–433.

Brett-Jones, J., Garety, P. A., & Hemsley, D. R. (1987). Measuring delusional experiences: A method and its application. *British Journal of Clinical Psychology, 26,* 257–265.

Broome, M. R., Woolley, J. B., Tabraham, P., Johns, L. C., Bramon, E., Murray, G. K., et al. (2005). What causes the onset of psychosis? *Schizophrenia Research, 79,* 23–34.

Carr, V. J., Lewin, T. J., Neil, A. L., Halpin, S. A., & Holmes, S. (2004). Premorbid, psychosocial and clinical predictors of the costs of schizophrenia and other psychoses. *British Journal of Psychiatry, 184,* 517–525.

Chadwick, P., Lees, S., & Birchwood, M. (2000). The revised Beliefs About Voices Questionnaire (BAVQ-R). *British Journal of Psychiatry, 177,* 229–232.

Chadwick, P., Newman Taylor, K., & Abba, N. (2005). Mindfulness groups for people with psychosis. *Behavioural and Cognitive Psychotherapy, 33,* 1–9.

Fowler, D., Freeman, D., Smith, B., Kuipers, E., Bebbington, P., Bashforth, H., et al. (2006). The Brief Core Schema Scales (BCSS): psychometric properties and associations with paranoia and grandiosity in non-clinical and psychosis samples. *Psychological Medicine, 36,* 749–759.

Fowler, D., Garety, P., & Kuipers, E. (1995). *Cognitive behaviour therapy for psychosis.* Chichester, UK: John Wiley and Sons.

Freeman, D., & Garety, P. A. (2003). Connecting neurosis and psychosis: the direct influence of emotion on delusions and halluncinations. *Behaviour Research and Therapy, 41,* 923–947.

Freeman, D., Garety, P. A., & Kuipers, E. (2001). Persecutory delusions: developing the understanding of belief maintenance and emotional distress. *Psychological Medicine, 31,* 1293–1306.

Freeman, D., Garety, P. A., Kuipers, E., Colberta, S., Jolley, S., Fowler, D., et al. (2006). Delusions and decision-making style: Use of the Need for Closure Scale. *Behaviour Research and Therapy, 44,* 1147–1158.

Frith, C. D. (2004). Schizophrenia and theory of mind. *Psychological Medicine, 34,* 385–389.

Garety, P. A. (1991). Reasoning and delusions. *British Journal of Psychiatry, 159* (Suppl. 14), 14–18.

Garety, P. A., Bebbington, P., Fowler, D., Freeman, D., & Kuipers, E. (2007). Implications for neurobiological research of cognitive models of psychosis: a theoretical paper. *Psychological Medicine, 37*(10), 1377–1391.

Garety, P. A., Fowler, D., Kuipers, E., Freeman, D., Dunn, G., Bebbington, P., et al. (1997). London-East Anglia randomised controlled trial of cognitive behavioural therapy for psychosis. II. Predictors of outcome. *British Journal of Psychiatry, 171,* 420–426.

Gaudiano, B. A., & Herbert, J. D. (2006a). Acute treatment of inpatients with psychotic symptoms using Acceptance and Commitment Therapy: Pilot results. *Behaviour Research and Therapy, 44,* 415–437.

Gaudiano, B. A., & Herbert, J. D. (2006b). Believability of hallucinations as a potential mediator of their frequency and associated distress in psychotic inpatients. *Behavioural and Cognitive Psychotherapy, 34,* 497–502.

Gilleen, J., & David, A. S. (2005). The cognitive neuropsychiatry of delusions: From psychopathology to neuropsychology and back again. *Psychological Medicine, 35,* 5–12.

Gray, J. (1998). Integrating schizophrenia. *Schizophrenia Bulletin, 24*(2), 249–266.

Gray, J. A., Feldon, J., Rawlins, J. N. P., Hemsley, D. R., & Smith, A. D. (1991). The neuropsychology of schizophrenia. *Behavioral and Brain Sciences, 14*, 1–84.

Haddock, G., Slade, P. D., Bentall, R. P., Reid, D., & Faragher, E. B. (1998). A comparison of the long-term effectiveness of distraction and focusing in the treatment of auditory hallucinations. *British Journal of Medical Psychology, 71*, 339–349.

Hayes, S. C., Luoma, J. B., Bond, F. W., Masuda, A., & Lillis, J. (2006). Acceptance and commitment therapy: Model, processes and outcomes. *Behavior Research and Therapy, 44*, 1–25.

Hayes, S. C., Strosahl, K. D., & Wilson, K. G. (1999). *Acceptance and commitment therapy. An experiential approach to behavior change*. New York: Guilford Press.

Hayes, S. C., Wilson, K. G., Gifford, E. V., Follette, V. M., & Strosahl, K. (1996). Experiential avoidance and behavioral disorders: A functional dimensional approach to diagnosis and treatment. *Journal of Consulting and Clinical Psychology, 64*(6), 1152–1168.

Hemsley, D. R. (2005). The development of a cognitive model of schizophrenia: Placing it in context. *Neuroscience and Biobehavioral Reviews, 29*, 977–988.

Hunter, M. D., Griffiths, T. D., Farrow, T. F. D., Zheng, Y., Wilkinson, I. D., Hegde, N., et al. (2003). A neural basis for the perception of voices in external auditory space. *Brain, 126*, 161–169.

Jones, S. R., & Fernyhough, C. (2007). Neural correlates of inner speech and auditory verbal hallucinations: A critical review and theoretical integration. *Clinical Psychology Review, 27*, 140–154.

Kapur, S. (2003). Psychosis as a state of aberrant salience: a framework for linking biology, phenomenology, and pharmacology in schizophrenia. *American Journal of Psychiatry, 160*, 13–23.

Kinderman, P., Kaney, S., Morley, S., & Bentall, R. P. (1992). Paranoia and the defensive attributional style: deluded and depressed patients' attributions about their own attributions. *British Journal of Medical Psychology, 65*, 371–383.

Lecomte, T., & Lecomte, C. (2002). Toward uncovering robust principles of change inherent to cognitive-behavioral therapy for psychosis. *American Journal of Orthopsychiatry, 72*(1), 50–57.

Lowe, C. F., & Chadwick, P. D. J. (1990). Verbal control of delusions. *Behavior Therapy, 21*, 461–479.

Maher, B. A. (1992). Delusions: Contemporary etiological hypotheses. *Psychiatric Annals, 22*, 260–268.

National Institute for Clinical Excellence. (2003). *Schizophrenia: Core interventions in the treatment and management of schizophrenia in primary and secondary care*. London: Gaskell and the British Psychological Society.

Nelson, H. E. (2005). *Cognitive–behavioural therapy with delusions and hallucinations: A practice manual* (2nd ed.). Cheltenham, England: Nelson Thornes.

Ost, L.-G. (2008). Efficacy of the third wave of behavioral therapies: A systematic review and meta-analysis. *Behaviour Research and Therapy, 46*(3), 296–321.

Pankey, J., & Hayes, S. C. (2003). Acceptance and commitment therapy for psychosis. *International Journal of Psychology and Psychological Therapy, 3*(2), 311–328.

Shawyer, F., Ratcliff, K., Mackinnon, A., Farhall, J., Hayes, S. C., & Copolov, D. (2007). The Voices Acceptance and Action Scale (VAAS): Pilot data. *Journal of Clinical Psychology, 63*(6), 593–606.

Smith, B., Fowler, D. G., Freeman, D., Bebbington, P., Bashforth, H., Garety, P., et al. (2006). Emotion and psychosis: Links between depression, self-esteem, negative schematic beliefs and delusions and hallucinations. *Schizophrenia Research, 86*(1–3), 181–188.

Startup, M., Jackson, M., & Pearce, E. (2002). Assessing therapist adherence to cognitive–behaviour therapy for psychosis. *Behavioural and Cognitive Psychotherapy, 30*, 329–339.

Tarrier, N., Beckett, R., Harwood, S., Baker, A., Yusupoff, L., & Ugarteburu, I. (1993). A trial of two cognitive–behavioural methods of treating drug-resistant residual psychotic symptoms in schizophrenic patients: I. Outcome. *British Journal of Psychiatry, 162*, 524–532.

Tarrier, N., & Wykes, T. (2004). Is there evidence that cognitive–behaviour therapy is an effective treatment for schizophrenia? A cautious or cautionary tale? *Behaviour Research and Therapy, 42*, 1377–1401.

Turkington, D., Kingdon, D., & Weiden, P. J. (2006). Cognitive behavior therapy for schizophrenia. *American Journal of Psychiatry, 163*, 365–373.

van der Gaag, M. (2006). A neuropsychiatric model of biological and psychological processes in the remission of delusions and auditory hallucinations. *Schizophrenia Bulletin, 32*(s1), s113–s122.

Wykes, T., Steel, C., Everitt, B., & Tarrier, N. (2008). Cognitive–behavior therapy for schizophrenia: Effect sizes, clinical models, and methodological rigor. *Schizophrenia Bulletin, 34*(3), 523–537.

Zigler, E., & Glick, M. (1988). Is paranoid schizophrenia really camouflaged depression? *American Psychologist, 43*, 284–290.

chapter twelve

Beyond the Fragmented Self: Integrating Acceptance and Psychodynamic Approaches in the Treatment of Borderline Personality

Ann Bailey, Dianne Mooney-Reh, Lisa Parker and Sonja Temelkovski

Borderline Personality Disorder (BPD) is a complex and serious mental disorder. It affects approximately 2% of the general population, about 10% of psychiatric outpatients and about 20% of psychiatric inpatients (American Psychiatric Association, 2000). Individuals with the disorder can experience life as tumultuous, and extreme, in terms of both their internal and external world. The inner and outer turmoil experienced by individuals with BPD is a great source of suffering, not only for them but also for those around them. Practitioners often view the borderline condition as frustrating and difficult to treat. In recent years, however, several models of treatment for BPD have demonstrated some effectiveness in ameliorating psychological functioning for individuals diagnosed with the condition, such as Linehan's (1993a,b) Dialectical Behavior Therapy (DBT), Bateman and Fonagy's Mentalization-Based Treatment (MBT; 2004), and Clarkin, Yeomans and Kernberg's (2006) Transference-Focused Psychotherapy (TFP).

Fundamental to Linehan's DBT is mindfulness. Mindfulness and acceptance-based approaches have permeated and expanded the cognitive–behavioral therapy tradition in the last decade. At the forefront of this permeation is acceptance and commitment therapy (ACT) as proposed by Hayes, Strosahl and Wilson (1999). Both DBT and ACT emphasize mindfulness in the treatment of psychopathology. While DBT is a population-specific treatment modality, ACT has been used across a number of Axis I conditions in the DSM-IV-TR (American Psychiatric Association, 2000), such as psychosis (Bach & Hayes, 2002), anxiety and stress (Bond & Bunce, 2000; Zettle, 2003), and depression (Zettle & Hayes, 1986; Zettle & Raines, 1989). More recently, acceptance-based strategies have been effective in reducing deliberate self-harm behaviors in a group of women diagnosed with BPD (Gratz & Gunderson, 2006). To our knowledge, however, ACT has not been used in the treatment of borderline personality per se.

The current chapter outlines a treatment model that integrates DBT and psychodynamic theory with the principles of ACT. The proposed model is the culmination of several years experience working with borderline patients within a public mental health setting. It evolved from a purist DBT model to that which now features self-discovery, cognitive defusion and valuing as key therapeutic strategies for change. Despite significant outcomes being obtained for our clients following a DBT intervention, particularly on measures of depression, anxiety, dissociation, alexithymia, global functioning and psychiatric hospital admissions (Mooney-Reh, in preparation), we were concerned about client dropout, as well as maintenance of treatment outcomes. Clinically, we were finding that a number of clients were not responding to DBT and/or were dropping out of therapy prematurely. Longitudinally, we were also observing that some clients were re-presenting for treatment or acute care at varying periods subsequent to DBT, usually after a substantial period of maintaining treatment outcomes (e.g., 12 months).

On review of these outcomes, we decided to reformulate our treatment approach. Our goals were, first, to enhance therapeutic engagement, minimize dropout, and maximize and maintain treatment outcomes. Essentially, we wanted to infuse hope in a client group commonly viewed by self and others as hopeless and thus retain them in therapy. Second, DBT, while effective in treating the symptomatic manifestations of BPD, was not specifically addressing what we believed to be the core psychopathology — identity diffusion. We wanted to use psychodynamic theory to elaborate this important component. Third, being philosophically aligned to the principles of ACT meant that we, as practitioners, could enhance our authenticity in treatment. With these considerations in mind, we set about conceptualizing BPD from an ACT/DBT/psychodynamic perspective. We then combined the core processes of each approach, developing a graded exposure model (GEM-ACT) treatment for BPD.

The current chapter aims to describe this integrated approach to understanding and treating individuals with BPD. To accomplish this goal, we will consider BPD from both categorical (i.e., DSM-IV-TR) and dimensional (psychodynamic) approaches to diagnosis, and then describe how it can be reconceptualized within an ACT framework. This will facilitate the identification of core processes underpinning the BPD behavior pattern and enable a conceptual foundation for discussing an ACT intervention. The current chapter also aims to provide an overview of the clinical application of GEM-ACT, drawn from our experience in working with clients diagnosed with BPD.

BPD Description and Criteria

Diagnostic and Statistical Manual of Mental Disorders (4th ed.) —
Text Revision (DSM-IV-TR; American Psychiatric Association, 2000)

The DSM-IV-TR defines BPD as a disabling Axis II personality disorder characterized by a 'pervasive pattern of instability in interpersonal relationships, self-image, affect, and marked impulsivity beginning by early adulthood and present in a variety of contexts' (2000, p. 706). BPD is indicated by the presence of five or more of the following nine symptoms:

- frantic efforts to avoid real or imagined abandonment
- a pattern of unstable and intense relationships
- an identity disturbance characterized by markedly and persistent unstable self-image or sense of self
- impulsive behaviors that are potentially self-damaging (e.g., gambling, spending money irresponsibly, binge eating, abusing substances, engaging in unsafe sex or driving recklessly, shoplifting)
- recurrent suicidal or parasuicidal behavior, gestures or threats
- affective instability due to marked reactivity of mood
- chronic feelings of emptiness
- inappropriate and intense anger (e.g., frequent displays of temper, extreme sarcasm, enduring bitterness, verbal outbursts, recurring physical fights)
- transient, stress-related paranoid ideation or severe dissociative symptoms (e.g., depersonalisation).

The DSM-IV-TR identifies a number of associated features of BPD, including a pattern of sabotaging opportunities for achieving goals just prior to that goal being realized, destroying potentially good relationships, an intolerance to being alone, chronic feelings of boredom, and social inhibition and fear. These symptoms make it difficult for the individual to function in family/social, school and workplace contexts.

BPD, like other personality disorders, is most commonly diagnosed using the DSM-IV-TR categorical approach (i.e., present vs. absent). However, there is no agreement that a categorical approach to diagnosis is the most appropriate. Bateman and Fonagy (2004) argue that a dimensional (i.e., psychodynamic) approach to BPD diagnosis removes some of the heterogeneity that arises from categorical approaches, and limits the loss of the more subtle features of symptom patterns.

Psychodynamic Diagnostic Manual (PDM; PDM Task Force, 2006)
Distinct from the symptom- and behavior-based BPD diagnosis identified by the DSM-IV-TR, is the conceptually and clinically-based construct of borderline personality organisation (BPO) described by the PDM.

The PDM uses a multidimensional approach to the diagnosis of mental disorders. It begins with a classification of the spectrum of personality patterns and disorders (Dimension I/Axis P), followed by a more detailed profile of mental functioning (Dimension II/Axis M), and ending with an assessment of symptom patterns (Dimension III/Axis S). The PDM is based on the fundamental premise that one can only understand personality and its pathology by examining observable behavior with reference to subjective experience and the underlying psychological structures. Unlike the DSM-IV-TR, which assigns people to a diagnostic category based on overtly observable clusters of symptoms and attributes, the PDM aims to ascribe meanings to the individual's observed and described phenomena (i.e., symptoms, behaviors, traits, affects, attitudes, thoughts and fantasies).

According to the PDM, BPO represents a level of personality functioning located on a continuum from healthy (absence of personality disorder), to neurotic, to severely borderline (toward the psychotic end of the borderline spectrum). The term 'borderline' therefore denotes a level of severity of personality structure, rather than a discrete, mutually exclusive type of borderline organisation or personality as described by the DSM-IV-TR.

Individuals with BPO are characterized by diffuse identity, the use of primitive or immature defenses (predominately splitting and projective identification), generally intact yet fragile reality testing, impairments in affect regulation, inconsistent internalized values and recurrent relational difficulties (Clarkin et al., 2006). Psychodynamic opinion holds that identity diffusion, or lack of an integrated concept of self and others, is central to BPO pathology. Clinically, identity diffusion is evident in individuals' non-reflective, contradictory, or chaotic descriptions of self and others, and the inability to integrate or be aware of these contradictions.

Behavioral correlates of the BPO pathology include interpersonal chaos; emotional lability; anger; impulsive self-destructive behaviors such as gambling, binge eating, self-mutilation, sexual risk-taking and substance abuse; and a propensity to lapses in reality testing (i.e., the types of symptoms described in the DSM-IV-TR). Based on clinical experience and observation, we believe that these behavioral symptoms are manifestations of an underlying lack of self or diffuse identity, and that for treatment to be effective in the long term it must target this core pathology.

Contrasting Approaches to Treatment

A meta-analysis by Leichsenring and Leibing (2003) indicates that both psychodynamic and cognitive–behavioral approaches are effective in the treatment of personality disorders. Although it is not our intention to present a scholarly review of the many treatments developed for BPD, it is useful to briefly review the three manualized approaches to treatment that have influenced and informed the development of the GEM-ACT model of treatment for BPD that will be presented later in this chapter. Dialectical behavior therapy (DBT; Linehan, 1993a,b), mentalization-based treatment (Bateman & Fonagy, 2004), and transference-focused psychotherapy (TFP; Clarkin et al., 2006) are each gathering support and prominence in the literature, and represent either a cognitive–behavioral or psychodynamic approach to the treatment of borderline pathology.

Dialectical Behavior Therapy (DBT)

Linehan's (1993a, b) dialectical behavior therapy (DBT) was originally developed for the treatment of chronically suicidal and parasuicidal females, and represents an adaptation of cognitive–behavioral therapy. It is currently receiving considerable attention for its application with individuals meeting DSM-IV-TR criteria for BPD. DBT is grounded in the biosocial theory of BPD, which asserts that the core pathology in BPD is emotion dysregulation. The theory posits that dysregulation of the emotional system results from a transaction between a biological tendency to emotional vulnerability and an invalidating rearing environment. Essentially, the borderline individual's intense emotional reactions in early childhood elicit invalidating behaviors in caregivers, which leads to further emotional dysregulation and further invalidation. This cycle leaves the individual with inadequate skills for coping with the normal stresses and challenges of life, and maladaptive patterns of responding to intense affect (e.g., self-injury, suicide attempts, binge eating).

There are four primary modes of treatment in DBT: individual therapy, group skills training, telephone contact and therapist consultation. Skills training is carried out in a group context, with a focus on four groups of skills: core mindfulness, interpersonal effectiveness, emotion regulation and distress tolerance skills. Between sessions, individuals are offered phone contact with their therapist. Clear limits on such contact is defined. The core mindfulness skills enable the individual to become more clearly aware of the content of experience in the present moment. The focus of the interpersonal effective-ness skills is on maintaining relationships and self-respect via assertiveness and problem solving. Emotion regulation skills include strategies for changing distressing emotional states, and distress tolerance skill includes strategies for coping with difficult emotional states if these cannot be easily changed (Linehan, 1993a,b).

Studies have reported the efficacy of DBT in reducing self-destructive and suicidal behavior (Linehan, Armstrong, Suarez, Allmon, & Heard, 1991; Verheul et al., 2003). Specifically, when DBT was compared with community-based treatment as usual (TAU), participants who were assigned to the DBT condition were found to have significant reductions in the frequency and medical risk of parasuicidal behavior, less days of inpatient psychiatric hospitalization, and a substantially lower 12-month attrition rate. Throughout a naturalistic follow-up year, DBT subjects were found to have significantly higher Global Assessment Scale scores; significantly less parasuicidal behavior, less anger and better self-reported social adjustment during the initial 6 months; and significantly fewer psychiatric inpatient, better interviewer-rated social adjustment during the final 6 months, compared to TAU subjects (Linehan, Heard, & Armstrong, 1993).

Across studies, however, DBT has not been effective in reducing depression and hopelessness (Linehan et al., 1991; Scheel, 2000), or in improving survival and coping beliefs or overall life satisfaction (Scheel, 2000). Verheul et al. (2003) report that, while DBT was effective in reducing self-harm in chronically parasuicidal individuals, its impact on individuals in the low-severity group was similar to that for TAU. These authors suggest that DBT should be the treatment of choice for individuals with BPD who are chronically parasuicidal in the first instance, followed by another treatment that focuses on other features of BPD once the high-risk, impulsive behaviors have reduced. Clinically, Verheul and colleagues (2003) state that there is a lack of evidence to support the efficacy of DBT for other core features of BPD, such as interpersonal instability, chronic feelings of emptiness and boredom, and identity disturbance.

Mentalization-Based Treatment

Bateman and Fonagy's (2004) mentalization-based treatment is a psycho-dynamic therapy grounded in attachment theory and developmental psychopathology. Fonagy and Bateman posit that borderline pathology has its source in the failure of mentalization (2004, 2007). Mentalization refers to the capacity to understand behavior in terms of the associated mental states in self and others. According to the mentalization theory of BPD, individuals who are constitutionally vulnerable and/or exposed to neglect in early relationships develop an enfeebled or fragile capacity to represent affect, and effortfully control attention (Fonagy & Bateman, 2007). Fonagy and Bateman (2007) argue that dysfunctional attachment relationships are not only the consequence of the difficulty in holding a stable and consistent representation of self and other in mind, but also the cause of distortions in self-organization (2007). Fonagy and Bateman (2007) suggest that 'enhancement of mentalization and the reduction of the predominance of non-mentalizing modes of experiencing internal reality represent the path to a cure [for BPD]' (p. 414).

The key features of MBT as summarized by Fonagy and Bateman (2007) are:

- The therapist focuses exclusively on the patient's current mental state (their thoughts, feelings, wishes and desires) with the aim of building up representations of internal states.

- The therapist avoids situations in which the patient talks of mental states that he or she cannot link to subjectively felt reality.

- Therapy acts to create a transitional area of relatedness in which thoughts and emotions can be 'played with'.

- Inevitable enactments over the course of treatment are not interpreted or understood in terms of their unconscious meaning but in terms of the situation and affects immediately occurring before the enactment.

MBT deviates from traditional psychodynamic techniques on several counts: it de-emphasizes unconscious concerns in favor of conscious or near conscious content; focuses less on the past as it is represented in the present; aims to recover mentalization rather than improve insight; avoids describing complex mental states and discourages interpretation (Fonagy & Bateman, 2007).

MBT's main aims are to foster the development of stable internal representations, aid the formation of a coherent sense of self and to enable the borderline patient to form more secure relationships in which the motivations of the self and other are better understood. Change occurs through techniques such as the therapist maintaining a mentalizing stance, retaining mental closeness via empathic response, focusing on current mental states and how these are influenced by events in the past; avoiding the use of metaphor; and paying careful attention to the transference and countertransference.

Bateman and Fonagy (1999) compared a psychoanalytically-oriented partial hospitalization program (MBT) with general psychiatric care (control group) for patients with BPD. Treatment was of 18 months duration and consisted of both individual and group psychoanalytic psychotherapy. Outcome measures included frequency of attempted suicide and acts of self-harm, number and duration of inpatient admissions, use of psychotropic medications, and self-report measures of depression, anxiety, general symptom distress, interpersonal function and social adjustment. Patients assigned to the partial hospitalization program showed significant reductions on all measures compared to the control group, which showed no change or had deteriorated over the same period. Further, improvement in patients in the partial hospitalization program began after 6 months of treatment, and continued until the program ended at 18 months. Bateman and Fonagy (2001) investigated patients' progress posttreatment and found that those in the partial hospitalization group not only maintained treatment gains at 18 months but also showed statistically significant improvement on most measures compared to the control group, who showed limited change in functioning during the same period. These results suggest a rehabilitative effect of the psychoanalytically-oriented treatment (Bateman & Fonagy, 2001). Bateman and Fonagy (2003) also found that the psychoanalytically-oriented treatment program provided considerable cost savings during the 18-month follow-up period with patients requiring less inpatient care and emergency room treatment compared to those in the control group. Although limited, research to date provides some evidence for the effectiveness of MBT.

Transference-Focused Psychotherapy (TFP)

Transference-focused psychotherapy (TFP) is a unique psychodynamic approach to the treatment of borderline personality with a coherent theoretical frame of reference and a manualized set of procedures (Clarkin et al., 2006). It is based on contemporary psychoanalytic object relations theory as developed by Kernberg (1984, 1992).

Object relations theory (Jacobson, 1964, Kernberg, 1980; Klein, 1957; Mahler, 1971) emphasizes that the basic drives described by Freud — libido and aggression — are always experienced in relation to a specific other: an object. Internal object relations are the basic building blocks of psychological structure and serve as the organizers of motivation and behavior. The basic building blocks of psychic structure are representatives of the self, an affect related to or representing a drive, and a representation of the other (the object of the drive). These units of self, other, and the affect linking them are object relations dyads. The 'self' and the 'object' in the dyad are not necessarily accurate, but rather are representations of the self and other as they were experienced at specific moments in time in the course of early development.

Object relations theory posits that in the course of the infant's development, multiple affectively charged experiences are internalized in such a way that a segment of the psyche is built up with idealized images based on satisfying experiences on one side, and another segment is built up with negative, aversive, devalued images based on unsatisfying experiences on the other. An active separation of these segments develops within the psyche. In the normally developing child, there is a gradual integration of these extreme good and bad representations of self and other during the first few years of life. Such integration occurs in the context of a secure attachment to the primary caregiver, and results in internal representations of the self and others that are more complex and realistic. In children who go on to develop borderline pathology, this process of integration does not evolve. It is suggested that this lack of integration is the result of distorted interactions between infant and caregiver caused by abnormal attachment.

The lack of integration of the internal object relations dyads corresponds to a split psychological structure, in which totally negative representations are split off/segregated from idealized positive representations of self and other. Individuals with BPD have difficulty integrating disparate representations of themselves and others, partly because negative emotions (i.e., aggression), disrupt their capacity to integrate these partial representations. Strong unprocessed emotions have the capacity to overwhelm positive representations. The individual may then become motivated to keep these representations separate or split in an effort to protect the positive representations of themselves and others. This inability to process emotional experience may result in global, undifferentiated affective states that do not direct the individual to effective behavioral or coping responses and, instead, elicit a range of emotional control strategies, including impulsive or self-destructive actions.

According to objects relations theory, the core pathology in BPD is the lack of differentiation and integration of internal images of self and others (i.e., identity diffusion). This lack of differentiation and integration leads to affective instability; the use of primitive defenses such as splitting (the tendency to see self and others in moralized, all-good and all-bad categories, or in an oscillating fashion between good and bad) and projective identification (the tendency to experience one's own negative affect/undesirable qualities as belonging to the other); rapidly shifting roles; deficits in social reality testing and a sense of inner emptiness.

TFP aims to integrate unintegrated conceptions of self and others via clarification, confrontation and transference interpretation and, in doing so, reduce symptoms (e.g., affect dysregulation, depression, anxiety, interpersonal difficulties), and increase the individual's capacity for self-reflection and acceptance (Clarkin et al., 2006). The treatment model comprises four therapeutic strategies:

1. Definition of the dominant object relations, which involves experiencing and tolerating confusion of the borderline individual's inner world as it is played out in the transference, identifying the dominant object relations, naming the actors and attending to the borderline individual's reaction.

2. Observation and interpretation of the borderline individual's role reversals.

3. Observing and interpreting linkages between the object relations dyads that defend against each other, and maintain internal conflict and fragmentation.

4. Working through the borderline individual's other significant relationships in light of this change.

Essentially, TFP fosters change by reactivating primitive object relations within a safe and controlled environment (the therapeutic relationship) allowing the borderline individual to act out, and reflect on, their internal representations of past experiences in the here and now.

TFP focuses on both external behavior and inner reality, and emphasizes the importance of the therapist's monitoring of his or her own counter-transference as information about the borderline individual's object relations. Duration of treatment is variable depending on the individual's level of borderline personality organisation (BPO; i.e., high or low — low-level BPO individuals being those who are actively suicidal, self-destructive, and whose psychological structure is infiltrated with aggression).

Evidence for the efficacy of TFP to date is limited, but promising. Borderline individuals who had received a 1-year outpatient TFP program were less suicidal, engaged in lower risk parasuicidal behaviors, had less hospitalizations, and less days in hospital when compared to their pretreatment status (Clarkin et al., 2001). In addition, Clarkin and his colleagues (2001) found that there were no patient suicides, no deterioration in functioning and no adverse effects of TFP among those who had completed treatment. In a randomized clinical trial comparing outpatient treatments for BPD, TFP was found to be as effective as DBT and psychodynamic supportive therapy in the domains of anxiety, depression and global functioning; and more effective than supportive therapy in the area of suicidal behavior (Clarkin, Levy, Lenzenweger, & Kernberg, 2004). In a more recent study, comparing 3 years of TFP with 3 years of schema-focused psychotherapy (SFP; Young, Klosko, & Weishaar, 2003), TFP was found to be effective in reducing BPD psychopathology and in improving quality of life, but less effective than SFT across all measures (Geisen-Bloo et al., 2006). The finding that SFP was more effective than TFP in treating borderline psychopathology, however, has been questioned — particularly in light of a lack of treatment equivalence (SFP allowed between-session telephone contact with therapists) and therapeutic and researcher allegiance (Grenyer, 2007a).

Summary

Both MBT and TFP posit an internal psychic structure as central to their treatment models for borderline personality. Linehan's DBT, on the other hand, focuses on the behavioral correlates of BPD. Clarkin and Levy (2006) argue that each of these approaches is appropriate as each attends to different aspects of the borderline pathology. Livesley (2005) suggests that evidence for both psychodynamic and cognitive–behavioral therapies outcomes point to the need for a practical, integrative, clinical approach to treating personality disorder in which the clinician matches problem areas unique to the individual patient (i.e., behaviors, symptoms, core issues in self-definition) to a combination of cognitive–behavioral and dynamic techniques. We support Livesley's view and propose a treatment model that not only combines cognitive–behavioral and psychodynamic techniques but embeds them within an ACT framework, thus adding a dimension to treatment for borderline pathology not currently present in existing models.

Table 12.1 compares and contrasts DBT, MBT, TFP and ACT. The components presented in bold italics represent those on which the GEM-ACT model of treatment for borderline personality has been based and developed.

Borderline Personality Disorder: An ACT Conceptualization

Hayes et al. (1999, p. 8) state that '*most* humans are hurting ... some more than others'. From an ACT perspective, human suffering is underscored by ordinary psychological processes and is not limited to syndromal categories (Hayes et al., 1999). Based on this fundamental premise, the six core ACT processes are considered functionally relevant to all conditions, regardless of diagnostic category or DSM-IV-TR axis. Essentially, acceptance, mindfulness, valuing, commitment, self-as-context and defusion are relevant to both personality and non-personality disordered clients. However, despite fundamental similarities, there are a number of differences between personality disordered and non-personality disordered populations that have important implications for treatment.

From an ACT perspective, then, it could be argued that borderline individuals differ from non-personality disordered individuals on two counts: (1) the nature of their experiential avoidance; and (2) the level of stability and constancy in their sense of 'self'. These will now be discussed in turn.

Experiential Avoidance in Borderline Personality Disorder

Experiential avoidance occurs when a person is unwilling to remain in contact with their private, internal experiences (e.g., thoughts, feelings,

TABLE 12.1
Comparison of Treatment Approaches

	DBT	TFP	MBT	ACT
Client population	Subgroup of borderline clients with suicidal behavior	Borderline personality organisation	Borderline personality disorder	DSM-IV Axis I disorders
Etiological theory	The biosocial theory of BPD; emotion dysregulation occurs in the context of an invalidating environment	Borderline personality organisation core construct; identity diffusion core pathology	BPD is the result of negative experiences with primary attachment figure	Relational frame theory
Modalities	Individual; social skills group; homework	Individual	Individual; group; psychoanalytic; expressive	Individual; group
Patient–therapist relationship	Dialectical relationship of acceptance and change	Therapeutic neutrality and exploration of relationship	Tactful exploration of relationship	Radical respect; mindful acceptance emphasizing the similarity of experience; undermining of therapist authority
Treatment goals	Reduction of symptoms	Identity integration; Reduction of symptoms	Reduction of symptoms	Willingness; Acceptance; Behavioral commitment to living a valued life
Core techniques	Mindfulness; validation; affect regulation; skills training	Clarification and confrontation, integration of split-off mental states by interpreting motivations for primitive defenses	Enhancing mentalization; bridging affect and meaning; interpretation	Acceptance of internal experience; identification of valued life goals; committed action
Mechanisms for change	Reduction of ineffective action tendencies linked with dysregulated emotions	Increased coherence and integration of conception of self and others	Enhanced mentalization	Development of the observer self; valuing

Note: (Adapted from Clarkin et al., 2006, p. 35)

memories or physical sensations), and subsequently take action to alter or change these experiences and the circumstances in which they arise (Hayes et al., 1999). These internal experiences are avoided via engagement in a range of behavioral responses. Borderline clients differ in their degree of experiential avoidance compared to Axis I populations in a number of ways:

Pervasive quality of avoidance. Eighty-seven per cent of clients diagnosed with BPD have suffered some type of childhood trauma, 40–71% have been sexually abused, and 25–71% have been physically abused (Perry & Herman, 1993). These figures correspond with rates of abuse found in a sample of clients who presented to our clinic for assessment and treatment of BPD (Mooney-Reh, in preparation). Beyond this, neglect, hostile conflict, early parental loss or separation, inconsistent treatment by a caretaker and witnessing sexual violence as a child are also common in the histories of people diagnosed with BPD (Perry & Herman, 1993). Such histories can create a learning environment that contributes to a more pervasive form of experiential avoidance (Gottman, Katz, & Hooven, 1996). When the internal experience is chronically invalidated, punished or trivialized, the person's own experience of their internal world can become confusing, threatening and, as a consequence, habitually avoided.

Reactivity in the affective response. Borderline individuals are often extremely sensitive and reactive to their internal experience; their early childhood histories having cemented a learned response of fear and confusion in relation to it. When an emotion, thought and/or physical sensation occurs, it is often experienced as intensely aversive, and sets in motion a series of reactive and avoidant responses.

Severity in the means of avoidance. The reactivity to, and rapid avoidance of, one's internal experience can manifest in the severity of means. Axis I clients may wash compulsively or count; borderline clients, on the other hand, will self-harm, or attempt suicide in order to avoid their internal world.

It can be argued that this learned pattern of pervasive, reactive and severe experiential avoidance results in an impoverished attribution of affect tolerance skills. Linehan (1993a,b) argues that the invalidating environment fails to teach the biologically vulnerable child to regulate their emotions, tolerate distress, or to trust their own emotional responses. Borderline individuals' skill deficits are evident in their inability to relate to, label and/or tolerate aversive internal experiences, and are less developed when compared to individuals meeting criteria for a DSM-IV-TR Axis I disorder. This is supported by findings that individuals diagnosed with BPD are significantly more alexithymic, have greater difficulty identifying and describing feelings, and have a lower capacity for reflective functioning when compared to individuals diagnosed with generalized anxiety disorder (GAD) (Mooney-Reh, in preparation).

Making the clinical distinction between BPD and DSM-IV-TR Axis I conditions highlights the need for grading an ACT intervention in the treatment of borderline individuals. Borderline individuals' inability to have and to hold their painful and aversive internal states, and their reactive and often impulsive attempts to avoid them, calls for a step-wise approach to treatment. Unlike individuals with an Axis I disorder who are clinically more robust, constitutionally more stable and therefore more apt to tolerate exposure to their internal states, borderline individuals require a much softer, more graded approach.

The Self: Identity Disturbance

One of the nine DSM-IV-TR criteria for BPD is identity disturbance, characterized by an unstable sense of self. As previously discussed, treatment approaches for borderline personality have declared identity disturbance or identity diffusion as the primary focus for treatment (Bateman & Fonagy, 2004; Clarkin et al., 2006). We support this view, and believe that ACT interventions can serve to facilitate the development of a more stable sense of self. The use of ACT interventions will be discussed later in this chapter. At this point, however, it is necessary to provide an overview of an ACT conceptualization of the self, followed by an ACT conceptualization of the borderline self.

The Self: An ACT Conceptualization

An ACT perspective conceptualizes the self as consisting of three states. These are referred to as: 'self-as-concept', 'self-as-process', and 'self-as-context'.

Self-as-Concept (I am a Person who is ...)

Self-as-concept, or the 'conceptualized self' is a position from which we define ourselves according to our temperament, values, tastes, habits, convictions, virtues, shortcomings and so forth. For example, 'I am a person who has black hair', 'I am a person who enjoys playing tennis'. A traditional cognitive–behavioral therapy (CBT) approach would focus on this particular aspect of the self, with the objective being to explore the self, improve it and change it. In contrast, an ACT approach prefers to reduce the emphasis placed on the conceptualized self. An ACT position argues that it is the investment in these self-concepts that can contribute to human suffering. Consider a woman who has a self-concept that she is a 'great mother'. When faced with evidence to the contrary, her conceptualized sense of self becomes threatened. The woman will then distort or reinterpret events in order to maintain the integrity of her self-categorization and evaluation as a 'great mother' and, thus, foster a pattern of self-deception. ACT aims to minimize intervention around the conceptualized self, preferring to undermine its importance rather than enhance it (Hayes et al., 1999). It is argued that releasing psychologically from the self-concept enables psychological flexibility to become more achievable.

Self-as-Process (I am Noticing I am Having the Feeling of …)

Self-as-process is a position from which internal experiences are watched and noticed as they occur in the moment. For example, self-as-process would be present when 'I am noticing I am having a feeling of… . ' Linehan (1993a,b) alludes to the self-as–process position via a set of three interrelated mindfulness skills: observing, describing and participating. 'Observing' involves the nonjudgmental awareness of internal experience; 'describing' places words around what is being observed; and 'participating' is being fully present in each moment-to-moment experience. Linehan's (1993a,b) DBT focuses on the development of self-as-process to enhance internal awareness with the view to modifying behavioral reactivity. ACT interventions focus on self-as-process to enhance awareness of internal experience with the view to promoting mindful choice around behavior.

Self-as-Context (I am Noticing that I am Noticing …)

Self-as-context allows one to experience the distinction between the self and one's private experiences. For example, 'I do not equal my self-evaluations; I do not equal my pain'. Therefore, the concept of 'I' does not equal any self-concept. Contacting the self-as-context also gives people a stable place from which to observe self-evaluations as they come and go.

Intervening in the area of the self can be a risky goal when working with borderline individuals. Ultimately, the goal of an ACT intervention is to increase and improve psychological flexibility. In terms of development of the 'self', this is achieved by releasing the self-as-concept, and making contact with the self-as-context, or the 'observer'. Ironically, releasing the self-as-concept, and making contact with the self-as-context can threaten to further destabilize the borderline individual's already fragile sense of 'self', particularly, if attachment to their conceptualized self is undermined too directly and/or too assertively. Even when this is not the case, ACT 'self' interventions can induce higher levels of anxiety in borderline clients compared to clients with an Axis I disorder (Deane, F., personal communication to A. Bailey, March, 2008). This is a crucial factor in treatment planning for borderline clients, and underpins the necessity for grading the intensity of ACT processes.

An ACT Conceptualization of the Borderline Self
Borderline Self-as-Concept

It has been argued that individuals with BPD have an early traumatic history and/or environment of serial invalidation from primary caregivers that leads to an impoverished and unstable sense of internal experiences and preferences (Grenyer, 2007b). Consider, for example, a child who was repeatedly and consistently told s/he was 'evil', 'bad', 'broken', or damaged'; or who was treated in such a way that lead them to perceive themselves as such. This type of learning environment can undermine the development of an elaborated self-concept. The afflicted individual fails to develop the ability to know and delineate their overall temperament, values, tastes, habits, convictions, virtues and/or shortcomings with any sense of long-range stability. Thus, they fail to develop any solid sense of conceptualized self, or who they are.

Borderline clients can demonstrate excessive levels of fusion with these impoverished self-concepts and/or self-evaluations, even when they are clearly unhelpful. For example, a client may perceive themselves as evil, and rigidly defend this self-concept when it is challenged or threatened. Why? For the borderline client, having some sense of a conceptualized self, even if bad or negative, is experienced as better than having none all. The alternative seems almost life threatening or psychologically annihilating. Hayes et al. (1999, p. 182) describe such a relational frame as 'Me = conceptualization', and its derived alternative being 'Eliminate conceptualization = eliminate me'. Defensive behavior, from this perspective can therefore be viewed as functional, in that it is 'self' preserving. Borderline clients frequently cling to a life story and self-concept that is mutually confirming, and often polarized and distorted, in order to maintain what little sense of self they have. Interestingly, it is their attachment to these self-conceptualizations, together with their ongoing avoidance of disturbing private experiences that maintains psychological pain and suffering. According to Hayes et al. (1999), fragmentation of the self (or identity diffusion) is the most destructive form of experiential avoidance an individual can employ. Paradoxically, the individual avoids greater awareness of 'self' at the expense of the self, and in doing so establishes and reinforces a perpetuating cycle of dysfunction. It is the extremity of the attachment or fusion to self-concepts, and the avoidance of private experiences, that poses the greatest challenge in the treatment of individuals with BPD/borderline personality.

Borderline Self-as-Process

It could be argued that the serial invalidation often present in the history of a borderline individual may have directly interfered with their development of self-as-process, also known as 'ongoing-self-awareness'. A caregiver who serially invalidates their child's expression of internal events (e.g., 'you don't feel upset', 'you don't want to feel anxious') effectively fails to provide accurate information and appropriate feedback in response to their child's experience. This results in a general mistrust of, and confusion in relation to, the internal world; in addition to a hypersensitivity to cues of invalidation. Accordingly, when painful or disturbing internal content is experienced, avoidance strategies are immediately employed in order to escape the perceived threat of insurmountable distress. Experiential avoidance subsequently becomes the learned behavioral response, thus reducing contact with one's internal states, and his/her ongoing awareness of self (self-as-process). For the borderline individual this is reflected in their inability to tolerate and/or regulate affect, and their extreme attempts to experientially avoid the associated distress (e.g., cutting, burning).

The borderline individual's inability to view self-as-process manifests in the form of rapid shifts and changes to self-concepts, which are strongly defended when present, but short lived and inconsistent. For example, a borderline client attending our clinic initially presented as a devout Christian, rigid and conforming in her beliefs, only to make a dramatic shift to a motorcycle riding, highly rebellious atheist some months later. Such rigid, yet rapidly shifting self-concepts contribute to the difficulty in employing ACT self-interventions with borderline individuals. If the goal is to release self-concepts in order to move to greater psychological flexibility, and self-awareness, such interventions again need to be chosen carefully and implemented in a graded and step-wise fashion in order to prevent further fragmentation.

Borderline Self-as-Context

Due to the absence of the ability to observe internal experience (self-as-process), there is an absence of observed continuity of self through time. Consequently, borderline individuals have great difficulty making the step toward contacting the observer self when the preliminary states of self, that is, self-as-concept and self-as-process, have not been fully developed.

Summary: ACT Self-Interventions With BPD

In summary, clients diagnosed with BPD have a profound self-disturbance. Clients diagnosed with a DSM-IV-TR Axis I disorder, on the other hand; have a more stable and less disturbed sense of self. This must be taken into account when planning treatment with these populations.

The ultimate goal of ACT self-interventions is to increase psychological flexibility. This is done by releasing self-as-concept, and allowing greater access to self-as-process, and self-as-context. In relation to DSM-IV-TR Axis I populations, this can be done directly and assertively because of their more robust and cohesive sense of self. Such an approach with borderline populations, however, could be harmful and lead to further fusion with existing self-concepts, increased experiential avoidance (e.g., self-harm, dissociation), and greater self-fragmentation.

The authors propose an ACT intervention for borderline clients that grades exposure to the self. It is argued that a graded approach to treatment minimizes therapeutic threat, inhibits the potential for defensive reactivity and aids treatment retention. The GEM-ACT treatment model for BPD will now be presented and discussed.

The GEM-ACT Model of Treatment for Borderline Personality Disorder

We have developed the GEM-ACT model of treatment for BPD/borderline personality to respond to the specific clinical and therapeutic challenges posed by this population. In this chapter, we will describe the application of the model in a group setting. This model, however, is equally relevant to individual psychotherapy, and can be adapted accordingly. Group psychotherapy comprises up to 8 participants, is facilitated by two clinicians, and takes the form of weekly, 90-minute sessions over a period of 6 months.

The GEM-ACT model is arbitrarily divided into three phases of treatment, each aligned to an assumed level of participant skill and/or 'self' development, and corresponding to an appropriate level (or grade) of therapeutic approach and/or intervention. As previously argued, borderline clients, because of their impoverished sense of self, are highly sensitive to and intolerant of affect. The GEM-ACT model therefore grades the emotional intensity of interventions with the aim of developing these areas of deficit. The grading of interventions is based on clients' phase of treatment, as determined by the treating clinicians, and ranges from benign experiencing to more intense or extreme experiencing. The grading and delivery of all interventions occur within a carefully regulated therapeutic frame, the structure of which conforms to each phase of treatment. Table 12.2 provides an overview of the GEM-ACT model of treatment for BPD/borderline personality.

We will now discuss the phases of the GEM-ACT model of treatment for BPD/borderline personality as outlined in the table.

The Therapeutic Frame

The therapeutic frame refers to the conditions, both practical and clinical, under which psychotherapy can occur (Langs, 1973). It is defined by the therapist(s), and consists of the time, place, and length of treatment;

TABLE 12.2
GEM-ACT Model of Treatment for BPD/Borderline Personality

	Phase of Treatment		
	1 (Beginning)	2 (Middle)	3 (Final)
Therapeutic frame	Firm, highly structured, consistently applied, uncompromising	Highly structured, reinforced/enforced when needed	Highly structured, more subtly applied, less apparent
Exposure to self and affects: Experiential exercises	Benign; innocuous; focused on internal experience of external stimuli; mild exposure to self-states	More emotionally evocative; moderate exposure to self-states	Provocative; more intense and direct experiencing of self-states
Behavioural skills	Extensive training in and utilization of skills to support exposure to self-states	Moderate application or utilization	Little to no application or utilization

rules/codes of conduct; client and therapist responsibilities; and fees (if applicable). Individuals entering therapy will, at some level, question whether they can trust the therapist to do no harm. This is particularly prevalent in the case of the borderline client who has often experienced severe interpersonal failings and trauma. Defining the therapeutic frame for the client brings about a sense of consistency and safety that promotes the psychotherapeutic relationship (Epstein, 1994). For the borderline client, the therapeutic frame can also provide an external structure to a chaotic and fragile internal world.

Grading the Therapeutic Frame

The therapeutic frame can be varied in terms of its structure and application. In a highly structured frame, group rules tend to be emphasized and routinely mentioned. The therapist is firm and uncompromising on such rules and seeks to control and modify client behavior through behavioral principles (e.g. reinforcing prosocial behavior). A less structured frame may involve therapists being less explicit and rigid in their rule governance, and increasingly flexible, collaborative and creative in their facilitation toward behavioral change.

Our experience with borderline clients suggests that a highly structured therapeutic frame provides consistency and predictability in therapy and, therefore, greater safety and containment of affect. Essentially, it provides the constancy and stability often understood to be internally absent in these clients. Conversely, a less structured therapeutic frame creates an environment in which the therapeutic endeavor is experienced as threatening and unsafe. Such a structure can further destabilize the borderline client and lead to increases in maladaptive coping strategies to stabilize the self and regulate affect (e.g., self-harm, dissociation), as well as experiential avoidance in the form of poor attendance or dropout.

Invariably, the borderline client will act to test the established frame. On one level this may reflect the borderline clients' difficulty in trusting others. Since they cannot trust people to be reliable and/or consistent in their caregiving, they feel they have to control others in order to avoid being abandoned or hurt by them. Given this dynamic, the test of the frame may be an indirect attempt to control the therapist(s). Alternatively, pressure may be applied to the therapeutic frame to test the therapists' ability to confront and contain the client's psychological pain and suffering. Fundamentally, borderline clients challenge the frame to test the safety of the therapeutic environment. Metaphorically, they are testing the water before diving in. Maintaining a firm hold on the therapeutic frame, especially in the early phases of treatment, is therefore essential to supporting and securing clients in therapy.

Within the GEM-ACT model, the therapeutic frame is graded from highly structured in the first phase of treatment, to less structured in the final phases. The initial firm structure is to address the abovementioned issues of engagement and therapeutic safety. The gradual loosening of the frame serves to strategically facilitate the emerging autonomy and development of the borderline client's sense of self.

During phase 1 of treatment the therapeutic frame provides safety, and acts as an external scaffold to the borderline client's affective instability and unstable sense of self. In this phase, clients are less able to modulate and contain their affect. Emotions are experienced as intense and overwhelming, and are experientially avoided. Consequently, skills for affect tolerance are poorly developed. A highly structured therapeutic frame serves as an external container for the overwhelming affect, and a 'holding' environment for internal experience. This therapeutic 'holding' is crucial in the initial phases of therapy; however, its 'hold' can be loosened as therapy moves through the middle to final phases of treatment. This is because, as therapy progresses, so too does the borderline client's capacity for tolerating affect and, ultimately, contacting their sense of self. Accordingly, clients become less reliant on external factors (therapeutic frame) to provide affective stability and internal cohesion. Instead, such experiences become internalized. It is at this later point in the therapeutic process (phase 3) where the client's internal agency, or personal values, can step into the orienting role, taking the place of the therapeutic frame.

It is important to note that the group rules remain the same regardless of phase of treatment. Differences lie in the manner in which they are applied. In phase 1, they are explicitly articulated in an uncompromising style. In phases 2 and 3, they are addressed in a more flexible and collaborative manner.

The following is an example of grading the therapeutic frame:

> Mary was in phase 1 of treatment. She actively violated the therapeutic frame by challenging the group rules and expectations. She would often turn up late, giggle and/or whisper during important points of therapy, and be hostile and verbally aggressive towards the facilitators. Mary's behavior was interpreted as an expression of her fear and anxiety in relation to therapeutic process, driven by an unstable sense of self. Mary's disruptive behavior served to test the strength and resilience of the therapeutic frame, in order to assure its capacity to provide safety and affective containment. In accordance with phase 1 of the GEM-ACT treatment model for BPD/borderline personality, the facilitators/therapists responded to Mary's behavior by increasing the firmness of the frame via explicit reinforcement of group rules, and the use of behavioral contingencies to extinguish behavior (e.g., 'Mary, let us again reiterate the group rules, which include no disruptive behavior ... we request that you utilize a skill you have learned in the program to try and manage the urges underlying your behavior ...').

> By the time Mary had entered the final phase of treatment (phase 3), her disruptive behavior had reduced significantly in line with her developing sense of self and affect tolerance. On the rare occasion when Mary demonstrated disruptive behavior, the facilitators/therapists, in accordance with phase 3 of treatment, chose not to explicitly reaffirm the therapeutic frame (group rules, etc.) but, rather, chose to use Mary's internalization of her values to reduce disruptive behavior and maintain group compliance (e.g., 'I notice Mary, that you have been giggling and whispering throughout the last 5 minutes, and have missed important parts of the discussion. Help me understand how that is in line with your value of learning as much as you can so you can get your kids back?').

Grading Experiential Exercises

Experiential exercises can be graded according to the intensity of affect they elicit. Due to histories of serial invalidation (Linehan, 1993a,b) borderline clients can be highly reactive to external threats to their identity (or sense of self). Therefore, for the borderline client, the most intense interventions are ones that seek to explicitly target the self. For example, the ACT Observer Exercise, as traditionally implemented, asks the client to notice that their 'self' is not equivalent to their self-evaluations (e.g., 'I'm having the feeling I'm damaged goods'). For the individual experiencing identity disturbance, this kind of intervention, if introduced prematurely, can be experienced as highly threatening due to an absence of sense of self beyond that being experienced in the moment (e.g., 'If I am not damaged goods then I am nothing'). This type of intervention may lead to an experience of self-annihilation, or an invalidation of the entire sense of being. Naturally, efforts will be made by the borderline client to avoid this experience and, therefore, such self-interventions may result in defensive behaviors such as cutting or dissociation. This experience may also give cause for the client to dropout of the program.

Therefore, the GEM-ACT model aims to very gradually and, at first, indirectly approach the client's sense of self. We can achieve this by following the principles of graded exposure. This is considered to be the GEM-ACT model's mechanism of change. In light of this principle, we are essentially grading the borderlines' exposure to two internal experiences: their identity (or sense of self) and their related affects. It is anticipated that the ability to tolerate a stimulus will increase as exposure continues. To make the endeavor more manageable, the exposure is graded in terms of intensity. This approach may be necessary when using a highly experiential therapy such as ACT, as a nongraded version of the therapy may risk emotional flooding, further self-fragmentation, and therapy dropout.

Graded exposure to self-states and affect are simultaneous and interwoven throughout the GEM-ACT model. It is therefore difficult to separate out one component from the other. Similarly, ACT processes are simultaneous and intertwined, and often overlap during this phasic intervention. We will now discuss a sampling of the graded intervention through the ACT process of mindfulness, and outline the manner in which the model targets two important and difficult components of the borderline psychopathology: the self and intolerance to affect.

Mindfulness and the Self

Mindfulness interventions, based on those routinely used in Linehan's (1993a,b) DBT, are used in the initial phases of the GEM-ACT model of treatment for BPD/borderline personality. These DBT interventions are then interwoven with ACT interventions toward the later phases of therapy. These interventions deviate from their traditional applications in that they are graded in terms of intensity, ranging from mild (e.g., notice yourself washing the dishes) to evocative (e.g., the Sweet Spot exercise). The GEM-ACT model aims to integrate the borderline individual's fragmented sense of self via gradual exposure to self-states within a con-trolled and contained environment. Let us demonstrate this through a sampling of mindfulness strategies.

Phase 1: Greeting the Self

Eating a raisin. In this mindfulness activity, clients are aware of the present moment by focusing sensory attention on the activities of eating a raisin. Throughout the process, clients become aware of the self through noticing the continuity of self-awareness in relation to only the raisin. At this early phase of treatment, it is necessary to contain the exposure to this external form of stimuli, as more evocative, internally focused exposure may raise affects, shut down awareness and undermine self-development.

Focused mindfulness (e.g., focusing on the breath). In this mindfulness activity, we increase the intensity by moving the focus from external stimuli to internal stimuli. However, we are grading the level of intensity to internal stimuli by using a nonthreatening focus (e.g., the breath). Again, this task enables the client to become introduced to self-experiences, this time in the process of mindful attention to one aspect of the internal landscape.

Phase 2: Noticing the Experiences of Self (Self-as-Process)

Conveyor Belt (Linehan, 1993a,b). The mindfulness exercises in phase 1 have opened up initial self-contact, and enabled an awareness of self-continuity to be introduced. This is evidenced by clients' demonstrated capacity to tolerate phase 1 mindfulness exercises and generalize the skills accordingly. It is now time to move to phase 2 of treatment, by increasing the intensity of the mindfulness interventions. This is achieved by turning the focus of attention further inward, to a 'mindful' contemplation of sensations, thoughts and affects (in this order) via a conveyor belt meditation. Self-as-process or ongoing self-awareness is beginning to form, laying the ground-work for self-as-context work to begin.

Phase 3: Having Perspective on the Experiences of Self (Self-as-Context)

Observer Exercise. With the development of internal (self) awareness in the preceding phases, the focus now turns to the development of the self as a constant and coherent entity in the face of internal content. The work in the current and final phase of treatment aims to establish the distinction between self, and one's inner experience and evaluations. This is achieved by exploring the concept of an observer self — a state of ongoing self, that exists beyond passing internal experiences — via the traditional observer exercise. This is the most intense intervention for a borderline client, and completion of the self-awareness skills in the first two phases of treatment is recommended prior to commencing this final stage.

The following is an example of grading mindfulness exercises to target the self:

> Mary demonstrated extreme and pervasive experiential avoidance on initial presentation for group therapy. Behaviorally, she would self-harm (cut), gamble and/or dissociate when confronted with difficult affects. A chronic

sense of emptiness pervaded her life. The facilitators embarked on mindfulness training to assist in the development of self and affect tolerance. The conveyor belt exercise was introduced to the group's participants, and Mary's observed response during the exercise was one of agitation. When completed it was clear that Mary had become dissociative. At this point the facilitators became aware that the phase 2 level of intervention was too extreme for Mary. Clearly, the level of exposure to the self was too high, and resulted in a defensive narrowing of awareness via dissociation. The facilitators chose to respond to Mary's behavior by titrating the intervention, and diluting the level of exposure by moving back to phase 1 mindfulness in the form of focus on external stimuli.

After some months in therapy, Mary, in her homework discussion, stated that she could now successfully utilize mindfulness skills in a variety of situations such as washing the dishes, having a shower, eating raisins. Mary noted that she could utilize these skills during neutral moments, but also during moments of distress. Mary was, in fact, demonstrating that mindfulness skills had replaced her previous self-harm behaviors. She had developed a basic awareness of self, and developed a formative capacity for the tolerance of affect. Given Mary's development, and that of her fellow group members, it was decided that the intensity of the exposure could increase, and the group could move to a phase 2 form of mindfulness intervention.

As therapy progresses, it is anticipated that the borderline individual's sense of self will become more coherent and stable. It is argued that the borderline client, through use of graded mindfulness strategies, develops their self-as-process, and ultimately their self-as-context. The skill of focusing on stimuli, mindfully, enables the client to become aware of a continuity of self beyond immediate affects, sensations and cognitions.

Values and the Self

Borderline clients have such a profound self-disturbance that in the early phases of therapy they have difficulty contemplating what it is they want for their lives. In fact, values work can, when ill-timed, be experienced as highly threatening to the borderline client. This is because values clarification can intensify the experience of internal emptiness, and emphasize the costs associated with not living a value-driven life. In light of this, it is suggested that values exploration be graded in accordance with the client's level of sense of self or self-development. This can be difficult as values and self are often inseparable and intertwined. The following section illustrates the process of grading values.

Phase 1: Greeting the Self
Planting the seed. In this initial phase, values work is approached indirectly. We begin the process by wondering what the therapeutic journey is about for participants. We pose this in a nondirective, rhetorical way. This serves

the function of allowing clients to choose to begin the process of exploring values if ready, and to postpone it if they are not. Essentially, we are setting up a context where they can moderate their level of exposure. Therefore, grading phase 1 of values can be achieved by (1) modulating the way values exploration is expressed (rhetorical/indirect as opposed to direct and expressive) and/or (2) narrowing the field that is being explored (e.g., focus on goals before values, or on only one value domain instead of many). This flexibility opens up space for clients to set the 'size of the jump' when it comes to contemplating/exposing to the 'self' via values.

Phase 2: Noticing the Experiences of Self

The sweet spot. In this phase, clients would have started a preliminary orientation toward what it is they want from the therapeutic experience in terms of goals or domain-specific values. From this position, we have introduced the internal compass, and set the platform for more intense contemplation of values. This is where we move toward interventions that encourage clients to connect with previously experienced moments of meaning and vitality. The function of this phase is to help clients become aware of what valued living feels like (which can often be outside their awareness due to their chaotic, traumatic lives). This phase also helps to further elaborate the sense of self by connecting self-awareness with experiences of meaning.

We place this intervention at phase 2 in therapy due to potential intensity of the exercise and the strong affects it can trigger. Most often, borderline clients have had difficulty living their lives in accordance with their values, due to the trauma and invalidation they have endured. In our experience, we have observed that bringing a moment of meaning and vitality into awareness with a borderline client also has the effect of bringing into awareness the costs of living a life that has been impoverished of such meaning. This awareness is pertinent to all of us at some level, but for the borderline client it is often experienced as an overwhelming loss in that they realize life, thus far, could have been so much more. This realization can often trigger quite extreme responses, and requires a level of affect tolerance to contain such intensity. This is why the sweet spot intervention is left until the second phase of therapy, and not introduced initially.

Phase 3: Having Perspective on the Experiences of Self

The Survey of Life Principles. In this phase, more direct values work is conducted. This is based on the assumption that a greater stability of self and improved tolerance for affect has been developed. In this phase, it is recommended that values exercises that directly target and clarify meaning and vitality in clients' lives be used. For example, the Survey of Life Principles (SLP; Ciarrochi & Bailey, in press) is useful for sampling/choosing a range of value domains, and for exploring motivations for each choice. For example, assume that a client values 'helping others'. The SLP helps identify the extent that 'helping others' is done because of pressure from others (a 'controlled' value) or because the client finds it personally meaningful (an 'authentic' value'). The SLP can help further develop clients' sense of self as they learn to distinguish between their own inner voice and the voices of other people. That is, they discover their own preferences and the sort of person they want to be.

The following is an example of grading values exercises to target the self:

In the initial stages of therapy, Mary complained of feeling hollow inside. She likened it to an empty coffin, which could never be filled. Mary found internally focused mindfulness/self-as-process tasks difficult, and responded with increases in defensive (dissociative) behavior, and numerous frame violations (distracting, arguing). On this basis, it was apparent that Mary did not have the affect tolerance or stability of self to manage anything more than a phase 1 values intervention. In the initial stages of therapy, facilitators began to approach the process of values by making very general comments to the group members, such as 'I wonder what it was that brought you all in today? … you are all here for a reason … we may not be sure of what that is right now … and that is OK … but you must all be here for something … or else you wouldn't be here.' Mary did not comment or elaborate on these musings, and did not react or respond to them disruptively either. This was interpreted as a sign that Mary was tolerating the material to some level, and thus, in weeks to come, the facilitators slightly intensified the values contemplation. In this next endeavor, facilitators started talking about goals for therapy, and what people wanted more tangibly from the process of being in the program. Facilitators did not target clients and directly question them, but rather wondered out loud what those goals may be … and asked clients to contemplate them if they felt able. Mary stayed silent. In weeks to come, when invited, Mary did not offer any goals or evidence that she had considered them. This was interpreted as Mary titrating the level of exposure, inherent in the intervention, to her own tolerance level. Facilitators, in accordance with phase 1 principles, did not expand or intensify the values intervention with Mary at this time.

After some months in therapy, Mary was regularly referring to her goal of 'screaming less at the kids' when she had visitation rights, and talked in general terms about her relationship with her children in the past and currently. Mary was much less disruptive during sessions and her dissociative and self-harm behavior had reduced substantially. Mary was able to tolerate various levels of internally based mindfulness interventions, and in light of these factors, facilitators deemed Mary to be at a phase 2 level of values work. On this basis, the sweet spot intervention was delivered. It was delivered early in the session to allow time for processing and grounding, if required. Mary responded emotionally to a memory of her children. She noted the memory was of a time when she felt truly connected to them; where they shared laughter, joy and a sense of family. Mary was moved by this memory; by its beauty, and by the deep sense of loss, guilt and regret it evoked in having lost her children to community services. By being in contact with the thing that was most important to her, Mary was also forced to be in contact with the costs of not living a value-driven life. Facilitators spent the remaining session, and some sessions afterwards, assisting Mary to process her experience of her values, in the midst of mindfulness-based grounding, and self-as-process work.

Many months later, Mary spoke openly about her feelings for her children, cried in session regularly, and often reflected on her feelings of guilt, rage and regret. Mary no longer dissociated, or engaged in self-harming behaviors. Similarly, Mary no longer disrupted the group with difficult behaviors but was an active and engaged contributor to the group process. This was interpreted by facilitators as progress. Rather than acting out her affects in an attempt to avoid them, Mary was able to reflect on them internally, and express them appropriately. Facilitators determined that, on the basis of these indicators, Mary was ready for phase 3 of the values intervention. Mary was given the Survey of Life Principles to complete and, over the next few sessions, facilitators assisted Mary and other group members to explore the facets and subtleties of chosen life principles and values. This served to further facilitate development of self-as-context, and enhance Mary's behavioral repertoire and psychological flexibility.

Within the current chapter, we have limited our discussion of the GEM-ACT model of treatment for BPD/borderline personality to the processes of mindfulness, values and, in particular, development of self-as-context. This focus, however, does not undermine the relevance of the remaining ACT processes of defusion, acceptance and committed action. The authors suggest that each of these processes can be applied in a similarly graded fashion to account for the complexities of the borderline population.

Summary and Conclusion

BPD/borderline personality is a complex and difficult condition to treat. Cognitive–behavioral and psychodynamic approaches to treatment have shown some efficacy (e.g., DBT, MBT, TFP) in ameliorating psychological functioning, with each approach attending to different aspects of the borderline pathology. The current chapter introduced and described GEM-ACT — an integrated model of treatment for BPD/borderline personality. This model combines cognitive–behavioral and psychodynamic techniques, and embeds them within an ACT framework.

As outlined in the chapter, the complexities of a borderline presentation include an unstable sense of self and related difficulties in tolerating affect. It is these issues that the GEM-ACT model has been designed to address. Specifically, the model aims to develop self-as-context (sense of self), affect tolerance and valued living. The GEM-ACT model does this by grading, incrementally, parameters of the therapeutic frame and the emotional intensity of interventions over the course of treatment.

The GEM-ACT model of treatment for BPD/borderline personality is currently being used by the authors with clients in a public mental health setting and, anecdotally, is showing signs of promise in terms of therapeutic engagement, retention rates and outcomes maintenance. The efficacy of the model is currently the subject of empirical research.

References

American Psychiatric Association. (2000). *Diagnostic and statistical manual of mental disorders* (4th ed.), *Text Revision*. Washington, DC: Author.

Bach, P., & Hayes, S. C. (2002). The use of acceptance and commitment therapy to prevent the rehospitalization of psychotic patients: A randomized controlled trial. *Journal of Consulting and Clinical Psychology, 70*(5), 1129–1139.

Bateman, A. W., & Fonagy, P. (1999). The effectiveness of partial hospitalization in the treatment of borderline personality disorder: A randomized controlled trial. *The American Journal of Psychiatry, 156*, 1563–1569.

Bateman, A. W., & Fonagy, P. (2001). Treatment of borderline personality disorder with psychoanalytically oriented partial hospitalization: An 18-month follow-up. *The American Journal of Psychiatry, 158*(1), 36–42.

Bateman, A. W., & Fonagy, P. (2003). Health service utilization costs for borderline personality disorder patients treated with psychoanalytically oriented partial hospitalization versus general psychiatric care. *The American Journal of Psychiatry, 160*(1), 169–171.

Bateman, A. W., & Fonagy, P. (2004). *Psychotherapy for borderline personality disorder: Mentalization-based treatment.* Oxford: Oxford University Press.

Bond, F. W., & Bunce, D. (2000). Mediators of change in emotion-focused and problem-focused worksite stress management interventions. *Journal of Occupational Health Psychology, 5*, 156–163.

Ciarrochi, J., & Bailey, A. (in press). *Integrating acceptance and commitment therapy and cognitive behavior therapy: A practical guide.* Oakland, CA: New Harbinger Publications Inc.

Clarkin, J. F., Foelsch, P. A., Levy, K. N., Hull, J. W., Delaney, J. C., & Kernberg, O. F. (2001). The development of a psychodynamic treatment for patients with borderline personality disorder: A preliminary study of behavioural change. *Journal of Personality Disorders, 15*(6), 487–495.

Clarkin, J. F., & Levy, K. N. (2006). Psychotherapy for patients with borderline personality disorder: Focussing on the mechanisms of change. *Journal of Clinical Psychology, 62*(4), 405–410.

Clarkin, J. F., Levy, K. N., Lenzenweger, M. F., & Kernberg, O. F. (2004). The Personality Disorders Institute/Borderline Personality Disorder Research Foundation randomized control trial for borderline personality disorder: rationale, methods, and patient characteristics. *Journal of Personality Disorders, 18*, 52–72.

Clarkin, J. F., Yeomans, F. E., & Kernberg, O. F. (2006). *Psychotherapy for borderline personality: Focussing on object relations.* Washington, DC: American Psychiatric Publishing, Inc.

Epstein, R. (1994). Keeping the boundaries: *Maintaining safety and integrity in the psychotherapeutic process*. Washington, DC: American Psychiatric Association.

Fonagy, P., & Bateman, A. W. (2007). Mechanisms of change in mentalization-based treatment for BPD. *Journal of Clinical Psychology, 62*(4), 411–430.

Geisen-Bloo, J., van Dyck, R., Spinhoven, P., van Tilburg, W., Dirksen, C., van Asselt, T., et al. (2006). Outpatient psychotherapy for borderline personality disorder: Randomized trial of schema-focused psychotherapy vs transference-focused psychotherapy. *Archives of General Psychiatry, 63*, 649–658.

Gottman, J., Katz, L. F., & Hooven, C. (1996). Parental meta-emotion philosophy and the emotional life of families: Theoretical models and preliminary data. *Journal of Family Psychology, 10*, 243–268.

Gratz, K. L., & Gunderson, J. G. (2006). Preliminary data on an acceptance-based emotion regulation group intervention for deliberate self-harm among women with borderline personality disorder. *Behavior Therapy, 37*, 25–35.

Grenyer, B. F. S. (2007a). Hope for sustaining a positive 3-year therapeutic relationship with patients with borderline personality disorder. *Archives of General Psychiatry, 64*, 609.

Grenyer, B. F. S. (2007b). *Principles of supportive-expressive dynamic psychotherapy for borderline personality disorder*. Unpublished manuscript, University of Wollongong, Australia.

Hayes, S. C., Strosahl, K. D., & Wilson, K. G. (1999). *Acceptance and commitment therapy: An experiential approach to behaviour change*. New York: The Guilford Press.

Jacobson, E. (1964). *The self and the object world*. New York: International Universities Press.

Kernberg, O. F. (1980). *Internal world and external reality: Object relations theory applied*. New York: Jason Aronson.

Kernberg, O. F. (1984). *Severe personality disorders: Psychotherapeutic strategies*. New Haven, CT: Yale University Press.

Kernberg, O. F. (1992). *Aggression in personality disorders and perversions*. New Haven, CT: Yale University Press.

Klein, M. (1957). *Envy and gratitude, a study of unconscious forces*. New York: Basic Books.

Langs, R. J. (1973). *The technique of psychoanalytic psychotherapy: The initial contact, theoretical framework, understanding the patient's communications, the therapist's interventions* (Vol. 1). New York: Jason Aronson.

Leichsenring, F., & Leibing, E. (2003). The effectiveness of psychodynamic theory and cognitive behaviour therapy in the treatment of personality disorders: A meta-analysis. *American Journal of Psychiatry, 160*, 1223–1232.

Linehan, M. M. (1993a). *Cognitive–behavior treatment for borderline personality disorder*. New York: The Guilford Press.

Linehan, M. M. (1993b). *Skills training manual for treating borderline personality disorder*. New York: The Guilford Press.

Linehan, M. M., Armstrong, H. E., Suarez, A., Allmon, D., & Heard, H. L. (1991). Cognitive-behavioral treatment of chronically parasuicidal borderline patients. *Archives of General Psychiatry, 48*, 1060–1064.

Linehan, M. M., Heard, H. L., & Armstrong, H. E. (1993). Naturalistic follow-up of a behavioural treatment for chronically parasuicidal borderline patients. *Archives of General Psychiatry, 50*, 971–974.

Livesley, W. J. (2005). Principles and strategies for treating personality disorder. *Canadian Journal of Psychiatry, 50*(8), 442–450.

Mahler, M. S. (1971). A study of the separation–individuation process and its possible application to borderline phenomena in the psychoanalytic situation. *Psychoanalytic Study of the Child, 26*, 403–424.

Mooney-Reh, D. M. (in preparation). *Identity diffusion in borderline clients: A study of differentiation of self.* Unpublished doctoral dissertation, University of Wollongong, Australia.

Perry, J. C., & Herman, J. L. (1993). Trauma and defense in the etiology of borderline personality disorder. In J. Paris (Ed.), *Borderline personality disorder: Etiology and treatment* (pp. 123–140). Washington, DC: American Psychiatric Press.

PDM Task Force. (2006). *Psychodynamic Diagnostic Manual.* Silver Spring, MD: Alliance of Psychoanalytic Organizations.

Scheel, K. R. (2000). The empirical basis of dialectical behaviour therapy: Summary, critique and implications. *Clinical Psychology: Science and Practice, 7*, 68–86.

Verheul, R., Van Den Bosch, L. M., Koeter, M. W., De Ridder, M. A., Stijnen, T., & Van Den Brink, W. (2003). Dialectical behaviour therapy for women with borderline personality disorder: 12-month, randomised clinical trial in The Netherlands. *British Journal of Psychiatry, 182*, 135–140.

Young, J. E., Klosko, J. S., & Weishaar, M. E. (2003). *Schema therapy: A practitioner's guide.* New York: The Guildford Press.

Zettle, R. D. (2003). Acceptance and commitment therapy (ACT) versus systematic desensitization in treatment of mathematics anxiety. *The Psychological Record, 53*, 197–215.

Zettle, R. D., & Hayes, S. C. (1986). Dysfunctional control by client verbal behaviour: The context of reason giving. *The Analysis of Verbal Behavior, 4*, 30–38.

Zettle, R. D., & Raines, J. C. (1989). Group cognitive and contextual therapies in treatment of depression. *Journal of Clinical Psychology, 45*, 438–445.

chapter thirteen

Acceptance and Commitment Therapy for Comorbid PTSD and Substance Use Disorders

Sonja V. Batten, Jason C. DeViva, Andrew P. Santanello, Lorie J. Morris, Paul R. Benson and Mark A. Mann

Many arguments have been suggested against the current syndromal classification structure employed in most mental health systems. For example, the frequent overlap of diagnostic categories leads to lack of specificity in both case conceptualization and treatment planning, especially for psychological presentations that include multiple Axis I disorders (Hayes, Wilson, Gifford, Follette, & Strosahl, 1996). For example, posttraumatic stress disorder (PTSD) and substance use disorders (SUDs) are commonly co-occurring, but generally seen as separate problems that require different interventions, often in unconnected treatment systems. We argue that the lack of coherence in treating these two problems separately can lead to both inefficiency and inconsistency in the treatment messages provided. In this chapter, we will provide a rationale for ACT-based treatment designed to address comorbid PTSD and SUDs, as well as an overview of one treatment program that has been developed to treat these comorbid problems in a military veteran population.

Extent of the Problems: PTSD and Substance Use Disorders

Exposure to potentially traumatic events is extremely common in the general population, and both PTSD and SUDs have high prevalence rates. For example, studies using current criteria for diagnosing PTSD have found that the likelihood of having experienced at least one potentially traumatic event in one's lifetime ranges from 81.3% to 92.2% for men and

74.2% to 87.1% for women (Breslau, 1998; Stein et al., 1997). Further, approximately 17% of men and 13% of women will experience more than three potentially traumatic incidents in their lifetime (Breslau, Davis, Andreski, Peterson, & Schultz, 1997). As a result, approximately 5% of men and 10% of women will meet full criteria for lifetime diagnosis of PTSD (Kessler, Sonnega, Bromet, Hughes, & Nelson, 1995). Many more will suffer from posttraumatic symptoms that do not meet full criteria for PTSD, such as intrusive and distressing recollections of thoughts (66.5%), hypervigilance (65%), distressing dreams of the trauma (48.2%), and physiological reactions to trauma cues (36%; Breslau, Davis, & Andreski, 1991). For military veterans, these numbers are even higher, both in past (Schlenger et al., 1992) and current conflicts (Hoge et al., 2004). The prevalence of SUDs in the general population is also high; for example, one study found that 8% of the US population suffers from substance abuse problems in any given year, and 15% of men and 8% of women have a substance use problem in their lifetime, resulting in significant economic cost to society (Harwood, Fountain, & Livermore, 1998).

Among individuals who meet diagnostic criteria for PTSD, rates of SUDs are generally higher than in the general population. One study found drug abuse or dependence rates of 34.5% for men and 26.9% for women with PTSD (Kessler, Sonnega, Bromet, Hughes, & Nelson, 1995). Further, in a large sample of combat veterans with PTSD, 75% met criteria for alcohol abuse or dependence (Kulka et al., 1990). In a large survey study of the general population (Helzer, Robins, & McEvoy, 1987), men with PTSD were five times and women twice more likely to have an SUD as compared to individuals without PTSD. Overall, it appears that there is up to a fourfold increased risk for alcohol/drug abuse or dependence in persons with PTSD (Chilcoat & Breslau, 1998). The analogous relationship between PTSD and SUDs also appears to be true, with the rate of PTSD among individuals with alcohol-related disorders ranging from 19% to 40% (Greeley & Oei, 1999). Overall, studies have shown that PTSD is a risk factor for substance abuse (Stewart, 1996), and substance abuse is also a risk factor for PTSD (Brady, 2001; Wilson & Raphael, 1993). Additionally, many have noted that the use of drugs and alcohol leads to an increased risk of traumatic exposure and ultimately an increase in PTSD (American Psychiatric Association, 1994; Tarrier & Sommerfield, 2003; Wilson & Raphael, 1993). Reviews of the literature show an overall comorbidity of the two disorders, ranging from 23% to 85% (Engdahl et al., 1991; Faustman & White, 1989; Stewart, 1996).

More recent research efforts have addressed the complex interaction between trauma exposure, PTSD and substance use. For example, treatment outcomes for individuals diagnosed with both SUD and PTSD have been found to be significantly worse than for individuals with SUD alone. Najavits and colleagues (2005) reported that the presence of both disorders is associated with greater impairment in mental health, physical health, work performance and general ability to cope, as well as higher rates of treatment utilization. Brown, Stout and Mueller (1996) reported that dually diagnosed women relapsed more quickly and reported more psychological distress. Ouimette and colleagues (1997) found higher readmission rates and poorer outcomes that appeared to be specific to PTSD in the presence of a substance use disorder. Further, Ouimette, Moos and Finney (2003) found that having PTSD treatment within 3 months of substance abuse treatment predicted improved SUD status 5 years later. The combined results of this research and increasing sophistication of treatment programs have led both clinicians and researchers to recommend treating both problems simultaneously whenever possible (Ouimette & Brown, 2002).

However, the approach of treating both disorders concurrently is not consistent with many mainstream treatment models. For years, clinicians and researchers were adamant that clients must be treated within a substance abuse setting first, because it was assumed that a person's PTSD could not be treated if there were continued use of drugs or alcohol. As a result, many individuals were turned away from trauma treatment or told that they needed to get 'clean and sober' for 6 months to 2 years before their PTSD symptoms could be addressed. Not surprisingly, this often led to individuals going without services at all; some individuals were unsuccessful in achieving sobriety without skills necessary to live with PTSD symptoms, and some 'fell through the cracks' because of lack of coordination between the systems providing PTSD and SUD treatment.

Over time, the interrelationship between these disorders became a focus of research, beginning with an examination of whether order of onset — whether SUD or PTSD came first — was significant in recovery. Additionally, researchers examined factors such as the presence of substance use and general adjustment prior to trauma. Seidel and colleagues (1994) noted a significant reciprocal relationship between SUD and PTSD in which increased anxiety increases vulnerability to use drugs or alcohol, and substance abuse can exacerbate symptoms of PTSD. As these examples clearly illustrate, treating SUD and PTSD separately fails to address the reciprocal relationship that exists between the two disorders.

In the last few years, the complex relationship between SUD and PTSD has been recognized as treatment developers have begun to combine components of successful treatments, such as coping skills and exposure, in hopes of addressing these disorders together. Examples of combined treatment approaches include Seeking Safety (Najavits, 2002), 12-session relapse prevention (Abueg et al., 1994), Transcend (Donovan, Padin-Rivera, & Kowaliw, 2001), and other concurrent treatment approaches (Brady et al., 2001; Triffleman, 2000). All of these show promise in addressing SUD and PTSD concurrently. However, we believe that some models may have inherent conflicts between different treatment components, which in turn may lead to providers giving mixed messages to their clients.

One example of potential conflicting messages can be seen with respect to the role of avoidance versus approach. Many substance abuse treatment approaches advocate avoiding people, places and things that trigger cravings. In trauma treatment, however, exposure is the most effective mode of psychotherapy (Institute of Medicine, 2007). In clinical application, dually diagnosed patients would thus be expected to implement two theoretically opposing techniques: avoidance strategies for substance triggers and exposure strategies for trauma triggers. This lack of consistency can be argued to result from a model of treatment development that focuses on SUDs and PTSD as separate but co-occurring disorders, rather than developing treatment based on a functional understanding of these two problems together. Although it can certainly be helpful to stay away from dangerous situations or individuals who engage in unsafe behaviors, it is not possible to stay away from all triggers for either substance use or trauma symptoms — these stimuli will be encountered as a natural part of living a full and vital life.

ACT as an Alternative Model to the Treatment of Comorbid PTSD and SUDs

If the field of comorbid PTSD–SUD treatment is to advance, it is essential that more integrated treatment models be developed that can account for the problems seen in both disorders. One example of such programmatic development can be found in the PTSD residential rehabilitation treatment program at the Baltimore Division of the Veterans Affairs Maryland Health Care System (VAMHCS). Historically, the program had provided assessment and short-term treatment for PTSD. However, in 2003, to address to the limits of treating PTSD and SUDs separately in dually diagnosed patients, the residential treatment unit was converted to a dual-diagnosis treatment program. Admission criteria were revised to include diagnosis of PTSD and substance abuse or dependence, as well as acknowledgment by the veteran that both problems were clinically significant. In addition, veterans had to be willing to work on both problems concurrently. Other changes in the admission criteria included opening the program to both women and men and allowing PTSD related to any traumatic event experienced while in the military (not restricted to combat trauma).

It was decided that in order to capitalize on the expertise of professionals who had long been treating SUDs, the dual-diagnosis program would partner with the VAMHCS substance abuse treatment program (SATP), which provides outpatient treatment to veterans with SUDs. The initial partnership between these two programs centered on the frequent approach to dual-diagnosis treatment in which treatments for PTSD and SUDs may be provided concurrently, but not in a truly integrated fashion. However, it was quickly determined that if this program were going to meet the needs of the complicated, dually diagnosed veteran population it was designed to serve, it would need to move to a truly integrated model that could be clearly understood by both veterans and staff. In deciding on a model for the program, it was obviously important to choose one that had an evidence base *and* that was relevant to the treatment of both PTSD and addiction.

After much discussion, the combined treatment team determined that all could agree that avoidance is a key process underlying both PTSD and SUDs. Thus, acceptance and commitment therapy (ACT; Hayes, Strosahl, & Wilson, 1999) was proposed as an appropriate treatment modality. ACT has been shown to be an effective treatment for a variety of problems related to experiential avoidance, ranging from depression to chronic pain to psychosis (for a full review, see Hayes, Luoma, Bond, Masuda, & Lillis, 2006). In addition, the results of mediational analyses are beginning to suggest that changes in outcome variables associated with participation in ACT may be due, at least in part, to changes in experiential avoidance.

Given that both PTSD and substance abuse can be conceptualized as disorders of experiential avoidance, it was argued that ACT could be a treatment model uniquely able to target these two problems in a coherent and consistent way (Batten & Hayes, 2005; Batten, Orsillo, & Walser, 2005). In support of this proposed approach, one would want to see evidence that ACT can be empirically demonstrated to be effective for PTSD and SUDs. In fact, there is preliminary evidence that ACT is a promising treatment specifically for substance abuse. In a sample of polysubstance abusing individuals enrolled in a methadone maintenance program, participation in an ACT intervention including both individual therapy and skills groups was associated with decreased substance abuse, as evidenced by self-report and objective (i.e., urinalysis) measures, at posttreatment and 6-month follow-up (Hayes et al., 2004). In addition, individuals receiving ACT in addition to methadone maintenance were less likely than those receiving only methadone maintenance to test positive for opiate use or to report any drug use at 6-month follow-up. A case study involving a male client who reported drinking alcohol to cope with social anxiety found that ACT was effective in increasing the client's willingness to experience anxiety as well as urges to drink alcohol, and in decreasing the frequency of the client's alcohol use (Luciano, Gómez, Hernández, & Cabello, 2001). ACT has also been shown as an effective intervention for smoking cessation at up to 1-year follow-up (Gifford et al., 2004).

Applications of ACT to PTSD are also beginning to be investigated. For example, the utility and acceptability of ACT have been examined in a sample of male and female veterans participating in an inpatient PTSD treatment program (Walser, Westrup, Gregg, Loew, Rogers, & Ulmer, 2006). Participation in ACT was associated with a decrease in thought suppression and experiential avoidance, and changes in psychological distress variables were moderated by those decreases in suppression and avoidance (R. Walser, personal communication, February 12, 2008). An uncontrolled trial of ACT for Australian Vietnam War veterans with PTSD found that 30 hours of group therapy with ACT was associated with reductions in PTSD scores, other psychiatric symptoms and levels of avoidance of disturbing thoughts at 3-month follow-up (Williams, 2007). In addition, at 3-month follow-up, all veterans had increased scores on mindfulness skills. Combining a focus on PTSD and SUD, Batten and Hayes (2005) report a case in which ACT was used successfully to treat a 19-year-old woman who met full criteria for PTSD related to childhood sexual abuse and who reported polysubstance abuse. At posttreatment, the results of several self-report measures indicated reductions in general psychopathology, depression and experiential avoidance compared to pretreatment levels. In addition, the client reported that she had completely stopped using substances of any kind after 7 months of treatment. Follow-up assessments demonstrated that these improvements were maintained at 3, 6, and 12 months after treatment was terminated. Considering the general effectiveness of ACT for disorders of experiential avoidance and the preliminary evidence that ACT may be an effective treatment for both substance abuse and PTSD, it is reasonable to suggest that ACT may be a useful model for a program designed to treat both PTSD and substance abuse in an integrated way.

In determining an appropriate treatment model for this novel dual-diagnosis program, compatibility with 12-Step philosophy was another important consideration, as many clients with substance abuse backgrounds have a connection to this tradition. In addition to its relevance to treating PTSD and addiction, ACT shares many concepts and principles with the 12-Step tradition, and these can be readily translated from one model to the other. As an example, a core aspect of both models involves honestly assessing how one's life measures up to a personally derived ideal. Twelve-Step proponents use the term 'manageability' to refer to this comparison. When individuals experience their lives as unmanageable or 'out of control', it implies that the strategies they are using to get what they want are not effective. ACT uses the term 'workability' to describe the degree of convergence between how things are and how one would like them to be, as measured by one's own values.

Furthermore, members of a 12-Step program evaluate the manageability of their lives as part of working the First Step. Admitting 'powerlessness' is a key component of this step, a provocative and often misunderstood aspect of the 12-Step tradition. The notion of 'powerlessness' is very much in line with the ACT concept of 'creative hopelessness', which also tends to be misunderstood by those unfamiliar with ACT. However, within the 12-Step and ACT approaches, respectively, 'powerlessness' and 'hopelessness' are not intended to describe absolute or global conditions, but rather refer to relative and specific experiences of living. Both models guide the client to recognize the futility of continuing behavioral patterns that they have already determined are not effective, particularly those involving experiential avoidance. Examples of such behaviors include problematic drinking or drug use, social isolation and narrowing the range of life choices to avoid taking risks. Acknowledging the hopelessness of 'doing the same thing while expecting different results' (or, in 12-Step terms, surrendering to the powerlessness inherent in this approach) frees the individual to try alternative behavioral strategies.

This process of giving up unworkable strategies and trying out new ones requires a large measure of 'acceptance' and 'willingness', two constructs that are prominent in both ACT and the 12-Step tradition. Both models also promote the practice of mindfulness — being fully present to one's experience without judgment — as a way of strengthening acceptance and willingness. Finally, ACT and the 12-Step tradition both strongly encourage individuals to identify what areas of living are really important to them, and to make commitments to act in accordance with those values. As a 12-Step member might say, the important thing is not whether one can 'talk the talk', but whether one can truly 'walk the walk'. ACT and 12-Step programs are not just effective at facilitating specific behavioral changes, they have the potential to be transformative in people's lives.

Implementation of the Program

Once it had been determined that staff with backgrounds in both PTSD and SUD treatment could see clear applicability of the ACT model to these populations, all staff were provided with training in ACT, through a 2-day experiential workshop led by a recognized ACT trainer. A weekly ACT consultation group was also developed, in which staff could come together to continue training on the application of and theory behind the use of ACT with this dual-diagnosis population. This multidisciplinary consultation group includes discussion of essential readings, experiential exercises, viewing of ACT videos and role plays of challenging clinical situations. A program was then developed that would incorporate ACT principles throughout a 6-week residential treatment stay. The details of the program as it currently runs, followed by preliminary data, are provided below.

Structure of the Program

Specific ACT Interventions

In order to ensure that participants are provided with the core ACT concepts, veterans attend a twice-weekly, hour-long ACT education group with the SATP patient population on general ACT principles. The purpose of this group is to introduce the principles of ACT so that veterans in both programs can apply those principles as an overarching treatment philosophy. Because the group is attended by veterans in both the dual-diagnosis program and the SATP, it was designed to accommodate rolling admissions. Due to the different lengths of the two programs (6 weeks for the dual-diagnosis program and 4 weeks for the SATP), a 5-week cycle of topics was developed. The topics include creative hopelessness (titled: 'How's that working for you?'), control as the problem/willingness, barriers to willingness/defusion, values, and committed action (titled: 'Just do it!'). [See Table 1 for more detail on topics covered and exercises used during each week of the program.]

In each ACT education group, veterans are introduced to key ACT metaphors (for example, the first session of the 'How's that working for you?' topic includes a thorough demonstration and discussion of the 'Person in the hole' metaphor) and are given homework assignments designed to help them focus the ACT principles on their own specific situations. Because all members of the group are working on substance abuse issues, but only some are also working on comorbid PTSD, the content matter of each session focuses on the ineffectiveness of substance use as a method for coping with problems and uncomfortable emotions. However, the fact that ACT core principles are not specific to any diagnostic category allows group leaders to discuss the general role of avoidance of uncomfortable internal experiences in increasing suffering. Most ACT education groups include discussions not only of avoidance strategies but also of the distressing experiences group members try to avoid, and the uncomfortable emotions associated with traumatic memories are often used as an example.

Three times per week, veterans participate in a 90-minute, process-oriented group, also with patients from the SATP, focusing on the specific issues that have contributed to each group member's use of substances, as well as current concerns in their daily lives. In each session, group members are asked to make a commitment to discussing a personally relevant topic, and facilitators continually frame veteran concerns from an ACT

TABLE 13.1
Objectives, Metaphors, and Exercises Used in Each Week of the Program

ACT theme of the week	General objectives	Sample metaphors/exercises
How's that working? (creative hopelessness)	• introduce concept of 'workability' • elicit specific examples of avoidance strategies (e.g., substance abuse, isolation) • identify avoidance as an 'unworkable' coping strategy • suggest willingness as an alternative to avoidance	• Person in the Hole • Driving with the Rear View Mirror • Quicksand • 'Identifying Shovels' Worksheet • Feedback Screech • Hitting a Baseball
Control as the problem/willingness	• identify efforts to control as contributing to the problem • introduce concepts of willingness and acceptance • investigate costs of unwillingness • encourage patients to practice willingness with negatively evaluated private events	• Two Scales • Tug-of-War with a Monster • Clean vs. Dirty Discomfort • Box Full of Stuff • In-vivo Willingness Exercises
Barriers to willingness/ defusion	• introduce defusion and mindfulness as willingness strategies • illustrate derived versus formal functions of language • encourage use of defusion with negatively evaluated cognitions	• Flyfishing • 'Eliminate the Negative'/'Holding onto the Good' Exercises • 'Name Tags' Exercise • 'Thoughts on Clouds' Exercise
Values	• introduce concept of values • discuss relationship between values and goals • discuss barriers to valued action • encourage identification of values in several life domains	• Tombstone/Eulogy • Path up the Mountain • Values Self-Assessment
Committed action (just do it)	• define commitment in terms of action in the service of values/goals • discuss relationship between commitment and willingness • encourage patients to make behavioral commitments in the service of values	• Swinging the Bat • Swamp • 'Stand Up and Make a Commitment' Exercise • Commitment Balance Worksheet

perspective. For example, facilitators often ask group members how a particular behavior is working for them or whether it is consistent with their long-term values. The process component of the group emphasizes experiencing difficult emotions in session instead of avoiding them, and when group members experience strong emotions during the session they are encouraged to engage with and not escape from those emotions. Facilitators also focus on the weekly ACT core principle being discussed in the education group. In this way, group members are encouraged to use ACT strategies within the session in the moment and, based on these experiences, learn to apply ACT concepts to current stressors in their lives.

Veterans with PTSD can choose whether they disclose details about traumatic events in the process group. However, all veterans are encouraged at least to discuss how trauma affects them in the present and to examine how they have struggled to cope through avoidance. Veterans are also encouraged to take risks in the process group in order to increase their level of trust in others, and these risks are framed according to the core principles of ACT. For example, a common goal identified by veterans in the program is decreasing isolation and developing closer relationships with family. Discomfort relating to difficulty trusting others often functions as a barrier to this goal. Veterans who report barriers to trust would likely be encouraged to engage with the trust-related discomfort and continue to discuss difficult topics in the small group, with the goal of developing willingness to accept that discomfort in the service of living more consistently with their values.

Dual-Diagnosis Interventions

In order to develop skills that can be useful with both PTSD and SUD-related problems, veterans in the program receive two 90-minute sessions per week of the Seeking Safety protocol for the treatment of dually diagnosed PTSD and SUDs (Najavits, 2002). Twelve modules of Seeking Safety are presented over a 6-week cycle, and the material focuses on identifying and coping with trauma and substance-related triggers, developing social support, finding new ways to respond to difficult thoughts and grounding skills. Veterans are given written assignments relating to each module. Facilitators focus on providing skills that can keep veterans safe in difficult situations in the program, as well as in everyday situations outside of the program. These skills are framed in an ACT-consistent way. For example, grounding skills are presented as a way of getting through a difficult moment without doing something destructive or impulsive — distraction in the service of one's values, not as a long-term way of coping or moving through life.

Veterans may also bring up the common strategy of avoiding 'people, places and things' associated with substance abuse. It is suggested that if avoiding a particular context does not interfere with a valued life, then this may be a reasonable strategy. However, if the contexts that occasion cravings to use substances are likely to continue to come up throughout the course of one's life (e.g., family celebrations, sporting events), then it is suggested that avoidance will not be a workable solution. In fact, it may lead to a constricting of one's life in a way that reduces quality of life and eventually increases the likelihood of substance abuse. Thus, the ACT program is not doctrinaire about whether or not one should avoid such situations — the answer depends on each individual's values and the resulting workability of such behaviors.

Trauma-Specific Interventions

Veterans attend a once-weekly trauma education group on the effects of traumatic events, the symptoms and associated features of PTSD, expectations about treatment, the role of avoidance in maintaining PTSD symptoms and ways to live effectively with guilt and shame. The material is presented in a 6-week, repeating cycle. The topics in this group are all described within an ACT framework. For example, in the group on what healing means in the context of PTSD, group members are instructed that 'healing' does not mean the absence of uncomfortable cognitive or emotional experiences, or the permanent disappearance of traumatic memories. Rather, veterans learn that through engaging with traumatic memories, they can increase flexibility enough to be able to live their lives in a values-consistent way. The session on avoidance and PTSD symptoms presents several ACT metaphors and relates them directly to PTSD.

Because of the prevalence of sleep problems and nightmares among veterans with PTSD, the program also includes a weekly 60-minute group providing empirically supported treatments for insomnia (stimulus control, sleep restriction) and nightmares (imagery rehearsal treatment). As with other groups, the material is presented in a 6-week cycle and from an ACT perspective. Metaphors about wanting control over inner experiences and experiential exercises focused on the effects of 'not thinking' about something are used to augment instruction in stimulus control and nightmare rehearsal procedures. In addition, veterans are encouraged to examine the longer-term consequences of unwillingness to tolerate discomfort in the short term, as it relates to the daily issues with sleep and nightmares.

To improve behavior relating to the experience of anger, veterans participate once per week in the 60-minute Honorably Experiencing Anger and Threat (HEAT) Group. The HEAT protocol applies ACT processes to anger-related problems in living (Eifert, McKay, & Forsyth, 2006) and includes elements of the cognitive–behavioral protocol for anger regulation in combat-related PTSD developed by Chemtob, Novaco, Hamada, and Gross (1997). The six-topic cycle includes sessions on self-monitoring of anger, the effects of struggling to control internal and external experiences, defusing from internal judgments, taking an objective perspective, using forgiveness to become untangled from unpleasant experiences and implementing acceptance in response to anger as it occurs.

Lifestyle interventions. Because the individuals in the program are seen as more than just their symptoms, treatment components also focus on functioning in daily life and improving physical health. Veterans in the program participate in a twice-weekly, 75-minute occupational therapy group that stresses development of functional skills (e.g., making a budget, organizing and cooking a meal). The group also provides training in assertiveness and teamwork. Veterans who are physically able also spend 60 minutes exercising in a gymnasium twice per week.

Individual case management. All veterans in the program are assigned a case manager who coordinates the veteran's care, provides individual therapy and develops a discharge plan with the veteran. Individual therapy focuses on identifying areas of the veteran's life that are not consistent with his or her values and developing plans for living more consistently with those values. Individual therapy is often skills-focused, with exposure-based interventions when appropriate.

Integration of ACT and PTSD/SUD Treatment

The integration of ACT core principles and techniques into treatments for PTSD, SUDs, and the comorbid presentation of the two serves three functions. First, the ACT core principles in general and the construct of experiential avoidance in particular provide a single conceptual framework for understanding this set of problems. The avoidance of internal and external trauma-related experiences is identified as a main factor that perpetuates the symptoms of PTSD, as well as the veteran's difficulties living a value-driven life. Substance use is conceptualized as a particularly unworkable way of dealing with these experiences. Across interventions, staff members help veterans to examine the consequences of familiar avoidance strategies and recognize when these strategies have been ineffective in the long term as methods for coping with PTSD symptoms. For example, the trauma education group presents PTSD as a syndrome driven by avoidance, some of which may have been learned during periods of traumatic exposure. Assignments given in the ACT education group ask veterans to list the coping strategies they have used that have interfered with living a life consistent with their values. This survey of maladaptive behavior is conducted in a nonjudgmental and validating way; for example, in the ACT education group, veterans are encouraged to assess their behavior not in terms of 'good or bad' or 'right or wrong,' but instead in terms of functionality (i.e., 'How's that working for you?').

Second, the core principles of ACT provide a common thread that runs through all treatment components and gives the program thematic continuity. The twice-weekly ACT Education Group and the HEAT Group are the two most explicitly ACT-based interventions in the program. However, ACT principles are also integrated into every other treatment component. All facets of the program emphasize sitting with, as opposed to avoiding, unpleasant internal states with the goal of living a life more consistent with one's values. For example, grounding skills in the Seeking Safety group are not conceptualized as ways to 'control' unpleasant emotions. Rather, staff present grounding as a way to facilitate being in the present moment with difficult emotions, people or situations without having to resort to behaviors that are not consistent with the veteran's values. In addition, veterans who experience strong emotions during process groups are encouraged to 'sit with' those emotions as opposed to moving away from them.

The program also focuses on developing a valued life as opposed to decreasing unwanted symptoms. Veterans are asked from the beginning of the treatment program to think about what their day-to-day life would be like if they were 'better'. Two of the ten sessions in the ACT education group cycle center on values clarification and group members are encouraged to identify their own set of values throughout the program. Group and individual therapists frequently refer back to values when veterans are making decisions or evaluating the functionality of behavior. Consistent with the recovery model, occupational therapy interventions specifically target skills for improving functionality in daily life, as opposed to 'symptoms'.

Third, ACT principles are frequently applied to increase the likelihood of veterans engaging with treatment recommendations. When suggesting tasks to veterans that involve working with uncomfortable emotions, staff often refer back to the results of values assessments or commitment exercises and encourage veterans to be mindful of the long-term consequences of their decisions. For example, the Sleep and Nightmares group includes imagery rehearsal therapy, a form of exposure treatment. Veterans often report reluctance to complete assigned work because of the discomfort they anticipate. Staff members conceptualize this reluctance with the veteran as an example of how avoidance of short-term negative consequences can interfere with the change process and keep the individual 'stuck'. Staff will then discuss with the veteran the potential value of willingness for initiating the change process. Veterans are encouraged to make choices not to avoid short-term discomfort but to approach longer-term desired life values and goals.

Preliminary Data

The program assesses veterans before and after treatment as part of an Institutional Review Board approved research study examining the effectiveness of the residential treatment program. During the first 15 months of this evaluation, approximately 90 veterans were admitted to the residential program, and 60 consented to be part of the research project. Of those 60, 20 completed both pre- and posttreatment assessments. The primary reasons for incomplete data were failure by veterans to complete the program (in which case posttreatment data could not be collected) and lack of dedicated research staff to collect data in a timely way.

Participants filled out a background questionnaire assessing demographic information and military history. They completed two measures of PTSD symptomatology, the PTSD Checklist (PCL; Weathers, Litz, Herman, Huska, & Keane, 1993) and the Mississippi Scale for Combat-Related PTSD (MISS; Keane, Caddell, & Taylor, 1988), as well as the Anxiety Sensitivity Index (ASI; Reiss, Peterson, Gursky, & McNally, 1986) and a measure of experiential avoidance, the Acceptance and Action Questionnaire-II (AAQ-II; Bond & Hayes, 2005). Participants also completed the Public Health Questionnaire, nine-item version to assess depression (PHQ9; Kroenke & Spitzer, 2002) and the Fear of Sleep Inventory (FOSI; Zayfert et al., 2006), an instrument assessing fear of sleep and trauma-related nightmares.

The 20 veterans who completed pre- and posttreatment assessment were predominantly male (90%) and had a mean age of 49.0 (SD = 9.4). The sample was predominantly African-American (50%), reported some college education (45%), and was not working at the time of assessment (55%). About half the sample served in a war zone, and 40% of the sample served during the Vietnam era. Two veterans (10%) reported military sexual trauma. Three-fifths of the sample reported some level of service-related disability, and 90% of the sample was planning to apply or in the process of applying for service-related disability or an increase in existing disability compensation.

Analyses indicated that scores on self-report measures of PTSD moved in the expected direction, with posttreatment scores on the PCL, M = 57.2, SD = 15.8 significantly lower than scores at pretreatment, M = 71.5, SD = 7.8, t (19) = 4.5, p < .001; and posttreatment scores on the MISS, M = 107.9, SD = 16.2, t (19) = 2.5, significantly lower than pretreatment scores, M = 115.9, SD = 14.5, p > .05. The AAQ-II scores showed a significant change in the desired direction, increasing from pretreatment, M = 25.5, SD = 8.9, to posttreatment, M = 33.0, SD = 12.7, t (19) = 2.7, p < .05. The ASI scores decreased significantly from pretreatment, M = 50.4, SD = 11.0, to posttreatment, M = 35.1, SD = 12.9, t (19) = 6.2, p < .001. The PHQ9 scores also decreased significantly from pretreatment, M = 19.3, SD = 4.9, to posttreatment, M = 12.1, SD = 7.2, t (19) = 4.4, p < .001. In addition, the FOSI total score decreased from pretreatment, M = 64.2, SD = 19.9, to posttreatment, M = 47.8, SD = 23.9, t (16) = 3.8, p < .01.

Although there was no control condition, experimental control was minimal and a large number of participants who consented to be in the study did not provide complete data, these initial results are promising and suggestive. Measures of PTSD symptom severity, fear of sleep and depression showed significant decreases from pretreatment to posttreatment, providing preliminary indications that the treatment program is effective at reducing symptomatology, even when that is not an explicit focus of the program. In addition, measures of experiential avoidance and sensitivity to anxiety showed significant changes in the desired direction, providing rough evidence of construct validity for the ACT-based treatment model.

Conclusion and Implications

The field of posttraumatic stress has made significant progress in the past decade in its awareness of the important comorbidity between PTSD and SUDs. It has become clear to most mental health professionals that the most effective treatment for this population will be one that is able to adapt to the needs of both sets of problems. We believe that ACT provides a coherent and innovative conceptual framework upon which to base such treatment. By viewing each of these problems as disorders of avoidance, ACT therapists focus on increasing willingness and working with the client toward a valued life, whether the tug-of-war of the moment is with cravings to use substances or with traumatic memories. The preliminary results presented here suggest that ACT may be effective in treating comorbid PTSD/SUD. The next phase of this treatment development should be on more controlled clinical trials to identify the effective components of ACT for this population and determine its large-scale applicability. Our evidence suggests that a model focused on reducing avoidance and increasing psychological flexibility may be uniquely suited for the complex PTSD/SUD population.

References

Abueg, F. R., Lang, A. J., Drescher, K. D., Ruzek, J. I. Aboudarham, J. F., & Sullivan, N. (1994). *Enhanced relapse prevention training for posttraumatic stress disorder and alcoholism: A treatment manual.* Menlo Park, CA: National Center for PTSD.

American Psychiatric Association. (1994). *Diagnostic and statistical manual of mental disorders* (4th ed.). Washington DC: Author.

Batten, S. V., & Hayes, S. C. (2005). Acceptance and commitment therapy of comorbid substance abuse and post-traumatic stress disorder. *Clinical Case Studies, 4,* 246–252.

Batten, S. V., Orsillo, S. M., & Walser, R. D. (2005). Acceptance- and mindfulness-based approaches to the treatment of posttraumatic stress disorder. In S. M. Orsillo and L. Roemer (Eds.), *Acceptance- and mindfulness-based approaches to anxiety: Conceptualizations and treatment* (pp.241–269). New York: Plenum.

Bond, F. W., & Hayes, S. C. (2005, July). *Here's the AAQ-2!* Paper presented at the ACT Summer Institute, Philadelphia, PA.

Brady, K. T. (2001). Comorbid posttraumatic stress disorder and substance use disorder. *Psychiatric Annals, 31,* 313–319.

Brady, K. T., Dansky, B. S., Back, S. E., Foa, E. B., & Caroll, K. M. (2001). Exposure therapy in the treatment of PTSD among cocaine-dependent individuals: Preliminary findings. *Journal of Substance Abuse Treatment, 21,* 47–54.

Breslau, N. (1998) Epidemiology of trauma and posttraumatic stress disorder. In R. Yehuda (Ed.), *Psychological trauma.* Washington: American Psychiatric Press, Inc.

Breslau, N., Davis, G. C., & Andreski, P. (1991). Traumatic events and posttraumatic stress disorder in an urban population of young adults. *Archives of General Psychiatry, 48,* 216–222.

Breslau, N., Davis, G. C., Andreski, P., Peterson, E. L., & Schultz, L. R. (1997) Sex differences in posttraumatic stress disorder. *Archives of General Psychiatry, 54,* 1044–1048.

Brown, P. J., Stout, R., & Mueller, T. (1996). Post-traumatic stress disorder and substance abuse relapse among women: A pilot study. *Psychology of Addictive Behaviors, 10,*124–128.

Chemtob, C. M., Novaco, R. W., Hamada, R. S., & Gross, D. M. (1997). Cognitive–behavioral treatment for severe anger in posttraumatic stress disorder. *Journal of Consulting and Clinical Psychology, 65,* 184–189.

Chilcoat, H. D., & Breslau, N. (1998). Investigations of casual pathways between PTSD and drug use disorder. *Addictive Behaviors, 23,* 827–840.

Donovan, B., Padin-Rivera, E., & Kowaliw, S. (2001). Transcend: Initial outcomes from a posttraumatic stress disorder/substance abuse treatment program. *Journal of Traumatic Stress, 14*(4), 751–772.

Eifert, G. E., McKay, M., & Forsyth, J. P. (2006). *ACT on life not on anger.* Oakland, CA: New Harbinger Publications.

Engdahl, B. E., Speed, N., Eberly, R. E., & Schwartz, J. (1991). Comorbidity of psychiatric disorders and personality profiles of American World War II prisoners of war. *Journal of Nervous and Mental Disease, 179,* 181–187.

Faustman, W. O., & White, P. A. (1989). Diagnostic and psychopharmacological treatment characteristics of 536 inpatients with post-traumatic stress disorder. *American Journal of Psychiatry, 14,* 501–503.

Gifford, E. V., Kohlenberg, B. S., Hayes, S. C., Antonuccio, D. O., Piasecki, M. M., Rasmussen-Hall, M. L., et al. (2004). Acceptance theory-based treatment for smoking cessation: An initial trial of acceptance and commitment therapy. *Behavior Therapy, 35,* 689–706.

Greeley, J., & Oei, T. (1999). Alcohol and tension reduction. In: E. E. Leonard & H. T. Blane (Eds.), *Psychological theories of drinking and alcoholism.* London: Guilford.

Hayes, S. C., Luoma, J. B., Bond, F. W., Masuda, A., & Lillis, J. (2006). Acceptance and commitment therapy: Model, processes, and outcomes. *Behavior Research and Therapy, 44,* 1–25.

Hayes, S. C., Strosahl, K. D., & Wilson, K. G. (1999). *Acceptance and commitment therapy: An experiential approach to behavior change.* New York: Guilford.

Hayes, S. C., Wilson, K. G., Gifford, E. V., Bissett, R., Piasecki, M., Batten, S. V., et al. (2004). A preliminary trial of twelve-step facilitation and acceptance and commitment therapy with polysubstance-abusing methadone-maintained opiate addicts. *Behavior Therapy, 35,* 667–688.

Hayes, S. C., Wilson, K. G., Gifford, E. V., Follette, V. M., & Strosahl, K. (1996). Experiential avoidance and behavioral disorders: A functional dimensional approach to diagnosis and treatment. *Journal of Consulting and Clinical Psychology, 64,* 1152–1168.

Harwood, H., Fountain, D., & Livermore, G. (1998). *The economic costs of alcohol and drug abuse in the United States.* Rockville, MD: National Institutes of Health.

Helzer, J. E., Robins, L. N., & McEvoy, L. (1987). Post-traumatic stress disorder in the general population: Findings of the Epidemiologic Catchment Area Survey. *New England Journal of Medicine, 31,* 1630–1634.

Hoge, C. W., Castro, C. A., Messer, S. C., McGurk, D., Cotting, D. I., & Koffman, R. L. (2004). Combat duty in Iraq and Afghanistan, mental health problems, and barriers to care. *New England Journal of Medicine, 351*(1), 13–22.

Institute of Medicine. (2007). *Treatment of posttraumatic stress disorder: An assessment of the evidence.* Washington, DC: National Academies Press.

Keane, T. M., Caddell, J. M., & Taylor, K. L. (1988) Mississippi Scale for Combat-Related Posttraumatic Stress Disorder: Three studies in reliability and validity. *Journal of Consulting and Clinical Psychology, 56,* 85–90.

Kessler, R. C., Sonnega, A., Bromet, E., Hughes, M., & Nelson, C. B. (1995) Post-traumatic stress disorder in the National Comorbidity Survey. *Archives of General Psychiatry, 52,* 1048–1060.

Kroenke K., & Spitzer R. L. (2002). The PHQ-9: A new depression diagnostic and severity measure. *Psychiatric Annals, 32,* 509–515.

Kulka, R. A., Schlenger, W. E., Fairbank, J. A., Hough, R. L., Jordan, B. K., Marmar, C. R., & Weiss, D. S. (1990). *Trauma and the Vietnam War generation: Report of findings from the National Vietnam Veterans' Readjustment Study.* New York: Brunner/Mazel.

Luciano, C., Gómez, S., Hernández, M., & Cabello, F. (2001). Alcoholism, experiential avoidance, and acceptance and commitment therapy (ACT). *Análisis y Modificación de Conducta, 27,* 333–372.

Najavits, L. M. (2002). *Seeking safety: A treatment manual for PTSD and substance abuse.* New York: Guilford Press.

Najavits, L. M., Schmitz, M., Gotthardt, S., & Weiss, R. D. (2005). Seeking safety plus exposure therapy: An outcome study on dual diagnosis men. *Journal of Psychoactive Drugs, 37*(4), 425–435.

Ouimette, P., & Brown, P. J. (2002). *Trauma and substance abuse: Causes, consequences, and treatment of comorbid disorders.* Washington, DC: American Psychological Association.

Ouimette, P. C., Finney, J. W., & Moos, R. H. (1997). Twelve-step and cognitive–behavioral treatment for substance abuse: A comparison of treatment effectiveness. *Journal of Consulting and Clinical Psychology, 65,* 230–240.

Ouimette, P., Moos, R. H., & Finney, J. W. (2003). PTSD treatment and 5-year remission among patients with substance use and posttraumatic stress disorders. *Journal of Consulting and Clinical Psychology, 71*(2), 410–414.

Reiss, S., Peterson, R. A., Gursky, D. M., & McNally, R. J. (1986). Anxiety sensitivity, anxiety frequency, and the prediction of fearfulness. *Behaviour Research and Therapy 24,* 1–8

Schlenger, W. E., Kulka, R. A., Fairbanks, J. A., Hough, R. L., Jordan, B. K., Marmar, C. R., et al. (1992). The prevalence of post-traumatic stress disorder in the Vietnam generation: A multimethod multisource assessment of psychiatric disorder. *Journal of Traumatic Stress, 5*, 333–363.

Seidel, R. W., Gusman, F. D., & Abueg, F. R. (1994). Theoretical and practical foundations of an inpatient post-traumatic stress disorder and alcoholism treatment program. *Psychotherapy, 31*(1), 67–78.

Stein, M., Walker, J. R., Hazen, A. L., & Forde, D. R. (1997). Full and partial post-traumatic stress disorder: Findings from a community survey. *American Journal of Psychiatry, 154*(8), 1114–1119.

Stewart, S. H. (1996). Alcohol abuse in individuals exposed to trauma: A critical review. *Psychological Bulletin, 120*, 83–112.

Tarrier, N., & Sommerfield, C. (2003). Alcohol and substance use in civilian chronic PTSD patients seeking psychological treatment. *Journal of Substance Use, 8*, 197–204.

Triffleman, E. (2000). Gender differences in controlled pilot study of psychosocial treatments with substance dependent patients with post-traumatic stress disorder: Design considerations and outcomes. *Alcoholism Treatment Quarterly, 18*(3), 113–126.

Walser, R. D., Westrup, D., Gregg, J., Loew, D., Rogers, D., & Ulmer, C. (2006, July). *ACT for men and women in the treatment of military trauma.* Paper presented at the ACT World Congress, London.

Weathers, F. W., Litz, B. T., Herman, D. S., Huska, J. A., & Keane, T. M. (1993, October). *The PTSD Checklist (PCL): Reliability, validity, and diagnostic utility.* Poster presented at the 9th annual meeting of the International Society for Traumatic Stress Studies, San Antonio, TX.

Williams, L. M. (2007). Acceptance and Commitment Therapy: An example of third-wave therapy as a treatment for Australian Vietnam War veterans with posttraumatic stress disorder (PTSD). *Salute, 19*, 13–15.

Wilson, J. P., & Raphael, B. (1993). International handbook of traumatic stress syndromes. New York: Plenum.

Zayfert, C., DeViva, J. C., Goodson, J., Pike, J. L., & Pigeon, W. R. (2006, November). *Fear of sleep and nighttime vigilance in trauma-related insomnia.* Paper presented at the annual meeting of the International Society for Traumatic Stress Studies, Hollywood, CA.

Contributors

Ann Bailey, MPsyc (Clin), Specialist Psychological Service,
South Eastern Sydney Illawarra Health

Dermot Barnes-Holmes, BSc, CertEd, DPhil, CPsychol,
Department of Psychology, National University of Ireland, Maynooth.

Sonja Batten, PhD, VA Maryland Health Care System
and University of Maryland School of Medicine.

Scott Bethay, MA, Department of Psychology,
University of Mississippi, Oxford, Mississippi.

Linda Billich, MSc, School of Psychology, University of Wollongong,
Australia.

John T. Blackledge, PhD, Department of Psychology,
Morehead State University, Kentucky.

Joseph Ciarrochi, PhD, School of Psychology,
University of Wollongong, Australia.

Joanne Dahl, PhD, Department of Psychology,
University of Uppsala, Sweden.

Frank P. Deane, MSc, Diploma in Clinical Psychology, PhD,
School of Psychology, University of Wollongong, Australia.

Natalie Glaser, MSc., University of Wollongong, Australia.

Steven C. Hayes, PhD, Department of Psychology,
University of Nevada, Reno, Nevada

Michael Levin, BA, Department of Psychology, University of Nevada,
Reno, Nevada.

Tobias Lundgren, MS, Department of Psychology,
University of Uppsala, Sweden.

Hamish McLeod, MA (Hons), DipApplPsych (Clinical), DIC, PhD,
School of Psychology, University of Wollongong, Australia.

Rhonda Merwin, PhD, Department of Psychiatry and
Behavioral Sciences, Duke University Medical Center.

Dianne Mooney–Reh, BPsyc (Hons), Specialist Psychological Service,
South Eastern Sydney Illawarra Health

Katherine Moyer, BA, Department of Psychology,
University of Mississippi, Oxford, Mississippi.

Lisa Parker, DPsych, Specialist Psychological Service,
South Eastern Sydney Illawarra Health

Patti Robinson, PhD, Mountainview Consulting Group, Moxee,
Washington.

Louise Shepherd, MSc, Counselling Service,
University of New South Wales

Kirk Strosahl, PhD, Mountainview Consulting Group,
Moxee, Washington.

Sonja Temelkovski, MPsych (Clin), Specialist Psychological Service,
South Eastern Sydney Illawarra Health

Kelly Wilson, PhD, Department of Psychology,
University of Mississippi, Oxford, Mississippi.

Index